PORTRAIT OF HENRY JAMES, JR. BY JOHN LA FARGE

Young Henry James

1843⊰1870

by

Robert C. Le Clair

BOOKMAN ASSOCIATES

New York

Copyright, 1955, by Robert C. Le Clair

To

Edward H. O'Neill

Preface

This study of the first three decades of Henry James's life was begun fourteen years ago, when the author found that, in the abundant material dealing with the novelist, very few essays and no books treated adequately James's formative years. In recent years, there have appeared several articles of importance and one distinguished book, Leon Edel's *Henry James, The Untried Years*. It is perhaps presumptuous to believe that there might be room for another study, after Mr. Edel's definitive treatment. A different approach, however, affords another point of view, and the author hopes that these chapters may offer some contrasting, even provocative, ideas on the development of Henry James from his birth in 1843 to what he called "the end of youth," 1870.

From the beginning, Henry James was a detached observer of life. As a child he was shy, hesitant, introspective, sensitive, and acutely intelligent. These qualities had much to do with the formation of his philosophy not only of life but of the art of fiction. Added to the forces of temperament were the powerful influence of his father and the devotion, the life-long friendship, between him and his brother William, the philosopher. In *Young Henry James*, the author has striven to treat as objectively as possible the intensely subjective nature of his material. A constant effort was made to avoid psychoanalysis, arbitrary interpretation, pet theories, and all the other glamorous but dangerous byways which often tempt the biographer beyond what he is able to bear.

In his essay, "The Art of Fiction," James gives a definition of experience that is highly significant of his life and work. More than

7

the sum total of the conscious events which compose an individual life, to him experience was "an immense sensibility, a kind of huge spider-web of the finest silken threads suspended in the chamber of consciousness, and catching every air-borne particle in its tissue." In reconstructing the story of young Henry James, one must penetrate into that chamber of consciousness and study the intricate, delicate web of experience, without breaking the threads.

There are two avenues of approach. The first is comparatively easy. It consists of sifting the documents that deal with the external events of James's life. To follow it is merely to fulfil what Virginia Woolf calls the first duty of a biographer, namely "to plod, without looking right or left, in the indelible footsteps of truth." The second is difficult. It demands standing aside and whenever possible letting James speak for himself. Of his adulthood, his fiction and letters tell much. Of the earlier years, however, little direct insight is offered by the boy and the youth. Those periods James gives us principally through reminiscences written in the crepuscule of old age. It is the task of the biographer, therefore, to compile accurately and thoroughly all data on the actual events of the years 1843-1870, touching James in any way, and to seek out every last word and syllable coming directly from him, which will reveal glimpses of that inner chamber, so infinitely more important in James than what "happened" to him.

The extensive use, made in this volume, of James's three auto-biographical works, *A Small Boy and Others,* 1913, *Notes of A Son and Brother,* 1914, and *The Middle Years,* 1917, is justified, the author believes, not only because these books offer the greatest amount of personal record set down by the novelist on his boyhood and youth, but because of the amazing accuracy of his recollections. It is astonishing that a man over seventy could recall even minute details of various incidents which occurred sixty or seventy years earlier. One assumes that he must have had access to a great deal of material contemporary with the events. When questioned on this possibility, his nephew, the late Henry James of New York, wrote:

I am very much interested and naturally pleased by your saying that an examination of the letters indicates that my uncle, writing in his old age, did stick to the "basic facts." I don't know for certain but am a little skeptical about his having consulted old letters and papers to check his recollections, for he never kept orderly files although bundles of letters were found after his death, tied up and put away in all sorts of places. His memory was, however, extraordinary and he may have gone over some bundles of letters, for his servant told me how at one time he destroyed a quantity of papers.*

The extraordinary memory was the result, in all probability, of Henry James's instinctive response to and consuming interest in whatever he observed or experienced. This hypersensitivity of reaction, evidenced from infancy, was a primary impetus in his development and accounts in large measure for his unique gifts as a man and as an artist. It became a basic axiom in his critical creed. In the Preface to *The Princess Casamassima,* he states: "This in fact I have ever found rather terribly the point—that the figures in any picture, the agents in any drama, are interesting only in proportion as they feel their respective situations; since the consciousness, on their part, of the complication exhibited forms for us their link of connexion with it."

James was deeply, keenly a feeling person. The spider-web of his consciousness was indeed spun of the finest silken threads, vibrant, strong. The impression, received at the age of eighteen months, of riding in a carriage past the Place Vendôme was as vivid and permanent as that of being introduced to Mr. Emerson, in the Fourteenth Street parlor in New York, a decade later. Nothing, especially of an asethetic nature, escaped his notice. The green veil of the Russian countess, in the garden of the Geneva pension; the sabots, black bodice, and red skirt of the French peasant, near the ruins of a castle at Nantua; the first installment of Flaubert's *Madame Bovary,* in the salon on the Champs Élysée; such things caught young James up in an excitement of thought and feeling which etched each impression vividly upon his mind.

Impressions are experience, James held. To follow the small boy, the youth, the struggling young author through three decades is to watch the unfoldment of his web of experience, to sense with him

---

* Letter to the author.

the degrees of feeling, from "the muffled, the faint, the just sufficient, the barely intelligent," to "the acute, the intense, the complete, in a word—the power to be finely aware and richly responsible." This is the story of *Young Henry James*.

Geneva, Switzerland
August 1, 1954

R. C. Le C.

Acknowledgments

During the decade or more in which this book has been in the making, innumerable people have contributed in many ways to its ultimate publication. Full acknowledgment can never be made, for the author's appreciation is boundless. Particular thanks are due, however, to Edward H. O'Neill of Philadelphia. Scholar, biographer, bibliographer, and friend, he has stood by the author from the beginning, giving generously of his time and thought, offering invaluable criticism and suggestions, as he read each chapter of the manuscript.

The late Henry James of New York, nephew of the novelist, and his sister, the late Mrs. Bruce Porter of San Francisco, who very kindly read the manuscript, both offered many helpful recollections of their uncle. Their brother, the present William James of Cambridge, very kindly read the manuscript and gave the author several helpful suggestions.

Appreciation is expressed to William A. Jackson, librarian, of The Houghton Library of Harvard University, for permission to use the collection of James Family Papers deposited there, and to Miss Carolyn E. Jakeman of the Staff for her kind services. To many unnamed librarians in New York, Philadelphia, Boston, Newport, Cambridge, St. Louis, and Geneva, who have helped the author in various phases of his work, he expresses heartfelt thanks.

The publication of this book would not have been possible without the encouragement and assistance of the author's colleague, Edwin S. Leonard, Jr., as well as the generous help and support of The Board of Trustees of The Principia and of William E. Morgan, President of The Principia College, Elsah, Illinois, to all of whom the author is deeply grateful.

For permission to use a photograph of the portrait of Henry James, by John La Farge, the author is indebted to The Century Association of New York. For permission to quote passages from various documents and publications, the author makes the following acknowledgments:

To Duke University Press and Miss Virginia Harlow for passages from *Thomas Sergeant Perry;* to Dodd, Mead & Company for quotations from *Alice James—Her Brothers—Her Journal,* by Anna Robeson Burr. Copyright 1934 by Dodd, Mead & Company, Inc.; to Harvard University Press and Ralph Barton Perry for passages from *The Thought and Character of William James;* to Raymond Emerson of Boston for a quotation from *The Early Years of the Saturday Club,* by Edward W. Emerson; to Houghton Mifflin Company for selections from *American Portraits* by Gamaliel Bradford and *The Heart of Emerson's Journals* by Bliss Perry, and for passages from *Rhode Island,* The American Guide Series; to Miss Mildred Howells for passages from *Life in Letters of William Dean Howells;* to Alfred A. Knopf, Inc., for selections from *The James Family* by F. O. Matthiessen; to The University of Illinois Press for quotations from *The Early Development of Henry James* by Cornelia Pulsifer Kelley; to The Macmillan Company, for passages from *Partial Portraits* by Henry James and from *The Memoirs of Julian Hawthorne* by Edith Garrigues Hawthorne; to Paul R. Reynolds & Son for quotations from *The Letters of William James,* edited by his nephew Henry James; to Charles Scribner's Sons for reprinting passages from *A Small Boy and Others* by Henry James; copyright 1913 by Charles Scribner's Sons, 1942 by Henry James, and from *Notes of A Son and Brother* by Henry James; copyright 1914 by Charles Scribner's Sons, 1942 by Henry James, and from *The Middle Years* by Henry James; to Odell Shepard of Hartford, Connecticut for passages from *The Journals of Bronson Alcott,* and for the same passages, to Frederic Wolsey Pratt of Concord, Massachusetts; to Yale University Press for quotations from *The Method of Henry James* by Joseph W. Beach.

ROBERT C. LE CLAIR

Contents

Book I

1843-1855

Chapter One

The Earliest Years

" . . . so fused and united and interlocked . . . "

Behind what Henry James called "the soft confusion" of his earliest recollections, stood William James of Albany, the handsome, square-jawed progenitor of the distinguished James family. In 1789, at the age of eighteen, he had come from Ireland "with a little money, a Latin grammar (which still exists), and a great desire to visit one of the Revolutionary battlefields." [1] The money grew into a large fortune; the grammar became symbolic of the family learning; and the desire to visit a battlefield of the American Revolution evidenced a spirit of adventure, freedom, and independence characteristic of many of the James progeny. No record has been found of the young man's life during his first four years in the New World, but all accounts agree that he settled in Albany in 1793.

From the beginning of his career, there was nothing either soft or confused about William James. Starting as a clerk, he advanced rapidly in the swelling tide of Albany's expansion, becoming master of a tobacco shop, then operator of an express business between Albany and Utica. Gradually, he acquired holdings in real estate and public utilities. Astutely supporting the Erie Canal project, he was the orator of the day at the official opening of that great water-way in 1823. His address reveals more common sense than literary ability. The talents of his son Henry as a religious and social philosopher can hardly be traced to the merchant father's orations. From this William James "of medium height, rather portly, clean-shaven, hearty, friendly, confident, and distinctly Irish" [2] came the strength of character and the keenness of mind, however, which were evidenced so strongly in his two grandsons, William, the philosopher, and Henry, Jr., the novelist. Amply compensating for his lack of learning and culture was his brilliant business sense. Combined with enormous industry, personal charm, and penetrating shrewdness, it enabled him to amass a fortune of three million dollars before his death in 1832. In New York State at that time, only John Jacob Astor had accumulated a larger estate.

William James also left to his heirs a deeply respected name, praises of which were widely published in Albany and New York papers.[3] Two of his heirs were to carry the name, though not the fortune, to far greater distinction; but they never forgot their indebtedness to the provider of that affluence which the family long enjoyed. The contrast between the life of this hard-working Albany merchant and the leisurely existence of his gentlemanly progeny was pronounced. Henry James, Jr., wrote: "The rupture with my grandfather's tradition and attitude was complete; we were never in a single case, I think, for two generations, guilty of a stroke of business." [4]

As in his business career, so in his domestic life, William James was expansive and prosperous. He married three times and begot thirteen children, of whom Henry James (1811-1882) was the second son of the third marriage, that to Catherine Barber. She was the daughter of Judge John Barber and his wife Jannet Rhea (or Rea) of Montgomery, New York, of Scotch-Irish stock with a creditable American pedigree, but without the English blood which her grandson Henry believed that she had.[5] She survived her husband William by more than a quarter of a century, always to be remembered by her large family as the "softly-sighing widowed grandmother" who dispensed a boundless hospitality to the very young Jameses and Temples, Barkers, and Van Burens, all of whom spent weeks, sometimes months, of happy holidays in the old James house at #62

North Pearl Street, Albany.[6] Her principal contribution to the James home was that of being a good wife and mother, a kindly friend and neighbor. She did much toward laying the foundation for the "intensely domesticated" affections of her children and grandchildren.

Her second son, Henry, received an especially large share of her care and devotion, for at the age of thirteen he met with an accident so severe that a boy less sturdy would hardly have survived. The unfortunate injury resulted from his attempting to stamp out a fire caused by a fire-balloon which had flown through the open window of a stable. His leg was so badly burned that it was twice amputated above the knee. For two years the boy was confined to his bed, recovering very slowly from the crude surgery of the times. For the rest of his life he was thus greatly restricted in his activities and the effects of this experience, both physical and psychological, cannot be overemphasized.[7] It is a strange coincidence that many years later his son, Henry James, Jr., was to meet with an accident at Newport, which, though not by any means so severe, greatly restricted his physical activities and threw the center of his interests on his inner life. In each case, the extraordinary intellectual development, with the father in religious and philosophical fields, with the son in a brilliant literary career, can be explained in some measure by the degree to which each was forced to forego an active life.

The natural physical force of Henry James, Sr., when a boy, was far greater than that of his novelist son. His strong animal spirits carried him through the intense suffering into a vigorous testing of his faith. The entire ordeal chastened the child, bringing a humility and spiritual strength which reshaped the direction of his life. The healing was discouragingly slow. Over two years after the accident, his sister Jannet James wrote to their sister-in-law, Marcia Ames James: "Henry's leg is not as well at present as it was in the Spring; instead of progressing it goes back and there is a greater space to heal now than there was before." [8] A few weeks later, the bedridden boy wrote to his half-brother, Reverend William James. The affection, admiration, and selflessness he expresses in a quaint, pious style are significant aspects of his developing thought:

ALBANY, NEW YORK
DECEMBER 14, 1827

MY DEAR BROTHER,

Since you have left us, we have heard very many testimonials to the character of your Sabbath evening discourse, to the elegance of its composition, and the truth of its sentiments. One gentleman, Cashier Gates, stated that if any man of established reputation, Dr. Chalmers for instance, had preached that sermon, it would be considered one of his finest efforts, and said further that when he hears one or two good passages in a sermon, he thought (sic) the sermon very good; but in your case there was such a continuous succession of brilliance, that one was constantly crowding its predecessor out of his mind, and that he could recollect no particular part. Dr. James, Harmanius Bleecker, John V. N. Gates and many other gentlemen expressed themselves in nearly the same way. Moss Kent (the Chancellor's brother) who has lately returned from England and Scotland, and one of our first men, says he cannot remember of ever having heard anything to compare with it, either in this country or abroad. Papa desires me to be particular in telling you that this ought to show you the capacity of increasing ardor in your studies, and of gaining the acquaintance of his most respected friends.

We hope you found Sister Marcia and little Hannah well, and Mamma wants very much that Sister M. should write often. As for herself, she has so large a charge, that she has hardly time to (do) anything but take care of the children. She hopes that Sister Marcia will not be so formal as wait for an answer to every letter before she writes again. However, she will promise to write as often as she can.

Jannet has just recovered from another of these very alarming attacks of spasms, etc. It is very necessary that she use every caution to prevent a return, as the least exposure to cold will invariably cause it. I am about as well as when you were here, and shall expect the books tomorrow evening. If I should not receive them at that time, do dispatch them next week. Write soon, and give our love to Sister Marcia.

Yours very affectionately,

BROTHER H. JAMES.[9]

The modesty, tenderness, affection, and solicitude expressed by the sixteen-year-old boy reflected his extraordinarily loving nature. This aspect of his temperament, partly inborn and partly the result of his prolonged illness, was to manifest itself throughout his life, becoming especially pronounced when he had a family of his own.[10] Moreover, this characteristic was transmitted to his children, to

William and Henry, Jr., in particular, whose mutual affection and loyalty were equálled only by their utter devotion to their parents.[11] Profound affection and faithfulness became fundamental traits of the James family, influencing their individual lives in infinite ramifications. The initial establishing of these qualities can be seen in the elder James during his invalid boyhood. Several years were to pass, however, before his religious thinking forced him to abandon completely the strict Presbyterian orthodoxy of his father. His half-brother William was also to turn from the unbending Calvinism of the Pearl Street home, eventually giving up the ministry and devoting himself to philosophical research.

In spite of an enforced inclination toward meditation and the inconvenience of his physical handicap, Henry James expressed a remarkable store of animal spirits during his undergraduate days at Union College, Schenectady, from which he was graduated in 1830, not, however, without some evidence of sowing wild oats, bringing down upon himself the Calvinistic wrath of his father in Albany. The young man was guilty of extravagance in delectable foods, flashy clothes, and general indulgence in worldly activities. While he fell just short of being elected to Phi Beta Kappa, he was one of the first American college students to wear a fraternity pin. His keen wit, buoyancy of spirit, and his gift for friendship combined to make him a campus figure quite different from either of his sons, William or Henry, Jr., at Harvard over thirty years later. He was, however, considerably sobered in the years following college by a futile attempt to study law and by being cut off, along with his half-brother William, in his father's will, which left only small annuities to these two rebels against Calvinism. Fortunately, the will was broken, with the result that both he and the Rev. William James received their share of the estate, along with the other children.[12]

In 1835, James entered Princeton Theological Seminary, apparently in an effort to find some answer to the turmoil of religious doubts which had been distressing him. Within two years he left the Seminary, convinced that the answers to his religious dilemma were not to be found in orthodoxy. One great blessing resulted from the

Princeton experience in the form of Hugh Walsh (1816-1859),
who shared James's doubts so strongly that the two young men
departed together. In the excitement of their drastic decision, they
took the coach to New York, young Walsh delighted with the
prospects of presenting his Albany friend to the unsuspecting Walsh
family at #19 Washington Square. Mrs. James Walsh, a widow
of several years, was immediately attracted to her son's companion,
as were her two eldest daughters, Mary Robertson and Catherine.
They were destined to play a major part in the life of this interesting
young man with a wooden leg, a contagious spontaneity of wit and
humor, and surprisingly unorthodox religious views. The Walsh
sisters, both in their middle twenties, soon found themselves involved
in discussions as disturbing as anything they had ever heard, and
the four young people enjoyed many stimulating hours together.
Their guest soon learned that he had found a family of delightful
individuals, charming in manner, intelligent in conversation, cultivated in taste, and, above all, in spite of their highly conventional
religious training, people who were more than sympathetic to him.
The background of the Walsh family was, in fact, not unlike that
of the Jameses.

Hugh Walsh, the founder of the American branch of his family,
came to the New World in the Eighteenth Century. His home originally was at or near Killingsley[13] on the west shore of Strangford
Inlet, County Down, Ireland. Leaving home in 1764, in his nineteenth year, he arrived presumably at Philadelphia, where he was
employed for a time by a shipping merchant, a Mr. Buchanan.
Before long, he was in business in New York. Later, he moved up
the Hudson to Newburgh, where he bought property and built a dock
and storehouse on the northeast corner of Water and Second Streets,
including the lands under water. In this manner he established himself, as did his fellow-countryman William James farther up the
River.

Hugh Walsh built up a prosperous general merchandise and
freighting business, the latter carried on by sloops which sailed from
Newburgh to New York and Albany. His merchandise store he
sold in 1799 and in 1804 disposed of his freighting business. In

1794 he constructed a large home (afterwards famous as the Mansion House), where he resided until 1808. He then occupied a handsome dwelling that he built on one of Newburgh's higher plateaus, fronting on Western Avenue, flanked by Grand and Liberty Streets. Here he died in 1817, in his seventy-second year, a prosperous and respected citizen.[14]

James Walsh, the eldest son of Hugh and Catherine Walsh of Newburgh, became a successful cotton merchant in New York City, where he married, on November 18, 1806, Elizabeth Robertson, tenth child of Alexander Robertson and Mary Smith, daughter of William Smith of Dumfries, Scotland.[15] Thus the Walsh grandparents of Henry James, Jr., united Irish-Scotch strains, just as did the marriage of William James and Catherine Barber on the paternal side of the family. Both grandmothers were left widows, but Elizabeth Walsh's plight was the more difficult as her husband, while on business in Richmond, Virginia died suddenly of apoplexy on March 5, 1820, leaving his widow with six children, the oldest eleven years and the youngest only five months. Fortunately, James Walsh left ample means, which were increased by income from the estates of Hugh Walsh and of Alexander Robertson, Elizabeth Walsh's father. Thus, the home which Henry James visited when he and Hugh turned their backs upon the Westminster confession in 1837 was one of affluence, culture, and refinement. It was, furthermore, extremely conservative, for the Widow Walsh had brought her children up in the strictest of codes, which did not include such worldly amusements as the theatre, the opera, or even oratorio concerts.[16]

This natural conservatism was much strengthened by a wave of old-fashioned, high-church Presbyterian piety upon which the entire family had been carried along so that Alexander Robertson Walsh, the first son, and James Walsh, the youngest boy, as well as Mary and Catherine, early became members of the Murray Street Presbyterian Church. They were rigidly devout, resting in the calm assurance that they were numbered among the elect who would inherit the kingdom of heaven. What sparks must have flown when the nonconforming Hugh and his equally rebelling friend, full of their break with the Seminary, came to grips with these ardent young parishioners! And what a blast of liberating ideas poured forth in the brilliant talk which filled the sedate front parlor of #19 Washington Square! As the two young ladies listened to the arguments of Henry James, with his easy, affable manners, his superior intellect and charming personality, they found themselves willing prey to the profound questionings that he presented. They questioned their own beliefs so seriously as a result of many discussions that, much to Mrs. Walsh's distress, both daughters withdrew from the Presbyterian Church. It is to the credit of the mother, however, that she never permitted her unhappiness over her daughters' action to interfere with her admiration and affection for Henry James. He was the type of young man whose spontaneous good nature automatically created reciprocal affections. The happy relationship was permanently established when Henry James married Mary Robertson Walsh on July 28, 1840 at the Walsh home, the marriage ceremony being performed not by an orthodox minister but by Isaac Leggett Varian, Mayor of New York City.

The young couple divided their time between New York and Albany, living mostly at the Astor House in New York. Here on January 11, 1842, their first child, William, was born. It became a well-known tradition in the James family that within a few months the proud young father escorted his recently acquired friend, Ralph Waldo Emerson, to see the child in their home on Washington Place, and that the Concord sage gave his blessing not only then but on many occasions when visiting the Jameses in New York during the next several years.[17]

In his Journal under March 18, 1842, Emerson recorded the fact that in New York he had met Henry James, John James, Horace Greeley, Albert Brisbane, and others.[18] James and Emerson experienced a strong mutual attraction which developed into a lasting friendship, with many notes and letters being exchanged, most of which are still extant. In response to an invitation from Emerson, James wrote on May 11, 1843 from New York:

Surely my heart goes forth to your invitation to Concord! We shall see. I am anxious to hear about the *Dial* from Mr. Thoreau . . . But I must stop ere I be stopped. My wife is grateful for your remembrances, and thinks nothing would so help me as a little intercourse with Concord. Another fine boy now lying in her lap preaches to me that I must become settled somewhere at home.[19]

The fine boy was Henry James, Jr., born April 15, 1843 at #2 Washington Place. A year earlier, in his first letter to Emerson, on March 3, 1842, James had described their residence, explaining that Washington Place "runs from Broadway to Washington Square and forms, or is formed by, the row of buildings between the University building and Broadway. My occupations are all indoors, so that I am generally at home—always in the evenings." [20] Thus located just around the corner from the Walsh home, with Grandmother Walsh and Aunt Kate Walsh conveniently available to help Mrs. James with Willy and Harry, both then under two, the young parents began to settle down to what might have become a permanent residence.

The neighborhood in the 'Forties couldn't have been more select or desirable, for Washington Square was then the *ultima Thule* of fashion. On one side was the dignified, gray structure of New York University (demolished in 1894); behind this was Waverly Place and Washington Place, as aristocratic as the Square itself on which then stood the New York Society Library in which Henry James owned shares. On the other side of the Square were the houses, built mostly in the 'Thirties, occupied by Commodore Vanderbilt, Mrs. Hicks Lord, Gen. George B. McClellan, the Coopers, DeForrests, Rhinelanders, DePeysters, and many other families of distinguished Dutch descent.[21] But social aspirations had small attraction for the Jameses, who were soon to give up their house in New York and go abroad for two years. In a postscript to his letter of May 11, 1843 to Emerson, James added these significant words:

I have advertised my house for sale—with a view either to go to France and Germany for a few years, or to pitch my tent in the country. I know not what is best for me to do. If your wisdom can resolve me write to me.[22]

Within six months the Jameses had given up their house and set forth on the international travels which played such a large part in the children's education. Fortunately there was seldom a question of money. Only James's crippled condition impeded his progress,. and that not very seriously.

For one unable to enter freely upon normal activities, James got about well, impelled by more than physical forces. At this time, he was particularly eager for personal contact with men like Carlyle, John Sterling, and Garth Wilkinson, whose works he had studied most devotedly. With characteristic enterprise he set off to see them. Emerson, who gave him much encouragement, wrote:

> Well, if you go to Europe, I shall rejoice in the opening of opportunities so rich and stimulating as the visit now will make for you . . . Do not fail to tell me what you decide and whither and when. Tell Mrs. Henry James that I heartily greet her on the new friend, though little now, that has come to her hearth . . . [23]

Quietly falling in line with her husband's plans, Mary Walsh James prepared for the voyage abroad. In 1843, she was thirty-three years old, one year older than her husband, retiring and quiet, intelligent, living entirely for her family. Her personality was, quite understandably, overshadowed from the beginning by the extraordinarily strong spirit of her husband and as a result there are very few accounts or sketches of her.[24] Adjusting her thoughts and feelings to those of her husband, Mrs. James never questioned his decisions but prepared her household according to his wishes. In the autumn of 1843, with two infant boys to manage, she closed the Washington Place house and bravely set sail on the first of several long journeys. He, in turn, left New York, caught between hope and regret, as the following letter to Emerson reveals:

NEW YORK, OCTOBER 3, 1843

MY DEAR FRIEND,

I believe we shall sail for Europe in the "Great Western" the 19th of this month. My affairs in various regards seem to indicate this as the advisable course. How long I shall stay, and whether I shall gain what I go for specially, or something instead which I have not thought of, and all questions of that clap—I am of course in the dark about. But I think it probable I shall winter in some mild English climate—Devonshire perhaps—and go on with my studies as at home. My chest is in an unsound condition someway, and if I can find a superior climate for it in England than I have at home, I think I shall then be much furthered also in my pursuits. In that case too I may print an Essay in England, if it finishes itself in time, and so get rid of one labour. I shall miss the stimulus of your candid and generous society and other friendly faces will be missed. I confess this aspect of the journey is not pleasant to think or talk of. One's destiny puts on many garments as it goes on shaping itself in secret—let me not cling to any particular fashion." [25]

After explaining at some length the nature of the essay he intended to write, he asks for letters of introduction to Carlyle and Sterling, apologizing in his charming way, for "it does appear a horrid boldness to present yourself in this roundabout way to a man, making a purchase of his friend in order to project yourself on to him." In closing, thoughts of separating himself for some time from Emerson, Margaret Fuller, Thoreau whom he only recently had met, Channing, and others, brought forth a burst of that generous and deeply affectionate nature for which he was beloved:

. . . Farewell then, my dear friend—many things spring up to my lips to say beside, but they are only variations of the tune *I love you.* I shall heartily (love) less the man I meet abroad who shall remind me of you. Please address me *Astor House,* N. York, as I shall probably be out of my house on the 10th instant. Say goodbye for both of us to good Margaret (Fuller).

Ever faithfully yours,

H. J.

Before leaving I shall send you my address in London, hoping some friendly angel may prompt you occasionally to make use of it. If I knew where to find such a servitor I should promptly *retain* him.[26]

Aboard the *Great Western*[27] on October 19, 1843, the James family sailed for England, Henry James, Sr., his wife, her sister, Catherine Walsh, their son William not yet two, their second son Henry, Jr., just six months old, and Fanny, a family servant. It was this Fanny who, in London, made the remark, classic in the James family lore, that the British Museum fell far short of the one in Albany. Armed with letters of introduction from Emerson to Carlyle and John Sterling, Henry James was filled with happy expectations. Even more important to him was to be the meeting with Garth Wilkinson, the noted Swedenborgian.

As preoccupied as he was with expanding intellectual horizons, the young husband and father never for a day neglected his family. The fullness of his love and happiness is expressed in the charming account of the crossing, and arrival in England, sent to his mother, Mrs. William James of Albany:

FROGMORE COTTAGE
WINDSOR, MAY 1, 1844

MY DEAR MOTHER,

Smith's letter by this packet will inform you sufficiently of our Parisian experience. We left that city on the 23rd, slept at Rouen, and came over to England on the 24th. The passage across the channel was very pleasant, none of us being sick but Fanny (family servant). When we were going to France the weather was rough, and we were all shockingly treated— from me down to poor little Harry. I never was so sea-sick before. Willy didn't know what to make of it, at all, and screamed incessantly to have "the hair taken out of his mouth." We were delighted enough to get back again to tidy old England.

The weather is perfectly delicious, foliage and flowers all out, the grass as green as summer, and the air equal to any barber's shop for fragrance. We went to Clifton after landing, but finding no precisely suitable lodgings there except in the town, we pushed on to Windsor, and here we have found a comfortable resting place at last. It is a little cottage standing between the Great and Little Parks, next to the residence of the Duchess of Kent, and fronting the entrance to the Little Park. The Little Park is called little because it is only four miles around, whereas the Great Park is twenty-three. Either of them will be quite large enough for the children's amusement. Let the Capitol Park (Albany) represent to your imagination the Great Park, and you may form some idea of our surroundings. But there is nothing in the aspect of City Hall to suggest an image of our beautiful cottage. A luxuriant hedge six feet high and two broad separates the courtyard from the road. An iron gate through the hedge gives admittance to the court which is filled with trees and flowers and shady walks, and a fine fruit garden running around the sides of the house to the rear gives further promise of a "glorious summer" to this son of New York.

The house is very convenient as to rooms, and very neatly and thoroughly furnished. The first floor has hall and dining room, study, kitchen, and servants' bed rooms; the second has a drawing room, four bed rooms, closets, etc. The butcher, milk man, grocer, and baker send for orders to the house and thus we are very snug as if we were in London itself. On our first entrance we were a little startled by the apparition of a huge watchman's rattle lying in the little room off the hall, and on inquiring its significance were told that it was to be used in case of an alarm from thieves at night. I have taken it to my room, determined to give it a fair trial at the first symptom of foreign invasion. It will be sure to arouse the Duchess of Kent whose bedroom is quite near and who will no doubt gratefully "use her influence" on our behalf. In any event the thieves cannot do much harm, unless their arms are long enough to reach over to our good and inexhaustible friend Hawley. (Hawley, one of the trustees of Wm. James's estate.) While *he* endures, the loss of one of my trifling pocketfulls now and then is a mere bagatelle, not worth the naming.

Our windows command a superb out look into the Little Park in front and the Great Park in rear. The latter comes "smack up" as Temple says, to the cottage hedge behind, and Willy and Harry from the nursery windows may hold concourse with the sheep and cattle browsing beneath, the livelong day. I have never seen a more enchanting spot. The long broad meadows of the Park dotted with the noblest oaks in England, and pasturing herds of the most beautiful cattle, deer, and sheep, stretch away for miles on one side; on the other the Duchess of Kent's gardens presenting an exhaustless variety of cultivated beauty; and again on the front the beautiful avenues of the Little Park sweeping over the hill and dale till they reach the Thames, the foresters lodges, the Queen's private gardens, her aviary and so forth—all these things combined with many others make Frogmore Cottage a desirable summer residence, even at 4.10 per week. This is much cheaper than we can get comfortable lodgings in London for at this season, indeed at any season. We have at present only a cook, whom we pay five shillings a week. We shall be obliged to get a chamber maid also, who will require three shillings. We also pay five shillings a week for plate and linen. Our living costs us *at the outside* two pounds. Altogether we consume 7.3 shillings a week—say thirty-six dollars. If Victoria, looking down from her castle windows upon our modest residence does not blush for herself, it is probably because these statistics have not been brought before her as they are now brought before you. But John and Temple and Gus and Smith (brothers and brothers-in-law to H. J., Sr.) should blush—each for himself first and then for each other. I am not so sure about Ed (another brother), as his expenses are much controlled by his residence with you— nor about William (a half-brother to H. J., Sr.) who I presume has some principle in the expenditure of his money. But clearly all the rest should blush and William Barker (another brother-in-law) among them, to observe how I support my entire family upon a sum which they probably throw away every week in superfluities. Let Mr. Hawley be appraised of the difference between us. Mary thinks I should allow three pounds

for living. Very well, that will be forty dollars only—still low enough
to justify the aforesaid fraternal blush, all around. Mary, however, is not
the most accurate person extant about figures, so you may look upon my
estimate if you please as the authentic one.

Mary Temple[28] (whom I will write to by next packet) and Smith
enlivened the somewhat dull current of our life by the hope their last
letters gave us, of seeing John and Mary (H. J.'s brother and sister-in-law)
in June. I am sorry the Great Western does not go over again, to afford
them choice of a passage in her. We saw Hoskens in Clifton who told
us that she would never again cross the Atlantic. He was very sorry, and
thought the company had not acted wisely in selling her. The last two
years she had paid very well, and would have done more in that way the
next two. The new steamer which we saw is the most magnificent vessel
I ever beheld.[29] They can't get water enough in the docks to float her
out into the river as yet, but are about making sure of that by some artificial means. And as to strength, no vessel that was ever built probably
can compare with her. Hoskens is full of enthusiastic expectations about
her. She will sail about the first of August. She offers a strong temptation to us to sail with her. I confess to some potent feelings now and
then dear Ma in your directions—"nursery" remembrances, and "little
back room" remembrances come over me not infrequently which make
Windsor Castle seem a great ghastly lie and its parks an endless sickness
not to be endured a moment longer. But these are only *feelings,* which
do not commend themselves to my judgment in sober moments, and they
therefore will not decide the question of our return.

The children are well in the main. Harry's teeth are troublesome at
times, but he is as good as the day is long, and the night on top of it.
Willy is very good too, when we are quietly settled. Our wretched Paris
excursion broke him up a little, but he is now on the mend. He is full
of fun—calls me "henwy" (he can't pronounce the *r* s) and his mother
Mawy—and talks frequently of his transatlantic experiences and acquaintances. I am anxious to learn about Loly and Bobby and Gus (niece and
nephews), and wish some of the girls would give me some account of
them. I wrote to Br. William before I went to Paris, and presume the
letter reached him in due season. Give my love and Mary's to Kate and
El and Mary and all the girls. Why doesn't Ed write me? When he was
in Europe I treated him a little differently I believe. Mary has become
so "pompious" with her new vocation as housekeeper in this regal neighborhood, that she quite disdains to write by this packet. So dear Ma, believe
me at least affectionately mindful of you all, and especially most tenderly
and truly

Yours,

H.

Kate Walsh and Mary have given me several messages the which I have unfortunately forgotten—but their general scope was amiable and affectionate.[30]

Certain passages and the general affectionate tenor of this letter were to be echoed twenty-five years later by Henry James, Jr., in writing to his mother from England and the Continent. It was characteristic of both father and son to be torn between a consuming love of family and home and strong attractions toward the delights of living and travelling abroad. Another similarity is seen in the natural gift of description, especially of the Windsor, Malvern, and the Cotswold country with which Henry, Jr., was so enraptured in 1869 and 1870.

There is absolutely no suggestion in this letter of May 1, 1844, of the profound crisis in his spiritual and intellectual life that Henry James, Sr., was facing. We know, however, from the detailed account which he left of the experience, that shortly afterward he passed through a kind of spiritual catharsis, not unlike Jacob's wrestling "until the breaking of the day." He states in part:

In the spring of 1844 I was living with my family in the neighborhood of Windsor, England, much absorbed in the study of the Scriptures. Two or three years before this period I had made an important discovery, as I fancied; namely, that the book of Genesis was not intended to throw direct light upon our natural or race history, but was an altogether mystical or symbolic record of the laws of God's *spiritual* creation and providence. I wrote a course of lectures in exposition of this idea, and delivered them to good audiences in New York. The preparation of these lectures, while it did much to confirm me in the impression that I had made an interesting discovery and one which would extensively modify theology, convinced me, however, that a much more close and studious application of my idea than I had yet given to the illustration of the details of the sacred letter was imperatively needed. During my residence abroad, accordingly, I never tired in my devotion to this aim; and my success seemed so flattering at length, that I hoped to be finally qualified to contribute a not insignificant mite to the sum of man's highest knowledge. I remember I felt especially hopeful in the prosecution of my task all the time I was at Windsor; my health was good, my spirits cheerful, and the pleasant scenery of the great Park and its neighborhood furnished us a constant temptation to long walks and drives.

One day, however, towards the close of May, having eaten a comfortable dinner, I remained sitting at the table after the family had dispersed, idly gazing at the embers in the grate, thinking of nothing, and feeling only the exhilaration incident to a good digestion, when suddenly—in a lightning flash as it were—"fear came upon me, and trembling, which made all my bones to shake." To all appearances it was a perfectly insane and abject terror, without ostensible cause, and only to be accounted for, to my perplexed imagination, by some damned shape squatting invisible to me within the precincts of the room, and raying out from his fetid personality influences fatal to life. The thing had not lasted ten seconds before I felt myself a wreck; that is, reduced from a state of firm, vigorous, joyful manhood to one of almost helpless infancy. The only self-control I was capable of exerting was to keep my seat. I felt the greatest desire to run incontinently to the foot of the stairs and shout for help to my wife,—to run to the roadside even, and appeal to the public to protect me; but by an immense effort I controlled these frenzied impulses, and determined not to budge from my chair till I had recovered my lost self-possession. This purpose I held to for a good long hour, as I reckoned time, beat upon meanwhile by an ever-growing tempest of doubt, anxiety, and despair, with absolutely no relief from any truth I had ever encountered save a most pale and distinguished glimmer of the divine existence, when I resolved to abandon the vain struggle, and communicate without more ado what seemed my sudden burden of inmost, implacable unrest to my wife.

Now, to make a long story short, this ghastly condition of mind continued with me, with gradual lengthening intervals of relief, for two years, and even longer. I consulted eminent physicians, who told me that I had doubtless overworked my brain,—an evil for which no remedy existed in medicine, but only in time and patience, and growth into improved physical conditions. They all recommended by way of hygiene a resort to the watercure treatment, a life in the open air, cheerful company, and so forth, and thus quietly and skillfully dismissed me to my own spiritual medications.[31]

Of his two small sons, William, then a little over two, and Henry, Jr., just past his first birthday, only William was ever to experience such spiritual torment, for he was more endowed than was his brother with their father's remarkable intuition and sensitivity to religious contemplation. William, ultimately the distinguished philosopher and psychologist, was to reveal the depths of his spiritual life in his *Varieties of Religious Experience*.

Deeply concerned over his perturbed condition, Henry James went to a famous water cure which did nothing toward helping his condition, but, as he states, enriched his memory "with a few morbid specimens of English insularity and prejudice" and increased his appreciation of "the exquisite and endless charm of English landscape." Almost a parallel situation occurred, though from a different cause, in Henry, Jr.'s life in 1869 and 1870 when he spent weeks at Malvern and other resorts seeking relief for his poor health. William, too, in 1867 while studying, as a young man, in Germany, occasionally was forced to give up his work and visit one of the many European watering places in search of better health.

Henry James, Jr., gives an interesting comment of this incident in his father's life, explaining how much he regretted not having witnessed the important meeting between the elder James and a certain Mrs. Chichester, residing near the watering place, who first told the ailing man that "the great Swedenborg, from whom she had drawn much light, might have something to say to his case." Immediately he went up to London and secured some of Swedenborg's works, beginning a study which influenced his life and thought profoundly. Swedenborg's writings were, from this time forth, an everpresent part of the James family household. Concerning this, Henry, Jr., states, that the works "ranged themselves before us wherever, and however briefly, we disposed ourselves, forming even for short journeys the base of our father's travelling library and perhaps at some seasons therewith the accepted strain of our mother's patience." [32]

The sojourn in England continued until early in 1845 when the Jameses went again to Paris before returning to America. It was on this visit to the French capital that Henry, Jr., received his first permanent impression, one so vivid and clear that in spite of the fact that he was not yet two years old he remembered it distinctly in later years. He first recalled the impression in 1848, at the age of five, upon hearing his parents discuss the news that the revolution had triumphed in Paris and Louis Philippe had fled to England. The highly sensitive child then startled his elders by stating to them quite certainly his recollection of being in Paris three years earlier:

. . . These last words, the flight of the king, linger on my ear at this hour even as they fell there; we had somewhat waked early to a perception of Paris, and a vibration of my very most infantine sensibility under its sky had by the same stroke got itself preserved for subsequent wondering reference. I had been there for a short time in the second year of my life, and I was to communicate to my parents later on that as a baby in long clothes, seated opposite to them in a carriage and on the lap of another person, I had been impressed with the view, framed by the clear window of the vehicle as we passed, of a great stately square surrounded with high-roofed houses and having in its center a tall and glorious column. I had naturally caused them to marvel but I had also, under cross-questioning, forced them to compare notes, as it were, and reconstitute the miracle. They knew what my observation of monumental squares had been—and alas hadn't; neither New York nor Albany could have offered me the splendid perspective, and, for that matter, neither could London, which moreover I had known at a younger age still. Conveyed along the Rue St. Honoré while I waggled my small feet, as I definitely remember doing, under my flowing robe, I had crossed the Rue de Castiglione and taken in, for all my time, the admirable aspect of the Place and the Colonne Vendôme.[33]

This peculiar trait of "taking in" impressions so acutely and permanently developed in Henry James, Jr., as one of his principal talents as a novelist. He was to become "an indefatigable gatherer of 'impressions.'" This keen susceptibility, even as a very small child, molded his equally acute imagination in directions and proportions that ultimately determined his whole career. And the process began literally in his infancy and quite significantly not in America but in Europe, seated on the lap of either Aunt Kate Walsh or the family servant, Fanny, riding in a carriage past the Place Vendôme.

NOTES

1. Katherine Hastings, *William James of Albany* (reprinted from the *New York Genealogical and Biographical Record*, LV, 1924), 3. William James (1771-1832) "was the son of William James (1736-1822) of Corkish (or, today *'Curkish,'* a townland a mile to the east of Bailieborough, Co. Cavan, Ireland), by his wife Susan McCartney (1764-1824) both of whom lie buried in Bailieborough, together with other members of the immediate family." *Ibid.*
2. *The Letters of William James*, edited by his son Henry James, New York, The Atlantic Monthly Press, 1920, I, 3.

3. One such account reads in part: "Of unaffected manners, generous, hospitable, public-spirited, open ever to claims of charity, prompt to participate in any enterprise of general utility or benevolence, Mr. James enjoyed, as he deserved, the sincere respect and esteem of his fellow citizens, and his loss was rightly considered a public calamity." Joel Munsell, *Annals of Albany,* Albany, Munsell and Rowland, 1858, IX, 259.

4. Henry James, *A Small Boy and Others,* New York, Charles Scribner's Sons, 1913, 190.

5. *Ibid.,* pp. 5, 6. See also *The Letters of William James,* I, 4, n. 2.

6. An interesting comment on the house appears in Joel Munsell's *Collections on the History of Albany,* Albany, N. Y., J. Munsell, 1865-1871, I, 487: "In tearing down the residence of the late William James, in Pearl Street, four copper plates were found embedded in the walls. The plates were about three inches long and two wide, bearing the following inscription in Roman letters: 'Daniel Hale, 1813.' This mansion was erected by him and after his death it passed into the hands of the late Mr. James." The house was torn down in 1860, after the death of Mrs. James on August 18, 1859.

7. For an account of the accident see *The Letters of William James,* I, 7, 8.

8. MS. letter from Jannet James to Marcia Ames James, Albany, N. Y., November 16, 1827, Houghton Library, Harvard University, Cambridge, Massachusetts.

9. MS. letter from Henry James, Sr., to Reverend William James, Albany, December 14, 1827, Houghton Library, Harvard University, Cambridge, Massachusetts.

10. A charming record of Henry James's deep affection for his wife and children was given many decades later by his daughter Alice in her Journal for November 18, 1889: "H(enry) says that certain places on the Continent bring up the old scenes so vividly: Father's sudden return at the end of thirty-six hours,—having left us to be gone a fortnight,—with Mother beside him holding his hand, and we five children pressed close round him, 'as if he had just been saved from drowning,' and he pouring out as he alone could the agonies of desolation through which he had come." Anna Robeson Burr, *Alice James—Her Brothers—Her Journal,* New York, Dodd, Mead & Company, New York, 11.

11. Almost a century later, in a critical sketch of the then celebrated novelist, Henry James, one critic wrote: "When those he loves are absent, he longs for them with a hungry longing which nothing else can satisfy, longs for news of them, longs for words of solicitude and thoughts of tenderness . . . He enters into their griefs and sufferings also, and with a comprehension and sweetness and tact of sympathy which must have been infinitely helpful . . . So it seems that the whole personal life of James, aside from his art,

centered in simply human affection . . . He was always a great writer, but the war revealed him to every one as a most lovable man." Gamaliel Bradford, *American Portraits*, Boston, Houghton Mifflin, 1922, 188, 189.

12. Concerning the strained relationship between William James of Albany and his two sons, William and Henry, see Austin Warren, *The Elder James*, New York, The Macmillan Company, 1934, 16-21.

13. In *A Small Boy and Others*, 6, Henry James states that Hugh Walsh, his great-grandfather, came from 'Killyleagh.' See William Walsh, *Hugh Walsh's Family*, Newburgh, N. Y., Newburgh Journal, 1903, 5. One of the few copies of this pamphlet may be found at The New York Genealogical and Biographical Society, New York City.

14. An interesting insight into Hugh Walsh's home and family life is given by one of his descendants who wrote:

"This house (on Western Avenue) was known for its open-handed hospitality, and to two quite different classes: one Presbyterian parsons, some of whom became eminent in New York, and the other officers and their families from West Point. Newburgh was in fact the nearest place for business and social life to West Point, and perhaps my uncle, Samuel A. Walsh, M. D., being Surgeon at the Point for some years, may have brought them to his father's house.

"Hugh Walsh's wife, Catherine, daughter of Mrs. Jane Armstrong, widow of Samuel Armstrong, was the mother of eight children, and died at the age of forty-six years, on the 27th of August, 1801. I think she was of a delicate physique, and for a few years rather an invalid. There seems to have been some fire in the Armstrong blood if this story be true, as I believe it is. She was in the habit of going to New York two or three times a year for shopping and securing a generous supply for family use. On one occasion, her husband, not having much money on hand, told her to call on Robert Boyd, a friend to whom he had loaned $10,000 without security or even a receipt of acknowledgment, and Mr. Boyd would give her all she wanted. Mr. Boyd, however, proved rather cranky, and declined unless she had an order. She therefore came back without her goods, vexed undoubtedly, and told her husband if Mr. Boyd would not credit her word, he was not to be trusted with an unsecured loan, and (the) result was that Mr. Boyd was obliged soon after to refund the loan."

Reverend William Walsh, *op. cit.*, 5, 6. Alice James, the iconoclast of family traditions, gives an interesting if somewhat satiric comment on the Walsh ancestry in her Journal for February 10, 1890, where she wrote: "The Ripleys write that great-grandfather, Hugh Walsh, left Ireland in a broken-hearted condition in his youth, because he was not allowed to marry a young lady with whom he was in love. What his social position was they know not, but he must have had some money, for he settled at Newburgh on the Hudson, and consoled himself by starting a soap (!) factory; he later took to building sloops. He married, and named one of his daughters after his first flame. He must have come, like grandfath♣ James, from that debased Ulster; what a humiliation for me. I suppose they didn't suspect what was to spring from them, or they would have managed better." Burr, *op. cit.*, 132, 133.

15. Concerning the Robertson forebears of the James family, Alice James wrote: "Katie and Henrietta Rodgers were very funny about great-grandfather Robertson, who came from Rannoch in Perthshire, they say. After he had made his fortune in linen in New York, he returned to Perthshire, and collected the bones of his forefathers and put a monument over them. He then took to his bosom his third wife and sailed away. After they had been at home a little while, he found that the bride had pinched Aunt Wyckoff (Cousin Helen Perkins' mother) who was his youngest and favorite daughter; so he rose in wrath and shipped her back to Scotland. They say that the blue Robertson Canton china, which came from cousin Helen, through Mother, to me, and which is now at Harry's, in DeVere Gardens, must be two hundred years old, quite." Burr, *op. cit.*, 133.

16. "Mrs. James Walsh was a person of marked individuality: warm-hearted, kind, hospitable, and a prudent dispenser of charities. If there was a thriftiness in her character it was of a harmless nature. For many years with her daughters she made a summer visit to her brother-in-law, John H. Walsh at New Windsor. Her second best was thought sufficient for the country, and was a matter of amusement to her nephews and nieces. The daughters were allowed to display their finery." Wm. Walsh, *op. cit.*, 10.

17. *A Small Boy and Others*, 8.

18. Bliss Perry, *The Heart of Emerson's Journals*, Boston, Houghton Mifflin, 1926, 173.

19. Quoted in Ralph Barton Perry, *The Thought and Character of William James*, Boston, Little, Brown, and Company, 1936, I, 47, 48.

20. *Ibid.*, I, 41.

21. Henry Collins Brown, *Old New York*, New York, Privately Printed, 1913, 60. In an account of life on Washington Square, Brown comments: "A man on an income of thirty or fifty thousand dollars a year in those days was considered very wealthy. The coachman and the footman were not above acting as butlers and waiters on occasion of hospitality. The groom did many other things than merely tend the horses—he brought wood for the fires, cleaned windows and made himself generally useful. Six servants were considered sufficient for a well-appointed household, and there were no such niceties of distinction in household service as exist today. Most of the houses had their own stables and gardens attached

and all the work incident to their upkeep was performed without outside assistance. The rooms above the stable made comfortable quarters for the coachman and his family, with accommodations for others when needed." *Ibid.*, 99.

22. MS. letter, Henry James, Sr., to Ralph Waldo Emerson, May 11, 1843, Houghton Library, Harvard University. This postscript is not included in the letter as published by Ralph Barton Perry *op. cit.*, I, 46-48, nor as published by F. O. Matthiessen, *The James Family*, New York, Alfred A. Knopf, 1947, 42, 43.

23. Quoted in Ralph Barton Perry *op. cit.*, I, 49, 50. The new little friend was, of course, Henry James, Jr.

24. The late Henry James of New York in the Introduction to his father's letters, gives the best account of Mary Walsh James. See *The Letters of William James*, I, 9.

25. Quoted in Ralph Barton Perry, *op. cit.*, I, 50.

26. *Ibid.*, I, 51, 52.

27. The *Great Western* was built in 1838 for the Great Western Steamship Company, at Bristol, England. It was a paddle-wheeler of 1,340 tons, 212′ by 35′, with four masts and one funnel. The ship ran regularly between Bristol and New York until the end of 1846; in 1847 she was sold to the West India Royal Mail Steam Packet Company and broken up in 1857, at Vauxhall, being then unable to compete with the newer steamers. She crossed the Atlantic in about fifteen days, a fast crossing in the 'Forties. See Eugene W. Smith, *Trans-Atlantic Passenger Ships Past and Present*, Boston, George H. Dean Company, 1947.

28. Mary Temple (Tweedy) was the sister of Robert Emmet Temple who married Catherine Margaret James, sister of Henry James, Sr. Mary Temple Tweedy, therefore, became the aunt of Minnie Temple, daughter of Robert Emmet and Catherine James Temple, who later played an important part in the life of Henry James, Jr.

29. The ship here referred to was probably the *Great Britain*, the keel of which was laid in July, 1839; the ship was launched on July 19, 1843. One account of the ship reads in part: "The 'Great Britain' was originally intended for a paddle-steamer, but the company having been unable to induce any forge-master to undertake the forgings required for the paddle-shafts, necessity compelled the adoption of of the screw-propeller. After her launch she was imprisoned several months in Cumberland dock, Bristol, owing to the locks being narrower than the ship, which necessitated their being widened. She was released from her long and ludicrous durance December 12, 1844, and early in 1845 steamed around to London . . . She was intended to be employed between Bristol and New York as the companion ship of the 'Great Western.' " See George Henry Preble, Rear Admiral, U. S. N., *A Chronological History of the Origin and Development of Steam Navigation*, Philadelphia, Hamersly & Co., 1883, 172, 173.

30. MS. letter from Henry James, Sr., to Mrs. William James of Albany, Houghton Library, Harvard University.
31. *The Literary Remains of Henry James,* ed. by his son, William James, Boston, James R. Osgood, 1888, 58-60.
32. *Notes of A Son and Brother,* New York, Charles Scribner & Sons, 1914, 158.
33. *A Small Boy and Others,* 53, 54.

Chapter Two

The New York and Albany Setting

" . . . his immediate native and domestic air . . ."

Upon their return to New York early in 1845, the James family entered into a new phase of experience and development. They were destined to remain on their native shores for ten consecutive years, the longest period of continuous American residence that Henry James, Jr., was ever to know. They were to be increased in number by three more children: Garth Wilkinson James, born in New York City, July 21, 1845; Robertson James, in Albany, August 29, 1846; Alice, in New York, August 7, 1848. They were to begin a long series of educational experiments, conducted through a maze of schools and teachers, at home and abroad, in English, French, and German, during the next twenty years.

After visiting with the Walsh relations in New York, Harry and Willy were taken to Albany where Grandmother James eagerly welcomed them into the bosom of her large family on North Pearl Street. Here, in a scene so permanently etched on their memories, the two boys were ushered into that richly domestic air, so alive with endless cousins, uncles, and aunts, which became the very atmosphere of their childhood. Here, too, they entered the first schoolroom of their long and varied process of education, with Harry trailing along behind the more certain steps of Willy. To all outward appearances, these elementary beginnings in Albany in no way suggested the immense complexity of the James boys' education, resulting ultimately in two such extraordinarily individualized men of genius.

During the first two or three years of this full decade of American residence, the home, not the school, played the more important role in the children's development, as it was to do increasingly throughout the next two decades. At the base of this matrix of formative experiences was the powerful force of Henry James, Sr., with whom no school was ever to compete in the children's education. Passionately devoted to his family, he returned to the Albany scene of his own childhood, brimming over with happy recollections. He loved the family tradition of charity and hospitality and carried it on abundantly. This ideal of love and generosity reached back many years to the days when his prosperous merchant-father had great quantities of beef and pork and potatoes laid aside each autumn for the winter's needy poor to whom these foods were distributed by the good wife and mother of the home.

The habit of caring for those in need was strongly established in Grandmother James, within, as well as outside of, her large family circle. In addition to her own eight children she had adopted the three children of William James's two previous marriages, making eleven sons and daughters, all but one of whom had married and were bringing up young children in 1845. Henry James, Sr., in an autobiographical fragment, wrote of the cordially affectionate relations he always enjoyed with his many brothers and sisters, "so much so, indeed, that I cannot now recall any instance of serious envy or jealousy between us. The law of the house, within the limits of religious decency, was freedom itself, and the parental will or wisdom had very seldom to be appealed to to settle our trivial discords." [1]

This same law of freedom, within even broader limits "of religious decency," was to be the outstanding characteristic of his own home, with such far-reaching effects upon his children. In a crystallization of this basic idea of freedom in his home, Henry James, Sr. wrote: "I desire my child to become an upright man, a man in whom goodness shall be induced not by mercenary motives as brute goodness is induced, but by love for it or a sympathetic delight in it. And inasmuch as I know that this character or disposition cannot

be forcibly imposed upon him, but must be freely assumed, I sur-
round him as far as possible with an atmosphere of freedom." [2]
As will be seen, this same principle was applied, as far as it was
humanly possible to do so, in the children's schooling, and at cost
of travel and instruction which only a man of considerable wealth
could afford.

The very first day of young Harry's schooling made such a vivid
impression upon his mind that for seventy years he could see himself, "crying and kicking . . . on the threshold of the Dutch House,"
making the first hour of his education a failure indeed. He retreated,
struggling, crying, even shrieking, from the Dutch House, with
Willy, sixteen months his senior, quite characteristically calm and
not a trifle amazed at his brother's performance. The differences
between these two brothers who were to experience an almost
identical training until adulthood was made apparent to sensitive
young Harry very early, and the psychological effect was immediate
and lasting. One of his first perceptions was that of his brother
"occupying a place in the world to which I couldn't at all aspire—
to any approach to which in truth I seem to myself ever conscious
of having signally forfeited a title." [3]

Willy's sixteen months' advanced experience in the world seemed
to put the younger brother at a disadvantage so "that I never for
all the time of childhood and youth in the least caught up with
him or overtook him. He was always round the corner and out
of sight, coming back into view but at his hours of extremest ease.
We were never in the same classroom, in the same game, scarce even
in step together or in the same phase at the same time; when our
phases overlapped, that is, it was only for a moment—he was clean
out before I had got well in. How far he had really at any moment
dashed forward it is not for me now to attempt to say; what comes
to me is that I at least hung inveterately and woefully back and
that this relation alike to our interests and to each other seemed
proper and preappointed." [4] Since such passages were a tribute to
his brother, a certain amount of self-abasement, even of distortion
may be allowed, but fundamentally the relationship between them
did exist in terms of Willy's quicker, more active responses causing

Harry to feel both slow and passive. Several factors contributed to this condition. In addition to the difference in age and temperament, there was a physical defect with which Henry, Jr., was to be afflicted most of his life, an impediment in his speech.

Many accounts of Henry James, Jr., in his mature years, make mention of the peculiar speech mannerism that was so often taken for an affectation. Actually it was a partial victory over a stammer which in his boyhood had been considered incurable and which became evident first during these Albany kindergarten days. It is not impossible that the elaborate politeness and the involved phraseology which he cultivated as an adult can be traced directly to this childhood affliction, for the ramifications of it, particularly in the case of an intensely sensitive boy, are legion. Oddly enough he developed a mastery of the French tongue, in spite of his speech handicap, which made a deep impression on French friends.[5] This speech defect remained as a barrier between him and friends, especially casual friends who could not know what lay behind his hesitancy. Yet it was not completely a handicap, for it very probably sharpened his innately keen sensitivity to people and his relation to them. Henry James, Sr., was also to some degree, at least in his earlier years, subject to a stammer. Carlyle, after first meeting the elder James in 1843 in England, wrote a highly favorable impression of him to Emerson, in part of which he states: "He confirms an observation of mine, which indeed I find is hundreds of years old, that a stammering man is never a worthless one. Physiology can tell you why. It is an excess of delicacy, excess of sensibility to the presence of his fellow-creature, that make him stammer . . . " [6] While Carlyle was speaking of the father, the "excess of delicacy" and "excess of sensibility" can be even more strongly applied to the son who as a man and as a novelist, consciously cultivated such refinement of feeling.

The pre-school, or dame's school as it was then called, to which the boys were sent, probably in 1846 when William was four and a half and Henry, Jr., just past three, was conducted by an impressive figure with an alien sounding name, "Miss Bayou," or "Miss Bayhoo." Her kindergarten was situated on North Pearl Street, facing their grandmother's house, and had the exotic charm of a Dutch gable, "of brick baked in the land of dykes and making a series of small steps from the base of the gable to the point." The pavement of uneven bricks and the cobblestone street left sharp images which broadened in memory to include the arching foliage on the avenue of trees, beyond which Steuben Street rose "very far away."

Then, in addition to the Dutch school-house and their grandmother's, there was one pinkish-red, standing back a little from the street, with a gate which worked by an iron chain weighted with a big ball, and high, white, perhaps marble steps, and a fan-lighted door. To such a house young Harry was taken on one of his first social calls, "paid visits" they were called, marking the birth of a social consciousness so intrinsically an ingredient in his development. The visit was paid to his aunt, Ellen King James Van Buren, the youngest of his father's three sisters, "lately married and who, predestined to an early death, hovers there for me, softly spectral, in long, light 'front' ringlets, the fashion of the time and the capital sign of all our paternal aunts seemingly; with the remembered enchantment of her living in Elk Street, the name itself vaguely portentous, as through beasts of the forest not yet wholly exorcised, and more or less under the high brow of that Capitol which . . . loomed, familiar yet impressive, at the end of almost any Albany vista of reference." [7]

The most impressive of these initial Albany experiences for the James boys was their introduction to the equally young but rapidly expanding labyrinth of cousinry which whirled about the old North Pearl Street house in concentric circles composed of little VanBurens, Barkers, Temples, and other Jameses in a profusion and confusion of happy family life. No less than twenty first-cousins were included in the immediate family group in 1845, with a series of second-cousins and even half-cousins adding much more to the bewilderment of Harry and Willy; and in the center of them all was Grandma James, "dear gentle lady of many cares," with her silk dress and peppermints, her lace mits and sweet smile, the embodiment of generosity, kindness, and common sense. The very atmosphere of her home permeated the minds of her children and grandchildren so deeply that twenty years later, her grandson William James, in describing Dresden to his brother-companion of kindergarten years wrote:

Dresden was a place in which it always seemed afternoon; and as I used to sit in my cool and darksome room, and see through the ancient windows the long dusty sunbeams slanting past the roof angles opposite, down into the deep well of a street, and hear the distant droning of the market and think of no reason why it should not thus continue in *secula seculorum*, I used to have the same sort of feeling as that which now comes over me when I remember days passed in Grandma's old house in Albany.[8]

The mood, the spirit of the place, still quaintly Dutch in spite of the inroads of commerce, of steamboats, of trains, made Albany a setting which lived on through all the changing years. And until old Mrs. James's death in 1859, her home meant vacations, and holidays, and fun, summed up in what Henry, Jr., called "the sweet taste of Albany."

The general impression that Mrs. Henry James devoted herself completely to her domestic duties and children, sharing not at all in her brilliant husband's intellectual activities is counteracted to some extent by the following letter written by her to Mrs. Garth Wilkinson. The Jameses had become intimately friendly with the Wilkinsons in England in 1843-1844, so that the relations between them extended happily over many years. Garth Wilkinson James, born in 1845, was named in honor of their English friend and in turn the Wilkinsons' daughter was named Mary, after Mary Walsh James. While living with grandmother James in the North Pearl Street house in Albany, on November 29, 1846, the younger Mrs. James wrote:

My dear Mrs. Wilkinson,

. . . Speaking about the future and the children, my dear Henry and I have lately been receiving a whole flood of light and joy upon this subject, by an insight into the glorious plans and prospects which Fourier opens upon the world. Henry has been reading to me a most charming little book by our friend Madame Gati de Gammon, and translated by our dear friend Mrs. Chichester. As a fiction it is more beautiful than any romance I ever read, but if true (and I *feel* that it must be so, or if not, as my hopeful loving Henry says, something better must be) it will not only banish from the world poverty with its long list of debasing evils but it will remove every motive to cruelty, injustice, and oppression, which the present disordered state of society has given birth to, and nourished in the selfish heart of man. Thus forms will be prepared into which the divine love and mercy may flow without measure, and this earth become a paradise indeed. These are bright prospects for our suffering race; but does not the word of God warrant us to look for just such a state of things upon earth? and does not Fourier prove that it may be brought about by means the most simple and rational, by merely taking advantage of certain laws of our nature which have been hitherto entirely overlooked, and which are doubtless implanted in us for this very purpose. Your dear husband seems from his recent letters and writings to be entering warmly into this subject. We expect great help from him in this way, as we do sympathy from both of you in the advances we make together in truth.

. . . One word about our dear Kate (Catherine Walsh) before I close. She spent a couple of days with us since the birth of the Baby (Robertson). When together we often talk of you, and she begs an especial and most affectionate remembrance to you and Mr. Wilkinson. I need not tell you what joyful occasions the arrivals of steamers have become to us, bringing to us with them your husband's letters. We have come to look for them regularly twice a month as our highest and choicest enjoyment. They have become to us something we could not do without, a sort of necessary ailment for our hearts and minds; so let him not dare to let us suffer for the want of it.[9]

Any young mother with four children under the age of six can hardly be expected to share in her husband's intellectual life to any great extent, yet from such a letter it is clear that Mrs. James did make an effort to enter into her husband's social and religious philosophies. And her style radiates that compassionate warmth and buoyant hope for mankind which characterizes his thinking and writing. Upon such strong bonds of affection and interest their marriage was most happily established.

With a rapidly increasing family, the Jameses could not prolong the Albany visit, particularly after the birth of Robertson in 1846; and thus there was no question about establishing a permanent home. Mr. James was very much occupied with his work as a writer and lecturer and needed a settled routine. A lecture, delivered before the Young Men's Association of Albany in December, 1845, resulted in his first publication, *What Constitutes the State,* printed in New

York in 1846. When the *Harbinger,* organ of the Fourierites and
first published at Brook Farm, was moved to New York in 1847,
Henry James's center of interest correspondingly moved from Albany
to New York. Here he could have intercourse with such outstanding
minds as Horace Greeley, Parke Godwin, George Ripley, William
H. Channing, Margaret Fuller, and Charles Dana, many of whom
had followed the *Harbinger* to its refuge in a small room at the top
of the *Tribune* building. In August, 1847, Garth Wilkinson, James's
English friend and fellow Swedenborgian, wrote, "rejoicing exceedingly at the prospects of your preaching and lecturing in New
York," [10] encouraging him to support the *Harbinger* in every way.
In the autumn of 1847, therefore, the Jameses and their four small
sons, all under the age of six, moved back to New York.

Until a satisfactory residence could be acquired, they lived for
several months during the autumn and winter of 1847-1848 at #11
Fifth Avenue. Years later, Henry, Jr., recalled that it was at this
address, "an apartment in one of the three Fifth Avenue houses
that were not long afterward swallowed up in the present Brevoort
Hotel," [11] that his uncles, "Gus" and John James from Albany,
announced to his parents that Louis Philippe had fled Paris for
England in March, 1848.[12] In the spring of that year, the family
moved to the house at #58 West Fourteenth Street which was to
be their home for the next seven years and the one in which, with
the birth of the beloved sister Alice in August, the children were
to spend the most settled and perhaps happiest years of their childhood. Probably no other year in the mid-Nineteenth Century was
quite so stirring or significant in the history of New York, for many
events, national and international, as well as local, bore rapid and
far-reaching effects upon the character, the size, and the future of
the city.

The discovery of gold in California and the revolutions sweeping
across Europe were the greatest topics of the day. The immediate
effect of the foreign upheavals was the influx of immigrants who
fled their homes and sought a new life in America, thousands of
them landing at the port of New York. Large numbers of these
foreigners went directly to the mid-west or to the inland areas of

the eastern seaboard, but a great percentage stayed in New York, creating social, economic, and political problems far removed from the comparatively simple life of "little old New York." Irish immigration had already been the largest of all foreign influx into the city, 50,000 having arrived during the previous decade. By the mid-Fifties, when the James family went abroad, Ireland had sent 1,073,065 people to America. New York's slums grew shockingly, since nearly all of these immigrants were illiterate, horribly poor, and subject to unbelievable conditions of squalor. Almost every country in Europe was represented in various degrees in the slum areas of New York. The good city of Father Knickerbocker and Washington Irving, so agreeable to the Jameses, was forever altered.

An exodus from the sprawling city, though disproportionately small, was caused by news of California gold. When the fabulous reports reached New York in September 1848, a fever of excitement and speculation swept through the entire population. On the Exchange and the streets, in theatres, shops, and drawing rooms, the new El Dorado was the exciting topic, with glowing accounts of vast fortunes to be washed from the golden sands. Men actually settled their affairs within a few hours, sold their property, often left their families and set out for the West. Within a year from September, 1848, it is estimated that 27,000 emigrants went by water to California, and nearly as many more by land.[13]

The advent of steamships and railroads of a few years previous coincided with the sweeping developments of the late 'Forties. In the steamships, the Jameses were especially interested, because Mr. James's lameness, occasioned by his wooden leg, necessitated the least strenuous means of travel; thus the Albany boat line was the preferred means of transportation up and down the Hudson. Henry, Jr., recalled that prior to the completion of the Hudson River Railroad line from Albany to New York "we always arrived by boat." He also recalled "the thrill of docking in dim early dawns, the whole hour of the Albany waterside, the night of huge strange paddling and pattering and shrieking and creaking once ended."[14] It was, in fact, aboard a River steamer that he, as a child of seven, hand held tightly by the elder James, had been presented to the celebrated Washington Irving, on an afternoon's sail from New York to Fort Hamilton in 1850. At that meeting Mr. Irving gave them news "of the shipwreck of Margaret Fuller in those very waters (Fire Island at least was but just within our Bay) during the great August storm that had within the day or two passed over us." [15]

The Hudson River Railroad Company, chartered in 1846, offered five years later much faster travel to and from the old family home on North Pearl Street. The boys were thrilled with the trains, which made all too frequent stops, in hot and glaring stations. Particularly impressive, though, was the panoramic sweep of the Hudson, flashing by the windows "so that the great swing of picture and force of light and colour were themselves a constant adventure." The fact that the boys had watched much of the actual construction of the line in the upper reaches of New York City made their trips all the more exciting, for they had made their way uptown through Fourth Avenue, in 1848 and 1849, to watch the work. It was "a riot of explosion and a great shouting and waving of red flags when the gunpowder introduced into the rocky soil was about to take effect. It was our theory that our passage there, in the early afternoon, was beset with danger, and our impression that we saw fragments of rock hurtle through the air and smite to the earth another and yet another of the persons engaged or exposed. The point of honor, among several of us, was of course nobly to defy the danger, and I feel again the emotion with which I both hoped and feared that the red flags, lurid signals descried from afar, would enable or compel us to renew the feat." [16]

Such marked evidences of the new order of things were counterbalanced by a number of picturesque figures of old New York, in particular the police. Until 1857, when the metropolitan police force was instituted, the ancient tradition of the Knickerbocker guard was continued. During the 'Forties and early 'Fifties, just as in Dutch times, a city watch began each day shortly after sunset and continued until dawn, a corps of about 1,000 men drawn from all vocations. No particular uniform was worn other than the old varnished fireman's hats, from which came the nickname "Leatherheads," as the watchmen were called. The duties were: to call out the hours of the night, give alarms of fire, cry out the name of the street in which the fire was raging, hang out a lantern to indicate the site of the flames, report disorderly persons and houses, and act as guardians for late travellers. Even ten years after the Jameses settled in Fourteenth Street, New York was considered "a huge semi-barbarous metropolis . . . not well-governed nor ill-governed, but simply not governed at all—with filthy and unlighted streets—no practical or efficient security for either life or property—a police not worthy of the name—and expenses steadily and enormously increasing." [17]

Yet the wealthy and fashionable sections of New York remained adequately secluded and select, though moving gradually to the upper portion of the city, farther and farther away from the old aristocratic strongholds of Bowling Green and Wall Street. Washington Square, Waverly Place, Astor Place, Bond Street, the lower part of Fifth Avenue, and East Broadway were the neighborhoods in which the well-to-do still resided in the 'Forties. Fourteenth Street was comfortably near Washington Square, yet also not too far from Twenty-third Street "parade" and the open areas of the city. A "country-place" on the northeast corner of Eighteenth Street and Broadway, was typical of the rural atmosphere in which the children roamed. Henry, Jr., recalled leaning against the iron rails, peering through to see two or three cows, some fawns, some peacock, guineafowl, and chickens.

No matter how ill-governed, unlighted, sprawling, and unsafe New York may have been in the mid-Nineteenth century, to the small boy, Harry James, it was a place of wonderful awakening, a setting against which he was always to see himself bewildered and delighted with his growing awareness, not only of the fascinating world about him but more especially of his wondering self. "I at any rate watch the small boy dawdle and gape again, I smell the cold dusty paint and iron as the rails of the Eighteenth Street corner rub his contemplative nose, and, feeling him foredoomed, withhold from him no grain of sympathy. He is a convenient little image or warning of all that was to be for him, and he might well have been even happier than he was. For there was the very pattern and measure of all he was

to demand: just to *be* somewhere—almost anywhere would do—
and somehow receive an impression or an accession, feel a relation
or a vibration. He was to go without many things, ever so many—
as all persons do in whom contemplation takes so much the place
of action; but everywhere, in the years that came soon after, and
that in fact continued long, in the streets of great towns, in New
York still for some time, and then for a while in London, in Paris,
in Geneva, wherever it might be, he was to enjoy more than anything
the so far from showy practice of wondering and dawdling and
gaping; he was really, I think, much to profit by it." [18] Every experience to the small boy enhanced his occupation of receiving
impressions; in this lies the key not only to an understanding of
the child but of the novelist he was to become. He was an individual
"in whom contemplation takes so much the place of action."

The instantaneousness, the vividness, the permanency with which
young Harry received impressions is illustrated in his account of
the first visit to the newly acquired Fourteenth Street house in 1848.
It was #58, on the south side of the street, fairly near Sixth Avenue,
in a row of houses already a few years old. His father took him
to inspect the house and to watch the workmen "in little caps
ingeniously formed of folded newspaper," standing on platforms
casting plaster into moulds and pasting long strips of yellowish
grained paper on the walls, with a pattern at the wainscoting level
"of dragons and sphinxes and scrolls and other fine flourishes . . .
a wonderful, sumptuous thing."

It was the beginning of the age of "brown stone" fronts, which
soon grew up in many of the vacant spaces between Fifth and Sixth
Avenues, changing the whole countenance of the city. Washington
Square, or Washington Parade as it was then still called, "a world
of quieter harmonies . . . so decent in its dignity, so instinctively
unpretentious," was enclosed with ancient wooden palings; but
Union Square, at what counted in 1848 as the top of the Avenue,
was more smartly encased in iron rails and adorned with a fountain,
frequented by "an aged amateur-looking constable . . . awful to my
generation in virtue of his star and his switch." Another reference
to the informal policing of the city is made as "the loose citizen

in the garb of a freeman save for the brass star on his breast—and the New York garb of the period was, as I remember it, an immense attestation of liberty." Such officers of the law wandered about the squares and avenues, having apparently little effect upon the milling people, the carts and barrows, boxes and baskets, the bumping hacks and more elegant carriages. Impressive above all were the enormous quantities of fruit which the James boys so fondly remembered at the corner groceries. Piles of Isabella grapes and Seckel pears, as well as huge mounds of peaches in profusion were carried home to Fourteenth Street. Peaches and cream, peaches with ice cream, "brandied" peaches lasting all through the winter, were the principal joy, with lesser ones crowding in, such as figs, bananas, watermelons, and coconuts. Even the small brothers recalled these days of abundant fruit and overflowing markets, for Robertson, the youngest son, years later, told of clutching his mother's shawl as she walked down Sixth Avenue to Washington market, with a basket on her arm, every week-day morning.[19]

Perhaps the most picturesque feature of New York City life in the mid-Nineteenth Century was the peddling of food from door to door by vendors who cried out their wares from morning till night. Each huckster had his special cry, according to what he offered for sale. The clam man sang out:

> Here's clams, here's clams, here's clams today,
> They lately came from Rockaway;
> They're good to roast, they're good to fry,
> They're good to make a clam pot-pie.
> Here they go!

Baker boys, with a tray of fresh tea rusk, went through the streets crying "tea ruk, ruk, ruk, tea ruk." Often Negro women were seen in the summer and fall, heads swathed in brilliant bandannas, on top of which each carried a pail, shouting "Hot corn, hot corn, here's your lily white hot corn; hot corn, all hot; just come out of the boiling pot!" Because of the general use of wood or bituminous coal, chimney sweeps were much in demand, calling "Sweep O!" competing with the junkman shouting "Rags, rags, any old rags— Scissors to grind, scissors to grind," all accompanied by the jingle

of the junk-cart bells. Adding to the general din were the voices of
vendors of oysters, fish, buns, yeast, hot spiced gingerbread, strawberries, ice cream, or other delectables.[20]

In this New York setting of their early years, the James children
were naturally more closely attached to the activities within the
home than with those out of doors. Much of their instruction during the first two or three years was carried on by governesses and
tutors. The fact that their father had no profession and spent most
of his time with his studies, his friends, and his family, caused the
home life to be unusually close and the relationship between the
father and the children very different indeed from that in other
families.

The realization that their father was without an evident profession suddenly struck the boys early in their New York experience.
Young Harry, hearing a boy say that his father was a stevedore, was
humiliated by the fact that no such fine and mysterious title belonged
to the elder James. In response to an appeal for some title, some
named profession upon which an explanation could be made to
playmates, very characteristically Henry James, Sr., replied: "Say I'm
a philosopher, say I'm a seeker for truth, say I'm a lover of my kind,
say I'm an author of books if you like; or, best of all, just say I'm
a student." The "student" plea young Harry found not at all satisfactory, but younger Robertson, or Bob, with all the confidence that
Harry lacked, announced boldly to the group of still curious playmates that his father was a student, and not only that, but "that
he had written *Lectures and Miscellanies James*." [21]

When the father happened to be an extraordinarily brilliant and
deeply affectionate man, the quality of the homelife was lifted to
a level that few children ever know. Many records bear testimony
to his devotion to the children whom he constantly instructed, often
by the mere flow of his conversation. They were to recollect, young
Harry in particular, that he brought them up "in horror of *conscious*
propriety . . . of 'flagrant' morality," yet with the deepest sense of
humanitarianism, of brotherhood and sympathetic understanding
of other people. Along such lines of thought and behavior he
taught them, not in a formal manner ever, but in the natural com-

panionship he offered them so that Henry, Jr., never forgot that
so many young impressions were gathered "at his side and in his
personal haunts."

It is interesting to note that he took these walks or had these
talks with the boys separately, so that neither Harry nor Willy
remembered going jointly with him, for "he seldom led us forth,
such as we were, together." The wise father early observed the
difference between them, but hypersensitive Harry was more aware
of this than his brother or father imagined. William "was to remember, as I perceived later on, many things that I didn't, impressions
I sometimes wished, as with a retracing jealousy, or at least envy,
that I might also have fallen direct heir to; but he professed amazement, and even occasionally impatience, at my reach of reminiscence
—liking as he did to brush away old moral scraps in favour of new
rather than to hoard and so complacently exhibit them. If in my
way I collected the new as well I yet cherished the old; the ragbag
of memory hung on its nail in my closet, though I learnt with time
to control the habit of bringing it forth." [22]

Even though Emerson was abroad in 1848, James kept up his
Boston connections.[23] Through his increasing acquaintances there
and in Cambridge he acquired some renown. In August, 1849,
James was invited to address the Town and Country Club of Boston.
He replied by accepting the invitation and enclosing to Mr. Alcott,
the treasurer, his five-dollars subscription. In writing to Emerson
about the nature of the talk he was to give, he included a paragraph
broaching the subject of another European trip then being considered by himself and Mrs. James with a view to the educational
and recreational needs of his family. When it is remembered that
the Jameses had just become established in New York and were
apparently settling down to a few years of uninterrupted home life,
this passage comes as a surprise:

My wife and I are obliged—so numerous has waxed our family—to
enlarge our house in town, and get a country house for the summer. These
things look expensive and temporary to us, besides being an additional
care; and so, looking upon our four stout boys, who have no play-room
within doors, and import shocking bad manners from the street, with much
pity, we gravely ponder whether it would not be better to go abroad for

a few years with them, allowing them to absorb French and German and get a better sensuous education than they are likely to get here. To be sure, this is but a glimpse of our ground of proceeding—but perhaps you know some decisive word which shall dispense it from any further consideration of the subject. When my paper to the Town and Country Club shall be read I shall be functionless, and may study as well, and better perhaps, abroad as here. Anyhow, and everywhere, I am, yours faithfully,

H. JAMES[24]

In response to a similar announcement in October, 1843, before the Jameses went abroad, Emerson had written, "I hate to have good men go out of the country which they keep sweet . . . " and in September, 1849, he wrote in similar words, "I hear with some terror that you are going to Europe, I who never see you, perhaps shall not, if you stay on this side. But New York looked amiable and intelligent whilst I knew you were in it. And now that we are to have a club, we might hope to see the members once a year. But you will not go till I have seen you, and learned to share in the project. So with kind remembrances to Mrs. James, Yours, R. W. Emerson." [25] On November 1, 1849 Henry James gave his lecture in Boston, on "Socialism and Civilization in Relation to the Development of the Individual Life," greatly strengthening his connections there.

This initial Boston lecture was followed by others with which the elder James established a reputation. Bronson Alcott recorded in his Journal for November 4, 1851: "Henry James advertises his lectures in the city papers, and is now coming to town (Boston) to read them. His audience will be small but intelligent and select, as was Emerson's, and essentially the same. But I cannot vouch for a very enthusiastic reception of him, or of his teachings. It would be too much to expect of our jealous and conservative Athenians. His themes, besides, are a little unpopular just now, and his bearing too consequential and knowing, as of a man with Kingdomcome in his brain, to make friends with any but the votaries of logic unadorned and of royal truth herself . . . A voracious intellect, subtle, sinuous, clear, forcible, and swift, voracious of guile as a cormorant of its prey. A terrible logician, and audacious even to the verge of duplicity. A fearless sham-shower of all visnomies, as of Medusian heads and Satan's, to his company. There is nothing so formidable, in his way, on this continent, and an over-match for any man—unless, perhaps, Carlyle—in the two hemispheres. It were safer for pretenders of all grades and complexions to keep out of his way on pain of being gobbled down by this glutton of deceits and fierce friend of truth and plain dealing . . . Perhaps this our New England is not quite the place for one of this Thracian mettle. Metropolitan New York were fitter, or the wild West . . . James is, perhaps, the best read of any American in those sovereigns of manifold thought— continents and seas each in himself—Swedenborg and Fourier, and needs all the room which these take and allow in which to move unencumbered and free." [26] Well could Henry James instruct his children to announce to their playmates that he was a philosopher, a seeker for truth, an author, a student.

In New York, the *Harbinger* expired in 1849, causing no small disappointment to the high hopes that had sustained the periodical through its brief existence. There were to be successors, *The Spirit of the Age,* and the *New Times,* the latter of which Henry James was to edit but it never appeared. The failure of these enterprises, however disappointing, did not dampen James's ardor for his study of Fourier and Swedenborg. He continued writing and lecturing, publishing in 1850 his *Moralism and Christianity; or, Man's Experience and Destiny.* This was composed of the lecture given in Boston before the Town and Country Club, combined with two lectures given in New York. Emerson too was lecturing in New York and staying as a guest in the James home. Such visits the boys well remembered, as did Emerson whose subsequent letters are filled with "kindest remembrances from me to your wife, and to your sister (Catherine Walsh); and give my love to the boys." [27] Under April 6, 1850, in his journal dated at Philadelphia, Emerson wrote:

I have made no note of these long weary absences at New York and Philadelphia. I am a bad traveller, and the hotels are mortifications to all sense of well-being in me. The people who fill them oppress me with their excessive virility, and would soon become intolerable if it were not for a few friends, who, like women, tempered the acrid mass. Henry James was true comfort,—wise, gentle, polished, with heroic manners, and a serenity like the sun.[28]

The joy which the older men found in their intellectual and social intercourse was felt by every member of the James household with little Harry, aged seven in 1850, retaining permanently awe-inspiring impressions "of the great and urbane Emerson's occasional presence in Fourteenth Street." [29] Many decades later the small boy was to recollect these visits in a manner and mood which catches much of the spirit of the James home in the mid-year of the nineteenth century:

I "visualize" at any rate the winter firelight of our back-parlour at dusk and the great Emerson—I knew he was great, greater than any of our friends—sitting in it between my parents, before the lamp had been lighted, as a visitor consentingly housed only could have done, and affecting me the more as an apparition sinuously and, I held, elegantly slim, benevolently aquiline, and commanding a tone alien, beautifully alien, to any we heard roundabout, that he bent this benignity upon me by an invitation to draw nearer to him, off the hearth-rug, and know myself as never yet, as I was not indeed to know myself again for years, in touch with the wonder of Boston. The wonder of Boston was above all just then and there for me in the sweetness of the voice and the finish of the speech—this latter through a sort of attenuated emphasis which at the same time made sounds more important, more interesting in themselves, than by any revelation yet vouchsafed us. Was not this my first glimmer of a sense that the human tone *could*, in that independent and original way, be interesting? and didn't it for a long time keep me going, however unwittingly, in that faith, carrying me in fact more or less on to my day of recognizing that it took much more than simply not being of New York to produce the music I had listened to. The point was that, however that might be, I had had given me there in the firelight an absolutely abiding measure. If I didn't know from that hour forth quite all it was to *not* utter sounds worth mentioning, I make out that I had at least the opposite knowledge. And all by the operation of those signal moments—the truth of which I find somehow reflected in the fact of my afterwards knowing one of our household rooms for the time—it must have been our only guest-chamber—as "Mr. Emerson's room." The evening firelight played so long for me upon the door—that is to the length probably of three days, the length of a child's impression.[30]

Within two years, by the same fire-side in the back-parlour of #58 Fourteenth Street, the celebrated Thackeray was to make an equally strong impression on the same small boy.

NOTES

1. *The Literary Remains of Henry James,* 151, 152.
2. Henry James, *The Nature of Evil,* New York, D. Appleton & Co., 1915, 99.
3. *A Small Boy and Others,* 8.
4. *Ibid.,* 9, 10.
5. Edith Wharton, one of Henry James, Jr.'s most intimate and devoted friends, states that French people told her that they never met an Anglo-Saxon who spoke French as did James, not only correctly but fluently. She also comments interestingly on his stammer and the way it would leave him under certain circumstances, as for example when he read certain poems, like Emily Bronte's "Remembrance"—"His stammer ceased as by magic as soon as he began to read, and his ear, so sensitive to the convolutions of an intricate prose style, never allowed him to falter over the most complex prosody, but swept him forward on great rollers of sound till the full weight of his voice fell on the last cadence." Edith Wharton, *A Backward Glance,* New York, D. Appleton-Century Co., Inc., 1934, 185. Concerning James's stammer see also 177, 178, 195.
6. Letter from Carlyle to Emerson, November 17, 1843, as quoted by C. Hartley Grattan, *The Three Jameses,* New York, Longmans, Green & Co., 1932, 45. Edward Emerson, describing a visit to the James home, in commenting on the elder James said: "For he was not only a humorist, but master of the superlative, and, after a little almost stuttering hesitation, he, like his sons after him would bring out an adjective or adverb, etc." Edward W. Emerson, *The Early Years of the Saturday Club,* Boston, Houghton Mifflin Co., 1918, 327.
7. *A Small Boy and Others,* 12.
8. *The Letters of William James,* I, 104, 105.
9. MS. letter from Mary Robertson Walsh to Mrs. J. J. G. Wilkinson, November 29, 1846, Houghton Library, Harvard University.
10. MS. letter from Garth Wilkinson to Henry James, Sr., August 17, 1847, Houghton Library, Harvard University.
11. *A Small Boy and Others,* 52, 53. The closing of this nearly century-old hotel was announced in the New York *Times,* Sunday, August 1, 1948: "The Brevoort ceased operations as a hotel yesterday in its ninety-fourth year at Fifth Avenue and Eighth Street."
12. Louis Philippe crossed the channel to Newhaven, after his flight from Paris, on March 3, 1848. An account of his arrival was given in the London *Times,* March 4, 1848.
13. James Grant Wilson, *The Memorial History of the City of New York,* III, 422, New York, New York History Co., 1893.
14. *A Small Boy and Others,* 178.
15. *Ibid.,* 61. In a letter to Edmund Tweedy, Henry James, Sr., wrote, September 5, 1852: "Steam boats are running mad on the rivers

and lakes, and people will shortly be obliged to take to lynching the captain and hands in order to protect themselves against violence. Yesterday the *Reindeer* blew up on the Hudson at Saugerties, killing 27 people, found; how many more no one knows. She had not let off steam once between New York and that point." MS. letter from Henry James, Sr., to Edmund Tweedy, September 5, 1852, Houghton Library, Harvard University.

16. *A Small Boy and Others*, 23.

17. *Harper's Weekly*, April 11, 1857.

18. *A Small Boy and Others*, 25, 26.

19. MS. letter from Robertson James to Alice H. James, February 24, 1898, Houghton Library, Harvard University. A guide book of the day describes Washington Market as being at the "corner of Vesey and Fulton streets, near the water's edge. It occupies a whole square, and is very similar to Fulton Market in its construction and internal arrangements. This market was formerly called the Bear market, from the fact that bear meat was there exposed for sale. The amount of business done there is less than at the Fulton, but the whole south and west population of the city frequent it— the products of the north river country find their principal sale in this market." *Francis' Picture of New-York. Strangers Guide.* New York, C. S. Francis & Co., 1851, 89.

20. Henry Collins Brown, *op. cit.,* 344. In writing of the hawkers, Brown continues: "They were a picturesque, hard-working lot with many a well-known character among them. So pronounced a feature of the city's life that curious drawings of them still exist; one in particular in the rooms of the New York Historical Society shows at least a dozen characteristic faces of these itinerant merchants. Strange to relate, the omnipresent newsboy of today had not made his appearance in any considerable number, but his beginning was noted." *Ibid.*

21. *Notes of a Son and Brother*, 64, 65.

22. *A Small Boy and Others*, 68, 69.

23. Bronson Alcott noted on March 24, 1848: "Took a morning walk around the Common before breakfast. Passed an hour at Parker's (Theodore Parker's house, 1 Exeter Place) where I met James who has spent some years in London and knows Wilkinson and Carlyle intimately. He told me of many things of both, and we had much to say on Swedenborg, of whose writings he is a student and whom he ranks first among modern minds. James intends to print a journal devoted to the views of Fourier and Swedenborg. His tracts called *Tracts for the Times* (N. Y., 1847) won him regard of the best people among us. I liked him well." *The Journals of Bronson Alcott,* ed. Odell Shepard, Boston, Little, Brown, & Co., 1938, 205.

24. Quoted in Ralph Barton Perry, *op. cit.,* I, 60.

25. *Ibid.,* I, 59, 60.

26. Bronson Alcott, *op. cit.*, 256, 257.
27. Quoted by Ralph Barton Perry, *op. cit.*, I, 62.
28. Bliss Perry, *The Heart of Emerson's Journals*, 248.
29. *A Small Boy and Others*, 8.
30. *Notes of a Son and Brother*, 204, 205.

Chapter Three

Experiments in Education

" . . . no education avails for the intelligence that
does not stir in it some subjective passion. . . . "

By 1850, the mind of the elder James had developed that "serenity of the sun" which Emerson noted and which the James children in retrospect were to appreciate so deeply. "It was a luxury, I to-day see," wrote Henry, Jr., many decades later, "to have all the benefits of his intellectual and spiritual, his religious, his philosophic and his social passion, without ever feeling the pressure of it to our direct irritation or discomfort." [1] This freedom from didacticism, the firm assurance that he was doing the right thing for his children in not submitting them to a rigid and prescribed academic training, can be understood only in terms of the elder James's spiritual convictions combined with his own experiences as a boy and young man. The magnanimity of his character had been developed rather early and under the pressure of some bitter incidents. His physical and mental agonies had played a large part in developing the fierce drive with which he had thought his way out of theological chaos into the peace and harmony of absolute faith.

"Father's *ideas,*" as they were affectionately and jokingly called within the family circle, supported and pervaded his very existence, and to a considerable extent that of his family. These "ideas" had crystallized by 1850 primarily as the result of the intellectual crisis he had suffered at Windsor in the spring of 1844, with the subsequent years of study of Swedenborg and Fourier. His friendship with such men as Wilkinson, Emerson, and Carlyle had so broadened and deepened his philosophic concepts that he was in these New York years coming into the fullness of his mental and spiritual powers. The bearing this had upon his relationship with his children is of paramount importance at this particular period of their early life. Henry, Jr., who was never fully to understand his father's religious philosophy, was none the less deeply cognizant of its effect. In spite of "a total otherness of contemplation" in the son during the years when he was closest to his father's ideas, he wrote: ". . . but the active, not to say the obvious, moral of them, in all our younger times, was that a life of the most richly consequent flowed straight out of them, that in this life, the most abundantly, and above all naturally, communicated *as* life that it was possible to imagine, we had an absolutely equal share." [2]

It seems characteristic of the Irish nature that it combines a native wit with a spontaneity of spirit and vitality often resulting in outstanding talent. William James of Albany had manifested such talent in terms of his extraordinary success as a merchant and business man. His son Henry, prior to the catastrophe which resulted in the loss of his leg at the age of thirteen, was possessed of corresponding strength and vitality, so much so, that he later wrote, "My boyish animal spirits, or my excessive enjoyment of life, allowed me no doubt very little time for reflection; yet it was very seldom that I lay down at night without a present thought of God, and some little effort of recoil upon myself." [3] With the amputation of his leg and the two years of confinement to his bed, the virile lad lost much of his animal spirits, but he developed a fine sense of contemplation. From this tragic event came a changed relation between William James, the busy merchant, and his crippled, convalescent son. "When I was very young I do not remember to have had much intellectual contact with my father save at family prayers and at meals, for he was always occupied during the day with business; and even in the frank domestic intercourse of the evening, when he was fond of hearing his children read to him, and would frequently exercise them in their studies, I cannot recollect that he ever questioned me about my out-of-door occupations, or about my companions, or showed any extreme solicitude about my standing in school. He was certainly a very easy parent, and I might have been left to regard him perhaps as a rather indifferent one, if it had not been for a severe illness . . . which confined me for a long time to the house, when his tenderness to me showed itself so assiduous and indeed extreme as to give me an exalted sense of his affection." [4] In another autobiographical passage he states: "My father was weakly, nay painfully, sensitive to his children's claims upon his sympathy; and I myself, when I became a father in my turn, felt that I could freely sacrifice property and life to save my children from unhappiness." [5]

The strong touch of Irish sentiment and sympathy that Henry James, Sr., noted in his father and expressed so fully with his own children was, however, counterbalanced by later, very intense incompatibilities, resulting from the intolerant Calvinistic views inflexibly held to by William of Albany. There is in the long story of the Henry James family no parallel situation of intolerance or incompatibility between father and son. The harrowing experience of estrangement from his father had so chastened and steeped him in the evils of intolerance that he went almost to the opposite extreme in dealing with his own children. Yet, he endeared himself to his family and friends with his extraordinary forces of sympathy and understanding without sentimentalism or any possessiveness in his relationships. He was able to do so because he consistently based his associations with his fellow men upon his idealistic social and religious principles. This foundation for human conduct was, therefore, far more durable than fleeting human sentiment and affections, and the practical, specific use he made of his faith and understanding are frequently mentioned in his correspondence. In 1854 he wrote to his friend and financial advisor, Samuel Gray Ward of Boston: " . . . So too in the education of children one gets great help from all this clear knowledge of spiritual laws. I am sure my paternity is daily softened and developed by it, and the dear chickens, it seems to me, come under my wing every night with an increasing sense of benediction." [6] The brilliant careers of his two eldest sons stand as unquestionable proof of the success of and reward for the years of applying his spiritual insight to their development; and the many letters, beautifully affectionate, between the sons and their father support in vivid testimony the "increasing sense of benediction" which his remarkable paternity pronounced.

In the introduction to *The Literary Remains of Henry James,* his son William has written an intimate and concise statement of the father's "clear knowledge of spiritual laws." But metaphysics and philosophy are complicated fields of thought which, however clear to the elder James himself, were ever difficult of presentation. "Oh, that I might thunder it out in a single interjection that would tell the *whole* of it, and never speak a word again!" he exclaimed in a frustrated moment of explanation. It is possible, nevertheless, to isolate some of his basic ideas, three of which in particular relate specifically to his theory of educating his children: (1) *God, the Creator, exists in everpresent unity with his Creation;* (2) *this unity of God and Man is hindered by nature and society; and* (3) *Man's innate spiritual spontaneity must be cultivated and protected against nature and society.* On these three basic points Henry James formed a system of training his children; to the application of this system he devoted over thirty years, from their infancy to their adulthood.

The first of these points was stated in his own words to a friend who had questioned the manner in which Harry and Willy were being trained in their youth: "The truth is . . . I have but one *fixed mind* about anything: which is that whether we stay here or go abroad, and whatever befalls our dear boys in this world, they and you and I are all alike, and after all, absolute creatures of God, vivified every moment by Him, cared for every moment by Him, guided every moment by Him, guided every moment by an infallible wisdom and an irreproachable tenderness, and that we have none of us therefore the slightest right to indulge any anxiety or listen in any conceivable circumstance to the lightest whisper of perturbation." [7] This is the central plank in his whole platform of convictions, that each individual is an absolute creature of God, in immediate and constant relation with God, guided and protected by His infallible wisdom and tenderness. This thesis of what seemed to Henry

James the true relation between the Creator and mankind appears in innumerable letters, and in nearly all the newspaper articles, essays, lectures, and books that he wrote. "Probably few authors have so devoted their entire lives to the monotonous elaboration of one single bundle of truths." [8]

Perceiving intuitively and adhering unfalteringly to this first conviction, the absolute unity between God and man, Henry James proceeded to the second point, expressed in his lecture, "Socialism and Civilization," given at Boston, on November 1, 1849: "Two things hinder the consciousness of this unity on the part of man—nature and society; the one by limiting his power, the other by limiting his sympathies; the one by finiting his body, the other by finiting his soul. Accordingly, the Christ, or representative Divine Man, is seen warring with and subjecting both nature and society . . . I repeat that the curse of our present ties, that which eliminates all their poetry, is our limited property in man and things, is the finite selfhood imposed on us by the present evil world. My internal property or selfhood, that which God gives me, is nothing short of infinite, is Himself in Truth. To match this divine internal, nature gives me my feeble body, society gives me a petty score of relatives and friends." [9] Thus, from the purely metaphysical thesis, first, of the unity of God and man, through the second point, the hindering of this unity by the action of nature and society, he comes to the third step in his system, bringing the train of ideas more definitely into closer relation to human experience.

In the Boston lecture of 1849, he arrives at the third point in the following words: "You all remember those grand mystic sayings of the Christ, 'whoso will lose his life in this world shall keep it unto life eternal,' and 'whoso will leave father or mother, or brother or sister, or wife or child, for my sake, shall find all these relations multiplied a hundred-fold.' Now what is the great spiritual burden of these divine words, for you know every divine word is so mainly from within. Is it not that our primal dignity is divine, and flows from God within us instead of from our outward relations? Is it not that each of us is under paramount allegiance to his own spontaneous life, and that if we insist first on the fulfilment of this allegiance, all these secondary or derivative relations will fall of themselves into harmony?" [10] Thus, this primal dignity, this spontaneous life within, flowing from God, is the paramount thing in man's experience and his allegiance to it must be maintained, even at the cost of sacrificing his outward or social relations.

There is a strong connection, one observes here, between this idea and Emerson's theory of self-reliance as "God-reliance." While it is, of course, merely a restating of the teaching of Jesus and is therefore in no way new, the degree to which Henry James would actually apply the idea in human relations was refreshingly new; it resulted, within his own family circle, in that law of freedom which was the key-note of the children's social and intellectual intercourse. This third point of the primal importance of man's innate spiritual spontaneity and his sacred allegiance to it, presented the problem of cultivating and protecting it from nature and society. This, then, is the point of contact between his spiritual convictions and the physical or natural problem of applying these "ideas" to his children's training as individuals and as members of society.

In enlarging upon this idea he continues: "We degrade by owning and just in the degree of our owning . . . We degrade and disesteem every person we own absolutely, every person bound to us by any other tenure than his own spontaneous affection. Of course one values one's brothers and sisters in the present state of things, if from nothing else, than from self-love; for society is so unfriendly and torpid to us that the domestic hearth gathers a warmth not wholly its own . . . It is the indispensable condition of a perfect respect, that a person be inwardly individualized, that is, possess the complete supremacy of his own actions. Then all his relations are of an inevitable dignity . . . So also one's child, how tiresome he grows when he does nothing morning, noon or night, but reflect the paternal dullness, when he is sedulous to do all the father prescribes and avoid all the mother condemns! Yet how beautiful he becomes, when he ever and anon flashes forth some spontaneous grace, some self-prompted courtesy!" [11] The watchword of the system and the ensuing educational experiments was "spontaneity." Whatever would cultivate and protect this inward grace and preserve the primal unity

of God and man must be secured at whatever sacrifice or cost. Furthermore, the whole process must begin at the earliest stages of training
and development. In fact, the childhood experiences were of even
greater significance than those of subsequent years.

The period of the New York residence in the early 'Fifties, when
the children were all under ten, marked the initial steps of the process.
In theory, at least, the elder James was perfectly certain of what he
desired at this time: "The great worth of one's childhood to his
future manhood consists in its being a storehouse of innocent natural
emotions and affections, based upon ignorance, which offer themselves
as an admirable Divine mould or anchorage to the subsequent development of his spiritual life or freedom. Accordingly in so far as you
inconsiderately shorten this period of infantile innocence and ignorance in the child, you weaken his chances of a future manly character." [12] This idea, as it was applied, explains the extremes to which
the parents went in their efforts to protect the children from importing
"shocking bad manners from the street," and to provide them with
tutors and companions whose influence would cultivate their minds
and at the same time prolong the innocence and purity of childhood.
The longer they could be protected from the gross and evil aspects
of society the stronger would be their manly characters and their
spiritual life or freedom. This sheltering from such mundane experiences as were the common lot of the average child was undertaken
not with a sense of fear but with the desire to preserve and cultivate
that innate spiritual spontaneity that is man's birthright. Thus, what
appears to be the delayed development of the careers of both William
and Henry James, Jr.,—for neither son became self-supporting until
he was well along in his thirties—is actually the resultant factor of
this particular phase of their father's "ideas." The use of the word
"ignorance" in the phrase "innocence and ignorance" must not be
misunderstood. By it is not meant intellectual ignorance, but rather
ignorance existing because of moral purity. No man was ever freer
or more honest with his sons than was Henry James. He was impatient with humbug of every sort, and, as already stated, Henry, Jr.,
testified, "in horror of *conscious* propriety, of what my father was
fond of calling 'flagrant' morality." [13]

In the realm of religious instruction, he afforded his children such a breadth of freedom that both Henry, Jr., and William were later to regret what they considered too much religious freedom and not enough coherent form of training. On this subject the second son wrote that " . . . our young liberty in respect to church-going was absolute and we might range at will, through the great city, from one place of worship and one form of faith to another, or might on occasion ignore them all equally, which was what we mainly did; . . . going forth hand in hand into the sunshine (and I connect myself here with my next younger, not my elder, brother, whose orbit was other and larger) we sampled, in modern phrase, as small unprejudiced inquirers obeying their inspiration, any resort of any congregation detected by us; doing so, I make out moreover, with a sense of earnest provision for any contemporary challenge. 'What church do you go to?'—the challenge took in childish circles that searching form; of the form it took among our elders my impression is more vague. To which I must add as well that our 'fending' in this fashion for ourselves didn't so prepare us for invidious remark—remark I mean upon our pewless state, which involved, in my imagination, much the same credit that a houseless or a cookless would have done— as to hush in my breast the appeal to our parents, not for religious instruction (of which we had plenty, and of the most charming and familiar) but simply for instruction (a very different thing) as to where we should say we 'went,' in our world, under cold scrutiny or derisive comment. It was colder than any criticism, I recall, to hear our father reply that we could plead nothing less than the whole privilege of Christendom and that there was no communion, even that of the Catholics, even that of the Jews, even that of the Swedenborgians, from which we need find ourselves excluded. With the freedom we enjoyed our dilemma clearly amused him: it would have been impossible, he affirmed, to be theologically more *en règle*. How as mere detached unaccompanied infants we enjoyed such impunity of range and confidence of welcome beyond comprehension save by the light of the old manners and conditions, the old local bonhomie, the comparative primal innocence, the absence of complications: with the several notes of which last beatitude my reminiscence surely shines. It was the theory of time and place that the young, were they but young enough, could take publicly no harm; to which adds itself moreover, and touchingly enough, all the difference of the old importances. It wasn't doubtless that the social, or call it simply the human, position of the child was higher than to-day—a circumstance not conceivable; it was simply that other dignities and values and claims, other social and human positions, were less definite and settled, less prescriptive and absolute. A rich sophistication is after all a gradual growth, and it would have been sophisticated to fear for us, before such bright and vacant vistas, the perils of the way or to see us received anywhere even with the irony of patronage. We hadn't in fact seats of honour, but that justice was done us—that is that we were placed to our advantage—I infer from my having liked so to 'go,' even though my grounds may have been but the love of the *exhibition* in general, thanks to which figures, faces, furniture, sounds, smells and colours became for me, wherever enjoyed, and enjoyed most where most collected, a positive little orgy of the senses and riot of the mind." [14]

It is highly significant that this freedom of choice in church attendance was intended by the elder James to offer the boys the widest possible individual experience by observation of a variety of church rituals, but for young Harry what it actually did was to afford an "orgy of the senses and riot of the mind" in the realms of imagination directed more toward his aesthetic than religious education. It was always to be so with Henry James, Jr., in such experiences, that the "figures, faces, furniture, sounds, smells and colours" were to mean far more to him than all the heterogeneous dogmas and creeds ever presented from pulpit or platform.

What the boys missed in their youthful religious experience, Harry especially, was the ritual, the traditional, the conventional pattern of regular church attendance with a recognized family pew and the ramifications of social activities that the ordinary family enjoyed as the accepted American way of life. In lieu of this element, however, they received at home the enlightening stimulation of the elder James's brilliant mind. All the children abundantly testified to this fact, Henry, Jr., with the statement: ". . . it would absolutely not have been possible to us, in the measure of our sensibility, to breathe more the air of that reference to an order of goodness and power greater than any this world by itself can show which we understand as the religious spirit." [15] Still, on the score of there being none of the conventional evidences of religious life, he continues in the same passage: "Wondrous to me, as I consider again, that my father's possession of this spirit, in a degree that made it more deeply one with his life than I can conceive another or a different case of its being, should have been unaccompanied with a single one of the outward or formal, the theological, devotional, ritual, or even implicitly pietistic signs by which we usually know it. The fact of course was that his religion was nothing if not a philosophy, extraordinarily complex and worked out and original, intensely personal as an exposition, yet not only susceptible of application, but clamorous for it, to the whole field of consciousness, nature and society, history, knowledge, all human relations and questions, every pulse of the process of our destiny." [16]

Henry James, Sr., so absolutely convinced of the inward goodness of man and so abundantly expressing that goodness and power in his own personal life and relations with his children, felt free to allow them such a scope in their religious training. It was always by works rather than words that he expressed his spiritual convictions to them. Henry, Jr., did recall that he occasionally read them stories from the Bible when they were small, but he also recalled that the elder James never imposed upon them the contents of his written works or lectures. The children were, of course, too young in the early 'Fifties to attend the lectures which their father was then engaged in giving. They remembered only his going forth in the early evening, their mother fluttering about him at the door, and the boys in procession on the stairs, pausing on their way to bed, in the excitement of the lecturer's departure.

Even a few years later, at Newport when the boys were in their teens and could well have exhibited some genuine interest in their father's study and writing, they came no closer to it than the door of the room in which he was working. He would then look up and remark a bit wistfully, "Oh I say, do look in a moment for manners if for nothing else!" He demanded of them hardly even the courtesy of their attention and never inflicted upon them directly his religious and philosophic convictions. It can be seen that in so refraining he was adhering to that principle which was so cardinal a point in his whole system of educating them, that the children must be free to cultivate and develop their own individual, natural spontaneity. The effort that this cost him, in relation to the question of religious instruction, must have been enormous in the light of the all-consuming fervor with which he pursued his research in that direction. Whether ultimately one consider it a fortunate or unfortunate thing for the children, there can be no question that they had extraordinary freedom of choice and that their father, with good reason, felt not the least fear in granting them such freedom.

When it came to the question of academic instruction, the very earliest years were the easiest ones in which to exercise an equal amount of freedom, for the situation was taken care of through the employment of governesses and tutors who were very carefully selected in terms of the elder James's ideas of qualifications. Most of them were chosen because of the purity of their French accent and the cultural degree of their training; this naturally directed the choice toward Europeans, although, for some reason or other, these departed as often as the Americans. The same basis of choice was followed in the selection of schools, when the boys came to an age at which it was more desirable for them to have regular classroom instruction and the group experience of competition and companionship.

The immediate successor to Miss "Bayou" of the Dutch House in Albany, was Mrs. Daly, the second in the "bevy of these educative ladies" who instructed the James boys, "literally with gloves." Her dame's school was a low house in a small row on the south side of Waverly Place. In visualizing Mrs. Daly and the vanished social order she represented, Henry, Jr., saw her as "a stout, red-faced lady with grey hair and a large apron, the latter convenience somehow suggesting, as she stood about with a resolute air, that she viewed her little pupils as so many small slices cut from the loaf of life and on which she was to dab the butter of arithmetic and spelling, accompanied by way of jam with a light application of the practice of prize-giving. I recall an occasion indeed, I must in justice mention, when the jam really was thick—my only memory of a schoolfeast, strange to say, throughout our young annals: something uncanny in the air of the schoolroom at the unwonted evening or late afternoon hour, and tables that seemed to me prodigiously long and on which the edibles were chunky and sticky. The stout red-faced lady must have been Irish, as the name she bore imported—or do I think so but from the indescribably Irish look of her revisited house?[17] It refers itself at any rate to a New York age in which a little more or a little less of the colour was scarce notable in the general flush." [18]

Waverly Place, in the autumn of 1848, when Willy, six and a half, and Harry, a little over five, strolled hand in hand down Fifth Avenue from Fourteenth Street to Washington Square, was far from the run-down area revisited fifty years later. It was indeed fashionable, making a strong stand against the tide moving uptown and the elegance of Union Square "situated at the termination of Broadway," with its oval form enclosed by an iron railing, and its center ornamented with a handsome fountain. On Washington Square, along the top of which Waverly Place crossed from Christopher Street to Broadway, was Grandmother Walsh's home where the small boys often stopped to pay a visit, or to play on the "Parade Ground." A guide book of the time describes it as in the northern part of the city, containing about 12 acres, "now a beautiful place of resort, and has of late undergone great improvement. An elegant iron fence is to supersede the antiquated wooden one which has surrounded it for many years past, the Common Council having recently appropriated $25,000 for that purpose." For years, Washington Square or Parade was the Potter's Field, "the general receptacle of the indigent and strangers, after the shackles of life had been thrown off," [19] but that time had long since passed and Mrs. Daly in her humble, red, two-story house, with its wrought-iron porch, was indeed well situated.

Significantly, the dame's school experiment did not last long, for Mrs. Daly's instruction gave way to that of Miss Rogers, "previously of 'Chelsea Female Institute,' " whose elegant gloves were strikingly impressive as the genteel Miss Rogers "beat time with a long black ferule to some species of droning chant or chorus in which we spent most of our hours . . . I see her very tall and straight and spare, in a light blue dress, her firm face framed in long black glossy ringlets and the stamp of the Chelsea Female Institute all over her." [20] In all probability, Miss Rogers possessed social graces with which Mrs. Daly was not sufficiently blessed.

Another reason for importing these instructresses into the home on Fourteenth Street in preference to sending Willy and Harry out to Mrs. Daly's or some other like establishment can be explained in terms of the two younger sons, Wilky, four, and Bob, three, in 1849, who were coming along to pre-school age. All four boys quite easily could be managed by one teacher at home where there were sure to be no undesirable companions or influences. Why Miss Rogers gave way to Miss Sedgwick and why Miss Sedgwick was not long retained within the ranks, as the procession of "educative ladies" moved along in 1849, 1850, and 1851, there can be no adequate explanation; but the ritual and the routine of home instruction were maintained over this period without unusual stress or impressiveness.

Things changed, however, when "small brown snappy Mademoiselle Delavigne" arrived on the scene, engaged because of her excellent French, a lady not without connections, being introduced into the James family as the niece, or probably grand-niece, of the celebrated Casimir. The charm and vivaciousness of Mlle. Delavigne stirred deeply young Harry's romantic imagination and he was forever after to think of her as "flitting in and out on quick, fine, more or less cloth-shod feet of exemplary neatness, the flat-soled feet of Louis Philippe and of the female figures in those volumes of Gavarni then actual, then contemporaneous, which were kept in a piece of furniture that stood between the front-parlour windows in Fourteenth Street, together with a set of Béranger enriched by steel engravings to the strange imagery of which I so wonderingly responded that all other art of illustration, ever since, has been for me comparatively weak and cold." [21] It was Mlle. Delavigne who played one of the earliest roles in the scene of "Europe," which began to form in young Harry's mind. Strikingly continental, "she was, besides not being at all pink or shy, oval and fluent and mistress somehow of the step—the step of levity that involved a whisk of her short skirt; there she was, to the life, on the page of Gavarni, attesting in reality, and there again did that page in return (I speak not of course of the unplumbed depths of the appended text), attest her own felicity. I was later on to feel—that is I was to learn—how many impressions and appearances, how large a sense of things, her type and tone prefigured." [22]

The vivacious Mlle. Delavigne was followed by a majestic Russian lady. So regal was she and so alien that her name was lost in the shadow of her overwhelming figure, the details of which were to remain permanently with Henry, Jr., even "to an extraordinarily short cape . . . of the same stuff as her dress, and Merovingian side-braids that seemed to require the royal crown of Frédégonde or Brunéhaut to complete their effect." Her accent was unquestionably good and her other assets of a fine order, but she too proved to be but "a creature of an hour" even though she lived with the Jameses during her term of employment, a sign of comparative security in the position. To Willy and Harry, the most outstanding fact about the Russian lady was that she came from Siberia; but she too was to leave, being "too big for a little job (she), towered over us doubtless too heroically."

Except for Mrs. Vrenenburg, who does not come into the chronology until the summer of 1854, very near the end of the New York scene, there remained but one other lady instructor, Mrs. Lavinia D. Wright, whose distinction for the children lay not in her ability as a teacher, so much, as in the situation of her school on East Twenty-first Street. En route each day, the boys had to pass the scene of the construction of the Hudson River Railroad which was nearing completion in 1851. There an education could be acquired more liberal than the offerings of "Lavinia D." Willy observed, however, "with characteristic authority . . . that that lady was a very able woman, as shown by the Experiments upstairs. He was upstairs of course, and I was down, and I scarce even knew what Experiments were, beyond their indeed requiring capability. The region of their performance was William's natural sphere, though I recall that I had a sense of peeping into it to a thrilled effect on seeing our instructress illustrate the proper way to extinguish a candle. She firmly pressed the flame between her thumb and her two forefingers, and, on my remarking that I didn't see how she could do it, promptly replied that I of course couldn't do it myself (as *he* could) because I should be afraid." [23]

As unsatisfactory as these schools and tutors all proved to be, there was no question of the children's being educated privately. Public schools in New York at that time were extremely poor. A Public School Society had been chartered in 1805 as a private corporation, organized by a group of public-minded citizens, DeWitt Clinton being the most prominent. In 1842, Governor Seward sent a message to the City urging the people to establish a school board elected by the people, with the result that for the first time, in that same year, the common-school system of the State was extended to the City of New York. The Society, however, was not dissolved until 1853, there being in the meantime a strong political and religious agitation on the part of the greatly increased Catholic population, to receive a share of public funds for the parochial schools in the City.[24] This movement, not unlike the present day situation in several states, aroused a storm of protests on all sides for several years. The general conditions in the public schools were therefore not propitious for the quality of education the Jameses were seeking for their children.

In the autumn of 1852, Willy and Harry were entered as day-pupils in the Institute Vergnès, situated on Broadway near Fourth Street. Each day they enjoyed this most stirring thoroughfare in the city. By 1850, Broadway had assumed a commercial and theatrical character, to some degree, in nearly every block from Canal Street to Bleeker Street, though much of the old residential character still remained. At Tenth Street, where Broadway changes its course, Grace Church was erected in 1846, the congregation having moved up from the far region of Rector Street near the Battery. During the next year, the New York Hotel was opened at 721 Broadway, between Washington Place and Waverly Place, an undertaking then considered by many as perilous, since the hotel was so far uptown. Inroads were also being made by places of amusement, with Tripler (or Metropolitan) Hall being opened in 1850 at 677 Broadway near Bond Street, the famous auditorium in which Jenny Lind was to have sung upon her arrival that September. Actually her first concert was given at Castle Garden, as Tripler Hall was not completed in time. The theatres were further down town; Brougham's Lyceum near Broome Street, the Park, the Broadway Theatre between Pearl and Worth Street were the leading houses. Institute Vergnès, thus impressed the boys as being very much in the center of things, the "liveliest conceivable" place in "the very pulse of traffic." Even though it proved as a school to be "a prompt disillusionment" the impression made was deep and permanent.

The rooms occupied by the Institute were situated on the first and second floors, overlooking the busy thoroughfare with its clattering "stages" and carts. M. Vergnès, highly irritated and bristling much of the time, catered mostly to small, homesick Cubans and Mexicans whose temperaments and conditions only intensified the general stir which prevailed. Most of the staff seemed constantly in a rage, as the James boys thought, expressing themselves in accents alarmingly shrill, with flushed complexions, tearing up hapless exercises and forever hurling more *dictées* at the cringing little Cubans, Mexicans, and Jameses bending before them. As the passion of instruction increased, one can imagine the retiring, hesitant Harry in a mounting state of terror and misery. Fortunately his inconspicuousness shielded him from the fray and he was able to play his favorite role of interested spectator in safe detachment. "In the Vergnès air at any rate I seem myself to have sat unscathed and unterrified—not alarmed even by so much as a call to the blackboard; only protected by my insignificance, which yet covered such a sense of our dusky squalor. Queer for us the whole affair, assuredly; but how much queerer for the poor petits pays chauds who had come so far for the privilege." [25]

How much Willy and Harry learned can hardly be judged. Some groundwork had been laid, Henry, Jr., felt in after years, for a "perfect assimilation of Alphonse Daudet's chronicle of 'Jack';" for Jack also was to learn the first lessons of life along with "petits pays chauds"—all of which was to see again the Institute Vergnès at once revived, swarming with poor little wretches in the second floor of that strange Broadway establishment of learning. Actually it was not so strange to the New York of that day, for there were many such boys' schools. Cousin Gus Barker from Albany, the orphaned nephew of Henry James, Sr., attended one entitled the Institute Charlier, and Gus's sister attended a fashionable finishing school, Madame Reichardt's in which only French was spoken on the premises. Harry, on a brief call there felt that he had crossed "the very threshold of 'Europe.' "

During 1853-1854 the boys attended the school of one Richard Pulling Jenks. This "select resort for young gentlemen" was then situated, as was the less select one of M. Vergnès, on Broadway near Fourth Street, and was composed, in the place of Latin Americans, of De Coppets and Van Winkles and Jameses. Much like the arrangements of the previous year, the rooms stretched from the Broadway front to the rear of the building and were closely packed with "young gentlemen" who were not always comfortable, even seated near the large stove which was silhouetted against gray, gritty oilcloth. Into such quarters the boys scrambled up out of Broadway, Harry forever afterward recalling the smell of the steep, cold, dusty wooden staircase, and back into Broadway they dropped each afternoon. The fascinations of this exciting thoroughfare were to Harry as educational as any lessons offered by Mr. Jenks or his assistants. "I literally conclude," he later wrote, "that we must have knocked about in Broadway, and in Broadway alone, like perfect little men of the world; we must have been let loose there to stretch our legs and fill our lungs, without prejudice either to our earlier and later freedoms of going and coming. I as strictly infer, at the same time, that Broadway must have been then as one of the alleys of Eden, for any sinister contact or consequence involved for us; a circumstance that didn't in the least interfere, too, as I have noted, with its offer of an entrancing interest. The interest verily could have been a *calculated* thing on the part of our dear parents as little as on that of Mr. Jenks himself." [26] The "earlier and later freedoms" and the stretching of legs and necks along Broadway were youthful enjoyments far more calculated by the parents than the boys had any reason to believe. It was always to urban environments that the parents directed the boys who were to stroll down Picadilly and saunter up the Champs-Élysées just as they stretched their legs up and down Broadway. Contact with the throbbing life of New York, London, and Paris was as important a part of the elder James's concept of the boys' education. The stimulation of mind, the enhancement of imagination, and the comparison of people that such contact afforded were to prove, in the case of Henry James, Jr., of inestimable value.

Two assistants to Mr. Jenks etched vivid vignettes in the mind of Harry and not without reason. One was Mr. Dolmidge, the writing master whom he describes as "inordinately lean, clean-shaved, as was comparatively uncommon then, and in a swallow-tailed coat and I think a black satin stock, was surely perfect in his absolutely functional way, a pure pen-holder of a man, melancholy and mild, who taught the most complicated flourishes—great scrolls of them met our view in the form of surging seas and beaked and beady-eyed eagles, the eagle being so calligraphic a bird—while he might just have taught resignation. He was not at all funny—no one out of our immediate family circle, in fact almost no one but W. J. himself, who flowered in every waste, seems to have struck me funny in those years; but he was to remain with me a picture of somebody in Dickens, one of the Phiz if not the Cruikshank pictures." [27]

Even more striking was the impression made by the drawing master, Mr. Coe. In view of the several years that William James was given over quite seriously to the study of art, with William Hunt at Newport especially, it is interesting to note how large a part Mr. Coe played in the minds of both boys during the winter of 1853-1854. Henry, Jr., was to recall brother William "drawing, and drawing, always drawing, especially under the lamplight of the Fourteenth Street back parlour; and not as with a plodding patience, which I think would less have affected me, but easily, freely and, as who should say, infallibly: always at the stage of finishing off, his head dropped from side to side and his tongue rubbing his lower lip." [28] To this natural talent, Mr. Coe must have added a touch of inspiration for he was "a worthy of immense stature and presence, crowned as with the thick white hair of genius, wearing a great gathered or puckered cloak, with a vast velvet collar, and resembling . . . the General Winfield Scott who lived so much in our eyes then." [29]

His works in water color, in oils, or charcoal were done on small sketch
blocks, the very smell of which lasted down through the years, so
impressed were the boys by their master's art. These "panel" pictures had the glamour of greatness about them, especially when
Willy brought some home, not from the atelier Jenks but from the
master's own place of instruction in the University building which
formed the east side of Washington Square.[30] Harry, too, trailing
along behind the "higher flights of power and promise" that Willy
was exhibiting in drawing, was making a certain advance with his
own sketch pad, "even if with less assured a hand," quite outside
of competition.

Richard Pulling Jenks himself, however, left the strongest imprint
of all; William James, years afterward, considered that of all the
masters and tutors the boys had had, Mr. Jenks was the most genial
and inspiring, worthy of adorning a higher sphere. The fact that
he may have gone up to greater altitudes of academic enterprise may
account for the James boys' breaking connections with him the next
year and "declining again upon baser things and a lower civilization." So much did Mr. Jenks mean to Harry and Willy that upon
returning to New York for a visit some years later, they called on
him one Sunday afternoon, finding him much altered, but profuse
in his recollections of their earlier association on Broadway. He
retained his dignity and his pride in the small but sound little academy
which stood up nobly against such competitors as Dr. Anthon's[31]
of Columbia College. Why the boys, upon severing ties with Mr.
Jenks in 1854, were not entered in the distinguished Professor
Anthon's rudimentary academy is explained in terms of a new development in their father's plans for their training.

During the summer vacation, which the James family spent at
New Brighton, then a fashionable resort on Staten Island,[32] Harry,
age eleven, and Wilky, two years his junior, were submitted to Mrs.
Vrendenburg for tutoring, while "no such trick was played" on
William who was sufficiently charged with learning to escape the
ordeal. This linking of Wilky with Harry in 1854, replacing the
former combination of Willy and Harry, was to carry on for several
years under the implication that the oldest son's capacities for study

were so advanced over Harry's that the latter was more comfortably
grouped with the younger Wilky. They were together again in the
fall of 1854 for what was to be their last winter of schooling in New
York, under the instruction of Messrs. Forest and Quackenboss who
conducted an establishment of long standing at which several of the
boys' New York uncles had received training for business careers.
It was, at this time, apparently, the elder James's plan to have the
boys given a grounding in the basic principles of commercial theory
and practice for Harry was to recollect " . . . the black bitterness of
our next ordeal . . . to have proceeded from some rank predominance
of the theory and practice of bookkeeping." [33]

This sudden turn from classic subjects to mundane bookkeeping
was precipitated not only by the elder James's desire that the boys
have some practical elements included in their curriculum but also
by the much-discussed and longed-for departure for Europe. Plans
were formulating during the winter and spring of 1854-1855, with
the actual date of departure being established as June 27, 1855.
With growing anticipation of the foreign fields to be travelled, not
merely for a short summer's holiday but for a period of several
years, the boys could hardly have been thoroughly devoted to their
studies under Messrs. Forest and Quackenboss. The academy was
not a mere "commercial school," for the roster was extensive and
met the needs of such a clientele as the little Hoes and Havemeyers,
the Stokes, Phelpses, Colgates, and other such best families of the
day, some of whom had good reason to be interested in bookkeeping.
But Willy and Harry were soon to be off for Geneva, London,
Paris, and Bonn, with enough cultural influences in store to counterbalance the heaviest schedule of commercial subjects. At the moment
they did not need whatever culture New York had to offer, and the
school attended seemed indeed limited in this respect.

The academy was much larger than the previous ones attended
and was situated on the northwest corner of Fourteenth Street and
Sixth Avenue, a short distance's walk from the James home. It had
the style of a shop, "a shop of long standing, of numerous clients,
of lively bustle and traffic." Harry remembered being seated "in
the vast bright crowded smelly smoky room, in which rusty black

stove-shafts were the nearest hint of architecture . . ." Here the "dreadful blight of arithmetic" was undergone, "filling all the air" which was already quite dense. The shy, hesitant, overly sensitive Harry, completely out of the orbit of his own individual talents and potentialities, presents a pitiful figure, a sore spectacle, seated among "strange neighbours and deskfellows who, not otherwise too objectionable, were uncanny and monstrous through their possession, cultivation, imitation of ledgers, daybooks, double-entry, tall pages of figures, interspaces streaked with oblique ruled lines that weirdly 'balanced,' whatever that might mean, and other like horrors. Nothing in truth is more distinct to me than the tune to which they were, without exception, at their ease on such ground—unless it be my general dazzled, humiliated sense, through those years, of the common, the baffling, mastery, all round me, of a hundred handy arts and devices. Everyone did things and had things—everyone knew how, even when it was a question of the small animals, the dormice and grasshoppers, or the hoards of food and stationery, that they kept in their desk, just as they kept in their heads such secrets for how to do sums—those secrets that I must even then have foreseen I should even so late in life as this having failed to discover." [34]

Swamped with a sense of his being lost amid such competitors and in such a subject, Harry was, in his own way, keenly taking in the human equation, especially as it was represented first by Mr. Forest, under whose immediate attention he "languished" and then Mr. Quackenboss, the junior partner. The former had lasted on from a plainer age "and was still of a *trempe* to whack in the fine old way." He stood "aloft, benevolent and hard, mildly massive, in a black dress coat and trousers and a white neckcloth that should have figured, if it didn't, a frill, and on the highest rostrum of our experience, whence he comes back to me as the dryest of all our founts of knowledge, though quite again as a link with far-off manners and forms and as the most 'historic' figure we had ever had to do with." [35] Mr. Quackenboss "a strange, curly, glossy, an anointed and bearded" junior partner, conducted the classical department and never whacked —"only sent down his subjects, with every confidence, to his friend." Willy, in all this experience, was occupied on upper floors, in higher

classes, in real pursuits, as his brother imagined, while Harry, despairing over ledgers, was often lost in dreams of a better world to come;
that was the world of "Europe" in which bookkeeping played no
part and in which one of his ilk, a spectator in life, would soon be
released from the ordeals at Sixth Avenue and Fourteenth Street.

By 1855 both William and Henry, Jr., thirteen and twelve, were
most certainly aware of the fact that their educational experience was
deviating far from the norm, even of the privileged group of well-
to-do boys with whom to make comparisons. They were also aware
of the far-reaching influence their father was playing, directly and
indirectly, in their whole scheme of things. As young Harry sat
dreaming, during the months before the rupture with New York took
place, "living by anticipation in another world" and feeling the un-
easy connections with New York already loosening, he had a sense
of the situation, perhaps never before quite consciously contemplated.
He was struck, in the light of the European plans, by the odd assort-
ment of experiences that had been their lot, taking the place of
education as more usually and conventionally understood. The deficiency of the whole arrangement, which William was later to deplore,
seemed to Harry, both then and in adult years, not at all deplorable,
for he was struck "with the rare fashion after which, in any small
victim of life, the inward perversity may work." His father would
have called it "inward spontaneity" rather than perversity, but the
meaning is identical; namely, that given whatever desirable influences and environments, the individuality of each child will develop
in accord with its own peculiar, inner self; in the case of Harry, whose
gifts of imagination and detached observation were so closely related
to his development as a novelist, the heterogeneous collection of
governesses, tutors, masters, and schools which had already, by 1855,
lent such extraordinary variety of stimulation to his mind, proved
the rightest kind of influence for him. The seemingly aimless, hap-
hazard direction of their schooling had for Harry especially great
value, for in retrospect he wrote: "It works by converting to its uses
things vain and unintended, which it by the same stroke so often
reduces to naught; with the result indeed that one may most of all see
it—so at least have I quite exclusively seen it, the little life out for

its chance—as proceeding by the inveterate process of conversion. As I reconsider my own and my brother's early start—even his too, made under stronger propulsions—it is quite for me as if the authors of our being the guardians of our youth had virtually said to us but one thing, directed our course but by one word, though constantly repeated: Convert, convert, convert!" [36]

It was not into gold that they were to convert their experiences. Of that sort of "success" in life they never heard a word at home, it being a presumption of their parents that they would hear word enough of that idea elsewhere, but, he continues, "We were to convert and convert, success—in the sense that was in the general air— or no success; and simply everything that should happen to us, every contact, every impression and every experience we should know, were to form our soluble stuff; with only ourselves to thank should we remain unaware, by the time our perceptions were decently developed, of the substance finally projected and most desirable. That substance might be just consummately Virtue, as a social grace and value—and as a matter furthermore on which pretexts for ambiguity of view and of measure were as little as possible called upon to flourish. This last luxury therefore quite failed us, and we understood no whit the less what was suggested and expected because of the highly liberal way in which the pill, if I may call it so, was gilded: it had been made up—to emphasize my image—in so bright an air of humanity and gaiety, of charity and humour." [37]

What then, the boys might well have asked, are we being educated for? Not for gold, not for materialistic gains, not for utilitarian ends. Could it be that they were being instructed to convert every moment, every incident into just Virtue? Could it actually be that their father meant literally what he said when he wrote: "I desire my child to become an upright man, a man in whom goodness shall be induced not by mercenary motives as brute goodness is induced, but by love for it or a sympathetic delight in it." [38] The evidence supports quite conclusively that Henry James, Sr., meant wholeheartedly those words, and the thousands of others which he wrote on the same theme; furthermore, he intended, as was shortly proved, to spare not a dollar to secure for his children absolute freedom from mercenary motives and to provide for them that atmosphere "of the best that has been thought and said" in which they would develop into upright men, men in whom goodness was induced by their natural sympathy toward it. Henry James, Jr.'s ultimate and consummate devotion to the art of the novel bears a basic relation to this axiom of his early training. Mercenary considerations, no matter how pressing, took second place with the novelist Henry James whose art was always the paramount objective.

Over fifty years after the New York residence was terminated in 1855, Henry, Jr., summarized his father's "ideas" as they related to his children's education, in the following words, "our father, caring for our spiritual decency unspeakably more than anything else, anything at all that might be or might become ours, would have seemed to regard this cultivation of it as profession and career enough for us . . . he held that there would always be enough; since the truth, the true truth, was never ugly and dreadful, and we didn't and wouldn't depart from it by any cruelty or stupidity . . . and might therefore depend on it for due abundance even of meat and drink and raiment, even of wisdom and wit and honour." [39]

The preservation and cultivation of that inward spontaneity was, therefore, not only the purpose of these experiments in education but actually the profession and career of these James children. It called for radical reliance upon his spiritual convictions for the elder James to sever the ties that a decade in America had established for himself and his family, to set sail for an indefinite period of years upon an uncharted journey across the Atlantic and much of Europe, all in the absolute faith that he would better find there "an atmosphere of freedom" so necessary in his plans for the children. He was doing much more than escaping from American vulgarity and grossness; he was taking a stand against those aspects of nature and society which at that time clearly indicated to him that Europe and not America was the more desirable place in which to work out his ideal.

NOTES

1. *Notes of a Son and Brother*, 157.
2. *Ibid.*, 165.
3. *Literary Remains*, 159.
4. *Ibid.*, 146, 147.
5. *Ibid.*, 170.
6. MS. letter from Henry James, Sr., to Samual Gray Ward, March 9, 1854, Houghton Library, Harvard University.
7. Letter to Mrs. Francis G. Shaw, quoted by Ralph Barton Perry, *op. cit.*, I, 186.
8. William James, *The Literary Remains of Henry James*, "Introduction," 9.
9. Henry James, "Socialism and Civilization," in F. O. Matthiessen, *op. cit.*, 53, 54, 55.
10. *Ibid.*, 56.
11. *Ibid.*, 57.
12. *The Literary Remains of Henry James*, 178.
13. *A Small Boy and Others*, 68.
14. *A Small Boy and Others*, 232-235.
15. *Notes of a Son and Brothers*, 163, 164.
16. *Ibid.*, 164.
17. In his chapter, "New York Revisited," in *The American Scene*, Henry James gives another account of Mrs. Daly and her school on Waverly Place, describing the school in a "shabby red house, with its mere two storys, its lowly 'stoop,' its dislocated iron-work of the forties, the early fifties, the record, in its face, of blistering summers and of the long stages of the loss of self-respect (making), it as consummate a morsel of the old liquor-scented, heated-looking city, the city of no pavements, but of such a plenty of politics, as I could have desired," 87, 88.
18. *A Small Boy and Others*, 17, 18.
19. W. Williams, *Appleton's New York City and Vicinity Guide*, New York, D. Appleton & Company, 1849, 14.
20. *A Small Boy and Others*, 16, 17.
21. *Ibid.*, 18, 19.
22. *Ibid.*, 19.
23. *Ibid.*, 21, 22.
24. Wilson, *op. cit.*, III, 389-391.
25. *A Small Boy and Others*, 200, 201.
26. *Ibid.*, 202, 203.
27. *Ibid.*, 204.
28. *Ibid.*, 205.
29. *Ibid.*, 204.
30. The University of the City of New York was located on the east side of Washington Square, between Washington Place and Waverly

Place. It was founded in 1831 and the building completed in 1836. The faculty lists do not include a Mr. Coe in the 'Fifties. In 1851, Samuel F. B. Morse was listed as Professor of the Literature of the Arts of Design. There were eleven professors with about one-hundred and fifty students enrolled. Connected with it was a large grammar school and a medical department.

31. Professor Anthon's grammar school "of rudimentary drill" was "of a higher grade and more comprehensive scope than any" others. "He gave instruction, but insisted upon education . . . By means of Latin and Greek he thus shaped the thought, the mental habits, and English style of many a small boy . . . " Wilson, *op. cit.*, III, 596, 597.

32. New Brighton, in the early 'Fifties, was described as "A village of country seats, erected for the accommodation of some of the 'best society' of New York. It occupies the most northern point of Staten Island, at the entrance of the 'Kills,' which separate the island from the Jersey shore. The town plot, which for the most part is the result of expensive excavation, descends rapidly from the base of the adjoining hills, and the buildings range in a line with, and at nearly an equal distance from the margin of New-York bay. The situation is very fine, commanding a view of the bay, with its islets, the city, Long Island, etc. The houses with their white fronts and massive columns, present a beautiful appearance from the water. There are two extensive hotels and several boarding houses. Population about 400 . . . Steam-boats leave the lower part of the city every hour during the day for New Brighton, the Quarantine Ground, and Tompkinsville." *Francis' Picture of New-York*, 21, 22.

33. *A Small Boy and Others*, 211.
34. *Ibid.*, 223.
35. *Ibid.*, 214.
36. *Ibid.*, 214.
37. *Ibid.*, 215.
38. See above, Chapter II, note 2.
39. *A Small Boy and Others*, 219, 220.

Chapter Four

New York Prosceniums and Marquees

1850-1855

" . . . I was with precocious passion 'at home' among the theatres. . . ."

Forty years after this mid-century residence in New York, Henry James, well established as a distinguished novelist, turned for a period of five years to the drama. The desire to write plays evolved from his early love of the theatre, acquired as a small boy of nine or ten, at the Park, or Burton's, or Wallack's Broadway Theatre in the "palmy days" of the New York stage. During the early 'Fifties, the drama was at its height, with Forrest, Macready, Laura Keene, James Hackett, Mrs. Hoey, Mrs. Holman, Mary Taylor, Fanny Wallack, Lester Wallack, and a host of others crowding the boards in a profusion of talent. Henry James, Sr.'s fondness for drama and his eagerness to have his children see the best plays and actors resulted in the frequent attendance of Willy and Harry, at first with their parents and later by themselves, "on non-dental Saturday afternoons."

It was characteristic of the elder James that he was not influenced by the current social stigma resting heavily on theatrical performances. While he never condoned evil of any sort and certainly would not expose his children to undesirable influences, he saw no harm in permitting them to attend good plays performed in reputable playhouses by distinguished or competent actors. To him, calling theatres "lecture halls" or "lyceums" was so much humbug, so much "flagrant morality" which was no part of his "ideas" for his boys. They were, consequently, frequent theatre-goers, often having the plays read and explained to them beforehand, being made increasingly aware of the difference between good and poor theatre. The boys were to be ever grateful to their parents for this "liberal law and happy view under which the addiction was shared with us, they never caring much for things we couldn't care for and generally holding that what was good to them would be also good for their children." [1]

In many pages of *A Small Boy and Others,* Henry James recorded, not always accurately, some very colorful and significant impressions of the mid-century New York stage. They range from Shakespearean comedy to some of Burton's wholesome fun in Chambers Street on down to a wholesale riotous and thrilling surrendering to Barnum's Museum and Franconi's Hippodrome with their endless spectacles and sideshows. The children's wanderings to such halls of amusement was as broad and winding as their religious meanderings of the same period, but with more concrete and, ironically enough in the case of Harry, more beneficial results. Being most impressed at church services by those things which contributed to his sense of exhibition, he found quite naturally that the theatre was a far greater stimulus to this same sense. The depth to which it contributed to the development of his imagination is unfathomable.

The first tangible recollections of the theatre came back to Henry James in the memory of the advertisements of current attractions. In wandering down Fifth Avenue, either to school in Waverly Place or to Grandmother Walsh's on Washington Square, the small boy observed many large oblong screens, propped up against trees and lamp-posts, walls and fences, announcing some of the same names he heard his parents mention at home. Wondering and gaping, Harry "stood long and drank deep at those founts of romance that gushed from the huge placards of the theatre." In those days advertisements were designed to convey information in full, with every member of the cast listed equally and every circumstance of time, place, and form presented minutely for the most inquiring mind. Before these "magnified playbills," the child's curiosity grew, increasing with the frequent changing of the placards, for they were changed often in that time of one or two night stands.

Then too, the air was full of theatrical excitements such as the Astor Place riot in 1849 and Jenny Lind's stupendous triumph at Castle Garden in September, 1850. While the boys were too young to catch the full import of such sensations, they acquired a general knowledge of these events from the conversations at home where everything worth talking about was discussed freely. Just when the first attendance at a play occurred is not clear, for, as Henry, Jr., stated, over sixty years later, "I fail doubtless to keep *all* my associations clear." In comparing his record of plays and actors with the playbills of the times, one is led to believe that he rather telescoped experiences and blended memories so that figures from different plays melt together into a cast which existed only in the golden haze of memory.

It has been demonstrated that the performance of *A Comedy of Errors* which James recalled as his first experience in attending the theatre occurred in 1855 and that he must have seen earlier productions which had telescoped into Burton's presentation.[2] Though the elderly novelist was confused about details, one is charmed by the image of the small boy transported with excitement and joy. Sixty years later he could feel "the sense of the sacred thrill with which I began to watch the green curtain, the particular one that was to rise to The Comedy of Errors on the occasion that must have been, for what I recall of its almost unbearable intensity, the very first of my ever sitting at a play. I should have been indebted for the momentous evening in that case to Mr. William Burton, whose small theatre in Chambers Street, to the rear of Stewart's big shop and hard by the Park, as the Park was at that time understood, offered me then my prime initiation. . . . The play had been read to us during the day; a celebrated English actor, whose name I inconsistently forget, had arrived to match Mr. Burton as the other of the Dromios; and the agreeable Mrs. Holman, who had to my relentless vision too retreating a chin, was so good as to represent Adriana. I regarded Mrs. Holman as a friend, though in no warmer light than that in which I regarded Miss Mary Taylor—save indeed that Mrs. Holman had

the pull, on one's affections, of 'coming out' to sing in white satin
and quite irrelevantly between the acts; an advantage she shared with
the younger and fairer and more dashing, the dancing, Miss Malvina,
who footed it and tambourined it and shawled it, irruptively, in
lonely state." [3]

Burton's Theatre was situated on the site originally occupied by
Stoppani's Arcade Baths, a fact adding an exotic touch to the later
colorful history of the place. On February 4, 1844, Sig. Ferdinand
Palmo, with ambitious dreams of establishing Italian opera in New
York, opened Palmo's Opera House at this same location, 39 and 41
Chambers Street, between Broadway and Centre Street. Sig. Palmo's
enterprise soon failed and the house became the cradle of Negro min-
strelsy, known as Dumbleton's Opera House, a far cry from Bellini's
"I Puritani," or "Il Barbiere di Siviglia," "La Sonnambula," "Lucia
di Lammermoor," and "L'Elisir d'Amore," of its original offerings.
After a turn at the ballet, and another attempt at Italian opera, this
time under Sig. S. S. Patti, father of Adelina Patti, the house declined
to German vaudeville and worse, until, terribly run-down, it was
leased by Burton and opened under his name on July 10, 1848.

The whole establishment was thoroughly renovated, a new proscenium arch being erected, private boxes constructed, and a new drop
curtain installed, painted by Hiegle. The theatre was thus launched
upon a series of seven or eight highly successful seasons, which
occurred in the very years the young Jameses were having their first
sight of such splendors. Actually the Chambers Street house in no
way compared with the elegance of the Park Theatre in Park Row,
famous since its beginning in 1795; however, Burton's was "the
resort of the most intelligent class of pleasure-seekers, and there
beauty, wit, and fashion loved to congregate, without the formality
or etiquette of attire, once deemed necessary at the Park." [4] Such a
theatre would have been very much to the taste and enjoyment of
the James family in 1850.

Seated in Orchestra chairs (with cushioned seats), or more probably in one of the private boxes if the view of the stage proved better
there, the parents and two oldest boys, with perhaps Aunt Kate
Walsh, awaited tensely the first scene. To Harry "the scarce tolerable

throb" of expectation increased every moment as his eyes glided
rapidly over the Dress Circle, the "Second Tier" or twenty-five cents
gallery, the Orchestra, Boxes, and the proscenium. But the green
curtain concealed the wonders to come. "One's eyes bored into it in
vain, and yet one knew it *would* rise at the named hour, the only
question being if one could exist till then." When the curtain did
rise on Mr. Burton's antics and the agreeable Mrs. Holman, in current fashion the performance was composed of more than Shakespeare's *A Comedy of Errors;* there were embellishments, entr'actes,
and interludes hardly in the Elizabethan manner, or at best mere
remnants, in form, of the delightful lyrics and lute songs of Shakespeare's stage. Mrs. Holman, actress and singer, and Miss Malvina
(Malvina Pray), dancer extraordinaire, were excellent representations of this mid-Nineteenth century "double feature" aspect of the
endlessly entertaining evening.[5] Miss Mary Taylor, a far greater
artist, the James boys later admired, for "at Brougham's, not at
Burton's, . . . we rendered *her* that tribute," where she played during
the 1850-1851 season.[6] Since she retired from the stage with a final
farewell performance at Burton's, on May 3, 1852,[7] and since Willy
and Harry enthusiastically attended her performances at Brougham's,
it can be assumed that his "first sitting at a play" probably occurred in
the season of 1849-1850, prior to Miss Taylor's going to Brougham's
Lyceum for 1850-1851.

As much as Mr. Burton delighted the boys, he could not compare,
in their estimation, with William Rufus Blake, "a much finer comedian, much more of a gentleman and a scholar—'mellow' Mr. Blake,
whom with the brave Mrs. Blake (*how* they must have made their
points), I connect partly with the Burton scene and partly with that,
of slightly subsequent creation, which, after flourishing awhile slightly
further up Broadway under the charmlessly commercial name of
Brougham's Lyceum (we had almost only Lyceums and Museums and
Lecture Rooms and Academies of Music for playhouse and opera
then), entered upon a long career and a migratory life as Wallack's
Theatre[8] . . . We rallied especially to Blake as Dogberry, on the
occasion of my second Shakespearean night, for as such I seem to place

it, when Laura Keene and Mr. Lester—the Lester Wallack that was
to be—did Beatrice and Benedick." [9]

Laura Keene was introduced to America at Wallack's on September
20, 1852, the evening being recorded as "being her first appearance
in America," so that the James boys must have seen her that season
in the very beginning of her famous career in New York. Born in
England, in 1820, she had had success on the London stage before
being engaged by Wallack to join his new company at the Lyceum
on Broadway. She was not, in 1852, very young, but she is remembered as being a very attractive woman, with a musical, sympathetic
voice, and charming carriage. She played during that first season at
Wallack's, such parts as *Beatrice,* to Mr. Wallack's *Benedick; Rosalind*
to his *Jacques; Rachel Heywood* to his *Martin* in the *Rent Day; Lady
Gay Spanker, Clara Douglas,* and *Lady Teazle,* giving him throughout most excellent support, and making the great mistake of her
life when she left his company.[10] By her managerial activities at the
Metropolitan Theatre in 1855, followed the next year by building
a new house, on Broadway near Houston Street, Laura Keene's
Theatre, she apparently sacrificed a great career as an artist for the
dubious career of becoming New York's first woman manager. In
contrast, J. Lester Wallack, the Benedick to her Beatrice in 1852,
was destined to achieve one of the highest positions among the
ranks of New York actors. Having played at the Broadway and at
Burton's, he was coming into his full promise at the Lyceum, building
up that reputation which resulted in his being called "the handsomest
man on our stage, the most graceful and gallant in his carriage and
bearing . . . he has had but one rival and no superior during all this
time . . . no one who can be justly called his peer." [11]

The third and last of the Shakespearean high-lights which were to
shine so long for Harry James was *A Midsummer Night's Dream,*
at the Broadway Theatre, "a confessed theatre," not masquerading
as a lyceum. This production so far surpassed all others in lavishness
of decor that to the boys in their "dazzled apprehension" the occasion was never to be forgotten. Records show that the Broadway
Theatre, the Old Broadway on the east side of Broadway between
Pearl and Anthony (later Worth) Streets, seating 4,500 people with

an immense pit to which only men and boys were admitted, was opened September 27, 1847. Forrest, Macready, Lester Wallack, William Blake, Charlotte Cushman, Kate Horn, Joey Gougenheim, Davidge, Mme. Ponisi and A. H. Davenport were among the host of splendid players who brought fame to the house and themselves over many seasons. It was highly appropriate, then, that "the most magnificent production of *A Midsummer Night's Dream* that had yet been seen in this city took place here February 6, 1854. The whole of Mendelssohn's music was given with it." [12] To the boys it was their "greatest conceivable adventure"; Harry's sense of exhibition could hardly have been more stimulated and it is not surprising to find him writing many decades later: "Everything here is as of yesterday, the identity of the actors, the details of their dress, the charm imparted by the sisters Gougenheim, [13] the elegant elder as the infatuated Helena and the other, the roguish 'Joey' as the mischievous Puck. Hermia was Mrs. Nagle, in a short salmon-coloured peplum over a white petticoat, the whole bulgingly confined by a girdle of shining gilt and forming a contrast to the loose scarves of Helena, while Mr. Nagle, not devoid, I seem to remember, of a blue chin and the latency of a fine brogue, was either Lysander or Demetrius; [14] Mr. Davidge (also, I surmise, with a brogue) was Bottom the weaver and Madame Ponisi Oberon." [15] These recollections, recorded nearly sixty years after the performances, testify to young Harry's extraordinary sensitivity to form, color, movement, and sound, to his already cultivated proficiency of "taking in" impressions and retaining them in amazing detail during many decades.

The James boys' appreciation covered a wide range from the distinguished Shakespearean actors to the celebrated and versatile Mr. William Burton. They saw him many times, "as Paul Pry, as Mr. Toodles and as Aminadab Sleek in The Serious Family, and we must have admired him very much—his huge fat person, his huge fat face and his vast slightly pendulous cheek, surmounted by a sort of elephantine wink, to which I impute a remarkable baseness, being still perfectly present to me." [16] One of the most popular comedies, *The Serious Family,* by Morris Barnet, was given for the first time in America at Burton's on December 3, 1849, during Burton's second season, which he opened "flushed with the success of the previous season," looking forward to many others of equal promise. From the first rising of the curtain the play was a most extraordinary success "being played one hundred and twenty-three times during the season, and Burton's *Sleek* being pronounced a masterpiece of canting hypocrisy." [17] For the following decade Burton exploited the comedy and particularly his role of Sleek. [18]

Closely competing with his role of Sleek was his Timothy Toodles in a comedy which had an interesting development under the master hand of Burton, who was shrewd in exploiting roles and plays which were suited to his peculiar talent. *The Toodles,* as the piece came to be called, was first played in New York at the Chambers Street house on October 27, 1848 and had much to do with getting Burton off for a good start as both manager and actor. It had been done in Baltimore under Burton's direction earlier in his career and was then known as *The Broken Heart, or the Farmer's Daughter.* By writing up the character of Toodles and cutting the play considerably, Burton extracted a maximum amount of fun from it. Actually *The Farmer's Daughter of the Severn Side, or Mr. and Mrs. Toodles,* by R. J. Raymond was the original piece, but by the time it reached the boards before the James boys' eyes such vast alterations had been made that except for one act there was little left of the original. When Burton played the part of Timothy Toodles he so embellished it with outrageously vulgar gags and inventions of his own that the gallery, as well as Willy and Harry in more select seats, went into waves of hopeless laughter. He played it in theatres all over America for over four hundred nights so that Billy Burton and his Toodles became a household word. No one who ever saw him ever forgot the character and the boys were then at an age when hilarious comedy is, perhaps, most appreciated. This broad-farce certainly did not have the quality of the Snug-Snout-Quince-Bottom element in *A Midsummer Night's Dream,* and was, in fact, questionable in its vulgarity so that one might wonder if the elder James had not given too much freedom to his boys in their theatre-going. As will be seen, several other plays and many of the side-show entertainments they attended at Barnum's and Franconi's were

far from genteel, but it can be pointed out that what Henry James,
Sr., wanted was to keep the boys from personal contact with vulgarity.
He obviously permitted them to attend performances in which vulgarity was enacted on the stage where they could observe it, developing thereby a sense of values and comparisons without being
contaminated as they might be by association with the type of person
represented in these plays and carnivals. The boys wandered freely
about Broadway and played over a wide area of streets so that one
notes in this New York period more license in the boys' experience
than many critics have implied they were permitted.

A perennial favorite dating from the heydays of the Park Theatre
two or three decades earlier was *The Cataract of the Granges*. The
boys thrilled to Madame Ponisi, very differently cast from the delightful Oberon role, as the white-veiled heroine of the Granges "where,
preferring death to dishonour, she dashes up the more or less perpendicular waterfall on a fiery black steed and with an effect only
a little blighted by the chance flutter of a drapery out of which
peeps the leg of a trouser and a male foot." [19] She appeared before
them many times in equally exciting assignments "as this and that
noble matron or tragedy queen. I descry her at any rate representing all characters alike with a broad brown face framed in bands
or crowns or other heavy headgear out of which cropped a row of
very small tight black curls. *The Cataract of the Grange(s)* is all
there as well, a tragedy of temples and idols and wicked rajahs and
real water, with Davidge and Joey Gougenheim again for comic
relief." [20] On November 24, 1851 it was given at the Old Broadway
with Mme. Ponisi as Tamine, Miss Gougenheim as Ulra, and W.
Davidge as Robinson and no live horses listed on the playbill.[21] On
December 26, 1854, however it was revived, again with Ponisi as
Tamine (or Zamine as it was sometimes spelled) but now accompanied by real horses which, in one scene were driven on the stage,
six of them, three abreast, drawing a triumphal car, the whole thing
being a novelty achieving wild acclaim from the pit and gallery.[22]

Another actress to whom the young Jameses were devoted was
Madame Celeste, a Parisian who had appeared in New York in 1827
as a dancer, not then able to speak a word of English but later, in

1834, returning to America, with sufficient control of the language
to play at the Bowery Theatre in *The French Spy.* By the early
'Fifties she was well established at the Old Broadway, doing such
things as Miami, in *Green Bushes,* captivating Harry with her "admired walk up the stage as . . . the huntress, a wonderful majestic
and yet voluptuous stride enhanced by a short kilt, black velvet leg-
gings and a gun haughtily borne on the shoulder." [23]   It was done
on September 13, 1851 at the Broadway with Mme. Celeste enthusiastically received after an absence of seven years.[24]   At the Bowery in
the 'Thirties she had danced before overflowing audiences. "Her
success was unbounded, perhaps more by the force and intensity of
her expressive pantomimic action than by the grace or elegance of
her dancing." [25]   Her dancing days were over when the boys saw her
twenty years later. They were content with her lingering charms of
form and costume.

Fanny Wallack, another of their favorites, was the daughter of
Henry Wallack and niece of the actor-manager James M. Wallack.
She was popular in the 'Forties, her career ending in New York, however, in June, 1852. She was acclaimed as Lydia Languish, Juliet,
Ophelia, and Lady Gay Spanker, the role which Harry long remembered, in *London Assurance,* by Boucicault, for she was "flushed and
vociferous, first in a riding-habit with a tail yards long and afterwards in yellow satin with scarce a tail at all." [26]   It was in this same
London Assurance that William Rufus Blake, whom the boys had so
admired as Dogberry, did his finest creation, the role of Sir Harcourt
Courtly.[27]   In the same category with Fanny was Mrs. Russell (later
Mrs. Hoey) who excelled in such things as *Love in a Maze,* in which
the stage was rather primitively arranged in the form of an intricate
garden-labyrinth much enhanced in charm by Mrs. Russell who, in
Harry's opinion, "wanted, especially for the low-necked ordeal, less
osseous a structure." [28]   She retired from the stage in 1851 for a period
of three years, reappearing in 1854 at Wallack's, at which time, in
all probability the boys saw her. *Love in a Maze,* also by Boucicault,
was offered at Brougham's Lyceum with Mrs. Russell as Mrs. Buck-
thorn on April 3, 1851, its first playing in New York having occurred
at the same theatre a short time earlier, on March 29th. In his recol-

lections of the play, Henry, Jr. wrote: "The piece in question was, I recall, from the pen of Mr. Bourcicault, as he then wrote his name— he was so early in the field and must have been from long before, inasmuch as he now appears to me to have supplied Mr. Brougham, of the Lyceum aforesaid, with his choicest productions." Dion Boucicault, the Irish playwright, was highly influential in the New York drama of the 'Fifties, not only for his original plays from his early writing in England from 1837-1844, but also for his adaptations of the French. From 1844 to 1848 he was in France, where he became intimately acquainted with the French language and theatre. By 1853, when he came to New York, he found a ready market for whichever type drama he produced.[29] Henry James's later interest in French literature, his year's residence in France, 1871-1872, his youthful studies of the French language during these New York years, 1847-1855, then in Geneva and Paris, all combined in retrospect to give a marked distinction to the dramas reflecting French influences in these early days of his going to the theatre.

An unidentified title of a play adapted from the French he connected with Miss Mary Taylor, first admired in *The Comedy of Errors* at Burton's but later again at Brougham's where she was highly effective as "the fond theatrical daughter in the English version of *Le Père de la Débutante* (by Theaulon), where I see the charming panting dark-haired creature, in flowing white classically relieved by a gold tiara and a golden scarf, rush back from the supposed stage to the represented green-room, followed by thunders of applause, and throw herself upon the neck of the broken-down old gentleman in a blue coat with brass buttons who must have been after all, on second thoughts, Mr. Placide. Greater flights or more delicate shades the art of pathetic comedy was at that time held not to achieve." [30] With another unidentified adaptation he associated a favorite actress, it being noted that the actresses far outnumbered the actors in his preference and recollection. It was a "drama of modern life and of French origin—though what was then not of French origin?—in which Miss Julia Bennett, fresh from triumphs at the Haymarket, made her first appearance, in a very becoming white bonnet, either as a brilliant adventuress or as the innocent victim of licentious design,

I forget which, though with a sense somehow that the white bonnet, when of true elegance, was the note at that period of the adventuress."[31] She had come from London in 1851, making her first American appearance as Lady Teazle at the Old Broadway on February 24th and enjoying repeated successes as a first class comédienne. This could, of course, hardly have been the French drama of modern life with which James's vague recollections connected her. The unidentified play in question could have been *Belphoeger, or the Mountebanke and His Wife,* translated from a French original and presented for the first time in New York at the Old Broadway with Julia Bennett as Madeline, on March 3, 1851,[32] only a few days following her debut there.

To some extent the boys were "taken in" by the French adaptations that they enjoyed, Harry especially not realizing that many of them were crude pieces compared with their prototypes with which he was in mature years to become so fastidiously familiar. Laura Keene, not yet given over to managing theatres in New York, was much demanded at Wallack's Lyceum where the boys enjoyed her doing Mrs. Chillington in *A Morning Call,* in which "she made delightful game of Mr. Lester as Sir Edward Ardent, even to the point of causing him to crawl on all fours and covered with her shawl after the fashion of a horse-blanket."[33] What shocked Henry, Jr., years later was the fact that the hilarious farce he had so enjoyed as a boy of nine or ten, proved to be a *pièce de résistance* of French literature, so much to his liking in later discerning years. In commenting on Laura Keene's robust handling of the play, he wrote: "That delightful impression was then unconscious of the blight to come— that of my apprehending, years after, that the brilliant comedietta was the tribute of our Anglo-Saxon taste to Alfred de Musset's elegant proverb of the Porte Ouverte ou Fermee, in which nothing could find itself less at home than the horseplay of the English version. Miss Laura Keene, with a native grace at the start, a fresh and delicate inspiration, I infer from the kind of pleasure she appears to have begun with giving, was to live to belie her promise and, becoming hard and raddled, forfeit (on the evidence) all claim to the higher distinction; a fact not surprising under the lurid light projected by

such a sign of the atmosphere of ineptitude as an accepted and condoned perversion to vulgarity of Musset's perfect little work. How
could quality of talent consort with so dire an absence of quality
in the material offered it? where could such lapses lead but to dust
and desolation and what happy instinct not be smothered in an air so
dismally non-conducting? Is it a foolish fallacy that these matters
may have been on occasion, at that time, worth speaking of? is it only
presumable that everything was perfectly cheap and common and
everyone perfectly bad and barbarous and that even the least corrup-
tible of our typical spectators were too easily beguiled and too helplessly kind? The beauty of the main truths as to any remembered
matter looked at in due detachment, or in other words through the
haze of time, is that comprehension has then become one with criticism, compassion, as it may really be called, one with musing vision,
and the whole company of the anciently restless, with their elations
and mistakes, their sincerities and fallacies and vanities and triumphs,
embalmed for us in the mild essence of their collective submission
to fate." [34]

In this same general group of theatrical performances, but of a
very different sort, was the intense rage of those years in the early
'Fifties for the dramatized versions of the universally popular Dickens
stories. Harking back to the curious, gaping, wondering small boy
who went from placard to placard in insatiable curiosity about plays
and players, James wrote: "It was the age of the arrangements of
Dickens for the stage, vamped-up promptly on every scene and
which must have been the roughest theatrical tinkers' work, but at two
or three of which we certainly assisted. I associate them with Mr.
Brougham's temple of art, yet am at the same time beset with the
Captain Cuttle of *Dombey and Son* in the form of the big Burton,
who never, I earnestly conceive, graced that shrine, so that I wander
a trifle confusedly. Isn't it he whom I remember as a monstrous
Micawber, the coarse parody of a charming creation, with the entire
baldness of a huge Easter egg and collar-points like the sails of
Mediterranean feluccas? Dire of course for all temperance in these
connections was the need to conform to the illustrations of Phiz,

himself already an improvising parodist and happy only so long
as not imitated, not literally reproduced." [35]

The confusion over Brougham and Burton here can be explained,
perhaps, in terms of the fact that *Dombey and Son* was a version of
Dickens's celebrated novel, adapted by John Brougham and presented
for the first time on any stage at Burton's Chambers Street Theatre
on July 24, 1848, the house having been opened on July 10th. Burton
originated Captain Cuttle with this first performance, hitting such
good fortune with it that he assiduously worked it for all it was
worth for many seasons. Brougham played Major Bagstock, also
Jack Bunsby, and Mrs. Brougham appeared as Susan Nipper. On
November 21, 1852, *Dombey and Son* was offered at Burton's with
Burton traditionally as Captain Cuttle, Miss Weston as Edith, and
Mary Taylor, the adored "Our Mary" of the day, doing Susan Nipper
for the first time.[36]

The whole James family may very well have been present on such
an occasion, for by that season the boys were regular theatre-goers and
the adaptation from Dickens was immensely popular, one of the
happiest and most successful of the many exploitations of the current
craze over anything connected with Dickens. Ten years before, on
Valentine's Day, 1842, New York society had held a ball in honor
of Dickens, the "Boz" Ball, which was the talk of the town for
months. With over two thousand people present amid magnificent
tableaux of scenes from Dickens, all decorations and ornaments being
strictly "Pickwickian," the Park Theatre presented a memorable occasion indeed. The subsequent publication of *Martin Chuzzlewit* cooled
the American ardor for Dickens considerably, but the immortal
characters of his novels continued the mania. Having been well established on the stage by Charlotte Cushman's portrayal of Nancy Sykes
in the adaptation of *Oliver Twist* at the Park Theatre, February 7,
1839, Dickens was in demand for several decades. J. W. Wallack, Jr., was acclaimed as Fagin in later productions, as was A. H.
Davenport as Sykes in still others. Brougham, in addition to his
Dombey and Son, adapted *Bleak House* and *David Copperfield* very
successfully. Dion Boucicault's *Nicholas Nickleby* in November,
1859, carried the tradition on into the 'Sixties, an earlier version hav-

ing been done at the Park, January 30, 1839 with Charlotte Cushman
as Fanny Squeers which was nearly as celebrated as her Nancy Sykes.
Henry, Jr., prior to his earliest experiences at the theatres, recalls
that he "languished at home when my betters admired Miss Cushman
as the Nancy of *Oliver Twist.*"

After 1850, when the boys no longer languished at home, there
was still plenty of Dickens to be seen on Broadway. "The second
definite matter in the Dickens connection is the Smike of Miss Weston
—whose praenomen I frivolously forget (though I fear it was Lizzie)[37] but who was afterwards Mrs. A. H. Davenport and then,
sequently to some public strife or chatter, Mrs. Charles Matthews—
in a version of *Nicholas Nickleby* that gracelessly managed to be all
tearful melodrama, long-lost foundlings, wicked Ralph Nicklebys
and scowling Arthur Grides, with other baffled villains, and scarcely
at all Crummleses and Kenwigses, much less Squeerses; though there
must have been something of Dotheboys Hall for the proper tragedy
of Smike and for the broad Yorkshire effect, a precious theatrical
value, of John Brodie. The ineffaceability was the anguish, to my
tender sense, of Nicholas's starved and tattered and fawning and
whining protégé; in face of my sharp retention of which through all
the years who shall deny the immense authority of the theatre, or
that the stage is the mightiest of modern engines? Such at least was
to be the force of the Dickens imprint, however applied, in the soft
clay of our generation; it was to resist so serenely the wash of the
waves of time. To be brought up thus against the author of it, or to
speak at all of the dawn of one's early consciousness of it and of
his presence and power, is to begin to tread ground at once sacred
and boundless, the associations of which, looming large, warn us off
even while they hold. He did too much for us surely ever to leave
us free—free of judgment, free of reactions, even should we care
to be, which heaven forbid: he laid his hand on us in a way to under-
mine as in no other case the power of detached appraisement. We
react against other productions of the general kind without 'liking'
them the less, but we somehow liked Dickens the more for having
forfeited half the claim to appreciation. That process belongs to
the fact that criticism, roundabout him, is somehow futile and taste-

less. His own taste is easily impugned, but he entered so early into
the blood and bone of our intelligence that it always remained better
than the taste of overhauling him. When I take him up to-day and
find myself holding off, I simply stop: not holding off, that is, but
holding on, and from the very fear to do so; which sounds, I recognize, like perusal, like renewal, of the scantest. I don't renew, I
wouldn't renew for the world; wouldn't, that is, with one's treasure
so hoarded in the dusty chamber of youth, let in the intellectual air.
Happy the house of life in which such chambers still hold out, even
with the draught of the intellect whistling through the passages." [38]

Unaccompanied by elders and with points of interest less literary
and, in a sense, more dramatic, Willy and Harry James, together with
one or two friends of the Fourteenth Street region set off on escapades of colorful amusement, during these same years of pre-
adolescence when circuses and side shows play their part in the
scheme of life for any American boy. Indelibly impressed upon shy
Harry's mind was an early outing of this sort in which he inadvertently became part of the entertainment. It took place "in Broadway, on the right going down and not much below Fourth Street
(except that everything seems to me to have been just below Fourth
Street when not just above), with the scene of my great public
exposure somewhat later, the wonderful exhibition of Signor Blitz,
the peerless conjurer, who, on my attending his entertainment with
W. J. and our frequent comrade of the early time 'Hal' Coster,
practised on my innocence to seduce me to the stage and there plunge
me into the shame of my sad failure to account arithmetically for
his bewilderingly subtracted or added or divided pockethandker-
chiefs and playing-cards; a paralysis of wit as to which I once more,
and with the same wan despair, feel my companions' shy telegraphy
of relief, their snickerings and mouthings and raised numerical
fingers, reach me from the benches." [39]

In a category with Signor Blitz in his house of tricks, but of far
greater range and variety, was P. T. Barnum's establishment at 537
Broadway, which together with Niblo's Garden at Prince Street and
Broadway, offered the James boys a combination of proscenium and
marquee, since the side-show section of Barnum's "museum" had,

in 1851 acquired an auditorium, a "saloon very beautifully decorated, and made capable of seating 2,000 persons." [40] These were the two most frequented resorts of the boys' more robust theatrical amusement, "Niblo's, which represented in our scheme the ideal evening, while Barnum figured the ideal day." Oddly enough it was at Barnum's that young Harry first came into the realization that one could approach the halls of amusement with something like critical detachment, with a sense of values and judgment which might protect one against the possibilities of being beguiled. The realization actually marks an important turning point in the small boy's development, though it came to him gradually and as a result of Willy's more mature and sophisticated appraisal of the entertainments they were attending.

In several passages, animated by the vividness of these events of his boyhood, Henry James, later wrote: "I turn round again to where I last left myself gaping at the old ricketty billboard in Fifth Avenue; and am almost as sharply aware as ever of the main source of its spell, the fact that it most often blazed with the rich appeal of Mr. Barnum, whose 'lecture-room,' attached to the Great American Museum, overflowed into posters of all the theatrical bravery disavowed by its title. It was my rueful theory of those days . . . that on all the holidays on which we weren't dragged to the dentist's we attended as a matter of course at Barnum's . . . (with) . . . the weary waiting, in the dusty halls of humbug, amid bottled mermaids, 'bearded ladies' and chill dioramas, for the lecture-room, the true centre of the seat of joy, to open: vivid in especial to me is my almost sick wondering of whether I mightn't be rapt away before it did open. The impression appears to have been mixed; the drinking deep and holding out in particular against failure of food and stage-fares, provision for transport to and fro, being questions equally intense: the appeal of the lecture-room, in its essence a heavy extra, so exhausted our resources that even the sustaining doughnut of the refreshment-counter would mock our desire and the long homeward crawl, the length of Broadway and further, seem to defy repetition. Those desperate days, none the less, affect me now as having flushed with the very complexion of romance; their aches and inanitions were part of the adventure; the homeward straggle, interminable as it appeared, flowered at moments into rapt contemplations—that for instance of the painted portraits, large as life, of the celebrity of the hour, then 'dancing' at the Broadway, Lola Montes, Countess of Lansfeldt, of a dazzling and unreal beauty and in a riding-habit lavishly open at the throat." [41]

"It was thus quite in order that I should pore longest, there at my fondest corner, over the Barnum announcements—my present inability to be superficial about which has given in fact the measure of my contemporary care. These announcements must have been in their way marvels of attractive composition, the placard bristling from top to toe with its analytic 'synopsis of scenery and incidents'; the synoptical view cast its net of fine meshes and the very word savoured of incantation. It is odd at the same time that when I question memory as to the living hours themselves, those of the stuffed and dim little hall of audience, smelling of peppermint and orange-peel, where the curtain rose on our gasping but rewarded patience, two performances only stand out for me, though these in the highest relief. *Love, or the Countess and the Serf,* by J. Sheridan Knowles—I see that still as the blazonry of one of them, just as I see Miss Emily Mestayer, large, red in the face, coifed in a tangle of small, fine, damp-looking short curls and clad in a light-blue garment edged with swansdown, shout at the top of her lungs that a 'pur-r-r-se of gold' would be the fair guerdon of the minion who should start on the spot to do her bidding at some desperate crisis that I forget. I forget Huon the serf, whom I yet recall immensely admiring for his nobleness; I forget everyone but Miss Mestayer, who gave form to my conception of the tragic actress at her highest. She had a hooked nose, a great play of nostril, a vast protuberance of bosom and always the 'crop' of close moist ringlets." [42]

" . . . To which I must add the other of my two Barnumite scenic memories, my having anciently admired her as the Eliza of *Uncle Tom's Cabin,* her swelling bust encased in a neat cotton gown and her flight across the ice-blocks of the Ohio, if I rightly remember the perilous stream, intrepidly and gracefully performed. We lived and moved at that time, with great intensity, in Mrs. Stowe's novel." [43] Both Willy and Harry had read *Uncle Tom's Cabin* soon after it became so popular. The first installment appeared in June, 1851, in the anti-slavery publication, the *National Era;* the first stage presentation appeared at Purdy's National Theatre, in Chatham Street, C. W. Taylor's original version, in August, 1852, followed by innumerable others, most notably that of Aiken, also at Purdy's National on July 18, 1853. [44] In relation to the "lecture-room version" of the novel, he wrote: ". . . the first was the fine free rendering achieved at a playhouse till then ignored by fashion and culture, the National Theatre, deep down on the East side, whence echoes had come faintest to ears polite, but where a sincerity vivid though rude was now supposed to reward the curious. Our numerous attendance there under this spell was my first experience of the 'theatre party' as we have enjoyed it in our time—each emotion and impression of which is as fresh to me as the most recent of the same family. Precious through all indeed perhaps is the sense, strange only to later sophistication, of my small encouraged state as a free playgoer—a state doubly wondrous while I thus evoke the full contingent from Union Square; where, for that matter, I think, the wild evening must have been planned. I am lost again in all the goodnature from which small boys, on wild evenings, could dangle so unchidden—since the state of unchiddenness is what comes back to me well-nigh clearest . . . The social scheme, as we knew it, was, in its careless charity, worthy of the golden age—though I can't sufficiently repeat that we know it both at its easiest and its safest; the fruits dropped right upon the board to which we flocked together, the least of us and the greatest, with differences of appetite and of reach, doubtless, but not with differences of place and of proportionate share. My appetite and my reach in respect to the more full-bodied Uncle Tom might have brooked certainly any comparison; I must have partaken thoroughly of the feast to have left the various aftertastes so separate and so strong. It was a great thing to have a canon to judge by—it helped conscious criticism, which was to fit on wings (for use ever after) to the shoulders of appreciation. In the light of that adventure I could be *sure* my second Eliza was less dramatic than my first, and that my first 'Cassy,' that of the great and blood curdling Mrs. Bellamy[45] of the lecture-room, touched depths which made the lady at the National prosaic and placid (I could already be 'down' on a placid Cassy); just as on the other hand the rocking of the ice-floes of the Ohio, with the desperate Eliza, infant in arms, balancing for a leap from one to the other, had here less of the audible creak of carpentry, emulated a trifle more, to my perception, the real water of Mr. Crummles's pump. They can't, even at that, have emulated it much, and one almost envies (quite making up one's mind not to denounce) the simple faith of an age beguiled by arts so rude.

"However, the point exactly was that we attended this spectacle just in order *not* to be beguiled, just in order to enjoy with ironic detachment and, at the very most, to be amused ourselves at our sensibility should it prove to have been trapped and caught. To have become thus aware of our collective attitude constituted for one small spectator at least a great initiation; he got his first glimpse of that possibility of a 'free play of mind' over a subject which was to throw him with force at a later stage of culture, when subjects had considerably multiplied, into the critical arms of Matthew Arnold. So he is himself at least interested in seeing the matter—as a progress in which the first step was taken, before that crude scenic appeal, by his wondering, among his companions, where the absurd, the absurd for *them,* ended and the fun, the real fun, which was the gravity, the tragedy, the drollery, the beauty, the thing itself, briefly, might be legitimately and tastefully held to begin. Uncanny though the remark perhaps, I am not sure I wasn't thus more interested in the pulse of our party, under my tiny recording thumb, than in the beat of the drama and the shock of its opposed forces—vivid and touching as the contrast was then found for instance between the tragi-comical Topsy, the slave-girl clad in a pinafore of sackcloth and destined to become for Anglo-Saxon millions the type of the absolute in the artless, and her little mistress the blonde Eva, a figure rather in the Kenwigs tradition of pantalettes and pigtails, whom I recall as perching quite suicidally, with her elbows out and a preliminary shriek, on that bulwark of the Mississippi steam-boat which was to facilitate her all but fatal immersion in the flood. Why should I have duly noted that no little game on her part could well less

have resembled or simulated an accident, and yet have been no less
moved by her reappearance, rescued from the river but perfectly dry,
in the arms of faithful Tom, who had plunged in to save her, without
either so much as wetting his shoes, than if I had been engaged with
her in a reckless romp? I could count the white stitches in the loose
patchwork, and yet could take it for a story rich and harmonious;
I could know we had all intellectually condescended and that we had
yet had the thrill of an aesthetic adventure; and this was a brave
beginning for a consciousness that was to be nothing if not mixed
and a curiosity that was to be nothing if not restless.

"The principal of this prolonged arrest, which I insist on prolonging a little further, is doubtless in my instinct to grope for our earliest
aesthetic seeds. Careless at once and generous the hands by which
they were sown, but practically appointed none the less to cause that
peculiarly flurried hare to run—flurried because over ground so little
native to it—when so many others held back. It is *that* air of romance
that gilds for me then the Barnum background—taking it as a
symbol; that makes me resist, to this effect of a passionate adverse
loyalty, any impulse to translate into harsh terms any old sordidities
and poverties? The Great American Museum, the downtown scenery
and aspects at large, and even the up-town improvements on them,
as then flourishing?—why, they must have been for the most part
of the last meanness: the Barnum picture above all ignoble and awful,
its blatant face or frame stuck about with innumerable flags that
waved, poor vulgar-sized ensigns, over spurious relics and catch-
penny monsters in effigy, to say nothing of the promise within of the
still more monstrous and abnormal living—from the total impression of which things we pluck somehow the flower of the ideal." [46]

Niblo's Garden was, by contrast, equally exciting but offering
presentations less bizarre than Barnum's. It had originated about 1800
as a circus and training ground for race horses, being called the
Stadium, on the northeast corner of Broadway and Prince Street.
After becoming a drill ground for militia officers at the time of the
War of 1812, it was opened as the Columbian Gardens, devoted to
summer-night entertainments, which William Niblo took over and
befitted with transplanted trees and splashing fountains. In 1827

it became the Theatre Sans Souci, but within a few years, with a
larger and well appointed auditorium it was opened as Niblo's and
continued through until 1895, seeing endless alterations and celebrities in every decade.[47]

Of their happy hours spent at Niblo's, James later wrote: "For
here, absolutely, *was* the flower at its finest and grown as nowhere
else—grown in the great garden of the Ravel Family and offered
again and again to our deep inhalation. I see the Ravels, French
acrobats, dancers, and pantomimist, as representing, for our culture,
pure grace and charm and civility; so that one doubts whether any
candid community was ever so much in debt to a race of entertainers
or had so happy and prolonged, so personal and grateful a relation
with them. They must have been, with their offshoots of Martinettis
and others, of three or four generations, besides being of a rich theatrical stock generally, and we had our particular friends and
favourites among them; we seemed to follow them through every
phase of their career, to assist at their tottering steps along the
tightrope as very small children kept in equilibrium by very big
balancing-poles (caretakers here walking under in case of falls); to
greet them as Madame Axel, of robust maturity and in a Spanish
costume, bounding on the same tense cord more heavily but more
assuredly; and finally to know the climax of the art with them in
Raoul or the Night-Owl and Jacko or the Brazilian Ape—and all
this in the course of our own brief infancy. My impression of them
bristles so with memories that we seem to have rallied to their different productions with much the same regularity with which we
formed fresh educational connections; and they were so much our
property and our pride that they supported us handsomely through
all fluttered entertainment of the occasional Albany cousins. I remember how when one of these visitors, wound up, in honour of New
York, to the very fever of perception, broke out one evening while we
waited for the curtain to rise, 'Oh don't you hear the cries? They're
beating them, I'm sure they are; can't it be stopped?' we resented
the charge as a slur on our very honour; for what our romantic relative had heatedly imagined to reach us, in a hush-up manner from
behind, was the sounds attendant on the application of blows to some

acrobatic infant who had 'funked' his little job. Impossible such
horrors in the world of pure poetry opened out to us at Niblo's, a
temple of illusion, of tragedy and comedy and pathos that, though
its *abords* of story brown Metropolitan Hotel, on the 'wrong side,'
must have been bleak and vulgar, flung its glamour forth into Broadway.[48] What more pathetic for instance, so that we publicly wept,
than the fate of wondrous Martinetti Jocko, who, after befriending
a hapless French family wrecked on the coast of Brazil and bringing
back to life a small boy rescued from the waves (I see even now,
with every detail, this inanimate victim supine on the strand) met
his death by some cruel bullet of which I have forgotten the deter-
minant cause, only remembering the final agony as something we
could scarce bear and a strain of our sensibility to which our parents
repeatedly questioned the wisdom of exposing us." [49]

One might, indeed, justly question the wisdom of the parents'
looseness of rein, particularly in the light of certain critical studies
of the James family which rather overstress the extent to which the
children were "kept from the streets," and bathed in an atmosphere
of purely European culture and influences. It is evident from the
variety of theatrical amusements that the boys freely enjoyed in New
York, prior to 1855, that Henry James, Sr., was not nearly so strict
in his limiting of their activities and that their environment was
overwhelmingly mid-Nineteenth Century American. Too often,
sweeping critical comment has given the general impression that
William and Henry, Jr., had practically no American influences or
experiences during these formative years before the Civil War other
than Newport, which was, of course, the most Continental and non-
American resort along the Atlantic coast. Such is actually not the
case. The eight years, from 1847 to 1855, during which the family
lived in New York, covered much of the boyhood of the two oldest
boys, William from five to thirteen, Henry, Jr. from four to twelve.
This period was the most non-European part of their lives, prior to
their attending Harvard in the 'Sixties, and the American elements
played a major role in their development, a role which needs to be
much more recognized particularly in the case of Henry James, Jr.,

whose ultimate expatriation has been so freely and often erroneously
interpreted.

In a concluding passage concerning their ramblings from halls of
tragedy and comedy to tents of elephants and monkeys, Henry James
supports further this contention that as boys he and his brothers
spent a great deal of time in pursuits that were already then, and
later even more so, classically American: "These performers and
these things were in all probability but a middling skill and splendour—it was the pre-trapeze age, and we were caught by mild marvels, even if a friendly good faith in them, something sweet and
sympathetic, was after all a value, whether of their own humanity,
their own special quality, or only of our innocence, never to be
renewed; but I light this taper to the initiators, so to call them, whom
I remembered, when we had left them behind, as if they had given
us a silver key to carry off and so to refit, after long years, to sweet
names never thought of from then till now. Signor Leon Javelli, in
whom the French and the Italian charm appear to have met, who
was he, and what did he brilliantly do, and why of a sudden do I thus
recall and admire him?[50] I am afraid he but danced the tight-rope,
the most domestic of our friends' resources, as it brought them out,
by the far stretch of the rope, into the bosom of the house and against
our very hearts, where they leapt and bounded and wavered and recovered closely face to face with us; but I dare say he bounded, brave
Signor Leon, to the greatest height of all: let this vague agility, in any
case, correct him with that revelation of the ballet, the sentimental-
pastoral, of other years, which, in The Four Lovers for example, a
pantomimic lesson as in words of one syllable, but all quick and gay
and droll, would have affected us as classic, I am sure, had we then
had at our disposal that term of appreciation. When we read in
English storybooks about the pantomimes in London, which somehow cropped up in them so often, those were the only things that
didn't make us yearn; so much we felt we were masters of the type,
and so almost sufficiently was that a stop-gap for London constantly
deferred. We hadn't the transformation-scene, it was true, though
what this really seemed to come to was clown and harlequin taking
liberties with policemen—these last evidently a sharp note to us

of that sort; but we had at Niblo's harlequin and columbine, albeit of less pure tradition, and we knew moreover all about clowns, for we went to circuses too, and so repeatedly that when I add them to our list of recreations, the good old orthodox circuses under tents set up in vacant lots, with which New York appears at that time to have bristled, time and place would seem to have shrunken for most other pursuits, and not least for that of serious learning. And the case is aggravated as I remember Franconi's, which we more or less haunted and which, aiming at the grander style and the monumental effect, blazed with fresh paint and rang with Roman chariot-races up there among the deserts of Twenty-ninth Street." [51]

In these full and varied introductions to American theatrical life and amusements, enjoyed under the elder James's understanding and benevolent eye even to the inclusion of the lurid realms of circuses and side shows, Willy and Harry James, the latter especially, became "with precocious passion 'at home' among the theatres." Their father's liberal law and happy view had afforded the boys ample opportunity to respond to the finer vibrations of Shakespeare, as well as the coarser excitements of Franconi's Roman chariots. In 1855, at the close of these years of New York life, when "London constantly deferred" was soon to become the scene of an entirely different life, twelve-year-old Harry James began to experience an inner struggle between these strong native ties and the sense of "Europe" which even then was growing in his consciousness. Against the backdrop of this New York setting he was slowly to work out the plot of his personal drama of expatriation. But in all the acts with their shifting scenes he was never to close the curtain on that inner stage of these New York lyceums and "lecture-halls."

NOTES

1. *A Small Boy and Others*, 101.
2. See Leon Edel, ed. *The Complete Plays of Henry James*, 22.
3. *A Small Boy and Others*, 104, 105. William E. Burton, 1804-1860, born in London where he had a brief career as a printer and an amateur actor, came to Philadelphia; here in the 'Thirties he established Burton's *Gentleman's Magazine*, of which Edgar Allan Poe

was for a time the assistant editor and leading contributor. He controlled the Chestnut Street and Arch Street Theatres in Philadelphia, and the National in New York before taking over Palmo's Opera House in 1848. As a comedian he excelled his successes as a manager: "Burton was probably the funniest man that ever lived. Certainly there lives no man today who can remember seeing or hearing of a man who was funnier than Burton. Burton in his day was the best known man in New York, if not in America, while Burton's Theatre in Chambers Street was better known throughout the United States, than any other public building in the Union . . . Burton's *Micawber* has never been equalled . . . Mr. Burton was a man of large culture, had collected a very extensive and valuable library; and the care and correct elaboration of many of his Shakespearean revivals will testify how great he was as a Shakespearean scholar . . . His *Caliban, Dogberry, Autolycus, Nick Bottom, Verges, Touchstone,* and his *Falstaff,* are by competent and impartial judges said to have been among the most complete embodiments of the great poet's ideas, that his works have ever seen." Laurence Hutton, *Plays and Players,* New York, Hurd and Houghton, 1875, 236, 237, 238, 240.

4. Joseph N. Ireland, *Records of the New York Stage from 1750 to 1860,* New York, T. H. Morrell, 1867, II, 237. The original Park burned completely to the ground on May 25, 1820; the New Park Theatre, on the site of the old one, opened September 1, 1821, but likewise was destroyed by fire, on December 16, 1848. Burton's had opened in Chambers Street in July, 1848 and benefited greatly by the ill fate of the Park.

5. Harriet Phillips Holman, wife of the tenor George Holman, popular at the Park a decade earlier, was born in New York and made her debut at the Walnut in Philadelphia in 1838. She joined Burton in the late 'Forties in Chambers Street, appearing with Blake, Lester Wallack, Fiske, Miss Fisher, Burton and others of the company. Malvina Pray, a popular dancer at Burton's at this same period, was later Mrs. William J. Florence, wife of the Irish comedian who supported Jefferson in some of his leading roles. Miss Malvina was also popular at Wallack's Theatre in 1853. Mary Taylor, born in New York in 1827, became popular as an actress at the Old Olympic, on Broadway between Howard and Grand Streets, in the 'Forties. So great was her popularity there and at Burton's that one critic writes of her: "Miss Mary Taylor . . . was one of the most deservedly popular actresses who ever appeared upon the stage . . . By the magnetism of her presence and the charm of her voice she seems to have carried everything before her . . . The boxes were nightly filled with her adorers, and she seems to have had as many worshippers as the pit would hold. The whole town seems to have wept with delight when she gave them a smile, and to have gone almost mad over 'Our Mary.'" Hutton, *op. cit.,* 30, 31.

6. *Ibid.,* 35.

7. Ireland says of her farewell: "She played her last engagement at Burton's Theatre, where (having married Mr. W. Ogilvie Ewen, on the seventh of November, 1851) she bade adieu to the profession in the third of May, 1852." Ireland, *op. cit.,* II, 243.

8. Brougham's Lyceum was situated on the west side of Broadway, two doors below Broome Street and was opened December 23, 1850. The venture failed, although the productions were of a high calibre and John Brougham, 1814-1880, was very popular as O'Trigger in "The Rivals," and Brulgruddery in "John Bull," etc. James Wallack became manager, with Brougham as a member of the company, opening on September 8, 1852 as Wallack's Lyceum.

9. *A Small Boy and Others,* 105, 106, 107. The new Wallack company opening in September, 1852, included Laura Keene, William Blake, and John Lester Wallack, all of whom appeared in "Much Ado About Nothing," on October 18, 1852 at Wallack's Lyceum, holding the stage for one week, during which, in all probability, Harry James was seeing it as his second Shakespearean production. See T. Allston Brown, *A History of the New York Stage,* 1732 to 1901, New York, Dodd, Mead & Co., 1903, I, 478. John Lester Wallack was a member of Burton's company during 1850-1851 and 1851-1852 seasons and not with Brougham, coming to the Lyceum when his father opened it at the beginning of the 1852-1853 season. See Hutton, *op. cit.,* 99.

10. Hutton, *op. cit.,* 101, 102.

11. Among the roles in which he was extremely successful were Orlando, Young Marlow, Captain Absolute in *The Rivals,* Charles Surface in *The School for Scandal,* and Count de Jolimatre in *Fashion.* See Ireland, *op. cit.,* II, 494, 500.

12. Brown, *op. cit.,* I, 397. In the same passage Brown continues: "The most interesting fact, perhaps, in connection with this event was the almost simultaneous production of the same work at Burton's Theatre, beginning on February 3 . . . The play at Burton's ran until March 6, and at the Broadway until March 11. In effectiveness of stage setting, and in the costuming, the comedy had an infinitely more brilliant showing here than at Burton's; in the acting, there was little left for critical cavil in the performance at either house."

13. James is apparently mistaken about Joey Gougenheim in the role of Puck; records indicate that "little Viola Crocker, as pretty as a pictured fairy, was the *Puck.*" Hutton, *op. cit.,* 177; see also Brown, *op. cit.,* I, 397 where Viola Crocker is listed as Puck. It is possible that Joey Gougenheim, who was a member of the Old Broadway company at this time, substituted for Miss Crocker at the performance the Jameses saw. One other role mentioned in James's reminiscence disagrees with the casts listed in accounts of the performance. However all others are identical with the playbill lists.

14. Again James's memory fails him, or a temporary substitution in the

part was made, for Joseph E. Nagle is not listed as a member of the cast. According to both Brown and Hutton, Lysander was played by Lanergan, Demetrius by Grosvenor, but Mrs. Nagle is listed as Hermia.

15. *A Small Boy and Others,* 107, 108. The Gougenheim sisters, of Jewish origin in England where they made London debuts, first performed in New York in 1850, remaining until 1856 when they went to Australia before returning to New York at Laura Keen's Theatre in 1859. They were very popular for several seasons in the 'Fifties, particularly "Joey" the younger one. William Davidge, also a favorite with the Jameses, was born in London in 1814 and first appeared at the Broadway Theatre as Sir Peter Teazle on August 19, 1850, staying with the company for five years playing "leading comedy" and "old men"' roles in the regular repertory. One critic wrote of the 1854 production of *A Midsummer Night's Dream,* " . . . the presentation of the part of *Bottom* by Mr. Davidge has had no equal before or since." Hutton, *op. cit.,* 178 (1875).

16. *A Small Boy and Others,* 105.

17. Ireland, *op. cit.,* II, 564. By many critics Burton was considered a great actor, in the limits of his sphere. "His facial power was greater than that of any other performer we ever saw. One fault of his was a habit of giving too much breadth—in fact, of throwing unnecessary coarseness into most of his impersonations." T. Allston Brown, *History of the American Stage,* New York, Dick & Fitzgerald, 1870, 58. In February, 1854, in the Chambers Street production of *A Midsummer Night's Dream,* Burton played the part of Bottom in a conscious and fairly successful attempt to compete with Davidge who was at the same time doing Bottom at the Old Broadway, "and the rivalry was prolonged throughout the season, both houses and both representations having their own partisans and strong admirers." Hutton, *op. cit.,* 178. Such rivalry between theatres and companies did much to stimulate the already wide activities of actors and playhouses of the 'Forties and 'Fifties.

18. *Ibid.,* 3. Joseph Jefferson states in his *Autobiography:* "Burton was thoughtful and saturnine . . . one of the funniest creatures that ever lived . . . As an actor of the old broad farce-comedy Mr. Burton certainly had no equal in his day . . . his face was a huge map on which was written every emotion that he felt." Quoted in Oral Sumner Coad, Edwin Mims, Jr. *The American Stage,* New Haven, Yale University Press, 1929, 186.

19. *A Small Boy and Others,* 108. Madame Ponisi, wife of James Ponisi, an English actor, was born in England and after her debut in London in 1848 came to America for a long and successful career. She appeared first at the Old Broadway, as Lady Teazle, on November 11, 1850, and continued there several seasons. See Brown, *History of the American Stage,* 293. She was popular in male roles, Romeo, Sir Edward Ardent in *The Morning Call,* and Faustus. Her Mrs.

Malaprop, however, was her highest accomplishment, it being considered "probably the best America has seen." Brown, *A History of the New York Stage*, I, 383.

20. *A Small Boy and Others*, 108.

21. Brown, *A History of the New York Stage*, I, 385.

22. *Ibid.*, I, 397.

23. *A Small Boy and Others*, 109. James wrongly attributed *Green Bushes* by J. B. Buckston to Boucicault. See Edel, ed., *The Complete Plays of Henry James*, 23.

24. Ireland, *op. cit.*, II, 593.

25. *Ibid.*, II, 119.

26. *A Small Boy and Others*, 109. Lady Gay was the first original character in high comedy in which Charlotte Cushman made a decided hit in 1841, so that the role was well established ten years later when Fanny Wallack, Mrs. Shaw, and Mrs. Blake did it frequently, the play continuing in demand until the 'Nineties.

27. William Rufus Blake, 1805-1863, was really a very fine artist. Oliver Wendell Holmes, in speaking of the interrelation of tears and laughter in *The Autocrat of the Breakfast Table*, says: "If you want to choke with stifled tears at the sight of this transition from laughter to weeping as it shows itself in older years, go and see Mr. Blake play Jesse Rural." This was the famous role in Boucicault's *Old Heads and Young Hearts*, so long a repeated success from its first performance at the Park Theatre on January 6, 1845.

28. Josephine Shaw Russell Hoey, born in Liverpool in 1824, made her debut in New York in 1839 at the National Theatre, Church and Leonard Streets, and later was very popular at Burton's in Chambers Street.

29. Arthur Hobson Quinn, *History of the American Drama*, New York, Harper & Brothers, 1923, 368, 369, 370. Boucicault's French adaptation succeeded for several reasons, the dialogue in which it particularly excelled being especially outstanding, as it was "fresh and racy, was his own and not a following of the original French. He translated with the ease and freedom born of a four years' acquaintance with the language . . . Instead of giving a literal translation, he rendered the sense of a passage while at the same time fitting the language of his adaptation to the character." Ralph Hartman Ware, *American Adaptations of French Plays on the New York and Philadelphia Stage from 1834 to the Civil War*, Philadelphia, 1930, 13.

30. *A Small Boy and Others*, 106.

31. *Ibid.*, 109, 110.

32. Ireland, *op. cit.*, II, 575.

33. *A Small Boy and Others*, 110.

34. *Ibid.*, 110-112. James's depreciation of Laura Keene is interestingly paralleled by contemporary critics who also saw her in those first

promising days at Wallack's Lyceum in 1852 and saw her decline as an actress as she rose in the role of manager, first at Laura Keene's Varieties, the Metropolitan Theatre, in 1855, and the following years at her own house, Laura Keene's New Theatre, on Broadway, near Houston Street. One critic writes: "Miss Keene made a most favorable impression, and had she remained in the establishment, under the guidance of Mr. Wallack, would probably have become the most elegant and favorite *artiste* in the city. She, however, threw up the advantage of her position, and after enjoying the dubious honor of management for a few seasons, is now a wanderer in the provinces." Ireland, *op. cit.,* II, 611.

35. *A Small Boy and Others,* 113.

36. Brown, *A History of the New York Stage,* I, 348. Accounts of the early productions of *Dombey* show that in characteristic fashion the play was altered and reconstructed from performance to performance, particularly when new members of Burton's company took over parts not previously well received. The first performance lasted four nights, after which, with certain fortunate changes, it was again offered on August 14, 1848 in Chambers Street with Mr. Jordan as Carker doing vastly better than his predecessor, Mr. Marshall; and Mr. Raymond as Toots was excellent; "Burton was incomparably great as *Captain Cuttle."* Ireland, *op. cit.,* II, 514.

37. Lizzie Weston was a member of Burton's company in Chambers Street in 1852, playing the Widow Delmaine, for the first time, in *The Serious Family* on March 5, 1852. She married the actor Davenport before becoming the wife of Charles Mathews, Jr., on February 16, 1858, also an actor but one whose career suffered by this marriage. "His social and professional career in this country he brought to a proper termination by getting well whipped with a cowhide in the hands of Mr. A. H. Davenport, whom he slandered with having sold to him his wife. The affair took place in front of the New York Hotel, and the ignominious chastisement was well deserved." Brown, *History of the American Stage,* 239.

38. *A Small Boy and Others,* 116-118.

39. *Ibid.,* 115, 116.

40. *Francis' Picture of New York and Strangers Guide,* New York, C. S. Francis & Co., 1851, xi.

41. *A Small Boy and Others,* 154-156. Lola Montes, notorious dancer, made her sensational première at the Old Broadway on December 29, 1851, a woman whose escapades had, for years, furnished scandalous topics at tea tables in Europe and America. For an account of the "Beautiful but Reckless" Lola Montes, see Coad and Mims, *op. cit.,* 191; also Charles H. Haswell, *Reminiscences of an Octogenarian,* New York, Harper and Brothers, 1896, 476.

42. *A Small Boy and Others,* 156, 157. Emily Mestayer, an oldtimer from the 'Thirties at the Park, was the leading lady at Barnum's

in the seasons of 1851-1852, 1852-1853, "When 'The Old Folks at Home' was produced, she made a hit by her singing of the song of that name." Brown, *A History of the Stage*, I, 74. She was popular at the Bowery Theatre in the early 'Thirties, especially as Rosalie Somers in *Town and Country*. In the 'Forties she enjoyed success at the Olympic in *Alpine Maid*, as Rosette, and in *Glance at New York*, as Lizey, with Chanfrau as Mose. See Ireland, *op. cit.*, II, 507, 508.

43. *A Small Boy and Others*, 158, 159.
44. Ireland, *op. cit.*, II, 158, 159.
45. Mrs. William Hoare Bellamy was born in Scotland and made her American debut in 1838 at the National Theatre, later playing in Philadelphia in 1842, then known as Mrs. Penson. She reappeared in New York and Philadelphia in the 'Fifties as Mrs. Bellamy. Her husband, born in Cork, Ireland, William H. Bellamy, also made his American debut in 1838. Neither actor achieved notable success.
46. *A Small Boy and Others*, 158-165.
47. A guide book of 1851 states: "This very popular place of entertainment is situated in Broadway, corner of Prince-street. The grounds of this establishment, which occupy nearly a whole city square, are laid out with great taste, and ornamented with the rarest of native and exotic plants. Besides the theatre there is a large saloon, for concerts and refreshments, and extensive covered walks, the whole open, during the summer months, to the outer air. The theatre is elegantly fitted up, and capable of seating three thousand persons. It has been for several years in most successful operation, commanding large and very fashionable audiences. It is open only during the summer months. Very expensive fireworks are occasionally given here, and add much to the variety of entertainment. Admission, 50 cents, to all parts of the house." *Francis' Guide*, 67.
48. From the first day of their arrival in America the Ravel family were a great success; for several decades, from 1832 to 1860 and beyond, some members being born and growing up while the family toured and performed, the youngest ones joining the troupe at the earliest possible age. They opened at the Park on July 16, 1832: "THE RAVEL FAMILY have just arrived from Paris, where they have performed with the greatest success. They have likewise performed in the principal Theatres of France, Germany, Italy, Prussia, Holland, and lastly, before the King of Sardinia. They wish to give a few performances in this city, that the nature of their Spectacle may be known and duly appreciated. The Spectacle consists of ROPE DANCING, HERCULEAN FEATS, and PANTOMIME BALLETS, in which the YOUNG GABRIEL RAVEL . . . will sustain the principal character . . . etc." Ireland, *op cit.*, II, 12; also Coad and Mims, *op cit.*, 104.
49. *A Small Boy and Others*, 165-167.

50. Leon Javelli was "a rope-dancer of the highest elegance and ability, who died of cholera July 13, 1854, aged thirty-nine years." Ireland, *op cit.*, II, 14.

51. *A Small Boy and Others*, 167-169. Franconi's Hippodrome was opened on May 2, 1853 when a syndicate of showmen secured the corner of 23rd Street and Broadway where they erected a large building for gladiatorial contests, chariot races, etc. In 1858 the Hippodrome was torn down to make way for the Fifth Avenue Hotel. One account reads: "Franconi's Hippodrome was opened where Corporal Thompson's Cottage had for a long time been sole occupant of the ground—the site of the Fifth Avenue Hotel of this day. The Hippodrome was of brick, two stories high, and about 225 feet in diameter. It enclosed an open arena. The performances were excellent and the place was in great favor during its existence of two years or thereabout . . ." Haswell, *op. cit.*, 487.

Chapter Five

The Sense of Europe

" . . . a tradition was thus fed, a presumption thus created, a vague vision thus filled in."

At the beginning of the first World War, when Henry James, the distinguished novelist and expatriate, had published two of his three volumes of reminiscences, he had lived in England nearly forty years and was to become a British subject in the year before his death in 1916. His recollections of the earlier years of his life were, therefore, seen in the perspective of an English tradition which he had consciously cultivated for many decades. It is understandable that in the circumstances many aspects of his childhood and youth took on, in his memory, a greater English coloring than they actually contained. One might query the speculation that had he made Paris his chosen home of exile instead of London he might have built up an equally effective French tradition, dating back also to the New York scene of 1850. Had there not been Mlle. Delavinge, in the Fourteenth Street days, and the volumes of Gavarni? On the shelves of the tall secretary between the front parlor windows, had there not been the beautiful set of Béranger with the excellent steel engravings so lingeringly pored over by young Harry James? And what of the Institute Vergnès, with the interminable *dictées,* and the large Russian instructress with her perfect French accent, domiciled with the Jameses? Even at Mr. Jenk's academy on Broadway, a strong

119

Swiss-French element of life was represented in the person of young Louis De Coppet with his fascinating French accent and manner, pressing home to Harry this "sense of Europe," this innate predilection for the rich experiences to be had across the Atlantic. Within two years, the apartment in Paris, the schools in Geneva, the French tutors and governesses were to carry this sense into partial realization, bringing to fruition the hopes and dreams of the small boy and others on Fourteenth Street to whom Europe was then a land of promise. Later on, in the 'Sixties when Henry, Jr., first ventured into print, the influences upon him of such authors as George Eliot, Dickens, Thackeray, Matthew Arnold, and Swinburne were counterbalanced strongly by Edmund de Goncourt, Daudet, Balzac, Flaubert, Zola, de Maupassant, and Ivan Turgenieff. And all through the years, the *Revue des Deux Mondes* counted more with the James family than the esteemed English and American reviews. If, in 1875, during his experiment of residing for a year in Paris, Henry James, Jr., had found there the intellectual, literary, the social stimulation and inspiration that he soon found in London, the French tradition rather than the English might well have carried him through a different expatriation. In the childhood years, however, although the English pull was perhaps more constant, the whole tradition and culture of the Continent offered infinite possibilities which flowed together in what he rightly called his "sense of Europe."

In view of the ten years spent in America, eight of them in New York, with no direct contact with Europe to account for the extraordinary obsession with foreign things which young Harry was developing, the question naturally arises as to the causes for this obsession. What were the ingredients which fed the tradition, filled in the vague vision and advanced the presumption that this American scene was only temporary, that it ultimately would give way to the richer life abroad? The cross-currents and interplay of American and foreign thoughts and fancies offer an interesting study, since they represent the birth of the dilemma in which he was caught, even as a child under twelve, with a growing division of interests and loyalties that was to harass him for the rest of his long life.

When only six months old, it will be remembered, young Harry had been taken to Europe in 1843 for a long residence at Windsor and visits to Paris so impressive that he later convinced his parents of remembering vividly the Place Vendôme, seen from a carriage on the Rue St. Honoré at the tender age of one year and a half. With such a prologue, his drama of Europe began, developing slowly at first, for Albany in 1845-1847 offered the antithesis of such Parisian vistas. Even there, however, Europe was present in the remnants of Dutch architecture and patroon life, lending a foreign note to the domestic scene, as did New York to a lesser degree in the next few years.

What so often sounded this note was the family conversations, especially with guests such as Emerson and Thackeray, Albany aunts and uncles, the Tweedies, and others returning from or en route to Europe. The pleasures of Rome and Florence, Pisa and Milan, Geneva and Vevey, Paris and London were painted in the brightest colors. But above all, Aunt Kate Walsh, an established member of the household and an announced Anglophile made the greatest contributions to the subject. As her nephew Harry remembered this "sole maternal aunt," she stood out in sharp relief amid the rosy memories of the Fourteenth Street house with her animated talk of European sights. With his parents she "was in a position to share . . . the treasures of these mild memories, which strike me as having for the most part, through some bright household habit, overflowed at the breakfast-table, where I regularly attended with W. J.; she had imbibed betimes in Europe the seeds of a long nostalgia, and I think of her as ever so patiently communicative on that score under pressure of my artless appeal. That I should have been so inquiring while still so destitute of primary data was doubtless rather an anomaly; and it was for that matter quite as if my infant divination proceeded by the light of nature; I divined that it would matter to me in the future that 'English life' should be of this or that fashion." [1]

To contrast Harry's reactions to these dreams of Europe with those of his brother William is to perceive even in their young boyhood the basic differences between them. Exposed to the identical influences at the same breakfast-table or back parlor, William was never to

develop the obsession for Europe which determined a large portion
of his brother's life. Many times William went abroad in later years,
but never with the least sense of expatriation. It was a matter of
temperament, of innate qualities and inclinations that reacted in
sharply divergent ways to this "sense of Europe." William was
prone to be active, to participate in whatever experiences might
be offered; Harry was markedly passive, detached, and observant.
They might be equally interested in a project, a journey, a game,
but only Willy would be impelled, with boyish vitality, to participate.
Harry invariably stood back, contemplative, analytical, often lost
in admiration for Willy's quick energy and originality, often exaggerating it, perhaps, in self-effacing admiration for the older brother.
Both boys must have been equally delighted with the prospects of
going abroad for several years, though for different reasons. With
Willy it was a matter of mere youthful curiosity. Harry's attitude
was almost mystical, toward the dreamy vision of Europe which he
had "filled in" with associations of ideas peculiarly his own and
toward which he came more and more to yearn to bring into reality.

In this strange preconditioning of thought, Harry absorbed avidly
every minute particle of information about Europe. Consequently,
when the De Coppets came into the swim of the James boys' schooling in New York, the impact of their "otherness" upon Harry was
staggering. "The De Coppets, particularly in the person of the
first-born Louis, had been a value to us, or at any rate to me—for
though I was, in common with my elders then, unacquainted with
the application of that word as I use it here, what was my insipient
sense of persons and things, what were my first stirred observant
and imaginative reactions, discriminations and categories, but a vague
groping for it? The De Coppets (again as more especially the most
impressively interpreted by the subtle Louis), enjoyed the pre-emi-
nence of being European; they had dropped during the scholastic
term of 1853-4 straight from the lake of Geneva into the very
bosom of Mr. Richard Pulling Jenk's select resort for young gentlemen, then situated in Broadway below Fourth Street; and had lately
been present at an historic pageant—whether or no celebrating the
annals of the town of Coppet I know not—in which representatives

of their family had figured in armour and on horseback as the
Barons (to our comprehension) de Coup or Cou. Their father was
thus of the Canton de Vaud—only their mother had been native
among ourselves and sister to the Colonel of the castellations (on
Staten Island). But what was the most vivid mark of the brothers, and
vividest on the part of the supersubtle Louis, was his French treatment of certain of our native local names, Ohio and Iowa for instance,
which he rendered, as to their separate vowels, with a daintiness and
delicacy invidious and imperturbable, so that he might have been
Chateaubriand declaiming Les Natchez at Madame Récamier's—
O-ee-oh and Ee-o-wah; a proceeding in him, a violence offered to
his serried circle of little staring and glaring New Yorkers supplied
with the usual allowance of fists and boot-toes, which, as it was
clearly conscious, I recollect thinking unsurpassed for cool calm
courage. Those *were* the right names—which we owed wholly to
the French explorers and Jesuit Fathers; so much the worse for us
if we vulgarly didn't know it. I lose myself in admiration of the
consistency, the superiority, the sublimity, of the not at all game-
playing, yet in his own way so singularly sporting Louis. He was
naturally and incorruptibly French—as, so oddly, I have known other
persons of both sexes to be whose English was naturally and incorruptibly American; the appearance being thus that the possession of
indigenous English alone forms the adequate barrier and the assured
racial ground. (Oh the queer reversions observed on the part of
Latinized compatriots in the course of a long life—the remarkable
drops from the quite current French or Italian to the comparatively
improvised native idiom, with the resulting effect of the foreign
tongue used as a domestic and the domestic, that is the original
American, used as a foreign tongue, or without inherited confidence!)
   "Louis De Coppet, though theoretically American and domiciled,
was *naturally* French, and so pressed further home to me that 'sense
of Europe' to which I feel that my very earliest consciousness waked
—a perversity that will doubtless appear to ask for all the justification I can supply and some of which I shall presently attempt to
give. He opened vistas, and I count ever as precious anyone, everyone, who betimes does that for the small straining vision; performing

this office never so much, doubtless, as when, during that summer, he invited me to collaborate with him in the production of a romance which *il se fit fort* to get printed, to get published, when success, or in other words completion, should crown our efforts. Our efforts, alas, failed of the crown, in spite of sundry solemn and mysterious meetings—so much devoted, I seem to remember, to the publishing question that others more fundamental dreadfully languished; leaving me convinced, however, that my friend *would* have got our fiction published if he could only have got it written. I think of my participation in this vain dream as of the very first gage of visiting approval offered to the exercise of a gift—though quite unable to conceive my companion's ground for suspecting a gift of which I must at that time quite have failed to exhibit a single in the least 'phenomenal' symptom. It had none the less by his overtures been handsomely *imputed* to me; that was in a manner a beginning—a small start, yet not wholly unattended with a bravery. Louis De Coppet, I must add, brought to light later on, so far as I know, no compositions of his own; we met him long after in Switzerland and eventually heard of his having married a young Russian lady and settled at Nice. If I drop on his memory this apology for a bayleaf it is from the fact of his having given the earliest, or at least the most personal, tap to that pointed prefiguration of the manners of 'Europe,' which, inserted wedge-like, if not to say peg-like, into my young intelligence, was to split the tender organ into such unequal halves. His the toy hammer that drove in the very point of the golden nail." [2]

This summer project of creating a publishable piece of fiction in partnership with the ambitious De Coppet was not the first of eleven year old Harry's original compositions. For more than a year he had plied the pen in secret passion for authorship, hiding his efforts from everyone, especially the older Willy and the younger boys who might be even more tormenting. It was, however, proved that Willy could be a demon of ridicule, for he "came upon them, and discovered that on one page Henry had made a drawing to represent a mother and child clinging to a rock in the midst of a stormy ocean and that he had incribed under it: 'The thunder roared and the lightning followed!' William saw the meteorological blunder immediately; he fairly pounced upon it, and he tormented the sensitive romancer about it so unmercifully that the occasion had to be marked by punishments and the inauguration of a maternal protectorate over the copy-book." [3] There were many other potential masterpieces undertaken in 1853 and later, though none of them suffered the agonizing exposure of the mother and child in the storm. "I was so often engaged at that period, it strikes me, in literary—or, to be more precise in dramatic, accompanied by pictorial composition—that I must again and again have delightfully lost myself. I had not on any occasion personally succeeded, amid our theatric strife, in reaching the footlights; but how could I have doubted, nevertheless, with our large theatrical experience, of the nature, and of my understanding, of the dramatic form. I sacrificed to it with devotion—by the aid of certain quarto sheets of ruled paper bought in Sixth Avenue for the purpose." [4] Working alone was exciting, but to be asked to write as co-author with a young European who had "found" young Harry was indeed pure joy.

Louis De Coppet was peculiarly qualified as a companion to eleven year old Harry, in the summer of 1854, on the two basic aspects: the writing urge and the sense of Europe. Not many of the boys within the family's circle of friends and acquaintances did qualify, or conversely, there were not many with whom Harry was constituted to play. He recalled that upon begging Willy to include him in some excursion with the neighborhood boys, Willy had pronounced the marked difference between them by stating with authority, "*I* play with boys who curse and swear!" Harry sadly reflected that he didn't, though he wanted to. He was drawn to Willy's "tough" friends (who couldn't have been so very tough), but was not acceptable to them on the grounds that his brother was. "All boys, I rather found, were difficult to play with—unless it was that they rather found *me*." His sensitive, hesitant, retiring nature, combined with the hesitation in his speech, his pensiveness and detachment, plus the tendency to stand passively by and observe, all combined to cut him off from being "one of the gang." Moreover, few ordinary lads of ten or eleven would take the trouble to "find" him, as he put it. His literary and artistic tendencies were too removed from the community of interests usual with boys who "curse and swear." Only a Louis De Coppet, product more of European than American life, found Harry's companionship rewarding. In this case the reward was definitely Harry's, for he never forgot the pleasurable excitement of his friend's "pointed prefigurement of the manners of 'Europe.' "

Throughout his youth, Henry James was faced with the conflict between a strongly aesthetic nature and adjustment to companions endowed with less sensitivity, for the De Coppets appeared rarely. Even at Newport, in 1858, when the Jameses had returned from three years in Europe to that select American resort, young Henry James, if not actually ostracized from the teen-age group that climbed the rocky bluffs and swam off the sandy beaches, was not fully taken in by the boys. Percy Mackaye, many years later, in interviewing the then distinguished novelist at the Players Club in New York, reminded him of the friendship between the James children and Steele Mackaye, the famous actor-to-be. "Henry James . . . recalled with deft strokes of reminiscence old pleasant associations of the two families at Newport and a fervent boyhood fellowship subsisting between 'Willie' and 'Jimmy,' albeit he did not refer to (though doubtless he would have smiled) the long-forgotten by-name of 'Sissy' which those incorrigible younger (sic) boys then used as epithet for the sensitively artistic, just-emerging author of fugitive short-stories, 'Harry' James himself." [5]

Thrown back upon his own resources, especially in the pre-Europe, New York days, the small boy found security and happiness in the warmly affectionate family circle. Here he was understood and encouraged. The dynamic but acutely refined spirit radiating from the elder James was in perfect accord with the literary urges that were stirring within Harry. The strong bookish atmosphere at home was reinforced at "the Bookstore, home of delights and haunt of fancy." It was located in the lower regions of Broadway and was frequented by the elder James who took Harry along as companion. The particularly English quality of the store was of great importance to the sense of Europe the child was developing as it was to his embryonic literary efforts. "My impression composed itself of many pieces; a

great and various practice of burying my nose in the half-open book
for the strong smell of paper and printer's ink, known to us as the
English smell, was needed to account for it. *That* was the exercise
of the finest sense that hung about us, my brother and me—or of
one at least but little less fine than the sense for the satisfaction of
which we resorted to Thompson's and to Taylor's:[6] it bore me company during all our returns from forages and left me persuaded that I
had only to snuff up hard enough, fresh uncut volume in hand, to
taste of the very substance of London. All our books in that age were
English, at least all our down-town ones—I personally recall scarce
any that were not; and I take the perception of that quality in them
to have associated itself with more fond dreams and glimmering
pictures than any other one principle of growth. It was all a result
of the deeply *infected* state: I had been prematurely poisoned—as
I shall presently explain. The Bookstore, fondest of my father's
resorts, though I remember no more of its public identity than that
it further enriched the brave depth of Broadway, as not less tonically
English was our principal host there, with whom we had moreover,
my father and I, thanks to his office, such personal and genial relations that I recall seeing him grace our board at home, in company
with his wife, whose vocal strain and complexion and coiffure and
flounces I found none the less informing, none the less 'racial,' for
my not being then versed in the language of analysis . . . The
true inwardness of these rich meanings—those above all of the
Bookstore itself—was that a tradition was thus fed, a presumption
thus created, a vague vision thus filled in: all expression is clumsy
for so mystic a process." [7]

The English smell in the Bookstore was supplemented by similar
English sounds at home, particularly one evening when Harry had
been sent to bed just as an Albany cousin had begun to read aloud to
Mrs. James the first installment of Dickens' latest novel, *David
Copperfield*. The temptation to hear the story at the sacrifice of all
scruples won a quick victory in the boy's conscience so that he,
feigning retirement, concealed himself by a screen, folded up behind
which and "glued to the carpet" he held his breath and listened.
The tenseness of his position combined with the strain of the Murd-

stones' situation proved too great for endurance and the highly-strung child burst into sobs of sympathy, giving away his eavesdropping and suffering amused banishment. Dickens, from that moment, became a far-reaching force in the literary current of Harry's imagination, and circumstances seemed to favor the English quality of such thoughts as Dickens alone was creating. "I remember indeed just afterwards finding the sequel, in especial the vast extrusion of the Micawbers, beyond my actual capacity; which took a few years to grow adequate—years in which the general contagious consciousness, and our own household response not least, breathed heavily through *Hard Times, Bleak House,* and *Little Dorrit;* the seeds of acquaintance with *Chuzzlewit* and *Dombey and Son,* these coming thickly on, I had found already sown. I was to feel that I had been born, born to a rich awareness, under the very meridian; there sprouted in those years no such other crop of ready references as the golden harvest of *Copperfield.* Yet if I was to wait to achieve the happier of these recognitions I had already pored over *Oliver Twist*—albeit now uncertain of the relation borne by that experience to the incident just recalled. When Oliver was new to me, at any rate, he was already old to my betters; whose view of his particular adventures and exposures must have been concerned, I think, moreover, in the fact of my public and lively wonder about them." [8]

Mid-Nineteenth century enthusiasm which first gathered momentum with Dickens' memorable visit to New York in 1842, topped by the brilliant "Boz" Ball on Valentine's Day at the Park Theatre, still held sway when young Harry became aware of Boz for himself. On Dickens' second visit to America in 1868, Henry, Jr., was to meet him at Charles Eliot Norton's home, but as a child of eleven or twelve Harry was just meeting the author's inimitable characters made frighteningly real by George Cruikshank's drawings. Each novel seemed more Cruikshank's than Dickens', the terribly vivid images depicted in the pictures being so undeniably the personifications of the fictional characters in the book. Inseparably entrenched in Harry's mind these figures so became that he was alarmed to find himself seeing his cousin as Mr. Dick, and another cousin, Miss Trotwood. It was even more alarming still to find that they seemed like real people only in terms of their staying in character with Miss Betsey and Mr. Dick, which, unfortunately, they very often didn't. With *Copperfield* read aloud in the front parlor and Micawber a vivid reality in the form of William E. Burton at the Chambers Street Theatre, the James boys were steeped in the Dickens tradition, and the Dickens world was the English world, growing more and more to be a large part of this sense of Europe.

There was an abundance of American literature available and consumed at the same time the "English smell" was being sniffed; it varied widely, from *Godey's Lady's Book,* glanced at inadvertently in the dentist's waiting room on Wall Street, to the poetry of Bryant and the stories of Irving, both of whom were at times guests in the Fourteenth Street home. Poe's "The Gold-Bug," "The Pit and the Pendulum," "The Murders in the Rue Morgue," "The Raven," and "Annabelle Lee," the last of which was recited by the children with a double, italicised *ee,* "falling thus into the trap the poet had so recklessly laid for us," were all as well known to Willy, Harry, and the younger children as the most current of the tales of Dickens. Hawthorne's *The Scarlet Letter,* and *The House of Seven Gables,* were an intrinsic part of the literary scene in America and well established classics in the James's library. Walt Whitman, of whom Henry, Jr., knew nothing until long after, was perhaps the most significant and important of all the American poets of the mid-century and had his *Leaves of Grass* reached the family conversations in the mid-Fifties, Henry, Jr., might have sooner reached a better understanding of the poet than his notorious review of *Drum Taps* was to reveal in 1865.[9] Mrs. Stowe's *Uncle Tom's Cabin* was Harry's "first experiment in grown-up fiction," and its stirring contemporariness was brought home to him sharply by the two slaves, Davy, and Aunt Sylvia (pronounced An'silvy), of the Norcoms, Fourteenth Street neighbors who had come from Louisville with their black retainers, who soon, however, ran away from the Norcom home. The very American quality of the book was thus carried on by the exciting escape of the slaves just a few doors from the Jameses at #58.[10] The Broadway bookstore with its English smell was no doubt a powerful factor in young Harry's imaginative and literary development,

but it was strongly balanced by many American agents, from Uncle
Tom to Leatherstocking.

Far removed from the Missouri Compromise with its tragic ramifications was the influence upon young Harry of the English magazine *Punch* of which he later wrote, in his essay on du Maurier:
"Many years ago a small American child, who lived in New York
and played in Union Square . . . was a silent devotee of *Punch* . . .
From about 1850 to 1855 he lived, in imagination, no small part of
his time, in the world represented by the pencil of Leech. He poured
over the pictures of the people riding in the Row, of the cabmen
and the costermongers, of the little pages in buttons, of the bathing
machines at the sea-side, of the small boys in the tall hats and Eton
jackets, of the gentlemen hunting the fox, of the pretty girls in striped
petticoats and coiffures of the shape of the mushroom. These things
were the features of a world which he longed to behold, so that the
familiar woodcuts . . . grew at last as real to him as the furniture
of his home . . . *Punch* was England; *Punch* was London; and England and London were at that time words of multifarious suggestion
to this small American child." [11]

Less generally known than *Punch* but of almost as thrilling an
interest to Harry was a small short-lived English magazine of which
he wrote: "My father had subscribed for me to a small periodical
of quarto form, covered in yellow and entitled *The Charm,* which
shed on the question the softest lustre, but of which the appearances
were sadly intermittent, or then struck me as being; inasmuch as many
of our visits to the Bookstore were to ask for the new number—only
to learn with painful frequency that the last consignment from
London had arrived without it. I feel again the pang of that disappointment—as if through the want of what I needed most for
going on; the English smell was exhaled by *The Charm* in a peculiar
degree, and I see myself affected by the failure as by that of a vital
tonic." [12] In the same category with these English magazines one
might class Nash's lithographed *Mansions of England in the Olden
Times,* kept on the shelves between the front parlor windows along
with the volumes of Gavarni and Béranger, for the magnificent pictures of English mansions fed richly the mind of the little boy lying

flat on his stomach on the floor, the large volumes spread open for him, kicking his heels backward in wrapt contemplation of such marvels of the English countryside. Here a tradition was being fed, a presumption created, a vague vision filled in. Also, bright, glittering postal cards of London's Crystal Palace of 1851 offered incidental food for thought, especially since the New York replica of the London Palace supported Harry's contention that English things were the genuine while American imitations were naturally only substitutions for the originals which he hoped very soon to see. Nevertheless the impressive Reservoir Square structure created an effective illusion of Europe, " . . . the Crystal Palace, second of its name, since following—not *passibus aequis,* alas—the London structure of 1851, this enterprise forestalled by a year or two the Paris Palais de l'Industrie of 1855. Such as it was I feel again its majesty on those occasions on which I dragged . . . after Albany cousins through its courts of edification: I remember being very tired and cold and hungry there, in a little light drab and very glossy or shiny 'talma' breasted with rather troublesome buttonhole-embroideries; though concomitantly conscious that I was somehow in Europe, since everything about me had been 'brought over,' which ought to have been consoling, and seems in fact to have been so in some degree, inasmuch as both my own pain and the sense of the cousinly, the Albany, headaches quite fade in that recovered presence of big European Art embodied in Thorwalden's enormous Christ and the Disciples, a shining marble company ranged in a semicircle of dark maroon walls. If this was Europe then Europe was beautiful indeed, and we rose to it on the wings of wonder; never were we afterwards to see great showy sculpture, in whatever profuse exhibition or of whatever period or school, without some renewal of that charmed Thorwalden hour, some taste again of the almost sugary or confectionery sweetness with which the great white images had affected us under their supper-table gas-light. The Crystal Palace was vast and various and dense, which was what Europe was going to be; it was a deep-down jungle of impressions that were somehow challenges, even as we might, helplessly defied, find foreign words and practices; over which formidably towered Kiss's mounted Amazon attacked by a leopard or whatever,

a work judged at that day sublime and the glory of the place; so that
I felt the journey back in the autumn dusk and the Sixth Avenue
cars (established just in time) a relapse into soothing flatness, a
return to the Fourteenth Street horizon from a far journey and a
hundred looming questions that would still, tremendous thought,
come up for all the personal answers of which one cultivated the
seed." [13]

Such forages into transplanted European art exhibitions were followed at home by exciting conversations and expressions of opinions,
varying in proportion to the divergence of age, taste, and individuality
represented at the dinner table or in the circle about the fireplace in
the back parlor. The subject of painting was to prove of special
interest to Willy in particular, within a few years when he studied
under Mr. Hunt at Newport, but to both Harry and Willy on their
European gallery tours painting occupied a prominent place in their
field of interest. In the mid-Nineteenth century that realm of art
was overwhelmingly European so that the Jameses' interest in it
naturally enhanced Harry's growing sense of Europe. Furthermore,
painting as a technique was to Harry so closely akin to the art of
writing that his early interest in painting had peculiar value to him,
although he had little talent with the brush. In speaking of this
joining together of his youthful concern with writing and painting,
combined with the strong connection with Europe the art world then
held, he later wrote: "I was capable of learning, though with inor-
dinate slowness, to express ideas in scenes, and was not capable, with
whatever patience, of making proper pictures; yet I aspired to this
form of design to the prejudice of any other, and long after those
primitive hours was still wasting time in attempts at it. I cared so
much for nothing else, and that vaguely redressed, as to a point, my
general failure of acuteness. I nursed the conviction, or at least I
tried to, that if my clutch of the pencil or of the watercolour brush
should once become intense enough it would make up for other weaknesses of grasp—much as that would certainly give it to do. This
was a very false scent, which had however the excuse that my brother's
example really couldn't but act on me—the scent was apparently
so true for *him;* from the moment my small 'interest in art,' that is

my bent for gaping at illustrations and exhibitions, was absorbing and genuine. There were elements in the case that made it natural: the picture, the representative design, directly and strongly appealed to me, and was to appeal all my days, and I was only slow to recognize the *kind,* in this order, that appealed most.[14] My face was turned from the first to the idea of representation—that of the gain of charm, interest, mystery, dignity, distinction, gain of importance in fine, on the part of the represented thing (over the thing of accident, of mere actuality, still unappropriated); but in the house of representation there were many chambers, each with its own lock, and long was to be the business of sorting and trying the keys. When I at last found deep in my pocket the one I could more or less work, it was to feel, with reassurance, that the picture was still after all in essence one's aim. So there had been in a manner continuity, been not so much waste as one had sometime ruefully figured; so many wastes are sweetened for memory as by the taste of the economy they had led to or imposed and from the vantage of which they could scarce look better if they had been current and blatant profit. Wasn't the very bareness of the field itself moreover a challenge, in a degree, to design?—not, I mean, that there seemed to one's infant eyes too few things to paint: as to that there were always plenty—but for the very reason that there were more than anyone noticed, and that a hunger was thus engendered which one cast about to gratify. The gratification nearest home was the imitative, the emulative—that is on my part: W. J., I see, needed no reasons, no consciousness other than that of being easily able. So he drew because he could, while I did so in the main only because he did; though I think we cast about, as I say, alike, making the most of every image within view. I doubt if he made more than I even then did, though earlier able to account for what he made. Afterwards, on other ground and in richer air, I admit, the challenge was in the fulness and not in the bareness of aspects, with their natural result of hunger appeased; exhibitions, illustrations abounded in Paris and London—the reflected image hung everywhere about; so that if there we daubed afresh and with more confidence it was not because no-one but because everyone did. In fact when I call our appetites appeased I speak less of our browsing vision, which was tethered and insatiable, than our sense of the quite normal character of our own proceedings. In Europe we knew there was Art, just as there were soldiers and lodgings and concierges and little boys in the street who stared at us, especially at our hats and boots, as at things of derision—just as, to put it negatively, there were practically no hot rolls and no iced water. Perhaps too, I should add, we didn't enjoy the works of Benjamin Haydon, then clustered at the Pantheon in Oxford Street, which in due course became our favourite haunt, so infinitely more, after all, than we had enjoyed those arrayed at the Düsseldorf collection in Broadway; whence the huge canvas of the Martyrdom of John Huss comes back to me in fact as a revelation of representational brightness and charm that pitched once for all in these matters my young sense of what should be.

"Ineffable, unsurpassable those hours of initiation which the Broadway of the 'fifties had been, when all was said, so adequate to supply. If one wanted pictures there *were* pictures, as large, I seem to remember, as the side of a house, and of a bravery of colour and lustre of surface that I was never afterwards to see surpassed. We were shown without doubt, under our genial law here too, everything there was, and as I cast up the items I wonder, I confess, what ampler fare we could have dealt with. The Düsseldorf school commanded the market, and I think of its exhibition as firmly seated, going on from year to year—New York, judging now to such another tune, must have been a brave patron of that manufacture; I believe that scandal even was on occasion not evaded, rather was boldly invoked, though of what particular sacrifices to the pure plastic of undraped shocks to bourgeois prejudice the comfortable German genius of that period may have been capable history has kept no record. New accessions, at any rate, vividly new ones, in which the freshness and brightness of the paint, particularly lustrous in our copious light, enhanced from time to time the show, which I have the sense of our thus repeatedly and earnestly visiting and which comes back to me with some vagueness as installed in a disaffected church, where gothic excrescences and an ecclesiastical roof of a mild order helped the importance. No impression here, however, was

half so momentous as that of the epoch-making masterpiece of Mr.
Leutze, which showed us Washington crossing the Delaware in a
wondrous flare of projected gas-light and with the effect of a revelation to my young sight of the capacity of accessories to 'stand out.'
I live again in the thrill of that evening—which was the greater of
course for my feeling it, in my parents' company, when I should otherwise have been in bed. We went down, after dinner, in the Fourteenth Street stage, quite as if going to the theatre; the scene of
exhibition was near the Stuyvesant Institute (a circumstance stirring
up somehow a swarm of associations, echoes probably of lectures discussed at home, yet at which my attendance had doubtless conveniently
lapsed), but Mr. Leutze's drama left behind any paler proscenium.
We gaped responsive to every item, lost in the marvel of the wintry
light, of the sharpness of the ice-blocks, of the sickness of the sick
soldier, of the protrusion of the minor objects, that of the strands of
the rope and the nails of the boots, that, I say, on the part of everything, of its determined purpose of standing out; but that, above all,
of the profiled national hero's purpose, as might be said, of standing
up, as much as possible, even indeed of doing it almost on one leg,
in such difficulties, and successfully balancing. So memorable was
that evening to remain for me that nothing could be more strange, in
connection with it, than the illustration of the admired work, on its
in after years coming before me, of the cold cruelty with which time
may turn and devour its children. The picture, more or less entombed
in its relegation, was lividly dead—and that was bad enough. But half
the substance of one's youth seemed buried with it." [15]

The Thomas J. Bryan collection of old masters in the famous
Bryan gallery was the center of interest for many of the James boys'
excursions among exhibited paintings. The collection was presented
to the New York Historical Society in 1857 after the death of Mr.
Bryan, but was intact and on full display earlier in that decade. Of
other pictorial evenings, the boys were to remember many "at Bryan's
Gallery of Christian Art, to which also, as for great emotions, we
had taken the omnibus after dinner. It cast a chill, this collection
of worm-eaten diptychs and triptychs, of angular saints and seraphs,
of black Madonnas and obscure Bambinos, of such marked and

approved 'primitives' as had never yet been shipped to our shores.
Mr. Bryan's shipment was presently to fall, I believe, under grave
suspicion, was to undergo in fact fatal exposure; but it appealed
at the moment in apparent good faith, and I have not forgotten how,
conscious that it was fresh from Europe—'fresh' was beautiful in
the connection!—I felt that my yearning should all have gone out
to it. With that inconsequence to handle I doubt whether I proclaimed
that it bored me—any more than I have ever noted till now that
it made me begin badly with Christian art. I like to think that the
collection consisted without abatement of frauds and 'fakes' and that
if these had been honest things my perception wouldn't so have
slumbered; yet the principle of interest had been somehow compromised, and I think I have never since stood before a real Primitive,
a primitive of the primitives, without having first to shake off the
grey mantle of that night. The main disconcertment had been its
ugly twist to the name of Italy, already sweet to me for all its dimness—even could dimness have prevailed in my felt measure of the
pictorial testimony of home, testimony that dropped for us from
the ample canvas of Mr. Cole, 'the American Turner' which covered
half a side of our front parlour, and in which, though not an object
represented in it began to stand out after the manner of Mr. Leutze,
I could always lose myself as soon as look." [16] The permanence of
the impression made upon him by the Cole landscape in the parlor
of the Fourteenth Street house is not so much a tribute to the genius of
the painter as it is an evidence of the acute imagination of the small
boy who was envisioning in his fancy the "dimness" of Italy. He
remembered the picture always, as it depicted Florence from one
of the neighboring hills, "Florence with her domes and towers and
old walls, the old walls Mr. Cole had engaged for, but which I was
ruefully to miss on coming to know and love the place in after
years. Then it was I felt how long before my attachment had started
on its course—that closer vision was no beginning, it only took up
the tale; just as it comes to me again today, at the end of time, that
the contemplative monk seated on a terrace in the foreground, a
constant friend of my childhood, must have been of the convent

of San Miniato, which gives me the site from which the painter wrought." [17]

Italy was also represented in the back parlor of the James home, a room in which Emerson, Thackeray, and less celebrated but equally interesting figures came to discuss for long hours with the elder James matters as philosophically beyond young Harry as the Italian landscapes were romantically dim to his yearning sense of Europe. Almost counterbalancing the Cole masterpiece of the front parlor wall was a large landscape over the sofa in the back parlor, by a French painter, M. Lefèvre representing a view in Tuscany, "a rural scene of some exuberance, a broken and precipitous place, amid mountains and forest, where two or three bare-legged peasants or woodmen were engaged, with much emphasis of posture, in felling a badly gashed but spreading oak by means of a tense rope attached to an upper limb and at which they pulled together. 'Tuscany?—are you sure it's Tuscany?,' said the voice of restrictive criticism, that of the friend of the house who in the golden age of the precursors, though we were still pretty much precursors, had lived longest in Italy. And then on my father's challenge of this demur: 'Oh in Tuscany, you know, the colours are much softer—there would be a certain haze in the atmosphere.' 'Why, of course,' I can hear myself now blushingly but triumphantly intermingle 'the softness and the haze of our Florence there: isn't Florence in Tuscany?' It had to be parentally admitted that Florence was—besides which our friend had been there and knew; so that thereafter, within our walls, a certain *malaise* reigned, for if the Florence was 'like it' then the Lefèvre couldn't be, and if the Lefèvre was like it then the Florence couldn't: a lapse from old convenience—as from the moment we couldn't name the Lefèvre where were we? All of which it might have been open to me to feel I had uncannily promoted." [18]

A further abundance of Italy existed in the back parlor in the form of a classic marble bust on a pedestal between the two back windows, "the figure, a part of the figure, of a lady with her head crowned with vine-leaves and her hair disposed with a laxity that was emulated by the front of her dress, as my next younger brother exposed himself to my derision by calling the bit of brocade (simulated by the chisel) that, depending from a single shoulder-strap, so imperfectly covered her. This image was known and admired among us as the Bacchante; she had come to us straight from an American studio in Rome, and I see my horizon flush again with the first faint dawn of conscious appreciation, or in other words of the critical spirit, while two or three of the more restrictive friends of the house find our marble lady very 'cold' for a Bacchante. Cold indeed she must have been—quite as of the tomb-stone temperament; but that objection would drop if she might only be called a Nymph, since nymphs were mild and moderate, and since discussion of a work of art mainly hung in those days on that issue of the producible name." [19]

Into both parlors with their Italian pictures and bust came the thrilling "Roman, Sorrentine, Florentine letters, letters in especial from the Baths of Lucca (that) kept open, in our air, more than any other sweet irritation, that 'question of Europe' which was to have after all, in the immediate years, so limited, so shortened, a solution." They were from Edmund and Mary Tweedy, the most intimate friends of Mr. and Mrs. James, Mrs. Tweedy being related to the James family of Albany. Many letters between Edmund Tweedy and Henry James, Sr., reflect not only the deep affection they felt for each other but the mutual interest in Europe. The Tweedies had gone abroad shortly after their marriage in the late 'Forties and remained in Europe for many years, frequently urging the Jameses to join them. The following letter from the elder James to Tweedy, dated from New York, May 30, 1851, shows how genuine was the family's interest in the possibility of leaving America for several years:

If I can find a pen on my table to second my inclination, I shall proceed to tell you that our affection for Paris and especially for our friends now luxuriating in all the delights of nascent domesticity there is waxing so great in this beautiful spring weather as to determine us to go out next summer—a year hence that is—if you and Mary will agree to stay in France, Germany, and Italy for 2 or 3 years longer. We make this condition because we so feel that the comfort we look to from your society after you shall have settled down in life, giving and taking dinners and suppers, comparing the style of babies' aprons and the cut of boys' jackets and trousers, discussing the prices of various coals and the merits of different tradesmen, etc., etc. would draw us home from the Tuileries themselves. Can you be induced to remain abroad? Short of a nomination for the presidency, which might keep me here, we will, if you will so conspire with us to turn life into a holiday for something like that time, come out and help with all our might and means;—not weans, though it looks like it and they are of course included, but means, which have been of late considerably—however, my sentence grows too long . . . Jenny Lind continues to carry all things before her, singing alternately at Castle Garden and in Tripler Hall.[20]

Permeating through the spirit of fun in which the letter is written is a seriousness of purpose which, four years later, was to take the Jameses to Europe and carry young Harry directly into the glories of London and Paris; it was not until several years after the Civil War however, that he was to see Rome and Florence.

In November, 1852, Thackeray arrived in New York with a contract to deliver his lectures on the "English Humorists of the Eighteenth Century" for the Mercantile Library Association, the first beginning on November 19th. Thackeray remained until April, 1853, making many friends including the elder James. Young Harry was to come into personal contact with the great novelist at this time in a manner that made the boy more than ever conscious of the difference between America and England, ". . . still present to me is the voice proceeding from my father's library, in which some glimpse of me hovering, at an opening of the door, in passage or on staircase, prompted him (Thackeray) to the formidable words: 'Come here, little boy, and show me your extraordinary jacket!' My sense of my jacket became from that hour a heavy one—further enriched as my vision is by my shyness of posture before the seated, the celebrated visitor, who struck me, in the sunny light of the animated room, as enormously big and who, though he laid on my shoulder the hand of benevolence, bent on my native costume the spectacles of wonder. I was to know later on why he had been so amused and why, after asking me if this were the common uniform of my age and class, he remarked that in England, were I to go there, I should be addressed as 'Buttons.' It had been revealed to me thus in a flash that we were somehow *queer*."[21] This first impression of the great humorist was followed by happier ones in Paris, during the spring of 1857,

when Thackeray was a frequent caller. All five children happened
to be present on one occasion when Alice became the center of a
remark not unlike the observation in the Fourteenth Street library
on Harry's buttoned jacket. "Our youngest was beside him, a small
sister, then not quite in her eighth year (sic), and arrayed apparently
after the fashion of the period and place; and the tradition lingered
long of his having suddenly laid his hand on her little flounced person
and exclaimed with ludicrous horror: 'Crinoline?—I was suspecting it! So young and so depraved.' " [22]

At the time when dancing school experience is certain to produce
the greatest of pain in a shy child, Harry along with Willy was sent
to "the halls of Ferrero," as they called it, to be instructed in the
charm and graces of ballroom demeanor. Edward Ferrero, "good-
looking, romantic and moustachio'd" became the commanding officer
of a New York regiment of volunteers in 1861,[23] and was as dashing
on the battle field as he had been in the ballroom, appearing in
Harry's eyes much as if he had been one of Bonaparte's young mar-
shals. As an instructor the boys found him not at all fierce or superior,
but most kind "to the sprawling youths," a charming man of the
world who gave the impression that he needed but to touch young
Harry to make him a man of the world also. The master's sister,
Madame Dubreuil, "a handsome authoritative person" carried the
brunt of actual instruction, however, calling out alarmingly in her
shrill Franco-American accent, "Don't look at *me,* little boy—look
at my feet." Not a detail was lost on the stumbling Harry, though
feet he was forced to attend. "I see them now, these somewhat fat
members, beneath the uplifted skirt, encased in 'bronzed slippers,'
without heels but attached, by graceful cross-bands over her white
stockings, to her solid ankles—an emphatic sign of the time; not
less than I recover my surprised sense of their supporting her without loss of balance, substantial as she was, in the 'first position';
her command of which, her ankles clapped close together and her
body very erect, was so perfect that even with her toes, right and
left, fairly turning the corner backward, she never fell prone on her
face." [24]

While dancing was the principal purpose and concern of the boys' attendance at the halls of Ferrero and though the atmosphere was strongly European, the association there with Madame Dubreuil was to lead Harry into a further enhancement of his sense of Europe. "There hovered in the background a flushed, full-chested and tawnily short-bearded M. Dubreuil, who, as a singer of the heavy order, at the Opera, carried us off into larger things still—the Opera, having at last about then, after dwelling for years, downtown, in shifty tents and tabernacles, set up its own spacious pavilion and reared its head as the Academy of Music: all at the end, or what served for the end, of our very street, where, though it wasn't exactly near and Union Square bristled between, I could yet occasionally gape at the great bills beside the portal, in which M. Dubreuil always so serviceably came in at the bottom of the case. A subordinate artist, a 'grand utility' at the best, I believe, and presently to become, on that scene, slightly ragged I fear even in its freshness, permanent stage-manager or, as we say nowadays, producer, he had yet eminently, to my imagination, the richer, the 'European' value; especially for instance when our air thrilled, in the sense that our attentive parents re-echoed, with the visit of the great Grisi and the great Mario, and I seemed, though the art of advertisement was then comparatively so young and so chaste, to see our personal acquaintance, as he could almost be called, thickly sandwiched between them." [25]

The children's freedom in attending theatres in New York at this time did not carry over to the opera and concerts, to which their parents went unencumbered. All the more stimulating, therefore, were such names as Bosio and Badiali, Ronconi and Steffanone, which young Harry heard echoed by his parents during their enthusiastic discussions of the great singers they had heard.[26] The romance and the exotic allure of such Italian names and operas and arias were intensified in Harry's imagination by the musical affairs which he was permitted to attend. Most memorable was the unique occasion at Castle Garden when he listened to "that rarest of infant phenomena, Adelina Patti, poised in an armchair that had been pushed to the footlights," where the charming child announced most captivatingly her incomparable selections. "She was about of our own age, she was one of us, even though at the same time the most prodigious of fairies, of glittering fables." [27] Her initial concert had been presented at Niblo's Garden, on December 3, 1851; the Jameses apparently attended one of her subsequent concerts at Castle Garden. Mme. Patti, many years later, was vividly clear in her recollections of the first concert, for she wrote of it:

> I sang on the stage from my seventh to my eleventh year, and carried on my doll when I made my first appearance in public at the former age, singing, "Ah! non guinge"—the finale of the third act of "La Sonnambula" in a concert at Niblo's Garden, December 3, 1851. I remember that occasion as well as though it were yesterday, and can even recall the dress I wore—a white silk with little trimming. [28]

In addition to attending a concert by the child Patti, the James boys were escorted by Mrs. James to Tripler Hall to hear the world-acclaimed Henrietta Sontag (Countess Rossi), who made her first appearance on that concert stage on September 27, 1852. She appeared in 'La Figlia del Reggimento' at Niblo's Garden, January 10, 1853, and achieved great success also as Lucrezia, Norma, Amina, Lucia, Linda, and Maria di Rohan. In his reminiscences, Henry, Jr., could not recall whether it was at Tripler Hall or Niblo's that he paid tribute to Mme. Sontag, tribute "quite other than critical . . . to the then slightly worn Henrietta Sontag, Countess Rossi, who struck us as supremely elegant in pink silk and white lace flounces and with whom there had been for certain members of our circle some contact or intercourse that I have wonderingly lost. I learned at that hour in any case what 'acclamation' might mean, and have again before me the vast high-piled auditory thundering applause at the beautiful pink lady's clear bird-notes; a thrilling, a tremendous experience and my sole other memory of concert-going, at that age, save the impression of a strange huddled hour in some smaller public place, some very minor hall, under dim lamps and again in my mother's company, where we were so near the improvised platform that my nose was brushed by the petticoats of the distinguished amateur who sang 'Casta Diva,' a very fine fair woman with a great heaving of the bosom and flirt of crinoline, and that the ringletted Italian gentleman in black velvet and a romantic voluminous cloak who represented, or rather who professionally and uncontrollably was, an Improvisatore, had for me the effect, as I crouched gaping, of quite bellowing down my throat." [29]

In the spring of 1855 many forces combined to push the doors of Europe definitely open, and what to young Harry was "a foreseen and foredoomed detachment" from America actually came to pass. The James family sailed from New York on June 27, 1855 on the *Atlantic,* not without deeply stirred feelings for all the American ties that they had established during the previous ten years. On the evening before the ship sailed, Henry James, Sr., expressed some of the depth of sentiment which filled his heart and hinted of a feeling that perhaps Europe would not always hold the power over them which it then held. To Samuel Gray Ward of Boston the elder James wrote: "We are having a golden sunset to grace our last evening at home. I wish we might be sure of as golden sunrises on the other side. But America evidently is the golden land now, and I feel it deeply as the hour of departure draws nigh." [30]

To twelve-year-old Henry James, Jr., the sailing brought no such doubts of Europe's golden treasures, nor of America's being the promised land. He was on the verge of that transition from his dreamworld of Europe to Europe realized. Within a few weeks he was to experience, like a crack of doom, in a tiny village along the carriage route from Lyon to Geneva, a brilliant crystallization of this constantly expanding sense of Europe. In Lyon a fever had kept the excited boy in bed for several days, detaining the family who, in desperation, arranged a wagon-lit for him by placing some boards and a mattress between the seats of their carriage. As the journey progressed through a tiny French village somewhere near Nantua, the road opened out into a low ranging mountain on the top of which was perched what the boy recognized with overwhelming joy as a real castle, a castle in ruins. Below the upper slope was a peasant woman, in a black bodice, a white blouse, and a red petticoat, laboring in the fields—a peasant, a real peasant in sabots. "Supremely, in that ecstatic vision, was 'Europe,' sublime synthesis, expressed and guaranteed to me—as if by a mystic gage, which spread all through the summer air, that I should now, only now, never lose it, hold the

whole consistency of it: up to that time it might have been but mockingly whisked before me. Europe mightn't have been flattered, it
was true, at my finding her thus most signified and summarised in
a sordid old woman scraping a mean living and an uninhabitable
tower abandoned to the owls; that was but the momentary measure
of a small, sick boy, however, and the virtue of the impression was
proportioned to my capacity. It made a bridge over to more things
than I then knew." [31]

NOTES

1. *A Small Boy and Others*, 83.
2. *Ibid.*, 32-35.
3. *Letters of William James*, I, 20, 21.
4. *A Small Boy and Others*, 260.
5. Percy M. Mackaye, *Epoch, the Life of Steele Mackaye*, New York,
   Boni & Liveright, 1927, I, 71.
6. Thompson's and Taylor's were popular ice cream parlors on Broadway to which Willy and Harry were escorted by their father after
   ordeals with the dentist. For a description of these popular eating
   places see Stephen Jenkins, *The Greatest Street in the World*, Broadway, New York, G. P. Putnam's Sons, 1911, 184, 185.
7. *A Small Boy and Others*, 80, 81, 82.
8. *Ibid.*, 119.
9. Ultimately Henry James, Jr., came to have a much better opinion
   of Whitman. In commenting upon the American soldier of the
   Civil War, he speaks of "the tender elegiac tone in which Walt
   Whitman was later on so admirably to commemorate him." *Notes of
   a Son and Brother*, New York, Charles Scribner's Sons, 1914, 311.
   In 1860, Henry James, Sr., revealed an appreciation of Whitman in a
   letter from Geneva in which he says: "You ask me 'why I do not
   brandish my tomahawk and, like Walt Whitman, raise my barbaric
   yawp over the roofs of all the houses.' It is because I am not yet
   a 'cosmos' as that gentleman avowedly is . . ." *Ibid.*, 233.
10. In describing the slaves, James wrote: "Davy mingled in our sports
    and talk, he enriched, he adorned them with a personal, a pictorial
    lustre that none of us could emulate, and servitude in the absolute
    thus did more for him socially than we had ever seen done, above
    stairs or below, for victims of its lighter form. What was not our
    dismay therefore when we suddenly learnt—it must have blown
    right up and down the street—that mother and son had fled, in the
    dead of night, from bondage? had taken advantage of their visit
    to the North simply to leave the house and not return, covering

their tracks, successfully disappearing . . . they escaped, on northern soil, beyond recall or recovery . . . Had Davy and An'silvy at least read Uncle Tom?—that question might well come up for us, with the certainty at any rate that they ignored him less than their owners were doing." *A Small Boy and Others,* 250, 251.

11. Henry James, "George du Maurier," *Partial Portraits,* New York, Macmillan Co., 1888, 327, 328.

12. *The British Museum Catalogue* (Periodical Publications, Part III, 447) lists this magazine as "The Charm: a book for boys and girls (Edited by J. C.) Series 1-3. London, 1853-1855, 8°."

13. *A Small Boy and Others,* 169-171. "On July 4, 1853, the first World's Fair ever held in America was opened in New-York by President Franklin Pierce with imposing ceremonies. The exhibition was held in the famous Crystal Palace, a beautiful edifice constructed wholly of iron and glass, cruciform in shape, and with a lofty translucent dome rising from its center. Thirty-nine thousand square feet of glass and 1250 tons of iron were used in its construction. It stood in the open space between the distributing reservoir and Sixth Avenue. In this beautiful gallery the largest and most notable collection of paintings and sculpture ever seen in New York remained open for several months, and was visited daily by throngs of interested people from all parts of the Union, as well as from foreign countries. The palace was reopened as a permanent exhibition on May 14, 1854, but the exhibition was not successful." Wilson, *op. cit.,* III, 444. See also Haswell, *op. cit.,* 488. The building was destroyed by fire on October 5, 1858 and with it Kiss's famous statue of the Amazon, valued by some people above the entire structure and all of its other contents.

14. Not until 1858 at Newport did Henry, Jr., realize fully that the pencil alone would be his medium of expression. John La Farge played an interesting part in this realization for he studied with Hunt at Newport when Willy and Harry were there. "The novelist had, he said, the painter's eye, adding that few writers possessed it. In La Farge's opinion the literary man did not so much see a thing as think about it. In those old days he advised Henry James to turn writer, but, he said, he did not offer his counsel dogmatically. He simply felt vaguely that in the conflict between the two instincts in his friend the writing one seemed the stronger." Royal Cortissoz, *John La Farge, A Memoir and A Study,* Boston, Houghton Mifflin & Company, 1911, 117.

15. *A Small Boy and Others,* 262, 268. In commenting upon American historical art in the mid-century one critic states: "Emmanuel Leutze, the painter of 'Washington Crossing the Delaware,' was probably our best artist in this branch in antebellum times. With all his faults, to a great extent those of conventionality, he was a painter of undoubted power, vigorous character, and a fervid imagination,

who won honor and respect both here and in Germany." Wilson, *op. cit.,* IV, 348.

16. *A Small Boy and Others,* 268, 269. In discussing the origin of American landscape painting one critic places Cole, Doughty, and Durand together as "a notable trio of New Yorkers. Character and energy, rather than good technique, are seen in the works of Thomas Cole. He was probably the first one to make a profession of landscape-painting in this country, and his great success was based upon series of allegorical compositions like the 'Course of Empire' and 'The Voyage of Life.' " Wilson, *op. cit.,* IV, 349, 350.

17. *A Small Boy and Others,* 269.

18. *Ibid.,* 271, 272. Henry James, Sr.'s growing interest in Italy was part of his as yet undeveloped plan to take his family abroad for several years, first expressed to Emerson in 1849 but not fulfilled until 1855. Among the books the elder James drew from the New York Society Library, of which he became a shareholder September 28, 1840, are many on travelling abroad. The records are partly illegible but read in part: "June 23, 1850, *English Civilization;* July 25, 1850, Ruskin's *Seven Lamps of Architecture;* September 1, 1850, Sanderson's *American in Paris,* 1, 2; September 27, 1850, Murray's *Italy;* March 2, 1851, Ford's *Gatherings in Spain;* March 9, 1851, Gray's *Rome,* 1; May 26, 1852, Husted's *Italy;* September 11, 1852, Tappan's *A Step from the New World." Charging Ledger,* New York Society Library (1839-1854), Shares A-J.

19. *A Small Boy and Others,* 270.

20. MS. letter from Henry James, Sr., to Edmund Tweedy, New York, May 30, 1851, Houghton Library, Harvard University. Jenny Lind, the Swedish nightingale, made her first American appearance at Castle Garden, September 11, 1850, under management of Phineas T. Barnum. She made a triumphal tour through the principal cities of the United States, returning for more concerts in New York. Castle Garden, a fortress in the American Revolution, had been converted into a summer garden; as Castle Clinton it thus soon became a popular place of amusement, being situated on the southwest point of Manhattan Island overlooking the bay. In 1845 the Castle was transformed into a theatre and by 1850 was used as an opera house, well suited to the debut of the great singer whose success there was unprecedented. Tripler Hall was situated on the west side of Broadway, nearly opposite Bond Street and was originally built as a music hall for Jenny Lind's debut, but was not ready in time, being opened on October 17, 1850. It was later damaged by fire and ultimately reopened as the Metropolitan Theatre. Hornblow, *op. cit.,* II, 208.

21. *A Small Boy and Others,* 87, 88, 89.

22. *Ibid.,* 88, 89. Alice James was born in 1848 and would have been in her tenth year in 1857.

23. See Wilson, *op. cit.,* III, 516.

24. *A Small Boy and Others,* 238, 239.
25. *Ibid.,* 239, 240. In 1854 the Academy of Music was built at the corner of Fourteenth Street and Irving Place, as a permanent home for opera, previously accommodated principally at Castle Garden. The Academy had a seating capacity of 4,600 and an immense stage. Under the management of James H. Hacket, it opened October 2, 1854, with Bellini's *Norma,* sponsoring both Madame Giulia Grisi and Mario, Cavaliere da Candia, whom he had brought to Castle Garden, prior to the opening of the Academy. Mario, the most famous tenor of the Nineteenth Century, was the most distinguished singer, together with Mme. Grisi, ever to appear on the Academy stage. Giulia Grisi, though somewhat past her prime as to both voice and appearance, was also received with great acclaim. See Ellen Creathorne Clayton, *Queens of Song,* New York, Harper & Brothers, 1865, 377-379.
26. Madame Angiolina Bosio, born in Milan in 1830, had achieved success in Italy, Spain, France, and Denmark as both an actress and soprano before arriving in New York, Philadelphia, and Boston, in the late 'Forties. "Her voice, a high, silvery soprano, was of the finest timbre, limpid, flexible, vibrating, and of great extent. She had a perfect method, and irreproachable good taste." Clayton, *op. cit.,* 453. In the summer of 1853, the prima donna Steffanone appeared at Castle Garden in an Italian opera company including Mmes. Sontage, Patti-Strakosch, Salvi and others of note, being well received during July and August. Mme. Steffanone had sung at Castle Garden in the summer of 1850 in company with Tedesco, Salvi, Bettini, Coletti, and Marini, all of whom did much to make the Italian opera a major part of the New York musical world in the mid-century. Clayton, *op. cit.,* 462-489.
27. *A Small Boy and Others,* 114.
28. Haswell, *op. cit.,* 476. The young genius appeared also at Tripler Hall often during these years, one account reading: "September 22, 1853, at a concert in Tripler Hall, Adelina Patti again sang in public, being then a child of about ten years; she displayed powers that confirmed the previous anticipations of her great future excellence. For a considerable time she continued to appear as a child performer, mostly in company with Paul Julien, a clever boy violinist." *Ibid.,* 490. Adelina Patti was exactly the age of Henry James, Jr., having been born in 1843. She died in 1919, three years after the death of the novelist. She made her New York debut as a mature artist on November 24, 1859, at the Academy of Music in *Lucia di Lammermoor,* four years after the James family had left New York for Europe.
29. *A Small Boy and Others,* 114, 115. Henrietta Sontag was born May 13, 1805 at Coblentz of actor-parents who trained the beautiful child for the opera; she studied at Prague with Mme. Czezka, developing remarkable capacity especially with German and Italian operas.

Upon her arrival in New York, September 19, 1851, she was slightly past her prime, with a voice, however, still extraordinarily fine and with which she completely won all of her American audiences. She died suddenly on tour in Mexico on June 17, 1854.

30. MS. letter from Henry James, Sr., to Samual Gray Ward, Houghton Library, Harvard University, dated from New York, June 26, 1855. A week earlier, on June 19th, he had written to Mr. Ward from 58 West 14th Street, New York: "My dear friend, We have taken passage for Europe in the *Atlantic,* which leaves here the 27th inst. and are going at last to place our dear boys at school in Switzerland. I wish to get a letter of credit upon the Barings, and upon making inquiries to that end of the good news, I am referred to you. This is charming, to go forth under your protection, and I accordingly make haste to request that you will give me a credit upon that house to the extent of ten thousand dollars per annum ($10,000). I do not intend that my drafts shall ever exceed my actual deposits in the hands of your agents here, which deposits will be carefully attended to by my brother-in-law, Mr. A. R. Walsh." MS. letter, Houghton Library, Harvard University.

31. *A Small Boy and Others,* 284, 285.

Book II

1855-1858

Chapter Six

The Geneva Illusion

" . . . that incorrigible vagueness of current in our educational drift . . ."

On June 27, 1855, as the *Atlantic* steamed out of New York, Henry James, Sr., was not alone in his misgivings of Europe's promise, or in his belated feeling that America might be the golden land. Such qualms were soon dispelled, however, in the hope and enthusiasm with which he looked forward to the development of his carefully laid plans. The rest of the party, not so reinforced with father's exuberance of spirit, were caught between anticipation of the journey and pangs of regret over the many ties being broken. To Mrs. James, mother of five children ranging from thirteen to seven, the undertaking caused a considerable upheaval, involving the termination of the eight-years residence in New York. To Aunt Kate Walsh, Mrs. James's sister, the sailing marked a turning point in life, for it brought to a definite conclusion her unfortunate marriage to Captain Charles H. Marshall, from whom she had been separated for some months, calling herself thereafter Mrs. Catherine Walsh.[1] Now a permanent member of her sister's family, she played an increasingly important part in the children's life.[2]

Not until long afterward were the children to realize fully that this sailing changed greatly the current of their lives. Their memories in 1855 stretched back barely beyond the years in the Fourteenth

151

Street house which had been such a full home to them. The two younger boys, Wilky and Bobby, as well as Willy and young Henry, retained hosts of images of these New York days: Alice and the nursery, scarlet fever and the measles; the Irish maid who wore a green crystal brooch; father's friends—Mr. Emerson, Mr. Thackeray, Charles Dana and George Ripley, Mr. Bayard Taylor and Mr. Thoreau; the Albany uncles, aunts, and cousins, especially young Gus Barker on visits from the Ossining School; Mary and Kitty Temple, Will and Bob Temple; the Van Burens and Van Zandts, Vanderpools and Van Winkles and De Coppets; General Kossuth parading down Broadway; there was no end to such kaleidoscopic visions.

Of the five children, only Willy and Harry had been abroad before, but then as very young children, having retained only the faintest recollections. *The Great Western,* 1843, had crossed to England in the record speed of fifteen days. The *Atlantic,* in 1855, landed the Jameses in Liverpool within twelve. On Sunday, July 8th, the weary party put up at the Queen's Hotel there, "in *every* respect a capital house." A few days later, Henry James, Sr., sent home an account of the voyage:

LONDON, JULY 11, 1855

MY DEAR MOTHER,

We arrived safely in England last Sunday morning, after a very unpleasant passage. The captain directed our course so far to the north, by way of avoiding icebergs, that we ran into cold weather and stormy seas for nearly all the voyage. We saw two or three icebergs; only Mary and the children were quite sick. Aunt Kate was well enough to nurse them, and with the aid of Annette, our French maid, kept things in tolerable cheer. Bobby (Robertson) remained intact, and kept me company at table, where he plied a knife and fork equal to those of his opposite neighbor, Sir Allen MacNab, who struck up a great friendship for him. The MacNabs were very nice people, and as they had seats opposite us at the Captain's table, we had much conversation with them. Prof. Renwick and family sat adjoining, and his wife worth fifty modern women, or say a hundred and fifty, by way of exactness. The son's wife, who was a Miss Aspinwall, belongs to the lower classes in manner and deportment, having been the only disagreeable person on board. Her husband, the architect, was jolly and boyish and there were multitudes of pleasant people besides. Indeed,

I never saw a better behaved company at sea. We spent Sunday in
Liverpool, and came here for Monday. We are stopping at the Euston
Hotel for a few days, when we shall start for Geneva. We find the
Wilkinsons well and glad to see us. London looks unchanged, except
that in riding about yesterday we saw in the neighborhood of the parks
marks of the violence of the mob on the preceding Sunday, in broken
windows, etc. The people are excessively incensed by some Sabbatarian
legislation which is said to bear very hard upon the poor, while leaving
the rich untouched, and they have undertaken to break the windows
of the latter by way of venting their indignation.

I will write again soon. Mary, Kate and the children join in love
to you all, and I remain, my dear Mother,

Ever faithfully yours,

H. JAMES.[3]

Grandmother James was for the present not told that young
Harry was suffering from some kind of malaria which had been
aggravated by the rough voyage. Never a strong child, he succumbed
to severe chills and fever, occurring intermittently, so that by the
time the family arrived in London it was obvious that the journey
on to Geneva would have to be postponed. With all possible care
and consideration he was confined to his bed, "a medieval four-poster
such as I had never seen," for several days. The fever intensified
his already excited state of imagination and the irony of being
actually in "Europe" but unable to see and enjoy it gave the situation a potency of effect which was to remain with him ever after.
In the intervals during which he was left alone, Harry overflowed
in response to "the thick and heavy suggestions of the London room
about me, the very smell of which was ancient, strange and impressive, a new revelation altogether, and the window open to the English
June (sic) and the far off hum of a thousand possibilities. I consciously took them in, these last, and must then, I think, have first
tasted the very greatest pleasure perhaps I was ever to know—that of
almost holding my breath in presence of certain aspects to the end
of so taking in. It was as if in those hours that precious fine art had
been disclosed to me—scantly as the poor place and the small occasion might have seemed of an order to promote it. We seize our
property by an avid instinct wherever we find it, and I must have

kept seizing mine at the absurdest little rate, and all by this deeply dissimulative process of taking in, through the whole succession of those summer days." [4]

Within a few days, it was possible to cross the Channel and continue on to Paris where the Jameses found that hotels exceeded "the London ones in the enormity of their present charges, and . . . do not serve you half so well." The Hotel Westminster on the Rue de la Paix proved to be in no respect "a capital house," except that of its location. The quality of accommodations interrupted not at all the continued responding to Europe which completely transported the ailing Harry as he stood on a balcony, in the soft summer night, overlooking the intoxicating Parisian scene moving beneath him. Oblivious even of the brothers and sisters also hanging over the ornate balustrade, he submitted himself willingly to the vast "Parisianism" flooding his consciousness. The perfectly tangible sense of Europe which Paris thus offered "filled out its frame or case to me from every lighted window, up and down, as if each of these had been, for strength of sense, a word in some immortal quotation, the very breath of civilized lips. How I had anciently gathered such stores of preconceptions is more than I shall undertake an account of—though I believe I should be able to scrape one together; certain it is at any rate that half the beauty of the whole exposed second floor of a *modiste* just opposite, for instance, with the flittings and figurings, as well as the intent immobilities, of busy young women descried through frank, and, as it were, benignant apertures, and of such bright fine strain that they but asked to work on the part of these things of so exactly crowning and comforting I couldn't have said what momentous young dream. I might have been *right* to myself—as against some danger of being wrong, and if I had uttered my main comment on it all this must certainly have been 'I told you so, I told you so!' What I had told myself was of course that the impression would be of the richest and at the same time of the most insinuating, and this after all didn't sail very close; but I had had before me from far back a picture (which might have been hung in the very sky), and here was every touch in it repeated with a charm. Had I ever till then known what a charm *was?*—a large, a local, a social charm, leaving out that of a few individuals. It was at all events, this mystery, one's property—that of one's mind; and so, once for all, I helped myself to it from my balcony and tucked it away. It counted all immensely for practice in taking in." [5]

From Paris to Lyon by train, from Lyon to Geneva by "travelling carriage," reclining much of the way in an improvised wagon-lit of boards and mattress placed between seats, Harry continued to absorb great sweeps of countryside, narrow village streets, broad poplar-lined roads. The ecstatic vision of "Europe," forever crystallized in his sight of the ruined castle near Nantua, with the colorful peasant figure in the foreground, indeed made a bridge over to more things than he knew. Over the Jura he carried the vision, vividly etched in his excited mind to the peace and beauty of Geneva.

By the mid-nineteenth century, Geneva had indeed acquired a very favorable reputation as a cultural center. The romantic glow of Byron, Shelley, Madame de Stäel, and other such luminaries still shone brightly on the charming city. Not insensitive to this attraction, the Jameses, however, thought of Geneva in terms of Calvin, Farel, John Knox, Voltaire, Rousseau, and Johann Heinrich Pestalozzi, whose theories and reforms in education had become widely known. They had, in fact, transformed Switzerland in a country of *pension-nats*. Moreover, in a Europe still reverberating from the revolutions of 1848, Geneva had achieved a political security which enhanced its cultural life. Calvin's "City of God" was rapidly becoming "a little Paris," but it had lost none of the beneficial effects of the Reformation. To the elder James, this latter point was of primary importance. True, he took his children to Europe "to absorb French and German and get a better sensuous education" than they were likely to get in New York; but the strong Protestant thought was the deciding factor in his choice of a European center.

Arriving in Geneva on July 26, 1855, the weary travellers took temporary accommodations at #3 Quai du Mont-Blanc, where friends from New York, Mr. and Mrs. Henry A. Stone, were residing. The building still stands, bordering the Lake of Geneva, not far from the present Hôtel de la Paix. It commands a fine view of the city, topped by St. Pierre Cathedral, and a breath-taking view of

Mont Blanc rising majestically, far over the border of France. After a minimum of sight-seeing, the family settled down to selecting a school for the boys and a nurse for Alice, still a small child. Three possibilities were considered: the pensionnat of Dr. Charles Haccius at the Chateau de Lancy, quite outside the city; that of M. Charles Diedrich, maître de pension at #44 Rue des Paquis, just a short distance away; and the Pensionnat Roediger, also called "La Châtelaine," situated mid-way between the hamlets of Aire and Châtelaine, just outside the present city limits, but at that time a good distance into the country. Dr. Haccius's school had already established a wide reputation. Though founded only two years earlier, it numbered among its students Baron de Malorne, nephew of Bismarck, and Samuel Vanderpool, son of Judge Vanderpool of New York, whom Mr. James knew. M. Diedrich's school was the least distinguished though most conveniently located. The decision to enroll the boys with M. Roediger was made apparently on the strength of that gentleman's dynamic personality, warm hospitality, and strong promises of first-rate instruction. Consequently, on Monday, August 6, 1855, William, the future philosopher, then thirteen, Wilkinson (Wilky), ten, and Robertson (Bobby), nine, entered Pensionnat Roediger as boarding students. Henry, Jr., however, had not yet recovered sufficiently to join the others and continued his convalescence untutored.[6] Of all these arrangements, Mr. James gave a full report to his family in Albany:

GENEVA, SWITZERLAND
MONDAY, 13TH AUGUST (1855)

MY DEAR MOTHER,

We have got the boys all nicely established at school at Mr. Roediger's, and last evening (Sunday) we dined there and passed a very agreeable evening. I should say, however, that Harry is not able to attend school, having not recovered as yet from his chills and fever. He is very nearly quite well, but he is obliged to be so very cautious of himself that it is impossible to separate him as yet from us. We like Mr. Roediger and his family extremely. He is a man of great sense and I should judge of enormous practical power, so that whatever he undertakes to do he is apt to succeed in. He is said to possess the power of ruling refractory boys in a very remarkable degree, and that without ever

going to extremities in the way of compulsion, but by perfectly gaining
their respect and confidence, and so binding them to his will. I certainly never met a man in my life of more powerful personal magnetism.
You feel that you could confide in him very thoroughly, were you called
upon to do so. His wife is a ladylike, motherly person, and his daughters
very sweet. The children have been there now a week, and are getting
very fond of the place. Bobby finds himself somewhat bumped and
thumped in the gymnasium but on the whole he gets on very well. I
have no doubt from the attainments they are already making (Willy
and Wilky especially) in the German and French, that they will speak
the latter with great fluency within a year, and the former nearly as
well. There are only five American boys besides mine in the school,
all the rest (40) being French and German. They have one English
lesson a day, but all the rest are conducted in French and German. On
Sunday, after going to church in the morning they return to lunch at
1 o'clock and have the rest of the afternoon to themselves. At 5 o'clock,
every Sunday, they have a very handsome dinner—judging indeed from
yesterday's specimen, one could desire nothing better—at which all the
pupils and the brother-in-law and sister of Mr. R., with such friends
of the pupils as may be in town, meet and enjoy themselves in the
merriest manner. After dinner, they have tea, after tea a concert of
music, and after the concert the children dance. This is the Swiss and
European method of passing the day, and though it strikes us as somewhat odd, I do not see that any serious damage is going to be done
by it either to soul or body. One thing is very clear, that if the little
fellows feel homesick at all, they will feel less of it on Sunday than
any other day.

I think you cannot do better than send Bobby and Willy Temple out
this fall.[7] I am not sure whether I had better put them at Mr. Roediger's
on some accounts, but when I consider how superior a person he seems
to be for the management of youth, I think that probably will be the
place. I am going to write Mr. Dexter by this steamer about it. I send
a letter to the *Tribune* also by this steamer, which sheds some light on
the schools.

We are never long without a sight of American faces here. Mr. Henry
Stone of New York, son of Mr. Araph Stone who with his wife was
lost in the *Arctic*, reside here most of the time while their children are
in school, and they are very civil to us. There are several others off
and on. Geneva is itself a lovely place, the environs being very English
in the number of their villas and the charming green lanes which
abound on every side. The Lake is very beautiful, and the climate
comfortably cool at the warmest. I do not know how we shall feel

about staying here all winter, but I think from present appearances we shall do so. The children do not need our presence, they are so well looked after at school; but nevertheless I fancy we shall find it hard to get away. We may possibly—or *I* may possibly—go to Paris for a month; but on the whole the chances are that we shall be all the time at Geneva. I had a letter from Howard (his brother) last week announcing his arrival in Paris. Give our love to all at home, the girls and John and Ed, and believe me, my dear Mother,

Ever faithfully yours,

H. JAMES.[8]

With his three brothers off at boarding school and his activities limited by his semi-invalid condition, young Henry James, more than at any previous time in his short lifetime, now felt increasingly the basic difference between himself and other people. "There was the difference and the opposition, as I really believe I was already aware— that one way of life was to go in for everything and everyone, which kept you abundantly occupied, and the other way was to be as occu- pied, quite as occupied, just with the sense and the image of it all, and on only a fifth of the actual immersion: a circumstance extremely strange. Life was taken almost equally both ways—that, I mean, seemed the strangeness; mere brute quality and number being so much less in one case than the other. These latter were what I should have *liked* to go in for, had I but had the intrinsic faculties; that more than ever came home to me on those occasions when, as I could move further and stay out longer, I accompanied my parents on afternoon visits to Châtelaine and the Campagne Roediger, a scene that has remained with me as nobly placid and pastoral. The great trees stood about, casting afternoon shadows; the old thick-walled green-shut- tered villa and its dépendances had the air of the happiest home; the big bearded bonhomie of M. Roediger among his little polyglot charges—no petits pays chauds these—appearing to justify, the more, the fond New York theory of Swiss education, the kind, à la portée of young New Yorkers, as a beautiful generalised, humanised, civil- ised, even romanticised thing, in which, amid lawny mountain slopes, 'the languages' flowed into so many beaming recipients on a stream of milk and honey, and 'the relation,' above all, the relation from master to pupil and back again, was of an amenity that wouldn't have been of this work save for the providential arrangement of a perfect pedagogic Switzerland. 'Did you notice the relation—how charming it was?' our parents were apt to say to each other after these visits, in reference to some observed show of confidence between instructor and instructed; while, as for myself, I was lost in the wonder of *all* the relations—my younger brother seemed to live, and to his own ingenuous relish as well, in such a happy hum of them. The languages had reason to prosper—they were so conspicuously represented; the English jostled the American, the Russian the German, and there even trickled through a little funny French.'' [9]

Achilles Heinrich Roediger, forced to give up his school in Hanau, Germany, because of political disturbances, had sought refuge in Geneva, the home of his sister, Madame Pelissier, wife of a prominent physician. With the kind aid of Professor Karl Vogt of the Academie, as the University of Geneva was then called, M. Roediger founded La Châtelaine on December 31, 1853, less than two years before the Jameses arrived. He had the good fortune to obtain a fine old *campagne,* surrounded by ample property stretching from a rise overlooking the city down to the sparkling, clear, fast-moving Rhone. Although today used as a four-family apartment house at #138 Chemin d'Aire near the Pont Butin, the building, with its lawns, trees, and gardens presents a view almost identical to pictures of the estate taken a century ago. One can readily visualize young Henry James and his parents, driving in the turning driveway to visit the three James boys, on a pleasant August afternoon and being cordially greeted by M. Roediger and his ''polyglot charges.''

In a letter to the New York *Daily Tribune,* in which he had invested $10,000 before leaving New York, Henry James, Sr., enlarged upon many points mentioned in the August 13th letter to his mother:

AN AMERICAN IN EUROPE   I

FROM NEW-YORK TO GENEVA — THE SCHOOLS THERE
Special Correspondent to the New-York *Daily Tribune.*

GENEVA, (SWITZERLAND) AUG. 13, 1855.

It is only very recently that I have got my boys placed *en pension,* and find myself honestly at liberty to begin epistolating . . . We are occupying an apartment of five or six beautiful rooms in the villa—or as villas are called in these parts, *Campagne*—Gerebsow: a lovely place within a stone's throw almost of Geneva, with grounds running down to the junction of the Arve and the Rhone, and commanding a very satisfactory view of Mont Blanc. My bedroom windows open full upon his majestic brow, and as I unclose them in the morning to inhale the delicious breath of the orange-blossoms which whiten our garden, night-cap nods to night-cap with the friendliest recognition. Such a snowy, spotless cap as the old fellow wears, to be sure! How it glistens in the morning sun, as no *blanchisseuse* here below can ever hope to make mine glisten! We pay at the Campagne Gerebsow—but this is the dear season—ten dollars a week, and we live in far more comfort than we have ever before enjoyed out of our own house. The table is ample without being luxurious, and the cooking entirely *comme il faut.* Our landlady moreover is a genuine lady, as motherly and human as though our tie was one of friendship instead of francs, bestowing every graceful and unstinted courtesy upon us through the day, and treating us at night to the most exquisite *morceaux* to be culled from the musical repertories of Italy and Germany.

From all I can learn here of John Calvin and his influence, I should regard him as a sort of model Bostonian—so entirely did his labors tend to the promotion of the municipal weal. I know that in Boston itself he is looked upon as twin-brother to Mont Blanc, only with more fire in the head and more ice at the heart; but the Bostonians knew only the theologian. As a civic ruler he was a man exactly after Boston's heart, and indeed worthy of all honor . . . We are concerned with our brother John only in his public aspect, or in relation to that great municipal wisdom of his which has impressed itself so lastingly on the educational institutions of Geneva. The college and academy are his standing and eloquent memorial. They are institutions which receive the homage of universal admiration; and I am informed by dispassionate persons that they are replete with the impress of Calvin's individuality. It is certainly highly honorably to his memory, that when his influence was unbounded, and he was free to do precisely as he liked, in establishing a college for the perpetuation of the Presbyterian faith, he not only made a provision for the strictly subordinate interests of letters and philosophy, but even stepped aside to organize two purely scientific chairs, one of Law and the other of Medicine. The physical sciences at that date (1560) were still in the hands of the Alchymists and Astrologers, and of course Calvin could make no provision for their extrication. But by founding the two professorships in question he evidently aspired to give theology a scientific footing, and anticipated time when men should be taught to expect a perfect harmony between the Word and the Works of God. Children found at the Hospital also, who manifested intelligence, were instructed at the College, and boarded with a governor until such time as they should discover their special aptitudes.

I should like to give you a full account of these schools, but I am not yet prepared to do so. Besides I wish at present to give you a rapid *coup d'oeil* of the private schools with which I have recently been brought in contact.

All these schools appear to me to be very nearly equal in substantial respects, the chief difference being in their external attractions. Mr. Diedrich, Dr. Haccius, and Mr. Roediger, conduct severally a distinguished *pension* for boys in this vicinity, and I hear nothing but good of any of them. The price of tuition *per annum*, at each, falls little short of $350, including washing and all necessaries. Every branch of study is vigorously prosecuted in these establishments under accomplished masters, while the physical education of the pupils is made a matter of unceasing and systematic obligation. For example, at Mr. Roediger's school, where I have placed my boys, the pupils have a play-ground as large very nearly as Washington-square, with all sorts of gymnastic apparatus, nine-pin alley, etc.; and here they play to their hearts' content, not apart from but in the company of their teachers, who lay aside the pedagogue and convert themselves into boys for the time being with a good will which would be surprising to one who did not know how much of limber and elastic boyhood survives in these ripe European constitutions. This imperishable juvenility, by the way, renders many of these people truly lovable. One can easily see how fresh and juicy and sweet it keeps them even through the winter of old age, and how often it may involve a sincere sentimental anguish to part with them. Madame ——————, our landlady, for instance, is a grandmother, and has seen, I am informed, great sorrows and reverses. A modester or less demonstrative person needn't exist, and yet life seems still so young and vernal with her that she no sooner comes in contact with children than you find her arms instinctively encircling them and theirs encircling her, and all manner of graceful frolic immediately blossoming forth as flowers blossom after rain.

But let us return to our lambs. The sport of the pupils is not only amply fostered and directed, their health is also carefully promoted by the general discipline of the school. They go down every fair day to the Rhone to bathe, of course under watchful care; they go twice a week to a swimming school upon the lake to practice swimming; they ramble all about the delicious neighborhood, in short excursions

with their teachers; they make long pedestrian tours in the Summer
vacation across the Alps; they sometimes visit Italy, sometimes some
German city; they invade the fastness of the Jura; they ride on mules
and donkeys; they pluck the wild strawberries; they drink at the wayside fountains; they eat the bread and honey of the mountaineers as
they pause to avoid the noon-day sun; they inhale all day the untainted
air of those grand solitudes; and they sleep at night in barn or chalet
a sleep so sweet, I am told, that every angel who waits on health and
innocence unquestionably conspires to minister it. At home they are
subject to the best influences. The teachers and pupils all make one
family. They have games and stories and plays to amuse themselves
with after nightfall, and on Sunday evenings they have charming concerts in which all voices are taught to join, and lift up to God the
incense of grateful hearts for all the goodness He showers upon them.
Music, I think, is one of the necessaries in Mr. R's school. However,
all the schools provide the best instruction in this respect.

Another point of interest is the extreme good manners nourished by
these institutions. All the pupils are made gentlemen in deportment.
Instead of the tyranny and oppression which is complained of in the
English Schools and to some degree in our own, the most rigid and
exact courtesy from each to all and all to each is here insisted on. A
son of Judge Vanderpool of New-York, who is at Dr. Haccius's school,
told me that on his joining the school, he was startled to find himself
the object of so many deferential attentions on the part of the older
pupils. He could hardly believe such amenity compatible with the boyish
bosom, and half expected to see the beautiful illusion suddenly dissipated
by a sly punch in the ribs, or the compulsory descent of his hat over
his eyes, all in the way of prospective good-fellowship. Certainly it is
very lovely to see youth preserving its ingenuousness; to see boyhood
wholly unused to the coarse and brutal commerce of the great world;
and from all I can learn I really think these schools do everything possible to secure that advantage. The whole tone of society around them,
too, strikes me as highly auspicious in this regard. I have seen no
rowdyism since I left England. It may doubtless exist, but it does
not come to the light on occasions when it would infallibly do so with
us. For example, last Sunday afternoon, I witnessed a regatta on the
lake. A great crowd of persons of the lower ranks were assembled
to look on, and every sort of boat from the costly yacht to a common
wash tub participated in the sport. There was no end to the fun, and
the heartiest enjoyment of it was manifested by the lookers-on. But I
perceived no symptoms of ribaldry or rudeness on any hand, nor heard
any angry tones, nor saw the least tendency toward that low and disgust-

ing practical joking which disfigures and embitters similar scenes with
us. Mr. Henry Stone of New-York, who is at present residing here,
and who, by the way, dispenses a liberal hospitality for which all his
compatriots are truly grateful, remarked on my making this observation
to him that he thought the difference lay in the absence of strong
drink. This may be. The drink of the people is a very light wine or
a lighter beer, and it would be hard to pump a black eye out of a
barrel of either. They both seem incapable indeed of doing aught but
add a little unction to one's politeness, and a slightly elevated flow
to one's eloquence, and are manifestly destitute of all malignity. But
then *per contra,* let us never cease to remember that rowdyism with us
is a sign of something which scarcely exists in these countries, namely
the *social* recognition of the masses. It is the method which the unlicked
cub of Democracy takes to proclaim its sense of deliverance from the
enveloping womb of the past. When this same unlicked cub shall have
got himself properly recognized on all hands, or admitted to the extremest social privileges, history will have exhibited no such staunch
or loyal conservator of order as he.

But the dinner bell rings, its clapper being the suavest of tongues
in the head of Francois, the waiter, who, with a bow which I doubt
not much virtue has been expended in the attainment of, says, "*Mesdames
et Messieurs, le diner est servi.*" Let us be off then, and drink your
health in a bottle of this harmless Genevese beer.

H. J.[10]

Such a glowing report of the family's situation in Geneva, the
very center of "a perfect pedagogic Switzerland," coincides in many
points with the elder James's theory of education. From Madame
Gerebsow, the hostess of their ideal pension and John Calvin, the
"model Bostonian," with his highly esteemed College and Academie
to M. Roediger's understanding faculty and well-mannered pupils,
plus the general high tenor of society in general—all these things
supported the religious, social, and intellectual convictions upon
which this European sojourn had been undertaken. Obviously the
strongly commercial and growing plebeian elements in New York
could in no way compete with Geneva's cultural advantages; yet,
Henry James, Sr., was far from becoming the expatriate his son Henry
was to be. A fastidiousness of taste is very evident in them both,
but the father's ideals of democracy and faith in America's future
seem akin to Walt Whitman's whose *Leaves of Grass* appeared that

very year, 1855. Whitman saw in America a new culture, based upon
the past to a degree, but original, dynamic, robust, and peculiar to the
United States. Unlike the elder James, he saw it cut off from European traditions, developing unique, independent standards and mores.
Emerson had cried out for cultural independence from the Old World,
as had Thoreau and others; the spirit of prophecy was in the air.
The Jameses, however, were already too Europeanized to take such a
radical position. From father to son was to pass the fascination of
contrasting American and European culture, seeing assets and liabilities on both sides of the Atlantic. From such interest ultimately
came *The Portrait of a Lady, The Ambassadors,* and the whole line
of "international" novels and short stories whose very substance was
in part "the extremest social privileges" of European society. From
his childhood, Henry James, Jr., was deeply drawn to the balance,
the form, the order of the old civilization, and form was to be a
primal ingredient in his art. The unlicked cub of democracy was to
remain for him far less interesting than "the enveloping womb of
the past."

Sixty years later, the novelist still retained such deep impressions
of these first few weeks in Geneva that he recollected with amazing
accuracy many things described by his father in letters of 1855. In
particular he remembered staying in the Campagne Gerebsow (which
he thought of as "Gerebsoff") and indeed with good reason. The
villa was situated on a large triangular property, bordered by Rue des
Charmilles, Avenue d'Aire, and the Rhone. It was demolished in
1949 to make way for apartment houses which now line Rue des
Treize-Arbres. In 1855, the site was surrounded by fields and ravines,
running down to the river. The property was not yet marred by the
railroad which was cut through that section of Geneva's suburbs in
1857. The villa was typical of the Genevese tradition of country
houses, with many generous-sized, high-ceiling rooms, great hall-
ways, balconies and terraces, all constructed solidly, with a certain
formal air, yet with an eye to comfort and gracious living.

The landlady was no ordinary person, being the Countess Maria
Amelia Hofrichter Gerebsow, a Viennese who had married a Russian colonel, Count Alexandre de Gerebsow.[11] Financial difficulties

had forced them to share their villa with paying guests and the James family occupied five or six rooms with splendid views of the estate and Mont Blanc. Their meals were served in the large dining room over-looking the gardens, and in the evening in the salon their hostess entertained them with music and conversation. Young Henry, confined at first to his room above, eventually joined these occasions and absorbed every aspect of the situation and especially of Madame Gerebsow. She was, in all probability, his first countess and no doubt supplied authentic background for the Russian princesses whom he notes sitting in the garden of the Hotel Trois Couronnes at Vevey, in the opening paragraphs of *Daisy Miller*.

As a hesitant, ailing twelve-year-old boy, he was a bit over-awed by his hostess, in later years thinking of her mostly as reclining "in her own quarter of the garden, on a chaise longue and under a mush-room hat with a green veil, and I, in the course of the mild excursions appointed as my limit, considered her from afar in the light of the legends supplied me, as to her identity, history, general practises and proceedings, by my younger brother Wilky, who, according to his nature, or I may say to his genius, had made without loss of time great advances of acquaintance with her. . . . " [12] Equally impressive was the grand villa itself: "Admirable the scale and solidity, in gen-eral, of the ancient villas planted about Geneva, and our house affected me as so massive and so spacious that even our own half of it seemed vast. I had never before lived so long in anything so old and, as I somehow felt, so deep; depth, depth upon depth, was what came out for me at certain times of my waiting above, in my immense room of thick embrasures and rather prompt obscurity, while the summer afternoon waned and my companions, often below at dinner, lingered and left me just perhaps a bit overwhelmed. That was the sense of it—the *character*, in the whole place, pressed upon me with a force I hadn't met and that was beyond my analysis—which is but another way of saying how directly notified I felt that such material condi-tions as I *had* known could have had no depth at all." [13]

Unaware of young Henry's exciting experience of absorbing never-to-be-forgotten impressions of everything he sensed, the elder James rejoiced in his own observations of this idyllic Swiss life. He was particularly impressed by the freedom with which Sunday was observed as compared with the blue-law traditions of New York at that time. As the second in a series of letters to the *Tribune,* he wrote:

AN AMERICAN IN EUROPE   NO. II

GENEVA, SWITZERLAND

FRIDAY, AUGUST 17, 1855

American parents in general are somewhat disposed to dread the holiday aspect which Sunday wears in most of the schools upon the Lake of Geneva. The pupils go to church in the morning, but for the rest of the day they amuse themselves, of course always under the surveillance of their teachers, pretty much as they please. The various schools differ no doubt among themselves as to the limits of the indulgence allowed the pupils in this respect—for example, Dr. Haccius does not allow dancing, but only music on Sunday evening; but there is absolutely none probably where the *spirit* of the observance of the day is not essentially different from that which obtains in our schools. In none of them whatever would the pupil *be instructed that it was unlawful to amuse himself on that day,* though some sort of amusement might doubtless be prescribed as preferable to others. Last Sunday we were invited to dine at one of these schools. The entire household of teachers and taught make one family every day, all their meals being taken together; but on Sunday afternoon they have a grand dinner, with a few relatives of the family, or perchance of the pupils also, as guests; and it was to one of these entertainments we were invited. The hour named was 5 o'clock. On alighting at the door we were cordially welcomed by our host and hostess, who, after the preliminary hospitalities had been attended to, led us out upon the grounds, where we found all the children in the full tide of successful recreation. Some were walking with their arms interlocked in playful converse; some were running, some swinging, some leaping, some playing chess; but all were plainly enjoying themselves without stint, and yet without rudeness. When the dinner-bell sounded, and we had got all seated at the luxurious table, I had an opportunity to observe the deportment of the children, and I could discover nothing indicating that their manners were practically disregarded. They were allowed to converse freely with each other, and there was a good deal of quiet laughter going on, but I observed no indecorum of any sort, nor any behavior which I should have felt bound to correct in my own children at my own table. The dinner was served in German fashion, and was a beautiful entertainment both in substance and form. After dinner the elders of the party took tea in the *salon,* and after tea the folding doors which connected that room with the dining-room, being opened, we found the latter converted into a concert hall, and for an hour or so we were agreeably regaled by the singing of pupils and teachers. To singing succeeded dancing, and there being some young misses present belonging to the house or to neighboring families, you may be sure that the young gentlemen showed no hearty disinclination to the exercise. The whole affair passed off without effort or embarrassment on any hand, and so far as the thing itself was concerned, I never spent an evening of more innocent and healthy gaiety. Yet if the scene had transpired at any of our American schools, one would apprehend an entire withdrawal of patronage from it. Now what is the exact truth about all this vexed question? Is there no way of approaching it? Let us see.

First, let us state the facts of the case, or the elements of the question to be resolved. Sunday is much more a day of pleasure among Europeans than it is with us. Even among the English it is a day of great *social* enjoyment; that is, they use it for friendly visiting, for family gatherings, for short rural excursions, and so forth, so that its weekly return even in England is associated with a good deal of cheerfulness. But on the Continent it comes near being regarded as a day of pure festivity, and is identified with simple physical recreation. Among Protestants indeed a strong effort has always been made to deprive the day of this holiday aspect, and give it a penitential character; but this is a strictly reactionary movement, and has therefore no absolute or permanent force. It is a reaction against the mere festal observance of the day toward which the whole original current of ecclesiastical life in Europe strongly sets. The tendency of the Romish Church is practically to desecrate the day by leaving out the divine element while giving the human one full play. Thus after mass in the morning the rest of the day is given up to any jollity which happens to come uppermost, horse-racing, boat-racing, cock-fighting, rifle-shooting, while shops are open in numbers, and the auction-sales frequently take place at the doors of the churches. Protestantism very logically denounces this observance of the day; but in its effort to correct the error runs to the opposite extreme, by unduly consecrating the day, or inflating the divine element to the comparative suffocation of the human. Thus in our country the day is too often one of gloom and moroseness, which make children hate it, and render domestic intercourse to the last degree sterile, unhandsome and oppressive. An immense amount of tobacco is chewed by the elders, and our good mothers doze persistently and pertinaciously behind their spectacles; but the day is a weary one in spite of all sedatives, and Monday morning invariably shines the brightest morning of all the week. The Protestant Sunday, then, is a reaction, and has no existence out of that light. Take away its Protestant or corrective force, and you deprive it of all meaning, for it has no positive force. It exists by simple antagonism to the Romish Sunday, so that in doing away with the latter, you necessarily do away with the antagonist. This is an honest historical judgment, for I am sincerely disinclined to either side in the quarrel. *Tros Tyriusve mihi nullo discrimine agetur.* (Let the Trojan and the Tyrian be impartially dealt with.) I am fully persuaded that we shall yet realize an observance of the day far more consonant with Christian truth, and far more beautiful, therefore, than that which has been bequeathed us either by Prelacy or Puritanism.

What was the purport of the aboriginal Sabbath? It was a representative or commemorative institution, designed to typify God's rest in creation. It was a symbol of the perfect contentment which the Divine love and wisdom find in the regenerate man, or the man who from being simply a subject of nature, which he is by birth, becomes first a spiritual man, or a subject of truth, and afterwards a celestial man, or a subject of good. The idea revealed in the symbol is, that the Divine love is dissatisfied with giving merely natural life to its creatures, because the creature by that gift remains nothing more than a superior sort of animal. This idea turns the natural life into a mere basement or culinary story for the true divine edifice in humanity, and makes the regenerate life alone to constitute the bedroom and parlor floors where the master chiefly inhabits. Now, inasmuch as man had forgotten this purpose of the Divine love in his creation, or had contentedly declined into his own lowest stories, the Sabbath was appointed to shield or symbolize the great truth, until such time as it might be unfolded in rational light, and the spirit of man become quickened to receive it. Abstinence from work accordingly was enjoined by the very typicality of the day. For as the day itself typified the regenerate state of man, or the state of perfect conjunction with God, it of course implied the cessation of his conflict with nature, or his exemption from the toils imposed upon him by his natural existence. Thus rest from labor constituted the distinctive morality of the day. "Six days shalt thou labor, but the seventh is the Sabbath of the Lord thy God, etc."

(After a detailed discussion of the Christian and Jewish traditions of the Sabbath the letter continues) . . .

Under the Christian dispensation, accordingly, instead of the Sabbath at the close of the week, we have the Lord's Day at the beginning of the week, the seventh day being no longer sacred save with the sanctity which it and all its fellows derive from the first day. The obvious meaning of this is, that in the regeneration effected by Christ, the natural life itself, typified by the working-days of the week, becomes sanctified and yields only the fruits of innocence and use. It teaches us that this great work of redemption shall purge our very nature itself of whatsoever renders it common, or unclean, and clothe it with a distinctive divine beauty. Hence under the Christian dispensation we lose our hold of the shadow, and grasp only the substance. For we perceive that the only worship acceptable to God is a spiritual worship, or that which consists in a heart at peace with God and our fellow men. Proper Sabbatical observance under the present dispensation then is easily determined. The Lord's Day refuses to be sanctified by any formalities merely, by the most assiduous attendance upon church, by the longest prayers, by the demurest postures of the body, by the utmost dejection of the visage, because all these things may consist with an intense and subtle deviltry. It refuses to be sanctified by anything short of that which equally sanctifies all the succeeding days of the week, namely, a heart of love to God and man, and a course of conduct exactly congruous with that of love. It allows, nay prescribes, every mode of activity which consists with such a heart, and forbids, nay excludes, every mode which does not consist with such a heart.

As to the *conventional* consecration of the first day of the week, it is immediately obvious from what has gone before that any consecration of it must be extremely faulty which represents the Divine and Human natures as still unreconciled, or urges man *to do* anything toward a purchase of the Holy Ghost. Sunday or the first day of the week, being now the Lord's Day, and therefore governing or controlling all its successors, we see that we have no right to speak of the secular life, which is represented by the working days, as any longer estranged from the divine cognizance and blessing. On the contrary, we have every right to speak of it as intimately related to Him, and as amply entitled through His own measureless condescension to the experience of an endless harmony and order. The attitude of the technical church is extremely careless and slovenly on this subject. I wish it would wake up and endeavor to organize a festal worship on Sunday which should in some sense befit the splendid symbolism of the day. If we were rightly instructed in that symbolism, the day would glow and burn with all the poetry of the human heart, bequeathing a lingering savor to its successors which would be sure to sweeten all their hours by stimulating memory and anticipation. Art is feeling in every direction for some adequate religious experience, and finds itself shockingly befogged and belittled when restricted as it is to the inanities of architecture, painting, etc. Where is the great theological artist, who, despising the solemn fopperies of Mr. Ruskin, and leaving all the mock-heroics of our ecclesiologists to the bats and owls whom they disturb, shall set himself to extricating God's only living and true temple, which is the human mind, from the rubbish of ignorance and unbelief, and giving it expansion in the way of a grand unitary worship, which shall at last adequately reflect and celebrate the distinctive Christian truth of the entire reconciliation of the Divine and human natures?

                                                                    H. J.[14]

Within six weeks from the writing of this letter, Henry James's marked enthusiasm for the Pension Roediger, his buoyant hopes that his children's educational problems were being solved, his healthy delight in every aspect of their situation at Geneva, began to cool rapidly. At first consideration, one would expect some drastic incident, some shocking exposé of undesirable conditions to be offered in explanation. As far as can be discovered, such was not the case. Henry James, Jr., in recalling the abrupt change of arrangements, says merely that "We had fared across the sea under the glamour of the Swiss school in the abstract, but the Swiss school in the concrete soon turned stale on our hands; a fact over which I remember myself as no further critical than to feel, not without zest, that, since one was all eyes and the world decidedly, at such a pace, all images, it ministered to the panoramic." [15] To a twelve-year-old boy, already given over to this fascinating process of taking-in impressions as varied, as stimulating as his brief travels had then afforded, the prospects of moving again across Europe, to Lyons, to Paris, to London quite outweighed any question as to the reasons for such a move. Suffice it to know that the elder James was not satisfied, that he hoped better arrangements could be made in England. To Harry the fact was simply that he was to "minister to the panoramic," to enhance further his vision of his sense of Europe. Art, to the future novelist, was not, as his father had recently stated, "feeling in every direction for some adequate religious experience." On the contrary, as stated in his preface to *The Ambassadors*: "Art deals with what we see, it must first contribute full-handed that ingredient." He found that artistic experience stemmed from his sense of *exhibition*, figures, faces, furniture, sounds, smells, colors in an "orgy of the senses and riot of the mind." As long as the property, the material, was unfolding before him, the boy little cared whether he remained in Geneva or left for London, though these three months in Geneva had enhanced his awareness of himself and of those things which were to take on renewed significance upon the family's return to the Swiss city, four years later.

From the elder James, far more reason and explanation for this disruption of what apparently had promised to be an ideal arrangement for the entire family can be expected. In a letter to the children's grandmother in Albany he wrote:

GENEVA, SEPTEMBER 25, 1855

MY DEAR MOTHER,

We are living on comfortably enough here in Geneva, but have come to the conclusion that the schools are greatly over-rated. We do not find the advantages we had expected in them; or rather we did not anticipate the sacrifices by which in respect especially to the younger children, these advantages are to be bought. The children seem happy enough at school. They have enjoyment enough, and live better than is common with these schools, but Mary never sees them without feeling how much they need her personal care, and how little they get in exchange for that lack. We have come to the conclusion that home tuition will be the best for all of them; that while it will be much the least expensive, it will also be greatly to the interest of the children both in moral and intellectual regards. Teachers abound so in this country, and we hear such encouraging things about the methods of private education, that I think we shall very soon make that experiment. We have a young Swiss lady, for Harry and Alice's sake, and I think she will very probably be all that is requisite for Wilky and Bobby as well. We have been for a couple of weeks living in an apartment just vacated by Mr. Henry Stone of New York but the expense of housekeeping is nearly as great as in Paris. We are inclined to leave here in the course of next month for Paris, if Mr. Roediger is willing to waive his rule of three months notice for the removal of pupils; but if he is not, we shall be obliged to leave them another quarter. However, I am anxiously awaiting tidings from Mr. Dexter about the Temple boys, whom, if they come, I think I shall place with Dr. Haccius, the head of the school where Sammy Vanderpool is. He is highly esteemed as a teacher and as a man, and his school has some advantages for boys of Bobby's and Willy's ages. But I will make the best arrangements I possibly can for them, whether I place them there or not. I hope I may get letters by the next steamer, letting me know what to expect in this behalf . . .

I hope you are better dear Ma than you were in the early part of the summer; and that the girls have recovered from their chills and fever. Harry is better, but Alice has been quite unwell. She has now recovered and I am in hopes will go on to confirmed health. The climate of this place is very good in many respects, but it has a wind from the North called the *Bise* which is extremely unpleasant and stirs up a perpetual tooth ache. The town is besides very dull for one who has no active pursuits, and I think we shall all feel better for a change.

Mary and Aunt Kate both join in love to you all and I remain, my dear Mother,

Yours ever faithfully,

HENRY JAMES[16]

This letter, upon careful study, expresses a kind of highly cultivated rationalization based upon the fundamental point that Henry James, Sr., could not bear the thought of being separated from his family. Geneva, it was obvious, did not offer the parents specially pleasant prospects for the long winter months approaching; and the idea of their going to Paris for the winter, taking Alice and probably Harry with them, leaving the remaining three boys in Geneva, even under the care of the capable M. Roediger, was actually too great a demand upon the elder James's extraordinary paternalism. His explanation, that private education in Europe would be "greatly to the interest of the children both in moral and intellectual regards," is a revival of the same theory on which the New York experiments were carried back and forth between private schools and tutors. Actually there existed no school or tutor that could provide the kind of education that Henry James was seeking for his children. The ideas he had developed in his theory of education were so inextricably entwined with his own moral and intellectual realms that he alone could be their teacher. His innate hopefulness, his belief in better things to come, and his determination to find for his children the right educational environment carried the elder James buoyantly from these disappointments to renewed optimism. However, the question in October, 1855, of an alternative to the Geneva experiment was particularly trying, for nothing definite seemed to offer a choice. With characteristic candidness and a genuine reaching-out for ideas, Henry James appealed to his friend in London, Garth Wilkinson. The following letter, equally candid and appealing, had much to do with the James family's settling in London for the autumn and winter of that year:

ST. JOHN'S WOOD
24 FINCHLEY ROAD
OCTOBER 13, 1855.

WELL BELOVED HENRY JAMES,

Rich people like you are sure to get the worse of nearly everything in this world, because you are always looking beyond obvious immediate good. This is a blessed thing for you all, for you want a deal of cooking before you are tender enough for the skies. I thought how it would be now if you would take my advice, you would locate yourself, (without any fantasies about Devonshire, which are really only so much second childhood) in the neighborhood of London, on the shore of a Railway: or else in the suburbs themselves. For less than £400 a year you could do everything, if you would administer affairs at home, or by occasional classes out; and you could yourself repose in congenial society. Then, as your main object is this same location, you will stick to that in the first place; and allow yourself a three months holiday in the best part of the year to go where you like. You will have enough of the best green lanes in that time. There are to my certain knowledge two places in the world for you for a year or two's permanence: New York and London; for pity's sake be faithful to one of them. Don't follow the theory of "spiritual wifery" in regard to place, flirting with one bit of sunshine after another: but marry one or the other of these fruitful plots of human life. Then you shall be like the Banian Tree, with sons and daughters in your sylvan shade.

There are few cheaper capitals than London; but it is the dearest of all places for the ambitious. When you are settled in Paris, if *you* will run over here for a week, we will give you a bed, treat you like a moderate man with all our friendship, and our plain fare, and talk over whatever you please to discourse about, but especially the way of managing the education. Now pray do come . . .

GARTH WILKINSON[17]

The tentative plans for sojourning in Paris, in the face of uncertainty, were soon discarded in consideration of the warm welcome and attractive suggestions from London.

Very early in an October dawn, with Mont Blanc misty in the background, Henry and Mary James, the four boys and Alice, Aunt Kate and Mademoiselle Cusin, the Swiss governess, rode slowly over the Alpine road from Geneva to Lyons. As the large, yellow *malls-poste*, heavily loaded with mail pouches, luggage, and the James party, rumbled along, few words were spoken. This return to Paris, within three months' time, seemed an ominous indication of the fitful, the improvised, yet reasoned variety of experiences through which the Jameses were to travel. Four years later they would return to Geneva, as though to prove that this attempt in 1855 had not been a failure, an illusion, in "that incorrigible vagueness of current" of their educational drift. Undaunted, hopeful, refusing to entertain regrets, Henry James, Sr., settled back comfortably in "the high haughtiness" of the mail coach, certain that London would be, as Wilkinson said, "the dearest of all places for the ambitious." To Harry, the least ambitious of all, Paris and London were magic places, Notre Dame, St. Paul's, a thousand spires, and bells, and steeples, and he rejoiced in such promise of delight.

NOTES

1. In letters to Edmund Tweedy and Emerson in 1851, Henry James, Sr., gives a colorful account of Captain Marshall's courtship of Aunt Kate and her ultimate acceptance of his proposal. Incompatibility of temperaments and complications over the Marshall children by a former marriage eventually resulted in her removal from the Captain's home and residence with her cousin Mrs. Helen Perkins, before going abroad with the Jameses. See Rev. William Walsh, *op. cit.*, 11.

2. While for the most part Aunt Kate is spoken of with affection and devotion by Henry, Jr., and William, there is a discordant note sounded by Robertson James in a letter of reminiscence written many years later: "You see this (recollection) goes far back and takes in the marriage of Captain Marshall and his subsequent discomfiture. I was a witness to his wooing, being near Aunt Kate at that time and not supposed to be an observer—sharing her bed in fact and carrying with me to this solemn hour the hurt I felt at her mandatory ways. A mother does wrong to confide her offspring recklessly to others than herself." MS. letter from Robertson James to Alice H. James, February 24, 1898, Houghton Library, Harvard University. Other portions of this letter appear in F. O. Matthiessen, *The James Family*, 270, 271.

3. MS. letter, Henry James, Sr., to his mother, Catherine Barber James, July 11, 1855; Houghton Library, Harvard University.

4. *A Small Boy and Others*, 279.

5. *Ibid.*, 280, 281.

6. Leon Edel, in *Henry James, The Untried Years*, 123, states that "William and Wilky were placed at a Swiss boarding school, the Pensionnat Roediger . . ." omitting the youngest boy, Robertson, who entered the same school with his two brothers. On the same page, Mr. Edel says: "In due course the boys were sent to the Institution Haccius, a celebrated establishment. . . ." There is no evidence that any of the James children attended Dr. Haccius's school, though it was one of those considered.

7. Robert and William Temple were nephews of Henry James, Sr., sons of his sister, Catherine Margaret James (1820-1854) and Col. Robert Emmet Temple (1808-1854). In addition to the two oldest sons there were four younger daughters, Kitty, Minny, Ellen, and Henrietta, all of whom played important parts in the James children's life at Newport and later at Cambridge after the Civil War. Their parents both died in the same year, 1854, leaving the five children to the care of Grandmother James and their various aunts and uncles. The Edmund Tweedys took most of the responsibility of the Temple children's care, Mrs. Tweedy having been Mary Temple and therefore the Temple children's aunt.

8. MS. letter from Henry James, Sr., to his mother, Catherine Barber James, August 13, 1855, Houghton Library, Harvard University, also published in part by Ralph Barton Perry, *The Thought and Character of William James*, I, 181, 182.

9. *A Small Boy and Others*, 290, 291.

10. New-York *Daily Tribune*, Sept. 3, 1855, courtesy of the New-York Historical Society, New York City.

11. An account of the Gerebsow family is found in *Archives du Bureau*, #9, 1946, in the State Archives of Geneva. For a description of The Campagne Gerebsow, see Edmond Barde, *Anciennes Maisons de Campagne Genevoises*, Geneva, 1937, 67.

12. *A Small Boy and Others*, 286, 287.

13. *Ibid.*, 289.

14. New-York *Daily Tribune*, Saturday, September 8, 1855. Courtesy of the New-York Historical Society, New York City. For a discussion of John Ruskin's residence in Savoy and his connection with Geneva see H. W. Häusermann, *The Genevese Background*, London, 1952, 157ff.

15. *A Small Boy and Others*, 294.

16. MS. letter from Henry James, Sr., to Catherine Barber James, September 25, 1855, Houghton Library, Harvard University.

17. MS. letter from Garth Wilkinson to Henry James, Sr., October 13, 1855, Houghton Library, Harvard University.

Chapter Seven

In Thackeray's London

" . . . I throbbed with the pride of a vastly enlarged acquaintance. . . . "

The failure of the Geneva experiment, following upon the unsuccessful New York attempts to work out the problem of education might have aroused in Henry James, Sr., a strong desire to discover some fundamental flaw in his method of approach. To a certain degree he must have struggled with the perplexing evidence that something was wrong with the procedures being employed, not with the goals or purposes of these experiments. The weakness which prevented his philosophical and metaphysical concepts from culminating in a recognized school of thought was basically the same weakness upon which his efforts to educate his children met with such difficulties. The crux of the matter was best expressed by the English philosopher, Shadworth H. Hodgson, in a letter written to William James in 1885, expressing appreciation for a copy of *The Literary Remains of Henry James,* published that year. Hodgson wrote: "What strikes me most forcibly and continually, as I read, is the reflection which constantly occurs to me: What a pity that all this deep and true insight into the moral and spiritual nature and wants and aspirations and faiths of man—man collectively—should be unaccompanied with a correspondingly complete framework of ideas and thoughts about the universe of things logically worked out and organized." [1]

In replying to Hodgson, William James wrote of his father: "He was the humanest and most genial being in his impulses whom I have ever personally known, and had a bigness and power of nature that everybody felt. I thank you heartily for your interest. I wish that somebody could *take up* something from his system into a system more articulately scientific. As it is, most people will feel the *presence* of something real and true for the while they read, and go away and presently, unable to dovetail it into their own framework, forget it altogether . . ." [2]

Although these comments are concerned with the elder Jame's ideas on religion and philosophy, they are clearly applicable to his ideas on education, the education he vainly sought for his children. As has been pointed out in a previous chapter, his one *fixed* point around which revolved and fluctuated all his efforts toward providing them with an ideal training was a metaphysical one. He believed that they, that all people, are "absolute creatures of God, vivified every moment by Him, cared for every moment by Him, guided every moment by Him . . ." His profound insight into the moral and spiritual nature and needs of his children was at all times the impelling force which drove him persistently from one place to another, seeking the institution, teacher, or situation wherein could be established this central plank of his *ideas*. One might say after Hodgson: What a pity that his deep and true insight, his "smiting *Ursprunglichkeit* of intuition" as William James called it, should not be accompanied with a complete framework of ideas about education, logically worked out and organized. Of such a framework or system Henry James, Sr., was devoid. As a result, much of the drifting from one teacher to another, from school to school, from country to country seems unorganized, even at times illogical. Paradoxically, for the two oldest boys, the whole experience was unpredictably fruitful.

Very often changes were brought about through impulses stirred by the suggestion of a friend, as in the case of Garth Wilkinson's urgings to come to London from Geneva in 1855. Such impulses were characterized by an indefatigable faith in goodness and an irrepressible buoyance of spirit. Regardless of disappointing results from any given arrangement, the next was sure to be better. There was nothing naive in such optimism. The elder James suffered from few illusions about mankind's weaknesses and foibles; but far outweighing such things was his magnificent spiritual faith in and understanding of man.

Into this atmosphere of geniality and hopefulness came a long line of French governesses: Augustine Danse, Amélia Fortin, Marie Guyard, Marie Bonningue, Félice Bonningue, Clarisse Bader—all of whom succeeded Mademoiselle Cusin in rapid succession. Henry, Jr., wrote that he was as mystified by the variety and frequency of their arrivals and departures as he had been in much the same degree by the "academic vicissitudes" he and his brothers had experienced in New York. "I can no more imagine why, sociable and charitable, we so often changed governesses than I had contemporaneously grasped the principle of our succession of schools: the whole group of phenomena reflected, I gather, as a rule, much more the extreme promptitude of the parental optimism than any disproportionate habit of impatience. The optimism begot precipitation, and the precipitation had too often to confess itself. What is instructive, what is historic, is the probability that young persons offering themselves at that time as guides and communicators—the requirements of our small sister were for long modest enough—quite conceivably lacked preparedness, and were so thrown back on the extempore, which in turn lacked abundance." [3]

One feels, upon studying the elder James's theory of education, that in all probability it was not so much that these young persons lacked preparedness as that they lacked the intuitive sense prerequisite to catching a glimpse of what the father was seeking for his children. One also feels, upon reading the novelist's reminiscences and letters, that he never completely "grasped the principle" of his father's inspired thought. William, more akin intellectually to their father, saw more fully the vision which led the family on so endless a journey for so many years.

Garth Wilkinson's encouraging letter of early October, 1855, brought the James family to London before the end of that month.

Much to young Henry's delight, they first stopped at the Old Gloucester House Coffeehouse on the corner of Piccadilly and Berkeley Street, the inn at which Pendennis stayed upon coming to London to study law. From the cold wind of the night, the party hurried into the warmth and glow of a roaring fire at the far end of the beamed-ceiling main room. After they had had a supper of cold roast beef, bread and cheese, and ale, the elder James turned expansively to the family group and exclaimed, "There's nothing like it after all." [4] To young Henry, the comment confirmed much of his pre-conditioned feeling about England, and he never forgot it.

Within a few days, a suitable house was found at #3 Berkeley Square, Thackeray's "Shiverley Square," in *Vanity Fair,* as the children already knew. They soon learned, too, that the plane trees under which they played were planted in 1789, trees which had looked down on many of England's literary figures; but the Square's history stretched back immeasurably, over Horace Walpole and Colley Cibber, Lord Clive and Beau Brummell, Lord Byron, Lady Mary Wortley Montagu, Dr. Johnson and Lord Bute, George Crabb, Lord Shelburne[5]—the line was endless in the mind of the future novelist to whom the Square took on increasing significance during the next half century. The intense charm of the neighborhood impressed him so deeply that in 1913 he could compare its appearance and see it as wearing "no very different face; the house that has risen on the site of ours is still immediately neighboured at the left by the bookseller, the circulating-librarian and news-agent, who modestly flourished in our time under the same name; the great establishment of Mr. Gunter, just further along, is as soberly and solidly seated; the mews behind the whole row, from the foot of Hay Hill at the right, wander away to Bruton Street with the irregular grace that spoke to my young fancy; Hay Hill itself is somehow less sharply precipitous, besides being no longer paved, as I seem to recall its having been, with big boulders, and I was on the point of saying that its antique charm in some degree abides. Nothing, however, could be further from the truth; its antique charm quite succumbed, years ago, to that erection of lumpish 'mansions' which followed the demolition of the old-world town-residence, as the house-agents say, standing on the south side, where Dover Street gives way to Grafton; a house of many histories, of vague importances and cold reserves and deep suggestions, I used to think after scaling the steep quite on purpose to wonder about it. A whole chapter of life was condensed, for our young sensibility, I make out, into a couple of months . . . spent by us in these quarters . . .'' [6]

History and literature blended together in these streets, creating an atmosphere which Harry's imagination found highly conducive to the best sort of gaping and wondering, as he strolled peacefully through them. John Campbell, second Duke of Argyll, had lived at #15 Bruton Street and it was here that Jeanie Deans, in Scott's *Heart of Midlothian,* came to see him and to plead for his sister Effie. Horace Walpole lived in this street in 1749, before he had inherited his title, and William Pitt lived there ten years later. Sheridan too, thirty years later, with his family in extreme need had been a virtual prisoner in Bruton Street, getting food and provisions through the area railings. Dover Street occupied the site of the wonderful Clarendon House, built in 1667 by Lord Clarendon and mentioned by both Pepys and Evelyn, the latter of whom had laid out the gardens which, after 1683, were turned into Albemarle, Old Bond, Stafford, and Grafton Streets, when the mansion was demolished. In Queen Anne days, John Evelyn in retirement lived in the house, nine doors in from Piccadilly on the east side, while across the street, a few doors down, Dr. Arbuthnot, "Martinus Scriblerus," had found retreat from St. James's Palace on the death of Queen Anne. As exciting to think of was Sir Joshua Reynolds, living in Dover Street and playing host often to Doctor Johnson and Bossy. Grafton Street, nearly as famous, farther away from Berkeley Square, met New Bond on the site of the Duke of Grafton's house and here Johnson's Boswell appeared with a letter from General Paoli, and was presented to Lord Chatham. Unconscious as the boy may have been of these personages and their roles in the life of a London long since passed, he was responsive to the depth of atmosphere to which their lives had contributed richly. In one of the last things that the future novelist wrote at the very end of his long career, he declared that though he had not been "to the manner born," he developed a realization of what it was on the part of others to be so. That realization was beginning in these earliest acquaintances with Berkeley Square and the Mayfair region and the realization ultimately became to him "the dearest and most precious of all native images." [7]

It has been suggested that for any real contact with London, this residence of the fall and winter of 1855-1856 was "a blank interlude" to Henry James, Jr.[8] To any ordinary child of twelve such might have been the case; but the evidence from the reminiscences of the James children and from family correspondence of that year indicates that the experience was far from blank. As Rebecca West expressed it, he "had been born with a mind that received impressions as if they had been embraces and remembered them with as fierce a leaping of the heart." [9] Thus, it mattered little to the preoccupied child that his parents were once again striving to find the right tutor or the best school, for he was daily embracing a legion of rich English impressions, almost effortlessly and quite without instruction. The elder James, in a letter to Grandmother James in Albany, indicated that the idea of a school was being given serious consideration:

> 3 BERKELEY SQUARE
> NOVEMBER 2, 1855
>
> MY DEAR MOTHER,
>
> . . . We are pleasantly settled in Berkeley Square for a month, *en attendant* more permanent lodgings in some less costly quarter of the town, and nearer to a good school for boys. I find that the English schools have the reputation of being better than the Swiss schools, as to all the solid parts of education, and I hope that the boys will be brought along rapidly. They are as good as they can be for the most part, and give us very little trouble while on our hands. In fact they undergo a regular schooling every day from their French governess, a Mademoiselle Cusin, whom we brought along with us from Geneva, and who is a very good teacher. I shall send them either to the London University Grammar School, or to a school of the Rev. Mr. Markly in St. John's Wood Park. both of which are considered first-rate institutions and which I find it hard to decide between. I shall probably decide on the latter . . . " [10]

Actually, neither school was decided upon and the problem, for the moment, was solved by engaging a first-rate tutor. Apparently, upon further investigation the Jameses found that the London private schools near home did not satisfy their requirements to a sufficient degree. As to the celebrated English schools away from home, there were two barriers involved: the entrance credit and preparation of the James boys whose schooling had been so extraordinarily varied and irregular; and, far more serious, the great English schools' curriculum designed for the English life and English career. It did not, therefore, offer young Americans a training in terms of either their backgrounds or future. In his autobiographical recollections, Henry, Jr., observed of his parents' reactions to this situation: "They had doubtless heard claimed . . . that no other method for boys *was* so splendidly general, but they had, I judge, their own sense of the matter—which would have been that it all depended on what was meant by this. The truth was, above all, that to them the formative forces most closely bearing on us were not in the least vague, but very definite by *their* measure and intention; there were 'advantages,' generally much belauded, that appealed to them scantily, and other matters, conceptions of character and opportunity, ideals, values, importances, enjoying no great common credit but for which it was their belief that they, under whatever difficulties, more or less provided." [11] It was just these "other matters," concerning character, ideals, values, intangible importances which were of paramount concern to the parents, and no school existed which could offer the children such training. Yet, the family life, the elder James knew, did not fully meet the needs of his children's training, even with the service of a tutor and governess; but for this London period such an arrangement seemed best.

Mlle. Cusin was retained and Mr. Robert Thompson, a Scotchman, was engaged. He was one of the many applicants calling at #3 Berkeley Square for an interview with the elder James. Harry was intrigued by them as "they hung about the door, cumbered the hall, choked the staircase and sat grimly individual in odd corners," having all read of the Jameses' need. An advertisement had been placed in The London *Times* to the effect that "an American gentleman . . . desired to arrange with a competent young man for the tuition of his three sons." Robertson and Alice, the two youngest children, were apparently to be provided for completely through the efforts of their governess, while Willy, Harry, and Wilky were submitted each morning to Mr. Thompson, from breakfast to lunch. This same competent young man later served as tutor to Robert Louis Stevenson, with whom Henry James, Jr., enjoyed comparing notes when the two celebrated authors discovered the coincidence. A memorable man was Robert Thompson, in his own quiet way, "so deeply solicitous, yet withal so mild and kind and shy, with no harsher injunction to us ever than 'Come now, be getting on!' that one could but think well of a world in which so gentle a spirit might flourish; while it is doubtless to the credit of his temper that remembrance is a blank in respect to his closer ministrations. I recall vividly his fresh complexion, his very round clear eyes, his tendency to trip over his own legs or feet while thoughtfully circling about us, and his constant dress-coat, worn with trousers of a lighter hue, which was perhaps the prescribed uniform of a daily tutor; but I ask myself in vain what I can have 'studied' with him, there remaining with me afterwards, to testify— this putting any scrap of stored language aside—no single textbook save the *Lambs' Tales of Shakespeare,* which was given me as (of all things in the world) a reward. A reward for what I am again at a loss to say—not certainly for having 'got on' to anything like the tune plaintively, for the most part, piped to me." [12]

The choice of the solicitous, mild, kind Mr. Thompson from among what was apparently a wide selection of applicants indicates further the elder James's disregard for the prescribed system of formal instruction during semesters or terms, of systematic drill or emphasis upon mere rote. His desire was that the boys be cultivated in broader terms, in the humanistic sense of versatile man, the *whole man,* in whom the range of human knowledge would be free from the limitations of specialization. This scheme of things was highly suitable to the peculiar temperament of Henry, Jr., who at once responded happily to the London arrangements; to William, the future philosopher and psychologist, the situation left much to be desired, for he was already aware of his instinctive dislike of so vague and general an approach. In later years Henry, Jr., wrote: "It was a very odd and yet to myself very rich and full reminiscence, though I remember how,

looking back at it from after days, W. J. denounced it to me, and
with it the following year and more spent in Paris, as a poor and arid
and lamentable time, in which, missing such larger chances and
connections as we might have reached out to, we had done nothing,
he and I, but walk together, in a state of the direst propriety, the
'little' black hats and inveterate gloves, the childish costume of the
place and period, to stare at grey street-scenery (that of early Victorian London had tones of a neutrality!) dawdle at shop-windows
and buy water-colours and brushes with which to bedaub eternal
drawing-blocks. We might, I dare say, have felt higher impulses
and carried out larger plans—though indeed present to me for this,
on my brother's so expressing himself, is my then quick recognition
of the deeper stirrings and braver needs he at least must have known,
and my perfect if rueful sense of having myself had no such quarrel
with our conditions: embalmed for me did they even to that shorter
retrospect appear in a sort of fatalism of patience, spiritless in a
manner, no doubt, yet with an inwardly active, productive and ingenious side." [13]

How inwardly active, productive, and ingenious these London days
of study and daubing, of walking and dawdling actually were to
young Harry, his father could not fully know, but he was much
pleased with his sons' competent young tutor as well as with Mlle.
Cusin. Especially happy was he about the prospects of accommodations for them all in St. John's Wood, not far from the Wilkinsons.
With the soaring of good spirits, so quickly called into action by
such pleasant arrangements, Henry James, Sr., wrote to his family
in Albany:

3 BERKELEY SQUARE, LONDON
NOVEMBER 30 (1855)

MY DEAR MOTHER,

I intended writing a long letter by this steamer, but we are all on the
jump today, preparing to move bright and early tomorrow morning to
St. John's Wood, and I have certain things to attend to which have completely occupied me until this late moment. . . . You are all quite wide
off of the mark in fancying that we are looking towards home. We are
delightfully situated here and shall be tomorrow even more so in all
probability. Our circle of acquaintances is extending among very nice

people, too, literary some of them and others well worth knowing. The boys have a capital tutor, and were never so sweet and good, all of them. The Francaise keeps them all up to their work in French, and I have no doubt we shall return home a well educated and polished family. Mamma is in capital health and spirits, and has on the whole a very jolly time of it. Aunt Kate is as dear and good as ever and does such justice to the good things of England that I have no doubt she will be a very near approach to Jannet Gomlay in breadth, by the time she gets back. Dr. Wilkinson and Mrs. are as full of kindness and hospitality as they can be. And on the whole I think we are very well off. It is greatly pleasanter in the domestic respects here than in Paris. We have a home-feeling in London, that is very agreeable and you do not feel yourself so constantly cheated as you are apt to in Paris. We have taken a delightful (furnished) house in Marlborough Place, St. John's Wood, larger than our house in New York, very considerably, for which we pay at the rate of £250 a year. Please direct our letters directly there hereafter. . . . Mary and Kate and all the little ones join me in the warmest love to you, Dear Ma, and I remain ever faithfully

Yours affectionately,

HJ.[14]

The joy, the sense of well being and domestic happiness which Henry James reflects in his letters suggest only a small degree of the depth and extent of the all-embracing love with which he and his wife gathered their children, their friends, their acquaintances to their hearts. Not fully appreciated at the time by any of the children, the loving consecration and devotion constantly emanating from the parents was beautifully recalled by their oldest son, William, twenty-five years later in a letter to his parents and sister, written from Amsterdam, July 13, 1880, telling of his visit in London with his brother Henry: " . . . in the vicinity of Clarges Street, ½ Moon Str., and Green Park, Piccadilly, I found myself thinking in a manner unexampled in my previous life, of Father and Mother in their youth coming to live there as a blushing bridal pair, with most of us children still unborn, and all the works unwritten; and my heart flowed over with a new kind of sympathy, especially for the beautiful, sylph-like and inexperienced mother. Then when I went into St. John's Wood and its monotony, and contrasted the life you led there with that which Harry is now leading in Bolton St., it made me feel how few things you laid claim to, and how entirely at that time your lives were given up to us. There is a strange inability on the part of children to project themselves out of their egoistic stand-point, so far as their parents are concerned. Perhaps my own parental condition makes me now more able to do so than before—at any rate, I have been almost shedding tears every day in London to think of you, my beloved old Mother and Father, standing in your youth before the great roaring foreign tide, often perplexed in the extreme, and wondering how you might best provide for us . . . St. John's Wood seemed terribly dreary to me, and I made no attempt to look up the Wilkinsons—having too much social activity anyhow and feeling no inward relation towards them . . ." [15]

Nine years after William James's visit to St. John's Wood, Alice James, in her journal for July 9, 1889 caught a fleeting glimpse of the same setting in the winter of 1855-1856, which she recorded: "There is a bit of brown wall that always brings up St. John's Wood so vividly, as I pass,—that winter of 1854-1855 (sic), all draped in December densities, with only three episodes standing out, as I remember: Mademoiselle C.'s bonnet, *Henry VIII*, and *Still Waters Run Deep*. Shall I ever forget Wolsey going to execution, or "My Sister is a Most Remarkable Woman"? The joy of *Henry VIII* was somewhat obscured by Aunt Kate's not being able to go. No greater misery ever befell a creature of woman born than that, thought I. I'm sure we went also to the pantomimes at Christmas, but I've completely forgotten it. Mademoiselle Cusin's bonnet is equally vivid, but a more mixed delight. In the grey dusk of our afternoon walks we discovered an artist, but the pangs of parturition were most severe, for the millinery point of view of Neufchatel and that of the Edgeware Road had not only to be revealed, but reconciled one to the other, by me, aged seven. It came forth green shirred silk and pink roses,—I can remember how my infant soul shivered, even then, at the sad crudity of its tone; it doubtless soon gathered depth as the atmosphere of the season enveloped it more and more." [16]

Quite understandably, these brief recollections of William and of Alice James are far outdistanced by the fuller reminiscences of their novelist brother to whom these winter months in London took on far greater value. The difference between the two oldest boys' reactions brings into sharper relief the marked difference of their temperaments and minds, and in further comment on their disagreement Henry, Jr., gives full consideration to his older brother's feelings: "It was just the fact of our having so walked and dawdled and dodged that made the charm of memory; in addition to which what could one have asked more than to be steeped in a medium so dense that whole elements of it, forms of amusement, interest and wonder, soaked through to some appreciative faculty and made one fail at the most of nothing but one's lessons? My brother was right in so far as that my question—the one I have just reproduced—could have been asked only by a person incorrigible in throwing himself back upon substitutes for lost causes, substitutes that might *temporarily* have appeared queer and small; a person so haunted, even from an early age, with visions of life, that aridities, for him, were half a terror and half an impossibility, and that the said substitutes, the economies and ingenuities that protested, in their dumb vague way, against weakness of situation or of direct and applied faculty, were in themselves really a revel of spirit and thought." [17]

In Geneva, when Harry had not been well enough to join Willy at the Swiss school, the growing divergence of their interests and attitudes had not been so evident to either of the boys. Now in London, thrown together in their study with their tutor and on their daily rambles, they were growing much more conscious of their individualities. Each boy had, fortunately, caught a sufficient degree of the father's extraordinary and abundant love and bigness of nature to maintain the deep mutual affection which they had enjoyed from earliest childhood. One critic says of Henry, Jr.: "He lacked initiative, and the capacity for bold and decisive action; but since his inclination here ran with his capacity, he suffered no self-disparagement. He was not envious of what he did not possess, having unassuming but sturdy confidence in what he did possess." [18] Thrown back upon "substitutes," Harry was seldom envious of Willy's tendency to participate actively; and he understood William's impatience with the comparative inactivity of this London experience. He himself was quite satisfied, however, for his preoccupation with observing and responding to all he saw and felt supplied, as he said, "a revel of spirit and thought" that only he fully appreciated. Never, in later years, was the great city to hold just the fascination or have exactly the quaintness that it had for him at this time: "I seem to see to-day that the London of the 'fifties was even to the weak perception of childhood a much less generalised, a much more eccentrically and variously characterized place, than the present great accommodated and accommodating city; it had fewer resources but it had many more features, scarce one of which failed to help the whole to bristle with what a little gaping American could take for an intensity of difference from *his* supposed order. It was extraordinarily the picture and the scene of Dickens, now so changed and superseded; it offered to my presumptuous vision still more the reflection of Thackeray—and where is the *detail* of the reflection of Thackeray now?—so that as I trod the vast length of Baker Street, the Thackerayan vista of other days, I throbbed with the pride of a vastly enlarged acquaintance.

"I dare say our perambulations of Baker Street in our little 'top' hats and other neatnesses must have been what W. J. meant by our poverty of life—whereas it was probably one of the very things most expressive to myself of the charm and the colour of history and (from the point of view of the picturesque) of society. We were often in Baker Street by reason of those stretched-out walks, at the remembered frequency and long-drawn push of which I am to-day amazed; recalling at the same time, however, that save for Robert Thompson's pitching ball with us in the garden they took for us the place of all other agilities. I can't but feel them to have been marked in their way by a rare curiosity and energy." [19]

The move from Berkeley Square to Marlborough Place, St. John's Wood, was made partly under consideration of expense but mainly in order to be nearer the Garth Wilkinson family who resided at #24 Finchley Road, St. John's Wood, a short distance from the Jameses. The general character of this section, furthermore, was more to the taste of Henry James, Sr., than was Mayfair and Berkeley Square in that it was a favorite resort of artists, literary men, musicians, and people interested in many phases of the liberal arts. Most celebrated of its residents was Sir Edward Landseer, who lived there from 1824 until his death in 1873. Among the well known works he did in his studio in St. John's Wood Road were, "High Life and Low Life," "Chevy Chase," "Flood in the Highlands," and the design for the lions in Trafalgar Square, the latter being made there in 1860. The Bohemian atmosphere bordered, in the minds of less imaginative people of nearby Marylebone, on the line of the socially questionable. The more modern villas with their cloistered privacy secured behind tall, substantial garden walls, suggested too much "free thought" to be considered "respectable." In 1863, George Eliot lived at North Bank, outraging Victorian London by her association with George Henry Lewes, arousing a storm of what the elder James called "flagrant morality."

Undisturbed by the growing doubts of St. John's Wood's respectability, the James family enjoyed an unusually happy winter and spring in Marlborough Place. Regent's Park, a short walking distance away, afforded the children endless strolls and outings, with the Zoological Gardens holding particular attraction for the younger ones. Just a few years earlier the Park had offered Elizabeth Barrett the quiet seclusion she sought from her father's displeasure over Robert Browning. Here, too, in 1846, she made her decision to marry the poet and flee to Italy. In 1856, at the age of thirteen, young Harry James wandered hazily about the very haunts of these literary figures with whom, in later years, he was to have such significant connections.

What Henry James, Jr., remembered most of the residence in St. John's Wood was the "considerable garden and wistful view, though by that windowed privilege alone, of a large green expanse in which ladies and gentlemen practised archery. Just *that*—and not the art even, but the mere spectacle might have been one of the substitutes in question; if not for the languages at least for one or another of the romantic connections we seemed a little to have missed: it was such a whiff of the old world of Robin Hood as we could never have looked up from the mere thumbed 'story,' in Fourteenth Street at any rate, to any soft confidence of. More than I can begin to say, that is by a greater number of queer small channels, did the world about us, thus continuous with the old world of Robin Hood, steal into my sense—a constant state of subjection to which fact is no bad

instance of those refinements of surrender that I just named as my
fond practice." [20]

The brief glimpse into the world of Robin Hood ballads gave
way to the immediacy of London's attractions, widely observed by
the boys, usually in company with their tutor, who went along with
the family, in the move from Berkeley Square to St. John's Wood.
It is a tribute to Robert Thompson that he so impressed the children
as to stand out in their memories from the host of others who came
and went so frequently. He did not live with the Jameses on Marlborough Place but occupied lodgings not far off, over a baker's
shop. Although it was more usual for him to come to the boys,
sometimes they had the pleasure of going to his quarters where a
mid-morning "break" was made the more enjoyable by "the appearance of a self-conscious stale cake, straight from below, received by
us each time as if it had been a sudden happy thought, and ushered
in by a little girl who might have been a Dickens foundling or
'orfling.' " [21]

Much more impressive than the stale cake intermissions were the
trips about the city, which they took under the direction of Mr.
Thompson "to the Tower, the Thames Tunnel, St. Paul's and the
Abbey, to say nothing of the Zoological Gardens, almost close at
hand and with which we took in that age of lingering forms no
liberty of abbreviation; to say nothing either of Madame Tussaud's,
then in our interminable but so amiable Baker Street, the only shade
on the amiability of which was just that gruesome association with
the portal of the Bazaar—since Madame Tussaud had, of all her
treasures, most vividly revealed to me the Mrs. Manning and the
Burke and Hare of the Chamber of Horrors which lurked just within
it; whom, for days after making their acquaintance (and prolonging
it no further than our conscientious friend thought advisable) I half
expected, when alone, to meet quite dreadfully on the stair-case or
on opening a door." [22]

The boys found, however, that the London streets, in certain areas
of the city far removed from Berkeley Square or St. John's Wood,
offered sights as exciting as any tableau exhibited at Madame Tussaud's. To Harry, always alert with the eye of the young artist, it

appeared that: "The London people had for themselves, at the same time, an exuberance of type; we found it in particular a world of costume, often very odd costume—the most intimate notes of which were the postmen in their frock-coats of military red and their black beaver hats; the milkwomen, in hats that often emulated these, in little shawls and strange short, full frocks, revealing enormous boots, with their pails swung from their shoulders on wooden yokes; the inveterate footmen hooked behind the coaches of the rich, frequently in pairs and carrying staves, together with the mounted and belted grooms without the attendance of whom riders, of whichever sex— and riders then were much more numerous—almost never went forth. The range of character, on the other hand, reached rather dreadfully down; there were embodied and exemplified 'horrors' in the streets beside which any present exhibition is pale, and I well remember the almost terrified sense of their salience produced in me a couple of years later, on the occasion of a flying return from the Continent with my father, by a long, and interminable drive west- ward from the London Bridge railway-station. It was a soft June evening, with a lingering light and swarming crowds, as they then seemed to me, of figures reminding me of George Cruikshank's Artful Dodger and his Bill Sikes and his Nancy, only with the bigger brutality of life, which pressed upon the cab, the early-Victorian four- wheeler, as we jogged over the Bridge, and cropped up in more and more gas-lit patches for all our course, culminating, somewhere far to the west, in the vivid picture, framed by the cab-window, of a woman reeling backward as a man felled her to the ground with a blow in the face. The London view at large had in fact more than a Cruikshank, there still survived in it quite a Hogarth, side— which I had of course then no name for, but which I was so sharply to recognize on coming back years later that it fixed for me the veracity of the great pictorial chronicler. Hogarth's mark is even yet not wholly overlaid; though time has *per contra* dealt with that stale servility of address which most expressed to our young minds the rich burden of a Past, the consequence of too much history." [23]

In New York, he had studied minutely the drawings of Leech in every copy of *Punch*. So acute had been these earliest devotions that in 1855 places and people in London had "an extravagant look of familiarity." Riding past in a carriage, or strolling along with his brothers and Robert Thompson, Harry took in vivid impressions which might themselves have been pages out of *Punch:* " . . . The expansive back of an old lady getting into an omnibus, the attitude of a little girl bending from her pony in the park, the demureness of a maid-servant opening a street-door in Brompton, the top-heavy attitude of the small 'Amerliar-Ann' as she stands planted with the baby in her arms on the corner of a Westminster slums, the coal-heavers, the cabmen, the publicans, the butcher-boys, the flunkeys, the guardsmen, the policemen . . . " [24] It has been suggested that the images he had fixed in his mind as a small boy in New York prevailed over the actualities that he met in the London streets, so that the real was more than real, or took on a kind of double vision peculiar to his own eye and mind.[25] Undoubtedly his view of the scene was far keener and more significant than those of the other James children, but it was a view in perfect focus, crystallizing even the smallest details, so that these people and places manifested themselves later in such fiction as *The Princess Casamassima,* as they could not otherwise have done.

With the family well established, Henry James, Sr., was free to carry on stimulating relations with Carlyle and Thackeray, with the Swedenborgian group centered about Wilkinson, and with Sir Arthur Helps, to whom he was presented by a letter from Emerson,[26] with Arthur Hugh Clough, and others of the world of literature and philosophy. On Christmas Day, 1855, James wrote another letter to the New York *Daily Tribune,* which reflects much of his current domestic happiness, his religious feelings on the European observance of Christmas, and his growing realization of his native land as "Happy America! where the people are superior to all mere classes of people, and where, consequently, Church and State are sure, in the long run to obey and reflect every expansion of the popular instinct." [27] It is important to note, at this point, the marked tendency of the elder James to see the United States in a brighter light in proportion to his discovery of some salient facts about English and European life. In contrast, his son Henry was at this time assimilat

ing and cultivating the seeds of his subsequent expatriation in which
his view of America took a diametrically opposite direction from that
of his father. After 1860, Henry James, Sr., was never to return to
Europe, whereas Henry, Jr., at the close of the 'Sixties was to approach
the decision which took him away from America for most of the
remaining years of his life. In both cases the reasons are significant;
for the son they multiplied from 1855 to 1875 into a complicated
web of intricate causes and effects; for the father they simplified
themselves from 1855 to the end of his life.

The residence in London during 1855-1856 brought home to the
elder James what to him was a basic deficiency in the English nature;
he commented upon this in "The Social Significance of Our Institutions," an address, "delivered by request of the citizens at Newport, R. I." on July 4, 1861. The impassioned, even at times caustic,
tone of the oration is explained partly by the circumstances surrounding its delivery, flowing with a patriotic fervor heightened by the
first year of the Civil War. Yet, this particular passage is based upon
a deeper aspect of his nature and would have been forthcoming even
under less patriotic conditions: " . . . I lived, recently, nearly a year
in St. John's Wood in London, and was daily in the habit of riding
down to the city in the omnibus along with my immediate neighbors, men of business and professional men, who resided in that
healthy suburb, and fared forth from it every morning to lay up
honest, toilsome bread for the buxom domestic angels who sanctified
their homes, and the fair-haired cherubs who sweetened them. Very
nice men, to use their own lingo, they were, for the most part; tidy,
unpretending, irreproachable in dress and deportment; men in whose
truth and honesty you would confide at a glance; and yet, after eight
months' assiduous bosom solicitation of their hardened stolid visages,
I never was favored with the slightest overture to human intercourse
from one of them. If ever I came nigh doing so, an instant film
would surge up from their more vital parts, if such parts there were,
just as a Newport fog suddenly surges up from the cold remorseless
sea, and wrap the organ in the dullest fishiest, most disheartening of
stares. They took such extreme pains never to look at one another,
that I knew they must be living men, devoutly intent each on dis-

owning the other's life; otherwise I could well have believed them
so many sad well-seasoned immortals, revisiting their old London
haunts by way of a nudge to their present less carnal satisfaction.
I had myself many cherished observations to make upon the weather,
upon the lingering green of the autumn fields, upon the pretty suburban cottages we caught a passing glimpse of, upon the endless
growth of London, and other equally conservative topics; but I got no
chance to ventilate them, and the poor things died at last of hope
deferred. The honest truth is what Dr. Johnson told Boswell, that
the nation is deficient in human sentiment. 'Dr. Johnson,' says Boswell, 'though himself a *stern, trueborn* Englishman, and fully preju-
diced against all other nations, had yet discernment enough to see,
and candor enough to censure, the cold reserve among Englishmen
toward strangers (of their own nation). "Sir," he said, "two men of
any other nation who are shown into a room together, at a house
where they are both visitors, will immediately find some conversation. But two Englishmen will probably go each to a different window
and remain in obstinate silence. Sir, we do not, as yet," proceeded the
Doctor, "understand the common rights of humanity." ' " [28]

As the winter of 1855-1856 passed, the elder James found the
"home-feeling in London" offset by the coldness of the British temperament, an aspect of character which was particularly offensive to
him in that the English thereby seemed shockingly indifferent to
what Doctor Johnson called "the common rights of humanity."
Furthermore, he was disappointed in his friend Wilkinson, about
whom he complained loudly to Emerson.[29] Another disturbing element in the London setting was the growing possibility of war
between the States, his concern over which is expressed to Grandmother James in a letter from St. John's Wood on February 4, 1856.
He mentioned the happy visit they had just enjoyed with Howard
James, his brother en route from Paris to Albany, and then wrote:
" . . . We are all well, but a little concerned at the symptoms of a
war spirit which break forth on your side of the waters. We should
dislike to be compelled just now to return home, when every thing
is going on so well with the boys. However, perhaps the outbreak
of a war, even if it should take place, would not necessarily force

our return . . ." [30] In spite of these disturbances of thought, the Jameses preferred to remain in London for the time being, and the boys continued to enjoy the diversions of the great city, especially the theatre to which their New York years had given them a generous introduction.

The very procedure of going to the theatre in London held a certain fascination in that it presented a serious business. In the first place the parents, five children, and Aunt Kate, with Mademoiselle Cusin and Mr. Thompson sometimes included, composed too large a party for one vehicle; thus a procession was formed of two "throbbing and heaving cabs over vast foggy tracts of the town . . . through twisting passages and catacombs," of city streets, and corridors of the theatre after crossing the magic threshold. The performance, on one occasion, must have been chosen out of consideration for the tastes of the younger members of the party in that it was not a play at all, but the popular lecture on the Panorama of the Ascent of Mont Blanc, by Albert Smith in the Egyptian Hall, almost opposite the Burlington Arcade, Piccadilly. Opening in 1852, the lecture, a kind of show in itself, was one of the most popular attractions of London entertainment during the next six years. The painting was by Beverley, a well-known panoramic artist, but it was Albert Smith's story with its mixture of humor and florid description which drew the crowds, among which were the Jameses in a party of nine, seated in a rustic balcony, constructed to give the effect of a Swiss châlet framed with creepers. Harry, overwhelmed by a sense of sudden publicity which the situation enforced upon him, felt that he was inadvertently a part of the boisterous show, perched as the group was on this improvised Swiss balcony. In view of the nature of the lecture, Harry's feelings are not surprising, for Smith, a large man, popped on to the platform out of a side door and leaned on the piano, pointer in hand, while he rattled off stories about his mountaineering experiences in the Alps. Down through the years, Harry was to remember him: "Big, bearded, rattling, chattering, mimicking Albert Smith again charms my senses . . . with the levity of his performance—a performance one of the great effects of which was, as I remember it, the very brief stop and re-departure of the train at Epernay, with the ringing of bells, the bawling of guards, the cries of travellers, the slamming of doors and the tremendous pop as of a colossal champagne-cork, make all simultaneous and vivid by Mr. Smith's mere personal resources and grace." [31]

The same "liberal law and happy view" of the theatre which Mr. and Mrs. James had held in New York prevailed in London. Here, however, the boys were not free to attend performances alone, as they had wandered up and down Broadway on "non-dental Saturday afternoons," attending Barnum's or Niblo's or Franconi's Hippodrome. London, with its vastness, was quite unlike the intimate, provincial, New York of the 'Forties and 'Fifties, so that even Willy and Harry attended performances only in company with their tutor, or, often with the entire family. The few London performances they did attend, however, represented the same broad interest which the parents had shared with the children during the New York years: the boisterous sort of humor offered by Albert Smith in the Egyptian Hall and the burlesque acting of Robson; the exciting melodramatic treatment of French adaptations such as Tom Taylor's *Still Waters Run Deep;* and the superb tragic acting of Charles Kean in Boucicault's *The Corsican Brothers,* or, above all, in *Henry VIII.* The James children had had, with the exception of Alice, rather unusual acquaintance with both tragedy and comedy, offered by some of the foremost players of the New York stage.

Charles Kean, famous son of the celebrated Edmund Kean, had opened the Princess's Theatre in joint management with Robert Keeley, on September 28, 1850, with *Twelfth Night.* [32] This marked the beginning of a long series of Shakespearean revivals by which Kean achieved an unprecedented success for several seasons. *Henry VIII* was revived at the Princess's on May 6, 1855, furnishing him, in the role of Cardinal Wolsey, with a part well suited to his powers, in which he reached the climax of his success. Just as had been their experience in New York, the James children had the play read to them and discussed by the family group before attending Kean's performance, during the season of 1855-1856, and the results, in terms of their reactions, were summed up decades later by Henry, Jr.: "Our enjoyment of Charles Kean's presentation of *Henry the Eighth* figures to me as a momentous date in our lives: we did nothing for weeks afterwards but try to reproduce in water-colour Queen Katharine's dream vision of the beckoning, consoling angels, a radiant group let down from the skies by machinery then thought marvellous—when indeed we were not parading across our schoolroom stage as the portentous Cardinal and impressively alternating his last speech to Cromwell with Buckingham's, that is with Mr. Ryder's, address on the way to the scaffold. The spectacle had seemed to us prodigious—as it was doubtless at its time the last word of costly scenic science; though as I look back from the high ground of an age that has mastered tone and fusion I seem to see it as comparatively garish and violent, after the manner of the complacently approved stained-glass church-windows of the same period." [33]

The Princess' Theatre, on the north side of Oxford Street some three hundred yards east of Oxford Circus, held for the children a fascination quite aside from Charles Kean's spectacles on its stage. Opened in 1840, first as a house for promenade concerts, it was adapted two years later for use as a theatre, housing an opera group which presented Italian operas in English.[34] The usual varied career, paralleling several theatres the boys had known on Broadway, the Princess' had its days of General Tom Thumb and similar attractions, mostly of screaming farces. In 1844, James Wallack, who had run Wallack's Lyceum so familiar to the Jameses, between 1852-1855 in New York, made a huge hit at the Princess' with *Don Cear de Bazan.* For the next two years, Edwin Forrest and Charlotte Cushman brought the house into popularity, the latter being an instant success but Forrest receiving a chilly reception which sent him back to American audiences mortified and revengeful. The hostility between Forrest and his English rival Macready culminated in the disgraceful Astor Place Riots in New York in 1849, at the very beginnings of the James children's acquaintance with the theatre. As had been the case in New York, the theatre in London in the 'Fifties was more or less unfashionable, but society, and even royalty, stirred by thrilling reports of Kean's productions, brought popular support to the theatre, while the players were several times summoned to Windsor to give court performances. It is small wonder that the children, from Willy, fourteen, down to Alice, seven, were to remember Kean's *Henry VIII* as a momentous event in their lives.

The other theatre which was to offer them an unforgettable experience was the Olympic, erected on Wych Street, in 1804, by Philip Astley. Until 1813 it was used for equestrian performances, then leased to the comedian, Robert William Elliston. Mme. Vestris, who leased it in 1831 and remained there until 1839, put the Olympic in the front ranks of London drama, the audiences rising under her magic wand "from cockneydom to aristocracy." [35] In the 'Fifties, with the passing of Mme. Vestris and others, the Olympic was on the downward way, though it lasted until 1899 when it was swept away in the building of Aldwych and Kingsway. Alfred Wigan, who specialized in plays from the French, achieved fame as John Mildmay in Tom Taylor's *Still Waters Run Deep,* creating the original role on January 23, 1855, and impressed young Henry James during the following season so that he carried in his memory many details of the play, down through the years. Later on, Fanny Kemble mentioned to the then celebrated novelist, that she had directed Tom Taylor to Charles de Bernard's novel *Un Gendre,* for the subject of the play which passed, in the 'Fifties, for a highly modern "social study." The play itself, the theatre, even the process of going to the theatre made an indelible impression, carrying about it suggestions of that antiquity, that "too much history" which made London, for Henry James, Jr., endlessly attractive. "It is perhaps in particular through the memory of our dismal approach to the theatre, the squalid slum of Wych Street, then incredibly brutal and barbarous as an avenue to joy, an avenue even sometimes for the muffled coach of Royalty, that the episode affects me as antedating some of the conditions of the mid-Victorian age; the general credit of which, I should add, was highly re-established for us by the consummately quiet and natural art, as we expertly pronounced it, of Alfred's Wigan's John Mildmay and the breadth and sincerity of the representative of the rash mother-in-law whom he so imperturbably puts in her place. This was an exhibition supposed in its day to leave its spectators little to envy in the highest finish reached by the French theatre." [36] For Victorian London of that day, the play was unusually candid and

'French' in its tenor and subject matter, hardly the sort of thing, one might say, for the James children to see. In the history of drama, it is interesting for, as one writer states: "In this play the most important thing is not the plot or the technique; it is the frankness with which the affairs of sex are discussed. In *The King's Rival,* Charles, it is admitted, had mistresses; in *Still Waters Run Deep* is the equally important admission that illicit love was a fact of life . . . the scope of the domestic play is being extended to include subjects and characters which before were taboo." [37] With parental authority and escort, Harry and the other children, ranging from fourteen down, were permitted to see such plays treating of the "facts of life." It will be recalled that from the earliest stages of their educational training, the children had been given unusual freedom by their parents, based upon the elder James's idea that the "great worth of one's childhood to his future manhood consists in its being a store-house of innocent natural emotions and affections, based upon ignorance . . . " but that by the word "ignorance" Henry James, Sr., did not mean intellectual ignorance, but rather the ignorance exist-ing as a result of personal moral purity. He did not, therefore, hesi-tate to take the children to any play which was well written and admirably presented, regardless of the candidness with which its subject matter might be treated. Not unrelated to this tolerant point of view is the profound admiration for French drama which Henry James, Jr., was later to cultivate and which had such a definite influ-ence upon his own literary development.

   The Discreet Princess; or, The Three Glass Distaffs, by James Rob-inson Planché, produced at the Olympic on December 26, 1855, as a Christmas production, presented especially to the Jameses "the strange and vivid little genius of Robson, a master of fantastic inten-sity, unforgettable for us . . . I still see Robson slide across the stage, in one sidelong wriggle, as the small black sinister Prince Richcraft of the fairytale, everything he did at once very dreadful and very droll, thoroughly true and yet none the less *macabre,* the great point of it all its parody of Charles Kean in *The Corsican Brothers;*[38] . . . a vision filled out a couple of years further on by his Daddy Hardacre and coarsely extracted from Balzac's *Eugénie*

Grandet. This occasion must have given the real and finer measure of his highly original talent; so present to me, despite the interval, is the distinctiveness of his little concentrated rustic miser whose daughter helps herself from his money-box so that her cousin and lover shall save a desperate father, her paternal uncle, from bankruptcy; and the prodigious effect of Robson's appalled descent, from an upper floor, his literal headlong tumble and rattle of dismay down a steep staircase occupying the centre of the stage, on his discovery of the rifling of his chest. Long was I to have in my ears the repeated shriek of his alarm, followed by a panting babble of wonder and rage as his impetus hurled him, a prostrate scrap of despair (he was a tiny figure, yet 'so held the stage' that in his company you could see nobody else) half way across the room." [39]

On a kind of double-feature evening, typical of the New York and London theatre bills of the time, the Jameses saw Charles Mathews in two plays, Sheridan's *The Critic,* and a comedy "botched from the French, like everything else in those days," called *Married for Money.* Charles Mathews was then about in his mid-career, offering to the highly receptive Henry James the effect "of a naturalness so easy and immediate, so friendly and intimate, that one's relation with the character, the artist thereby somehow positively suffering while the character gained, or at least while the spectator did—this comes back to me quite even of my earlier experience and as an attesting on behalf of the actor a remarkable genius . . . what I perhaps most retain, by the light of the present, of the sense of that big and rather dusky night of Drury Lane is not so much the felt degree of anyone's talent as the fact that personality and artistry, *with* their intensity, could work their spell in such a material desert, in conditions intrinsically so charmless, so bleak and bare." [40]

In addition to the exciting and instructive experiences at the theatre, the James boys, Willy and Harry in particular, developed in interest in drawing and painting, during this London year of 1855-1856, which had begun in the New York days and was to carry on to a serious degree in Paris and Newport, for William especially. The two boys, in their early 'teens, would have most serious discussions as to whether they should buy their "artists' materials" from Messrs. Rowney or from Messrs. Windsor and Newton; but in any event they strolled toward Rathbone Place, not far from Piccadilly Circus, more frequented by them than any other corner of the city, "the short but charged vista of which lives for me again in the tempered light of those old winter afternoons." Almost as frequently did the boys visit the old Pantheon of Oxford Street, "a place of fine rococo traditions, a bazaar, an exhibition, an opportunity, at the end of long walks, for the consumption of buns and ginger-beer, and above all a monument to the genius of that wonderful painter B. R. Haydon." [41] The Pantheon, at 173 Oxford Street, was the third such structure on the site, the first, opened in 1772 being visited by Boswell and Johnson, Gibbon and the fashionables of the day, also being mentioned frequently in the literature of that time. Fanny Burney's Evelina goes to the Pantheon with Captain Mirvan and his family, and meets there Lord Orville. Turner, inspired by the ruins of the building after its destruction by fire in 1792, chose it as a subject for his early painting, "The Pantheon the Morning after the Fire." The building to which the James boys were attracted was built in 1813 as an amusement place and survived until 1867. To them, it was a wonderful place, as it suited their tendency to relax in tired contemplating after long walks about the city; also, "Haydon's huge canvasses covered the walls— I wonder what has become now of 'The Banishment of Aristides' attended to the city gate by his wife and babe, every attitude and figure in which, especially that of the foreshortened boy picking up stones to shy at the all-too-just, stares out at me still. We found in those works remarkable interest and beauty, the reason of which was partly, no doubt, that we hung, to fascination, at home, over the three volumes of the hapless artist's *Autobiography,* then a new book, which our father, indulgent to our preoccupation, had provided us with;[42] but I blush to risk the further surmise that the grand manner, the heroic and the classic, in Haydon, came home to us more warmly and humanly than in the masters commended as 'old,' who, at the National Gallery, seemed to meet us so little half-way, to hold out the hand of fellowship or suggest something that *we* could do, or at least want to. The beauty of Haydon was just that he was new, shiningly new, and if he hinted that we might perhaps in some happy future emulate his big bravery there was nothing so impossible about it. If we adored daubing we preferred it *fresh,* and the genius of the Pantheon was fresh, whereas, strange to say, Rubens and Titian were not." [43]

Even the charm of the Pantheon yielded, in the eyes of Harry and Willy, to the greater attraction they found in the English collection, the Vernon bequest, then displayed at Marlborough House "to which the great plumed and draped and dusty funeral car of the Duke of Wellington formed an attractive adjunct. The ground-floor chambers there, none of them at that time royally inhabited, come back to me as altogether bleak and bare and as owing their only dignity to Maclise, Mulready and Landseer, to David Wilkie and Charles Leslie. *They* were, by some deep-seated English mystery, the real unattainable, just as they were none the less the directly inspiring and endlessly delightful. I could never have enough of Maclise's *Play-scene in Hamlet,* which I supposed the finest composition in the world (though Ophelia did look a little as if cut in silhouette out of white paper and pasted on); while as I gazed and gazed again, at Leslie's *Sancho Panza and his Duchess* (sic) I pushed through the great hall of romance to the central or private apartments." [44] The rather uncultivated taste of the two oldest James boys was to pass through some major changes within the next four or five years, eventually leading them, William in particular, to the studio of William Morris Hunt at Newport. The Pre-Raphaelite group they met within the next two years upon return visits to London, but the principal impetus to the sharpening of their taste as well as to their individual attempts at serious study of painting stemmed from their experiences in Paris and Boulogne from 1856 to 1858. London, for the time being, was to play a minor role in their lives.

Less sudden than the departure from Geneva the previous year, the move from London to Paris had been formulating in the mind of Henry James, Sr., for several weeks during the spring of 1856. He had tired of the English coldness of nature, the stiffness of manner, and the general insular tone of thought, even among his friends in London. His belief in the necessity of the study of foreign languages for his children, one of the original causes for the departure from New York, again seemed of major importance. After these eight months in London, the Parisian scene, with the treasures of the Louvre and the Luxembourg attracting the growing interest in painting, made a strong appeal. The value of this English experience, however, was not lightly dismissed. With characteristic geniality and kindness sparkling occasionally with his keen wit and warm humor, the elder James wrote, in part, to his friend Edmund Tweedy, from London, May 23, 1856:

. . . We are off to Paris on the 3rd of June. We have taken apartments for a month on the Avenue Champs-Elysées, and during that time I have no doubt we shall be able to find something capable of housing us very comfortably for two years longer. Aunt Kate and I went over the other day to look up apartments, but after traversing the town under Mr. Arthur's guidance, were obliged to accept of these provisional ones for the present. Paris is looking as gay and glittering as a fashionable upholsterer's shop, and all the world seems as usual all alive. I never was so sick as in crossing the Channel and silently vowed that if I lived to reach France I should never leave it. But I am back again, and we are now beginning the bustle of preparation for departure from these hospitable shores. We have really met with great kindness here—have made many acquaintances which one would gladly cherish, and on the whole have seen much that is admirable and lovable in brother Bull, and especially in sister Cow. There is no nobler ingredient going into the new humanity than that which comes out of these shy, sullen, honest men, and these ill-drest, energetic, long-striding and unaffected women . . . Remember me to all our friends, especially Ripleius (George Ripley). I have made an allusion to him, tell him, in a new edition of my tract on the church, just published here.[45] Goodbye, and receive my wife and Aunt Kate's love for you and Mary, and believe me ever my dear, *dear* old friend yours *faithfully*,

H. J.[46]

Lacking as these repeated moves were in any tangible framework of ideas about education, they were never disrupting to the extraordinary family spirit which the Jameses carried with them, radiated about themselves, whether residing in St. John's Wood or on the Champs-Elysées, in Boulogne or at Newport. This drifting from place to place strengthened their common bond, in fact. In the autobiographical fragment which the elder James wrote, he spoke of his family in Albany in terms of the peculiar way it seemed to dwell apart: "Our family at all events perfectly illustrated this common vice of contented isolation." [47] In subsequent years, he might have thought of his own family, continually en route, as a unit, as illustrating the common vice of *discontented isolation*. No matter where they settled or for how long a period, during these years when the children were growing up, they never actually became a part of the place; they were in it, but not of it. In the development of Henry James, Jr., this is an important aspect of his family's influence upon him, for it suited perfectly the strong inclination he manifested from earliest childhood to observe, and to observe in detachment. He was afforded, therefore, endless opportunities of carrying on his own inner education with frequent and profitable changes of scene, of milieu, of cultures, of languages, each individual one of which made its marked contribution to his growth as a man and as an artist. Thus on June 3, 1856, when he found himself "off to Paris" again, he suffered no sense of disruption, of interference, but, on the contrary a sense of pleasant expectancy. "We seize our property by an avid instinct wherever we find it," he wrote in later years. Paris was to become his "property" just as Thackeray's London had been during the previous eight months, though that London was never to be lost to him in its unique character or in its place in the unfoldment of his thoughts about it. There were London aspects, "Thackerayan vistas," which touched him nearly sixty years later as "sensible reminders of this hour of early apprehension, so penetrated for me as to have kept its ineffaceable stamp."

NOTES

1. *The Thought and Character of William James,* ed. Ralph Barton Perry, I, 148.
2. *Ibid.,* 149.
3. *A Small Boy and Others,* 306, 307.
4. *Ibid.,* 298.
5. George H. Cunningham, *London,* New York, E. P. Dutton, 1927, 40-42, 525.

6. *A Small Boy and Others*, 298, 299.
7. See "Within the Rim," *Fortnightly Review*, vol. 108 (July-Dec., 1917), 161-171.
8. Percy Lubbock, ed. *The Letters of Henry James*, New York, Charles Scribner's Sons, 1920, I, 4.
9. Rebecca West, *Henry James*, London, Nisbet & Co., 1916, 14.
10. MS. letter from Henry James, Sr., to Catherine Barber James, November 2, 1855, Houghton Library, Harvard University.
11. *A Small Boy and Others*, 312, 313.
12. *Ibid.*, 300, 301.
13. *Ibid.*, 301, 302.
14. MS. letter from Henry James, Sr., to Catherine Barber James, November 30, 1855, Houghton Library, Harvard University.
15. Anna Robeson Burr, *Alice James—Her Brothers—Her Journal*, New York, Dodd, Mead & Company, 1934, 41.
16. *Ibid.*, 101, 102. Robertson James's recollections of the London days were telescoped in a blurred vision which he jotted down in an autobiographical letter written to his sister-in-law, Alice H. James, many years later: " . . . a riot in Regent's Park where the mounted men charge the populace in the Bread Riots. The night in London when it was aflame with fireworks over the Crimean Peace. The Queen who sits in the gilded coach on her way to Parliament. The Christmas Pantomime—the Rat-Catcher's Daughter—Berkeley Square—Fanny MacDaniels—Dr. Wilkinson—the Horse Guards. Mr. Thackeray who carried me on his shoulders. . . . " MS. letter from Robertson James to Alice H. James, Houghton Library, Harvard University. Other portions of this letter appear in F. O. Matthiessen, *The James Family*, 270, 271.
17. *A Small Boy and Others*, 302.
18. Perry, *op. cit.*, I, 174.
19. *A Small Boy and Others*, 303, 304.
20. *Ibid.*, 303.
21. *Ibid.*, 305.
22. *Ibid.*, 305, 306. Mme. Tussaud's original wax-work establishment was located at #59 Baker Street in the Portland Rooms, not far from Portland Square. She died there in 1850. Her exhibition was housed on the first floor of the "Baker Street Bazaar," as it was called, and the little Frenchwoman used to sit at the door taking the entrance money. In the 'Fifties there were over 250 figures in the collection, arranged mostly in a large mirrored salon, opening off of which were three smaller rooms, the Chamber of Horrors, the Napoleon Room, and the Hall of Kings. See, Arthur L. Hayward, *The Days of Dickens*, London, Geo. Routledge & Sons Ltd., n.d., p. 173. Mrs. Manning, and Burke and Hare, were notorious criminals of the early 19th century, the latter two of Edinburgh; Mrs. Manning was a Frenchwoman, prototype of Mademoiselle Hortense in *Bleak House*. The Chamber of Horrors depicted in

gory details the hideous crimes of these murderers. Hayward, *op. cit.*, 173, 183, 194.

23. *A Small Boy and Others*, 309, 310.

24. "George du Maurier," *Partial Portraits*, New York, Macmillan & Co., 1888, 329, 330.

25. Van Wyck Brooks, *The Pilgrimage of Henry James*, New York, E. P. Dutton & Co., 1925, 80.

26. From Concord, July 17, 1855, Emerson wrote to Sir Arthur Helps; "My dear Mr. Helps,—Mr. Henry James, a valued friend of mine, and as I am wont to think, the best man in the city of New York, for all its millions of bodies, goes to London and to France, and though he hinted a wish for letters to 'souls in prison,' I think he might also go to enfranchised and palatial souls. You will find him well versed in what is good in America, and with a compass in his thought and his love of men that is rare here. He is meaning, I believe, to put his boys in school in Switzerland. I think I cannot do either of you a greater kindness than to present you to each other. I wish he may add motives to the inclination you professed to visit your friends and readers in this country. With kindest regards, yours faithfully, R. W. EMERSON" Perry, *op. cit.*, vol. I, p. 83. In a letter to Emerson from London in 1856 James wrote of Arthur Helps, as "an amiable, kindly little man with friendly offers. . . . He fancied a little that I was going to make a book, and might be indiscreet enough to put him in. . . ." *Ibid.*, vol. I, p. 85. In this same letter to Emerson he describes Carlyle as "the same old sausage, fizzing and sputtering in his own grease."

27. (CHRISTMAS AT LONDON. . . . A letter to the N. Y. *Daily Tribune*, from H. J., Sr. at L.) (Wed. Jan. 16, 1856)

London, Christmas-day, 1855

From the bobbery which the children have been making for several hours past up stairs, I conclude that St. Nicholas, the merry old elf, crossed the water to us last night, and that we are in for at least five stockings full of over-flowing jollification. European countries are full of traditional customs at Christmas, which indicate a sort of instinctive popular apprehension of the great mystery of Redemption. At Dewsburg, in this country, they toll the bell at midnight to celebrate *the death of the devil*, and in many other localities similar customs exist with a similar intensity of meaning. A beautiful custom prevails at *Tonneins* in France, which consists in multitudes of peasants, men and women, gayly scouring the fields the night before Christmas with lighted torches on high poles, "to announce to the earth the coming of the day of UNIVERSAL rejoicing." You will see a very spirited illustration of this custom in the *Almanach de l'Illustration* for 1856, worth a dozen ordinary sermons.

The sermons, in fact, are ordinarily very far below the theme. The Church has faithfully preserved to some extent the memory of the great service which Christ rendered to the private or individual soul; but it has utterly neglected the equally memorable work He accomplished in and for our common nature. . . .

. . . Human society, human fellowship, human equality, is fast becoming popularly recognized as a divine truth, and it finds the leaders in Church and State not giving it a cordial and generous welcome, but doing their best in many cases to defame and deny it altogether. The result cannot be doubted. Indeed, it is already evident on every hand. The people yield their leaders no longer the tribute of a hearty belief and admiration, but that of a well-merited contempt. Happy America! where the people are superior to all mere classes of the people, and where, consequently, Church and State are sure in the long run to obey and reflect every expansion of the popular instinct. . . .

28. Henry James, Sr., "The Social Significance of our Institutions" published in part by F. O. Matthiessen, *The James Family,* 63, 64.
29. "Wilkinson disappoints me, he is so eaten up with the spirits and all that. His imagination is so vast as to dwarf all the higher faculties, and his sympathy is as narrow as Dr. Cheever's or Brownson's. No reasonable man, it is true, likes the clergy or the philosophers, but Wilkinson's dislike of them seems to be as envenomed as that between rival tradesmen or rival beauties. One can't endure the nonsense they talk, to be sure, but when one considers the dear human meaning and effort that they are struggling at the bottom of all that nonsense, you can't feel any personal separation from the men. Wilkinson's sarcasm is awful, and on the whole he seems to be sowing his intellectual wild oats at present, and will grow more genial in good time. . . ." Quoted in Ralph Barton Perry, *op. cit.,* I, 84, 85.
30. MS. letter from Henry James, Sr., to Catherine Barber James, February 4, 1856, Houghton Library, Harvard University.
31. *A Small Boy and Others,* 317. An account of the first night of the lecture reads in part: "On his arrival at Chillon, Mr. Smith introduced us to an American, and a literary lady . . . The confusion of the American's mind relative to Lord Byron and his heroes, identifying the Prisoner of Chillon and Mazeppa with the poet, was rich in comic eccentricity . . . the second part commenced with the Village of Chamonix and the Cascade and Chatel de Pélerins; after which the celebrated ascent was proceeded with. Here it becomes impossible to follow Mr. Smith in his lively and graphic descriptions of the early difficulties and dangers in making the Pierre Pointue, Pierre a l'echelle and the Glacier des Bossons. Mr. Smith appears to have been quite exhausted just before he reached the summit, and to have experienced some of the phenomena of sleep-walking. But he was well protected by his friends, and at length he stood on top, in triumph, without feeling it, for he was

so overworn that he was unable to attend to the view, and fell off immediately to sleep. During this part, Mr. Smith treated his audience with a specimen of the hurdy-gurdy music of the guides, and the manner in which they sing scraps of Savoyard songs. The lecture itself concludes in a Parisian *café*, accompanied with a metrical description of an Englishman's way of behaving at a restaurant and at a theatre in Paris." Arthur L. Hayward, *op. cit.*, 175, 176.

32. George Henry Lewes, whose criticisms in the *Leader* frequently attacked Kean during the 'Fifties, wrote of the initial performance: "Never do we remember to have seen *Twelfth Night* so well played; never perhaps was it relished with such gusto. It showed how much could be done by casting a play well." He was pleased to find a "sufficient splendor of scenery and costume without prodigality of spectacle." *Leader*, Oct. 5, 1850, as quoted by Ernest Bradlee Watson, *Sheridan to Robertson*, Cambridge, Harvard University, 1926, 225, 226.

33. *A Small Boy and Others*, 318, 319. This same passage continues: "I was to have my impressions of Charles Kean renewed later on— ten years later, in America—without a rag of scenic reinforcement; when I was struck with the fact that no actor so little graced by nature probably ever went so far toward repairing it by a kind of cold rage of endeavour. Were he and his wife really not *coercively* interesting on that Boston night of *Macbeth* in particular, hadn't their art a distinction that triumphed over battered age and sorry harshness, or was I but too easily beguiled by the old association? I have enjoyed and forgotten numberless rich hours of spectatorship, but somehow still find hooked to the wall of memory the picture of this hushed couple in the castle court, with the knocking at the gate, with Macbeth's stare of pitiful horror at his unused daggers and with the grand manner, up to the height of the argument, of Mrs. Kean's coldly portentous snatch of them. What I especially owe that lady is my sense of what she had in common, as a queer hooped and hook-nosed figure, of large circumference and archaic attire, strange tasteless toggery, with those performers of the past who are preserved for us on the small canvasses of Hogarth and Zoffany; she helped one back at that time of her life to a vision of the Mrs. Cibbers and the Mrs. Pritchards—so affecting may often be such recovered links."

34. For an account of the Princess' Theatre see A. L. Hayward, *op. cit.*, 151, 152.

35. Watson, *op. cit.*, 191.

36. *A Small Boy and Others*, 320. Concerning Wigan and the Olympic, one critic writes: "In 1849 the original Olympic—or the 'Pic' as it was universally called—was burned to the ground. The new theatre erected on its site opened in gloom and was soon a failure. In 1850 William Farren vainly attempted to make a success of it but after three years he handed over the management to Alfred

Wigan, who opened with *The Camp at the Olympic,* with Mrs. Stirling and Frederic Robson in the cast. It was Robson—until then but little heard of—who saved Wigan from ruin. A ridiculous farce called the *Wandering Minstrel* gave the comedian his chance, and in the character of Jem Baggs he made an extraordinary and incomprehensible hit with the old song of 'Vilkins and his Dinah.' London went mad about it. From drawing-room to scullery, from Buckingham Palace to St. Giles, everyone was singing or whistling 'Too-roo-lal, too-roo-la, too-ral-li-da!' Then followed a series of burlesques which made the Olympic the most fashionable theatre in London, so that night after night Wych Street, Drury Lane, and Newcastle Street were jammed with carriages." A. L. Hayward, *op. cit.,* 148.

37. Allardyce Nicoll, *A History of Late Nineteenth Century Drama,* Cambridge, University Press, 1946, I, 101.

38. Dion Boucicault's *The Corsican Brothers* was first produced at the Princess' Theatre on February 2, 1852, by Charles Kean, whose masterful performance brought fame to the house. The play was a daring, ingenious, exciting melodrama, done in an elegance of spectacle, mingling the supernatural with the real, lending itself aptly to the sort of parody Robson could do to perfection. Thomas Frederic Robson (1822?-1864) whose real name was Thomas Robson Brownhill, was a born comedian who had got his start in Dublin at the Queen's Theatre, coming to the Olympic in London first in March, 1853. Under the management of Alfred Wigan, his marvelous gifts of burlesque brought him to the height of popularity, earning the title of "the greatest comic actor of his day." He was particularly known for the role of Prince Richcraft which the Jameses saw him do in *The Discreet Princess.*

39. *A Small Boy and Others,* 321, 322.

40. *Ibid.,* 322, 323. Charles James Mathews, Jr. (1803-1878), had made his debut on December 7, 1835 at the Olympic, abandoning law for the stage and marrying the celebrated Mme. Vestris who had made the Olympic famous in the 'Thirties, making an American tour with her. *The Merry Wives of Windsor, The School for Scandal,* and *The Critic,* were standard English works revived with much success by Vestris and Mathews and carried on by him after her death in 1854.

41. *A Small Boy and Others,* 313. Benjamin Robert Haydon (1786-1846), who lived for about ten years in Lisson Grove North, St. John's Wood, entertaining there such friends as Walter Scott, Charles Lamb, Hazlitt, David Wilkie, Leigh Hunt, Talfourd and Keats, held particular interest for Harry and Willy by the spectacles represented in many of his paintings.

42. Haydon's sincere and delightful autobiography was edited by Tom Taylor and published in 1853, two years before the Jameses came to London. Haydon is also remembered in literary circles for his

Lectures on Painting and Design, 1844-1846. His being called "hapless" is an allusion to the fact that Haydon's uneven career, one year of which he spent in the King's Bench Prison, painting while there his "Mock Election," ended by his committing suicide in 1846, at #12 Burwood Place, Edgware Road, which had been his residence for many years. See Cunningham, *op. cit.,* 56, 64, 93.

43. *A Small Boy and Others,* 313, 314.

44. *Ibid.,* 314, 315. Marlborough House, built by Christopher Wren in 1709-10 for John Churchill, the great Duke of Marlborough on the site of the old pheasantry of St. James's Palace, was used as a royal residence by Queen Adelaide, wife of William IV, until 1837. Queen Victoria allowed certain apartments in Marlborough House to be used for exhibits of the Government Fine Art Musuem and School of Design which included the Vernon Collection and the Turner paintings from about 1849 to 1859. In 1861 Marlborough House was remodelled as the London residence of the Prince of Wales, afterwards Edward VII. See G. H. Cunningham, *op. cit.,* p. 445. Daniel Maclise (1811-1870) painted *The Play-scene in Hamlet* in 1842, usually considered along with his other work as marred by "an unintelligent respect for detail." Charles Johnson, *English Painting,* London, G. Bell and Sons Ltd., 1934, p. 225; William Mulready (1786-1863), was an Irish painter whose works are "sincere if a little dull"; Sir Edwin Henry Landseer (1802-1873), did numerous and popular works which depended mostly upon their subject matter for interest and effect; Sir David Wilkie (1785-1841), was considerably more gifted than this group of English painters who "in insight into character indeed and in the power to record spontaneous poses . . . even equalled Hogarth, but never reached his level in pure painting." See Johnson, *op. cit.,* 224. Charles Robert Leslie (1794-1859), was born in London of American parents, spent most of his adult years in England, painting *Sancho Panza in the Apartment of the Duchess,* in 1844.

45. *The Church of Christ Not an Ecclesiasticism: A Letter of Remonstrance to a Member of the 'Soi-disant' New Church,* Second Edition, London, W. White, 1856, Sm. 8vo. 156. The first edition was published in pamphlet form in New York in 1854. In relation to the earlier edition, Mrs. Henry James wrote an interesting comment to her mother-in-law, Mrs. William James of Albany, dated from New York, January 14 (1854): "Dear Ma, Henry has, I believe, acknowledged the receipt of the basket of poultry, and thanks you for your kind remembrance of us at the New Year. He has wanted to go up to see you and would have done so had he not been —and still is—entirely engrossed with his book, which keeps him busy reading proofs for several hours every day. When it is out I wish you (would) read it for I am sure you will like it better than anything he has ever written. It is addressed to the church

and meets so rationally and satisfactorily so many of the difficulties
that one in the church, who is not a mere formalist, must some
times have felt in many of its teachings, that I am sure you will
read it with interest. It fills too with new meaning and beauty,
so many of the old Scriptures, which we have all been taught to
revere, by giving them their true spiritual significance that no one
I think can read it attentively without gaining new delight in their
Bible. . . ." MS. letter, Mrs. Henry James, Sr., to Mrs. William
James of Albany, January 14 (1854), Houghton Library, Harvard
University.

46. MS. letter Henry James, Sr., to Edmund Tweedy, May 23, 1856,
Houghton Library, Harvard University. Parts of this letter appear
in Perry, *The Thought and Character of William James,* I, 120.

47. Quoted by F. O. Matthiessen, *op. cit.,* 21. In this same work Henry
James, Sr., continued: "Our family righteousness had as little felt
relation to the public life of the world, as little connection with
the common hopes and fears of mankind, as the number and form
of the rooms we inhabited; and we contentedly lived the same life
of stagnant isolation from the race which the great mass of our
modern families live, its surface never dimpled by anything but
the duties and courtesies we owed to our private friends and
acquaintances."

Chapter Eight

Echoes of Old Paris

"Yes, small staring jeune homme, we are dignity and memory and measure, we are conscience and proportion and taste . . ."

In leaving the London of Queen Victoria for the Paris of Empress Eugenie, the James family in June, 1856 moved into a realm of art and history that was "educative, formative, fertilising, in a degree which no other 'intellectual experience' our youth was to know could pretend . . . to rival." In these early years of the Second Empire, the great alterations of parks and avenues, of the Louvre and other public monuments, were slowly going forward under the direction of Haussmann; yet, old Paris was still to be observed on all sides in the multitude of sounds and sights and smells which reached even the select Champs-Elysées. A few years earlier, in 1845, Balzac had written: "On the boulevards of Paris you find freedom of mind. You find life, a strange fertile life, a communicative life, a warm life, the life of the lizard in the sun, the life of the artist, an amusing life, a life of contrasts. The boulevards are never twice the same. They experience all the moods of Paris." Willy, Harry, and Wilky James, within the prescribed limitations of their activities, were also to experience the moods of Paris, which for Harry in particular created a permanent fascination. It was Paris which he was to consider, twenty years later, before settling in London, as the city of his expatriation. The brilliant literary figures who attracted him in the 'Seventies were just beginning, in the 'Fifties, to make Paris their home. Some, in this same year, 1856, were experiencing the very first surrenderings to the endless charms of the great city, charms which thirteen-year-old Harry James was then responding to so deeply. Others already knew her well.

Victor Hugo was living in exile, having been forced to flee from his home at #6 Place des Vosges in the Revolution of 1848.[1] Charles Dickens, in April, 1856, had given up his apartment on the Champs-Elysées, within a door or two of the Jardin d'Hiver, to return to England after a year's residence spent almost entirely among writers. Wilkie Collins and the Brownings were in Paris, as was frequently Thackeray, coming over from London to see his daughters, who were then living on the Champs-Elysées. Chopin had died in 1849, but George Sand was holding her salon, and had recently finished her *Histoire de Ma Vie*. Alexandre Dumas, *père*, returned to Paris in 1856 after two years in Brussels and was living at #77 Rue d'Amsterdam. In this same year, George du Maurier, later a beloved friend of Henry James, Jr., arrived in Paris and enrolled as a student in the Atelier Gleyre, later transformed into Atelier Carrel in *Trilby*. In 1856 also came Alphonse Daudet, an impressionable lad of sixteen, with his brother, fresh from the provinces, finding quarters in the Rue de Tournon. Emile Zola, also sixteen, was not to see Paris until two years later; but Gustave Flaubert, at thirty-five, in that very year produced *Madame Bovary* as his first published work, a novel for which, in 1902, Henry James, Jr., was to write a preface. Paris, indeed, was a city of promise for the young American boy, but not for almost two decades was he to realize fully how much it would affect him. At the moment he was quite preoccupied with that peculiar "sense of Europe" which the city expressed in "the very breath of civilized lips."

The short visits, en route to and from Geneva during the previous year, had offered the briefest of glimpses, mostly of the Rue de la Paix, but the vistas now broadened as the Jameses became established on the Champs-Elysées, between the Rond-Point and the

Rue du Colisée. The house belonged to an American planter from
Louisiana, and was serenely situated behind a "protuberantly-paved
and peculiarly resonant small court," accessible by a high grille which
opened in response to the jangle of bells and the clatter of feet
across the cobbled enclosure. It was an odd relic of a house, which,
like its owner, dated back to the turn of the century, with a kind
of old-world presence still lingering along the glassy polish of the
floors and on the winding staircase. Its formal elegance was reflected in a redundancy of mirrors, the elegance of china clocks and
ormolu vases, of walls lined in white and gold panels, of sofas and
chairs of red damask against gilt frames, of brocades and satins.

Amid such Parisian refinements, a family routine was soon established, but with some changes of personnel; Mlle. Cusin was replaced
by Mlle. Danse, Mr. Thompson by M. Lerambert whose connections lasted only four or five months and terminated by a "separation . . . attended with friction." He was "spare and tightly black-
coated, spectacled, pale and prominently intellectual," living in the
Rue Jacob with his mother and sister; he was the author of a volume
of verse, "sympathetically mentioned by the Saint-Beuve of the
Causeries in a review of the young poets of the hour ('M. Lerambert
too has loved, M. Lerambert too has suffered, M. Lerambert too
has sung!' or words to that effect)." His duties were strictly those
of academic instruction and Harry was ever to associate him "with
warm somniferous mornings by the windows that opened to the
clattery, plashy court," during which the tutor feigned an interest
he obviously did not feel. As usual, William provided the most
stimulating problems of instruction; Wilky offered the greatest cause
of distraction; Harry, meekly following directions, accomplished one
definite task, the translation into English of La Fontaine's fables,
rendered with a certain felicity of idiom. M. Lerambert, impressed
by Harry's marked ability, carried the word of praise to the elder
James, who, in turn, commended the boy; Harry, incidentally, had
thought the work not very well done. This lack of assurance, combined with the perfectionist's sense of falling short, characterized the
slow and prolonged development of Henry James, Jr., during the
remainder of his youth, extending even into the first period of his

success as a novelist. In thinking back on this incident of translating La Fontaine, he wrote: " 'Oh,' I seem inwardly to have said, 'if it were to be, if it only could be, *really* a question of rendering—!' and so, without confusion, though in vague, very vague, mystification to have left it: as if so many things, intrinsic and extrinsic, would have to change and operate, so many would have to happen, so much water have to flow under the bridge, before I could give primary application to such a thought, much more finish such a sentence." [2]

In London, the governess Mlle. Cusin, had played a minor role in the lives of the three oldest boys, being charged with the complete supervision of the youngest son, Robertson, and Alice. Robert Thompson had spent the afternoons with his pupils of the morning classroom hours, escorting them in wide range over the vast stretches of historic London. Mlle. Cusin had by happy matrimonial arrangements remained in England, rising to a higher sphere than service with the nomadic Jameses, but writing profusely to them and renewing connections with them, on a different social footing, during their subsequent return to London two years later. In Paris, Mlle. Augustine Danse carried on the work of her "brave Vaudoise predecessor" with the younger children but also assumed some of the responsibilities of Mr. Thompson, since M. Lerambert was not entrusted with all phases of the older boys' instruction. Mlle. Danse, consequently, became quite frequently and intimately associated with Willy, Harry, and Wilky, so that they were to remember her more vividly than anyone else in the endless line of "educative females," stretching from New York to various capitals of Europe. There were other reasons, however, that set Mlle. Danse apart. She possessed an all-knowing, all-imposing mind, a most flexible *taille,* and salient, smiling eyes more pleasingly green than those of Becky Sharp. These attributes were especially attractive to the boys, even down to "l'ingénieux petit Robertson," as she dubbed him. Her company, charmingly stimulating, on the long afternoon wanderings about Paris, "our first fine *flâneries* of curiosity," as Harry expressed it, offered far more genuine solicitude than Thackeray's Becky, lost in a cynical daydream, ever offered her neglected pupils. The Paris which the boys enjoyed under her remarkable guidance was slowly becoming, like Thackeray's London, a city of the past, with the newer Paris, conceived under the first Napoleon, taking on even more formal design and grander scale during the Second Empire.

The Revolution of 1848, terminating the reign of Louis Philippe, whose flight across the Channel the Jameses had learned of on Fifth Avenue, was followed by the short-lived Second Republic. In 1851, by a coup d'état, Napoleon III had established himself and the inimitable Eugénie, more or less securely, for the next eighteen years. In 1856 the Second Empire was still feeling its way "with the great free hand soon to be allowed to Baron Haussmann marked as yet but in the light preliminary flourish. Its connections with the past, however, still hung thickly on; its majesties and symmetries, comparatively vague and general, were subject to the happy accident, the charming lapse and the odd extrusion, a bonhomie of chance composition and colour now quite purged away. The whole region of the Champs-Elysées . . . was another world from the actual huge centre of repeated radiations; the splendid Avenue, as we of course already thought it, carried the eye from the Tuileries to the Arch, but pleasant old places abutted on it by the way, gardens and terraces and hôtels of another time, pavilions still braver than ours, cabarets and cafés of homely, almost of rural type, with a relative and doubtless rather dusty ruralism, spreading away to the River and the Wood. What was the Jardin d'Hiver, a place of entertainment standing quite over against us and that looped itself at night with little coloured oil-lamps, a mere twinkling grin upon the face of pleasure? Dim my impression of having been admitted—or rather, I suppose, conducted, through— . . . to view it by the colourless day, when it must have worn the stamp of an auction-room quite void of the 'lots.' More distinct on the other hand the image of the bustling barrière at the top of the Avenue, on the hither side of the Arch, where the old loose-girt *banlieue* began at once and the two matched lodges of the octroi, highly . . . architectural, guarded the entrance, on either side, with such a suggestion of the generations and dynasties and armies, the revolutions and restorations they had seen come and go." [3]

An insight into the domestic scene of the James family, at the time the children were so occupied with their new tutor and governess, is found in a letter from Mrs. James to Grandmother James in Albany, giving an account of the change of residence and some very American observations on the French and their ways. It is in such family letters that one catches, behind the brilliant, shifting scenes of the children's education, the firm, homely, durable spirit of the family, which grew stronger as the experiences became more complicated. A clear note of the Albany and New York background sounds throughout this letter, in sharp contrast to the Parisian setting in which it was written:

PARIS, AUG. 25TH (1856)

MY DEAR MA,

We have been disappointed in letters from Albany for several weeks, and have begun to feel most anxious to hear from you. Libby's letter of 16th of June was the last, with the exception of two brief epistles from Gus, principally on business matters.

Since I wrote last, we have changed our apartment and taken one for a year. We found great difficulty in getting one with a sufficient number of sleeping rooms to accommodate us. The French in the construction of their houses make provision it seems for very small families, the number of sleeping rooms seldom exceeding three and *very rarely* four. The means the French adopt to keep their families small is, I am told, sending their infants away into the country to be nursed, where eight out of ten die, or if they live, to send them to boarding schools to be educated. We have succeeded after a good deal of trouble in getting a most delightful and commodious apartment with six bedrooms (intended doubtless for some unlucky English or American family with a great many children *all* at home), and which accommodates us all most delightfully. But I am almost afraid to tell you what we have to pay for it. We saw this apartment on our first arrival, indeed it was offered to us last October (1855) when we were looking for rooms, and the price was so appalling that it fairly drove us off to England. But here we are, snugly ensconced in it, unable it seems to resist our destiny, and paying a rent of $2200 a year. This of course we will not be able to do for any length of time, securing as we do but $1400 for our house at home.[4]

The other expenses here are proportionately high, not to the French, but to strangers, upon whom the grossest extortion is practised at every turn. The most amazing part of housekeeping here consists in the petty theft practised upon you every day by the cook, who is the marketeer and provider in general. It is part of her business to double the amount of her wages at least by purloining from you, out of every breakfast and dinner she provides you. The first discovery of this is very vexatious, and one feels tempted to resist it, and to determine not to be made a fool of, and fleeced in this way every day; but a little experience teaches you that it is inevitable, that it is better to submit with the best grace you can, only keep your eyes open, lest the amount be adroitly doubled.

. . . The boys have good teachers and are well and happy. We have been most fortunate in a governess for Alice and Rob. She is a most sensible, ladylike person, and really quite an acquisition to the family circle. Wilkie, Bob, and Alice have commenced music with a good deal of enthusiasm . . .

. . . Henry (Sr.) is well, but I think experiences much more fatigue in walking than he used to do. The effort he had made in walking for so many years has occasioned a weakness in his back, which at times gives him great trouble . . . The boys miss their home companions more than any(thing) else. Just at the present moment perhaps the peaches at home more, and recall with longing desire the *baskets* full that are taken daily at Grandma's . . . [5]

The lack of companions was an aspect of these experiences in Europe which all of the James children felt keenly and the result of which had a very tangible effect upon the peculiar development of Henry, Jr. Not until the family settled in Newport were the children to have daily companions, and not until William and Henry, Jr., attended Harvard did they have any real group experience in their studies. As is indicated in their mother's letter, the boys were at this time beginning to feel quite seriously the need for a more normal, wholesome companionship which would include friends of their own age. Newport was to offer them a few friends, but even there they had no contact with young people outside of the very restricted social milieu in which the family constantly lived. In a sense, this side of their youth was a warped and unnatural one, but in the case of young Harry whose peculiar temperament and talents called for a detached and unmolested freedom from the demands of group activity, it can hardly be considered a misfortune.

The commodious and most delightful apartment to which the family moved from the Champs-Elysées was situated at #19 Rue d'Angoulême, St. Honoré, later called Rue La Boëtie. During the autumn and winter months, as brief as the residence there was to be, Harry took in certain impressions of the site, the neighborhood, the various aspects of the domestic elements of which it was composed: ". . . our many-windowed *premier,* above an entresol of no great height, hung over the narrow and, during the winter months, not a little dusky channel, with endless movement and interest in the vivid exhibition it supplied. What faced us was a series of subjects, with the baker, at the corner, for the first—the impeccable dispenser of the so softly-crusty crescent-rolls that we woke up each morning to hunger for afresh, with our weak café-au-lait, as for the one form of 'European' breakfast-bread fit to be named even with the feeblest of our American forms. Then came the small crêmerie, white picked out with blue, which, by some secret of its own keeping, afforded, within the compass of a few feet square, prolonged savoury meals to working men, white-frocked or blue-frocked, to uniformed cabmen, stout or spare, but all more or less audibly *bavards* and discernibly critical; and next the compact embrasure of the écaillère or oyster-lady, she and her paraphernalia fitted into their interstice much as the mollusc itself into its shell; neighboured in turn by the marchand-de-bois, peeping from as narrow a cage, his neat faggots and chopped logs stacked beside him and above him in his sentry-box quite as the niches of saints, in early Italian pictures, are framed with tightly-packed fruits and flowers. Space and remembrance fail me for the rest of the series, the attaching note of which comes back as the note of diffused sociability and domestic, in fact more or less aesthetic, ingenuity, with the street a perpetual parlour or household centre for the flitting, pausing, conversing little bourgeoise or ouvrière to sport, on every pretext and in every errand, her fluted cap, her composed head, her neat ankles and her ready wit. Which is to say indeed but that life and manners were more pointedly and harmoniously expressed, under our noses there, then we had perhaps found them anywhere save in the most salient passages of 'stories' . . . " [6]

While Mrs. James struggled with the problems of a French domestic staff and the children drank in deep currents of French culture, Henry James, Sr., was experiencing a stimulating consideration of England and the English from Emerson's recently published *English Traits*. His residence in London during the previous year had given the elder James a deeper insight into the English nature, and from his point of vantage now in Paris he was able to view his American friend's opinions with a detachment and perspective which added keenness to his already sharpened sense of John Bull. The general tone of his letter to Edmund Tweedy, who sent him a copy of the book, foreshadows the Fourth of July address he was later to make at Newport; it also suggests a growing awareness of American values, without, however, any indication that he was thinking of returning from Europe in 1856.

> PARIS, 19 RUE d'ANGOULEME,
> ST. HONORE
> SEPTEMBER 14, 1856

MY DEAR TWEEDIUS,—

Many thanks for Emerson! It came in most apropos to a great desire which I felt after it, and which had led me to go down to the Palais Royal bookseller the day before to look after it, but in vain. I am somewhat disappointed now that I have read it; the appreciation is so overdone. The study has been too conscientious. The manners—the life—he was investigating, haven't the depth either for good or evil he attributes to them. His own stand-point is too high to do justice to the English. They are an intensely vulgar race, high and low; and their qualities, good or evil, date not from any divine or diabolic *depths* whatever, but from most obvious and superficial causes. They are the abject slaves of routine, and no afflatus from above or below ever comes, apparently, to ruffle the surface of their self-complacent quietude. They are not worth studying. The prejudices one has about them, even when they are unjust, are scarcely worth correcting. There is nothing better supplied by the actual truth of the case, to put in the place of them. They belong, all their good and evil, to the past humanity, to the infantile development of the mind, and they don't deserve, more than any other European nation, the least reverence from a denizen of the new world. They are a solider, manlier race than the French, according to the old ideas of manhood: that is, they do not lie, cheat, commit adultery and murder with half so much good-will: but of the spiritual causes out of which these evil things proceed, pride and self-love and the love of domineering, they have their full share, and perhaps more than most other people. They lack heart. Their love is clanish. They love all that wear their own livery, but they don't even *see* anyone outside of that boundary.

Mrs. Cranch[7] wondered the other day, upon some new experiences of French perfidy, "what the Lord *would* do with these French people." I wonder what He will do with any European people. Or rather I don't wonder: for I see that they are all destined to be recast and remoulded into the form of a new and *de-nationalized* humanity, a universal form which, being animated by God's own infinite spirit, the spirit of human fellowship, will quickly shed all the soils it has contracted in the past . . . American disorder is sweet beside European order: it is so full of promise. . . .

Good-bye, my dear old Tweedius, and believe me ever faithfully yours,

H. J.[8]

Underlying his critical view was the spiritual idealism with which the elder James constantly evaluated all he surveyed; in the light of this fact, while his severe strictures on the English and upon Emerson's *English Traits* are not therefore without some foundation, the subsequent attachment which his son Harry formed with both the English and the French on a totally different basis points up the ever-widening chasm which was forming at this very time between the future novelist and his father. Henry James, Jr., was never to envision a *de-nationalized* humanity in Europe, animated by a universal spirit of human fellowship; in fact, the great fascination for him of both the French and the English people was their very nationalistic natures. In this light he was to weave about them the fabric of his fiction, and in this same light was he, during these particular childhood years in Europe, beginning to feel and understand them.

One of the most exciting spectacles for the James children upon their excursions up and down the boulevards was the sudden appearance of Empress Eugénie in her open carriage. Her youth and beauty, her dramatic sense of exhibition, her entourage of ladies-in-waiting, and attendants on horseback all rode straight out of a story book, and the public approval and enthusiasm intensified the excitement. Even more thrilling was her appearance with the baby Prince Imperial going forth for his airing, or on progress to Saint-Cloud in a splendid coach followed by the *cent-gardes,* in light blue and silver uniforms, pistols raised and cocked, intensely erect as they jolted up the Avenue in perfect formation. The Prince was born on March 16, 1856, three months before the Jameses arrived in Paris, where they witnessed, on June 14, 1856, the stupendous celebration in the great place before Notre Dame upon the occasion of the royal baptism. Three-hundred thousand people from the provinces and other countries had come to join the Parisians for this great event. In the vast square before the cathedral, high masts had been erected, from which floated banners bearing the Imperial arms; the ground was covered with smooth, clean, white sand, and masses of flowers and banks of ferns transformed the whole area about the square into a kind of fairylike garden. A large covered marquise had been erected in front of the main portals. The ceremony was appointed for six in the evening, but hours before, over four thousand people had assembled in the cathedral, while outside the multitude was so great that it was impossible to pass even on foot. Every window and roof-top on every thoroughfare for many blocks around was crowded to capacity, even to the tops of chimneys. At five o'clock, the military bands began the procession at the Pavillon de l'Horloge, through the Tuileries gardens, the Rue de Rivoli, the Place de l'Hotel de Ville, over the Pont d'Arcole and the Rue d'Arcole to the Place Notre Dame.

The procession was headed by the trumpeters and the band of the First Carabiniers, General Korte and his staff, followed by squadrons, officers and bands of several other regiments. Then came eight carriages each drawn by six horses, carrying the ladies of the Empress's household, chamberlains, the chief officers of the Crown, the Princess Mathilde in the seventh carriage, preceded by four postilions, and the Princess Marie of Baden, with cavaliers to the right of the carriage and on the left the Colonel of the Guards. The eighth carriage contained the Grand Duchess of Baden, King Jerome, Prince Oscar of Sweden and Prince Napoleon. Two splendid state coaches, after an interval, arrived, each drawn by eight horses, the first coach being the one used by Napoleon on his marriage to Marie Louise; now it contained Admiral Bruat's widow, Governess of the Children of France, holding the Prince Imperial in an ermine-lined cloak, attended by under-governesses. In the second state coach, the vehicle in which Charles X had been driven to his coronation, rode the Emperor and Empress. A squadron of the *Cent-Gardes,* officers of the Emperor, and other distinguished contingents completed the procession, all of which reached the doors of the cathedral by six o'clock, where the sovereigns were met by Msgr. Libour, surrounded by his clergy. With the most splendid and colorful ceremonies the baptism was performed, followed by roars of *"Vive le Prince Impérial"* as the Emperor raised his son aloft for the crowds to see. The little Prince was then escorted back to the Tuileries by way of the quays, while a grand banquet was held, after which the return to the Tuileries was effected in semi-State landaus amid loud and continuous cheering along brilliantly lighted streets hung with flags and banners. One of the ladies in Eugénie's suite, in a letter describing the entire celebration, commented in conclusion, "This is, indeed, a day that will be long remembered by Parisians and which will remain more deeply graven than any other in the heart of the Empress." [9]

Somewhere in the heaving throngs surging through the streets were the James family, with Harry, gaping as he had never gaped before, succumbing to the overwhelming splendor and intoxicating excitement of the whole tremendous spectacle. On his mind too the scene was graven forever, for he wrote of it: "Was a public holiday ever more splendid than that of the Prince's baptism at Notre Dame, the fête of Saint-Napoleon, or was any ever more immortalised, as we say, than this one was to be by the wonderfully ample and vivid picture of it in the Eugène Rougon of Emile Zola, who must have taken it in,[10] on the spot, as a boy of about our own number of years, though of so much more implanted and predestined an evocatory gift? The sense of that interminable hot day, a day of hanging about and waiting and shuffling in dust, in crowds, in fatigue, amid booths and pedlars and performers and false alarms and expectations and renewed reactions and rushes, all transfigured at the last, withal, by the biggest and brightest illumination up to that time offered even the Parisians, the blinding glare of the new Empire effectually symbolised—the vision of the whole, I say, comes back to me quite in the form of a chapter from the Rougon-Macquart, with its effect

of something long and dense and heavy, without shades or under-
tones, but immensely kept-up and done." [11]

When the city offered no such attractions and the weather became
too warm, the family often enjoyed excursions to Passy and Auteuil,
sometimes with fellow Americans whose gutteral French was a
revelation to Harry, to whom the French language was already becoming something of an accomplishment. There were picnics, also, in
the Bois de Boulogne, which to the James boys represented "the virgin
forest better than anything at our own American door had done."
Such a remark contains more truth than the modern reader might
understand, for until 1848 the Bois belonged to the crown-domains
and received little attention. It was known as the Forêt de Rouvray
and covered, as it still does, nearly all of the peninsula formed by
one of the endless windings of the Seine. As far back as Roman
days a colony of prisoners was employed in reclaiming the old forest;
in the Middle Ages lordly chateaux were constructed on its borders,
as well as a monastery, the Abbaye de Longchamp. In 1852 it was
presented to the city, on condition that a sum of two million francs
be expended on it within four years. Thus, what had been a waste-
land, the haunt of robbers and wild boars, a favorite resort of duel-
lists, was changed in the 'Fifties to a magnificent parkland, stretching
over two thousand acres. Actually the Bois appears to be much
larger than it is, because of the artful designs by Adolphe Alphand,
the landscape gardener who carried out the project. The many roads,
lanes, and footpaths, winding through the trees and dense under-
brush and wild-flowers, stretched through large areas of untouched
woods which may well have seemed a virgin forest to the James
boys in 1856.

As attractive as the Bois was on occasional picnics and drives,
the boulevards and great monuments of Paris offered Harry James
far more interest, for they contributed strongly to his growing sense
of the social aspect of the great city, ranging from the fashionable
throngs on the avenues and in the parks to the lower ranges of the
bourgeoisie crowded about the charmed circle of Polichinelle and
his puppets. "The 'amusement,' the aesthetic and human appeal, of
Paris had in those days less the air of a great shining conspiracy

to please, the machinery in movement confessed less to its huge purpose; but manners and types and traditions, the detail of the scene, its pointed particulars, went their way with a straighter effect, as well as often with a homelier grace—character, temper and tone had lost comparatively little of their emphasis. . . ." [12]

The difference between the ages of thirteen and fourteen-and-a-half marked a temporary lessening of companionship during the summer of 1856 between Harry, not quite into the full boyhood stage, and William, definitely beyond such childhood interest as puppets and merry-go-rounds. More significant, however, was Harry's preference for the "social aspect," the people and their shops and bourgeois lives, or their promenades and drives through the Bois and St. Cloud; while William's inclinations already took him toward "exact knowledge" with all due respect to Mlle. Danse and their tours of Paris. Yet, after the summer months had passed, as had also the services of M. Lerambert, the two oldest boys were drawn together again in their common experience as pupils in the Institution Fezandié, on Rue Balzac, a big square villa to which they turned "as pupils not unacquainted with vicissitudes." In all their complicated, checkered career, however, Willy and Harry and Wilky here found something entirely different: "It was a recreational, or at least a social, rather than a tuitional house; which fact had, I really believe, weighed favourably with our parents, when, bereft of M. Lerambert, they asked themselves, with their considerable practice, how next to bestow us. Our father, like so many free spirits of that time in New York and Boston, had been much interested in the writings of Charles Fourier and his scheme of the 'phalanstery' as the solution of human troubles, and it comes to me that he must have met or in other words heard of M. Fezandié as an active and sympathetic ex-Fourierist (I think there were only ex-Fourierists by that time), who was embarking, not far from us, on an experiment if not absolutely phalansteric at least inspired, or at any rate enriched, by a bold idealism. I like to think of the Institution as all but phalansteric—it so corrects any fear that such places might be dreary. I recall this one as positively gay—bristling and bustling and resonant, untouched by the strenuous note, for instance, of Hawthorne's cooperative Blithedale. I like to think that, in its then still almost suburban, its pleasantly heterogeneous quarter, now oppressively uniform, it was close to where Balzac had ended his life, though I question its identity—as for a while I tried not to—with the scene itself of the great man's catastrophe. Round its high-walled garden at all events he would have come and gone—a throb of inference that had for some years indeed to be postponed for me. . . ." [13] In view of the fact that as a distinguished literary critic Henry James, Jr. was to consider Balzac the greatest of all novelists, "the first and foremost member of his craft," these personal childhood experiences so close to the scene of his idol's poor and lonely life were to take on a very special coloring. Balzac's Paris of 1830-1840, the pre-Haussmann Paris, was still very much in evidence in 1856, including such sites as the Maison Vauquer, which James was later to speak of as the "most portentous setting of the scene in all the literature of fiction," at #24 Rue Neuve Sainte-Geneviève. Here *Le Père Goriot* was set; here old Goriot suffered and died in sharp contrast to the surroundings of the adored daughters for whom he stripped himself to the last sou; so, in 1856-1857, Harry James lived in similar luxuries, innocently unaware of the Balzacian section on the south side of the Seine, which he was later to know so well in its literary aspect.

The James parents must have had but one objective in mind during these months of residence in Paris, as far as the children's education was concerned—namely, the acquiring of the French language. This insistence upon the "languages" had impelled their departure from New York, had settled them in Switzerland, and caused them, in part at least, to leave London. The tutorial arrangements having failed with M. Lerambert, it mattered little what sort of school the boys attended as long as the instruction in French was of the best. On no other basis, even that of the wildest idealism of Fourier, would the elder James have sent the boys to the Institution Fezandié, for it was apparently one of the most experimental of progressive schools in 19th century France. It was not limited to children, but open to all ages of both sexes, nor did it offer the conventional curriculum of instruction; it was, rather, a sort of Parisian Brook Farm

in which all members of the institution met together in a kind of
glorified well-being of general intellectual, cultural, and spiritual
advancement, all conducted under the severe demands of the French
tongue. Its very freedom from regular classes and courses attracted
the interest of Harry, who never found ordinary rosters and cur-
riculums much to his liking or ability. While to William such schooling as that offered by M. Fezandié was far from attractive, Harry
thought back on it in a favorable light, remembering vividly its odd
procedures and one or two of its unique instructors: "I in any case
can't pretend not to have been most appealed to by that especial
phase of our education from which the pedagogic process as com-
monly understood was most fantastically absent. It excelled in this
respect, the Fezandié phase, even others exceptionally appointed,
heaven knows, for the supremacy; and yet its glory is that it was no
poor blank, but that it fairly creaked and groaned, heatedly overflowed, with its wealth. We were *externes,* the three of us, but we
remained in general to luncheon; coming home then, late in the
afternoon, with an almost sore experience of multiplicity and vivacity
of contact. For the beauty of it all was that the Institution was,
speaking technically, not more a *pensionnat,* with prevailingly English
and American pupils, than a *pension,* with mature beneficiaries of
both sexes, and that our two categories were shaken up together
to the liveliest effect. This had been M. Fezandié's grand conception;
a son of the south, bald and slightly replete, with a delicate beard, a
quick but anxious, rather melancholy eye and a slim, graceful, juvenile
wife . . . I see him as a Daudet *méridinal,* but of the sensitive, not the
sensual, type, as something of a rolling stone, rolling rather down
hill—he had enjoyed some arrested, possibly blighted, connection
in America—and as ready always again for some new application
of faith and funds. If fondly failing in the least to see why the
particular application in the Rue Balzac—the body of pensioners
ranging from infancy to hoary eld—shouldn't have been a bright
success could have made it one, it would have been a most original
triumph." [14]

The venture was original for all concerned, but hardly a triumph.
There were "lessons" from time to time, attended by ladies and

gentlemen, young men and young women, many of Anglo-Saxon
homes, seated along long boards of green cloth, all taking *dictées*
from M. Fezandié himself. Often, however, they were presented by
"the most remarkable M. Bonnefons, whom we believed to have
been a superannuated actor (he above all such a model for Daudet!)
and who interrupted our abashed readings aloud to him of the French
classics older and newer by wondrous reminiscences and even imitations of Talma. He moved among us in a cloud of legend, the
wigged and wrinkled, the impassioned, though I think alas underfed,
M. Bonnefons: it was our belief that he 'went back,' beyond the first
Empire, to the scenes of the Revolution—this perhaps partly by
reason, in the first place, of his scorn of our pronunciation, when
we met it, of the sovereign word *liberté,* the poverty of which, our
deplorable 'libbeté,' without r's, he mimicked and derided, sounding
the right, the revolutionary form out splendidly, with thirty r's, the
prolonged beat of a drum. . . . There were times when he but paced
up and down and round the table—I see him as never seated, but
always on the move, a weary Wandering Jew of the *classe;* but in
particular I hear him recite to us the combat with the Moors from
Le Cid and show us how Talma, describing it, seemed to crouch
down on his haunches in order to spring up again terrifically to the
height of 'Nous nous levons alors!' which M. Bonnefons rendered
as if on the carpet there fifty men at least had leaped to their feet.
But he threw off these broken lights with a quick relapse to indifference; he didn't like the Anglo-Saxon—of the children of Albion
at least his view was low; on his American specimens he had, I
observed, more mercy; and this imperfection of sympathy (the
question of Waterloo apart) rested, it was impossible not to feel,
on his so resenting the dishonour suffered at our hands by his beautiful tongue, to which, as the great field of elocution, he was patriotically devoted. I think he fairly loathed our closed English vowels
and confused consonants, our destitution of sounds that he recognised
as sounds. . . . We of the younger persuasion at least must have done
his ear less violence than those earnest ladies from beyond the sea
and those young Englishmen qualifying for examinations and careers
who flocked with us both to the plausibly spread and the severely

disgarnished table, and on whose part I seem to see it again an effort of anguish to 'pick up' the happy idiom that we had unconsciously acquired. French, in the fine old formula of those days, so much diffused, 'was the language of the family'; but I think it must have appeared to these students in general a family of which the youngest members were but scantly kept in their place. We piped with a greater facility and to a richer need of recognition; which sounds as if we might have become, in these strange collocations, fairly offensive little prigs. That was none the less not the case, for there were, oddly enough, a few French boys as well, to whom on the lingual or the 'family' ground, we felt ourselves feebly relative, and in comparison with whom, for that matter, or with one of whom, I remember an occasion of my having to sink to insignificance." [15]

Supporting the old adage that an Englishman is never so English as when he is abroad, Harry James found himself profoundly impressed by the extreme insularity of many of the sons of Albion with whom he daily associated in French instruction. The attitude of condescension which Lowell was to make so notorious in his famous essay seemed to reach unbelievable heights in these young men in their criticism of everyone and everything connected with the Institution. Conservative, retiring Harry found it all a trifle terrifying, this magnificent scorn on the part of "a mightier race," poured like hot lava upon poor old Bonnefons, on good ex-Fourierist Fezandié himself, on the "beggars and beasts" who comprised the staff of waiters and bonnes, on every dish served at every déjeuner, and still more at the later meal which the James boys did not attend. All, all was "rotten." Such attitudes and expressions were not part of the James family's domestic air, though the elder James was gifted in his capacity to rant and roar out against any sort of humbug or hypocrisy. These fine, handsome, knowing, superior young Englishmen extended for Harry the range of social resources, far more so than had any Englishmen he had observed during the previous year in London. They were especially formidable one afternoon on the Champs-Elysées, passing swiftly along with fine, long British strides and in the costume of the period, costumes out of *Punch* in the 'Fifties. Harry, in company with his mother and Aunt Kate, or even worse perhaps with the governess, saw them as supermen, lording it over the inferior race with whom they temporarily had condescended to reside, and casting casually a slight sign of recognition toward the embarrassed, hesitant young American and his escort of females.

On one other occasion was Harry to receive a flash of that insular superiority against a Paris setting, but with a kindlier gesture on the part of the lordly one. Mrs. James and her son had just emerged from a visit with Pendleton cousins, then living at the Hôtel Méurice. In the gaslit glare of the Rue de Rivoli, Mrs. James was anxiously urging Harry through the cross currents of the bristling traffic, rather than depending upon him for support and escort. There and then "swung into view the most splendid, as I at least esteemed him, of my elders and betters in the Rue Balzac, who . . . with his high hat a trifle askew and his cigar actively alight, revealed to me at a glance what it was to be in full possession of Paris. There was speed in his step, assurance in his air, he was visibly, impatiently on the way; and he gave me thereby my first full image of what it was exactly to *be* on the way. He gave it the more, doubtless, through the fact that, with a flourish of the aforesaid high hat (from which the Englishman of that age was so singularly inseparable) he testified to the act of recognition, and to deference to my companion, but with a grand big-boy good-humour that—as I remember from childhood the so frequent effect of an easy patronage, compared with a topmost over-looking, on the part of an admired senior—only gave an accent to the difference. As if he cared, or could have, that I but went forth through the Paris night in the hand of my mamma; while he had greeted us with a grace that was as a beat of the very wings of freedom." [16] Unendowed with a speed in his step, an assurance in his air, or the dash and flourish of wearing a high hat, Harry James was to pass so slowly through the awkward, uncertain, dependent years of youth and early manhood, through a very gradual process of winning his freedom; and even more prolonged was to be his way leading eventually into the very fabric of that English culture and grand style, the town club and country house society in which he was to achieve distinction as a man and as an artist. This youthful

awe, inspired in his eye and mind by these associations in Paris, in
all probability laid more of the groundwork for that intense attraction toward the English that he had already begun to cultivate. "Of
such shreds, at any rate, proves to be woven the stuff of young sensibility—when memory . . . rummages over our old trunkful of spiritual
duds and, drawing forth ever so tenderly this, that and the other
tattered web, holds up the pattern to the light." [17]

As the autumn months settled down into a different pattern and
tone, Willy and Harry undertook long walks, free from escort of
elders or company of their younger brothers. Mostly they seemed to
be measuring the space between their apartment on Rue d'Angoulême
and the gallery of the Luxembourg, a considerable walk, "every step
of which, either way we took it, led us with some interesting, some
admirable image. . . ." They would cross the Champs-Elysées to
the Seine, and go over the nearest bridge. The Pont de l'Alma,
constructed in 1856, was slightly out of their way, while the Pont
des Invalides made a direct line from the Rond-Point across to the
quays "with their innumerably old bookshops and print-shops";
these were displayed on the parapets, along which the boys sauntered,
stopping occasionally over a volume, or more probably over a print,
for their interest in art was coming into early bloom. At the "long,
black Rue de Seine" they turned right and felt emotion deepening
in the face of the perspective before them—"*such* a stretch of perspective, *such* an intensity of tone as it offered in those days; where
every low-browed vitrine waylaid us and we moved in a world of
which the dark message, expressed in we couldn't have said what
sinister way too, might have been 'Art, art, art, don't you see? Learn,
little gaping pilgrims, what *that* is!' Oh we learned, that is we tried
to, as hard as ever we could, and were fairly well at it, I always felt,
even by the time we had passed up into that comparatively short but
wider and finer vista of the Rue de Tournon, which in those days
more abruptly crowned the more compressed approach and served
in a manner as a great outer vestibule to the Palace. Style, dimly
described, looked down there, as with conscious encouragement, from
the high grey-headed, clear-faced, straight-standing old houses—
very much as if wishing to say 'Yes, small staring jeune homme, we

are dignity and memory and measure, we are conscience and proportion and taste, not to mention strong sense too: for all of which good
things take us . . . ' " The Rue de Tournon, on which the Daudet
brothers were then habitants, was heavily cobbled and a little grass-
grown, looking quite like a fine old street in some provincial town.
Then too the "wide mouth of the present Boulevard Saint-Michel,
a short way round the corner, had not yet been forced open to the
exhibition of more or less glittering fangs: old Paris still pressed
round the Palace and its gardens, which formed the right, the
sober social antithesis to the 'elegant' Tuileries." [18]

The approach to the gallery of the Luxembourg was made in part
under the guidance of a volume, *Les Français Peints par Eux-Mêmes,*
with fine woodcuts by Gavarni, Grandville, and Henri-Monnier, some
of which the boys copied in pen-and-ink sketches. "This gild-edged
and double-columned octavo it was that first disclosed to me, fore-
stalling a better ground of acquaintance, the great name of Balzac,
who, in common with every 'light' writer of his day, contributed
to its pages: hadn't I pored over his exposition there of the contrasted types of L'Habituée des Tuileries and L'Habituée du Luxembourg?—finding it very *serré,* in fact what I didn't then know enough
to call very stodgy, but flavoured withal and a trifle lubricated by
Gavarni's two drawings, which had somehow so much, in general,
to say." As in their approach to the theatre, so in their introduction
to a serious consideration of art, the James children were given a
helpful preconditioning at home, having access to books and plates
and above all to the stimulating commentary of their father. This
academic preparation took on immediate significance as they entered
the Gallery of Living French Artists (Musée du Luxembourg), which
contained what was considered in 1856 as the best work of living
French painters; with characteristic French règle, it was decreed that
"at the expiration of ten years from the death of an artist his works
may be transferred to the Louvre." [19] The work of contemporary
French artists was of particular interest because William James, during this Paris residence of 1857, was receiving lessons in painting
at the atelier of M. Léon Cogniet, whose *Marius among the Ruins
of Carthage* was exhibited at the Luxembourg and who was then one

of the best art teachers in Paris.[20] The fact that the oldest James boy
was accepted in the atelier indicates that his ability in drawing and
painting was above average and led, in the next few years, to his
considering art as a career. With Harry James there was never such
a question in relation to painting, for he showed no talent in spite
of his marked attraction toward the art.

"Most of the works of the modern schools that we most admired
are begging their bread, I fear, from door to door—that is from
one provincial museum or dim back seat to another; though we were
on much-subsequent returns to draw a long breath for the saved
state of some of the great things as to which our faith had been
clearest. It had been clearer for none, I recover, than for Couture's
Romains de la Décadence,[21] recently acclaimed, at that time, as the
last word of the grand manner, but of the grand manner modernised,
humanised, philosophised, redeemed from academic death; so that
it was to this master's school that the young American contemporary
flutter taught its wings to fly straightest, and that I could never, in
the long aftertime, face his masterpiece and all its old meanings and
marvels without a rush of memories and a stir of ghosts. . . . We
were in our immediate circle to know Couture himself a little toward
the end of his life, and I was somewhat to wonder then where he
had picked up the aesthetic hint for the beautiful *Page with a Falcon*
(sic), if I have the designation right, his other great bid for style
and capture of it—which we were long to continue to suppose perhaps the rarest of all modern pictures. The feasting Romans were
conceivable enough, I mean *as* a conception; no mystery hung about
them—in the sense of one's asking one's self whence they had come
and by what romantic or roundabout or nobly-dangerous journey;
which is that air of the poetic shaken out as from strong wings when
great presences, in any one of the arts, appear to alight. What I
remember, on the other hand, of the splendid fair youth in black
velvet and satin or whatever who, while he mounts the marble staircase, shows off the great bird on his forefinger with a grace that
shows *him* off, was that it failed to help us to divine, during that
after-lapse of the glory of which I speak, by what rare chance, for
the obscured old ex-celebrity we visited, the heavens had once opened.

Poetry had swooped down, breathed on him for an hour and fled." [22]

Eugène Delacroix, their next great admiration, was then in firm possession of his laurels and continued so on through the years. Though both boys were sure about Delacroix's work, Henry, Jr., was to recall that he was sure by way of his brother's sureness, especially about *La Barque du Dante* which Willy reproduced at home, from memory aided by a lithograph.[23] The older boy, with his gift for painting and a keener insight toward appreciation, saw beauty and living interest in *La Barque* and a certain queerness which caught his eye and interest beyond Harry's. To the younger boy, less discerning at the time, Paul Delaroche's *Les Enfants d'Edouard* was thrilling beyond comparison; at thirteen he "couldn't doubt that the long-drawn odd face of the elder prince, sad and sore and sick, with his wide crimped sidelocks of fair hair and his violet legs marked by the Garter and dangling from the bed, was a reconstitution of far-off history of the subtlest and most 'last word' modern or psychological kind. I had never heard of psychology in art or anywhere else—scarcely anyone then had; but I truly felt the nameless force at play." [24] Delaroche had died that year, 1856, and the Jameses attended a commemorative show of his works given soon after his death, "in one of the rather bleak salles of the Ecole des Beaux-Arts to which access was got from the quay. There was reconstituted history if one would, in the straw-littered scaffold, the distracted ladies with three-cornered coifs and those immense hanging sleeves that made them look as if they had bath-towels over their arms; in the black, the headsman, the bandaged eyes and groping hands, of Lady Jane Grey—not less than the noble indifference of Charles the First, compromised king but perfect gentleman, at his inscrutable ease in his chair and as if on his throne, while the Puritan soldiers insult and badger him. . . ." [25] It was to their Scotch tutor, Robert Thompson of the previous year in London, that the boys were indebted for the English history and lore. These things he had "rubbed into us more than anything else and all from a fine old conservative and monarchical point of view." To imaginative Harry, Delaroche's historical pieces were fascinating in context and sufficiently skilled in arrangement of detail and in the construction of groups to carry the message with a staggering impact. To William, Delaroche did not so speak and of him no reproductions were attempted at home or in the Atelier Cogniet, though he repeatedly tried his hand at Delacroix or Decamps whom he regarded as more or less of a same rare genius. Neither Willy nor Harry was actually as yet aware of style, though they were both on the way to some conscious definition of it; they were becoming acutely aware of that mystery with which the really great work of art is touched. Willy found in Delacroix and Decamps "the ineffable, the inscrutable, and Delacroix in especial . . . the incalculable," and in feeling out such categories the boys were making a transition toward that critical acumen with which they were both to find such individual value in their different ways.[26]

The great galleries of the Louvre contained such overwhelming and bewildering treasures, to the delight of these two young American dilettantes, that the long stretches seemed to be filled with a vast, deafening chorus. "I shall never forget how—speaking, that is, for my own sense—they filled those vast halls with the influence rather of some complicated sound, diffused and reverberant, than of such visibilities as one could directly deal with. To distinguish among these, in the charged and coloured and confounding air, was difficult—it discouraged and defied; which was doubtless why my impression originally best entertained was that of those magnificent parts of the great gallery simply not inviting us to distinguish. They only arched over us in the wonder of their endless golden riot and relief, figured and flourished in perpetual revolution, breaking into great high-hung circles and symmetries of squandered picture, opening into deep outward embrasures that threw off the rest of monumental Paris somehow as a told story, a sort of wrought effect or bold ambiguity for a vista, and yet held it there, at every point, as a vast bright gage, even at moments a felt adventure, of experience." [27]

In this mystic sort of transport, Harry James felt himself carried over the bridge of *style* which vaguely brought him into "not only beauty and art and supreme design, but history and fame and power, the world in fine raised to the richest and noblest expression." The world outside, of the Second Empire, new, radiant, and elegant, complemented the world of the Galerie d'Apollon which, in 1856, created a crisis in the inner life of the boy. The experience was like that of a dream fantasy; he imagined himself pushing his shoulder against the locked and barred door which excluded him from entering the fullest appreciation of these priceless treasures. Amid a great storm of thunder and lightning, flashing through the deep embrasures of the high windows at the right and vaulted arches above, his young imagination, in a sudden wild start, forced open the door through which he was, in this immense hallucination, carried forward down the glorious hall, over the polished floor, into the brilliant chamber of recognition. In the full illumination of this release, Harry stood gaping at Géricault's *Radeau de la Méduse,* "*the* sensation, for splendour and terror of interest, of that juncture to me, and ever afterwards to be associated, along with two or three other more or less contemporary products, Guérin's *Burial of Atala,* Prudhon's *Cupid and Psyche* (sic), David's helmetted Romanisms, Madame Vigée-Lebrun's 'ravishing' portrait of herself and her little girl, with how can I say what foretaste (as determined by that instant as if the hour had struck from a clock) of all the fun, confusedly speaking, that one was going to have, and the kind of life, always of the queer so-called inward sort, tremendously 'sporting' in its way . . . that one was going to lead." [28]

This sense of bliss was attended by the sense of a freedom of contact and appreciation which from that year grew steadily; at first, however, it was hampered by the realization that appreciation was an endless process, discouragingly boundless. Going to the Louvre became to Harry something far more than a routine part of the tutorial efforts of M. Lerambert or Mlle. Danse; he was permitted to go there and elsewhere unattended even by Willy. On such "uncorrectedly juvenile" visits "the house of life and the palace of art became so mixed and interchangeable . . . that an excursion to look at pictures would have but half expressed my afternoon. I had looked at pictures, looked and looked again, at the vast Veronese, at Murillo's moon-borne Madonna, at Leonardo's almost unholy dame with the folded hands, treasures of the Salon Caré as that display was then composed; but I had also looked at France and looked at Europe, looked even at America as Europe itself might be conceived so to look, looked at history, as a still-felt past and a complacently personal future, at society, manners, types, characters, possibilities and prodigies and mysteries of fifty sorts; and all in the light of being splendidly 'on my own,' as I supposed it . . . and of going and coming along that interminable and incomparable Seine-side front of the Palace against which young sensibility felt itself almost rub, for endearment and consecration, as a cat invokes the friction of a protective piece of furniture. Such were at any rate some of the vague processes—I see for how utterly vague they must show—of picking up an education . . ." [29]

Since the acquiring of the French language was the basic and most practical educational aspect for the James children during this year in Paris, the theatres presumably would have offered delightful opportunities of "picking up an education." The Paris stage, how-ever, quite free from the Victorian restrictions of drama in London and New York, presented moral issues which even the broadest views of the elder James could not ignore. In later years the boys could not remember whether or not their parents had set before them the reasons for slighting the theatre, but they grasped the situa-tion intuitively, and by occasional "depressing hearsay" that the French drama "great, strange and important, was as much out of relation to our time of life, our so little native strain and our culti-vated innocence, as the American and English had been directly addressed to them." [30] If they had been taken in the Paris of 1856-1857, as they had been during the previous years, in London and New York, they might have heard some of the finest theatrical celebrities of the times. Rachel was still alive, but dying of consump-tion, her brilliant career already becoming a thing of the past.[31] Mlle. Mars, "the idol of the Parisian public," had died nearly ten years earlier, but in spirit still hovered about the theatres in which, when she was well past sixty, she had played, to the unqualified delight of all, such ingenue roles as that of twenty-year-old Célimène in Moliere's *Le Misanthrope*.[32] Mlle. George, whose success stemmed partly from the favor she won as mistress of Napoleon Bonaparte, was living in retirement, having been pronounced by Théophile Gautier as *"la réalisation la plus complète du rêve de la muse tra-*

gique." [33] She had returned to the stage for a season in 1856-1857,
"a massive, a monstrous antique," Harry James then heard her
described, but the Jameses missed her, as they also missed Virginie
Déjazet, Frédérick Lemaître, Etienne Mélingue, Joseph Samson, and
a host of others whose performances were filling the boxes and stalls.[34]
The dramatists of the moment were Emile Augier, the younger
Dumas, Eugène Scribe, Madame de Girardin, and François Ponsard,
with Victorian Sardou struggling toward his first plays, written for
Déjazet in collaboration with Vanderbuch. But of such plays and
actors the children saw few. They were conducted for the most part
to the Cirque d'Eté, the Cirque d'Hiver, the Théâtre du Cirque, and
other such houses of entertainment whose names appeared a comparative safety.[35] What the quality of French was at these lesser
houses is a question. A guide book of the time comments on the
scope of instruction available in the thirty or more playhouses,
designed to amuse every class of people from the wealthy and noble
to the workman and his family of Faubourg St. Marceau: "To the
English or American visitor, or resident in Paris, the theatre is not
merely an amusement, it is one of the very best sources of instruction
and practice, in a language so difficult to acquire, without constant
exercise both of ear and tongue, as the French. He that comes fresh
from grammar and dictionary, and can read *Gil Blas* all through,
will by no means find himself at first up to the idioms of the Théâtre
Français, still less to the slang and brogue of the Porte St. Martin
and smaller houses of the Boulevards. His best plan will be to read
beforehand the play which he is going to see acted; cheap editions
of almost all the pieces in the repertoire may usually be bought at the
door, or at Barba's in the Palais Royal, Galerie de Chartres, 2 and
3." [36]

Such a suggestion very much resembles the system followed by
Willy and Harry in New York and London where their parents
read and discussed plays with them before the family attended the
productions. In this case, however, a warning note is sounded in this
same guidebook: "Most of the theatres are devoted to light comedy
with music (Vaudeville), and the subjects and treatments of many
of the pieces render them unfit for the ears of English ladies." What

was unfit for Victorian ladies was, at least to a degree, unfit for American boys entering their 'teens, particularly those being brought up in a "cultivated innocence." The seamy side of life, if it actually represented life, the elder James had little if any objection to, but immorality presented for its own sake, or merely for the sake of amusing, devoid of any comment on life, was highly objectionable. Unfortunately a good deal of French theatrical entertainment was more or less of this nature since the whole fabric of the Gallic ethical concept was quite different from the Anglo-Saxon. With caution and discrimination, then, the Jameses approached the Paris theatres.

When not presenting equestrian or gymnastic performances, much in the style of Niblo's, Barnum's, or Franconi's in New York, these Paris cirques offered a type of entertainment, glittering, enchanting, and full of a preponderant moral point. Harry was particularly impressed with one entitled *Le Diable d'Argent,* "a radiant revelation—kept before us a whole long evening and as an almost blinding glare; which was quite right for the *donnée,* the gradual shrinkage of the Shining One, the money-master hugely inflated at first, to all the successive degrees of loose bagginess as he leads the reckless young man he has originally contracted with from dazzling pleasure to pleasure, till at last he is a mere shrivelled silver string such as you could almost draw through a keyhole. That was the striking moral, for the young man, however regaled, had been somehow 'sold'; which *we* hadn't in the least been, who had had all his pleasures and none of his penalty, whatever this was to be." [37]

More in line with higher theatrical art was an evening at the Théâtre du Gymnase Dramatique, dating back to 1820 and built, ironically enough, on the site of the ancient cemetery of Notre Dame de Bonne-Nouvelle, on the Boulevarde Bonne-Nouvelle. The house in early years had been given over to vaudeville which was gradually abandoned for serious drama, Scribe having written most of his plays for it. Squeezed in between his mother and Aunt Kate, in a stuffy baignoire, Harry was transported by the delights of Madame de Girardin's *Une Femme qui Déteste son Mari* with a cast including Mesdames Rose Chéri, Melánie, Delaporte, and Victoria (afterwards Victoria-Lafontaine).[38] It was a thrilling story of an admirable lady

who, to save her loyalist husband, during the Revolution, pretends
to the most Jacobin opinions, representing herself as a loyal citoyenne
in order to keep him safely concealed in her house. He is kept
crammed behind a wainscot panel which the wife secretly opens to
give him food and air. Harry was reduced to a state of exhaustion
by the intense excitement of these secret moments of tremendous
strain, followed by the even worse strain of Madame's receiving the
investigating Terrorist commissaries, alertly suspicious but successfully baffled. In addition to this main theme of awful suspense was
the sub-theme of the husband's mother and sister who are not in the
secret but believe him concealed elsewhere and in more terrible
danger. Over and above the heights of such dramatic moments
appeared always the vision of Rose Chéri, acting rather finely the
emaciated woman with a high bulging forehead, an extremely odd
and osseous appearance not unlike that of Rachel's.

In the same class as Madame de Girardin's drama was that of
Francois Ponsard, *Ce qui Plaît aux Femmes,* which Willy and Harry
saw not in 1856 but in 1860, the year the play appeared.[39] The
Jameses were then en route to Newport, at the very end of this period
of European residence. While the play had scant success, it left upon
Harry "ineffaceable images." Mademoiselle Fargeuil[40] was the heroine, a fine lady whom a pair of rivals seek to win by offering her what
will most please her; one treats her to a brilliant fête, staged effectively
as a play within a play much to the boys' delight, and the other, by
contrast, an attic of misery "into which the more cunning suitor
introduces her just in time to save a poor girl, the tenant of the place,
from being ruinously, that is successfully, tempted by a terrible old
woman, a prowling *revendeuse,* who dangles before her the condition on which so pretty a person may enjoy every comfort. Her
happier sister, the courted young widow, intervenes in time, rein-
forces her tottering virtue, opens for her an account with baker and
butcher, and, doubting no longer which flame is to be crowned, charmingly shows us that what pleases women most is the exercise of
charity." [41] Thus, in the dingy, old Théâtre du Vaudeville, on the
Place de la Bourse, where Dumas, *fils,* achieved immortal fame with

his *Dame aux Camélias* in 1852, the James boys paid tribute to Ponsard and his moral piece.

In the cast of Ponsard's *Ce qui Plaît aux Femmes* with Mlle. Fargeuil was Mlle. Pierson, a juvenile beauty in her teens, to whom the James boys had taken a fancy in 1856 when she appeared first at the Théâtre de l'Ambigu Comique. In roles of the coquette or ingenue Mlle. Pierson brought a freshness of life to the old Ambigu on the Boulevard Saint-Martin, the original of which dated back to 1769, being one of the oldest strongholds of marionettes, vaudeville, and melodrama in all Paris. From her beginnings in the provinces, Mlle. Pierson made her way to the Ambigu and on to the Théâtre du Gymnase, and so to the Théâtre du Vaudeville, ultimately arriving on the stage of the Théâtre Français for a career whose span was to strike Henry James, Jr., as fabulous, in long after years. Mlle. Fargeuil he was also to admire in the after-time, "the time after she had given all Sardou's earlier successes the help of her shining firmness, when she had passed from interesting comedy and even more romantic drama—not less, perhaps still more, interesting, with Sardou's *Patrie* as a bridge—to the use of the bigger brush of the Ambigu and other houses of melodrama." [42] In looking back on this comparatively brief introduction to the French theatre of 1856-1857, it seemed that everything "but the 'interpretation,' the personal . . . had kinds and degrees of weakness and futility, say even falsity." The playhouses were places of almost physical torture, and the old thinness of the school of Scribe, the emptiness of the vaudeville tradition, plus the downright absurdity of the romantic and melodramatic fare offered little toward the education of the young Americans. At the time, however, Harry James was not conscious of such deficiencies in these experiences; they held for him, actually, a kind of intensity. Decades later, when his own efforts as a dramatist had failed, when he was acutely aware of dramatic values with which he might look sharply, in retrospect, at these Paris days, he wrote: " . . . All of which leaves us with this interesting vision of a possibly great truth, the truth that you can't have more than one kind of intensity—intensity worthy of the name—at once. The intensity of our period is that of the 'producer's' and machinist's, to which

add even that of architect, author and critic. Between which derivative kind of that article, as we may call it, and the other, the immediate kind, it would appear that you have absolutely to choose." [43]
There can be little doubt that, whether as a boy in his teens or a man
over seventy, Henry James would choose that immediate intensity
which established in him such strong currents of response to the
plays and players who stood before him, depending only upon their
good faith and his.

In March of 1857, with the passage of a new tariff measure in
the United States, a sharp commercial and banking panic occurred
with alarming effects which temporarily paralyzed manufacturing
and endangered many of the James family's investments. When
reverberations reached Henry James, Sr., in Paris, he felt it wise to
sub-lease the Paris apartment and withdraw to Boulogne, at least
for the summer months, enjoying the advantages of that resort and
at the same time economizing on family expenses. The move was
an enforced one, undertaken with the expectation of returning to
Paris when the crisis in America subsided. The stay at Boulogne
proved to be a much longer one than anyone imagined and resulted
in completely new arrangements for the children, arrangements very
satisfactory to Willy and the younger children but not for Harry.
To him it was simply a retreat from the most fascinating of cities.

One incident occurred, however, before they left Paris, which gave
Harry a literary stimulation that ultimately carried him far into the
art of fiction. On a table in his father's study, he saw a copy of the
Revue de Paris. Casually turning the pages, he chanced upon the
arresting words: "Madame Bovary: Moeurs de Province" by Gustave Flaubert. The moment was, for the boy, little short of historic.
Standing there before the fire, his back against the highly ornamental
French chimney-piece, the sunny little salon resounding faintly with
the cheerful outside clatter coming through the partly opened window, he was absorbed with what he could make out of the installment.[44] Ignorant of what had preceded and not to know until much
later what followed, he felt at once a closeness, almost a kinship
with the author. It was an intangible thing, vague and uncertain;
but the printed pages, the room, the window, the sunlight—every-

thing about the moment was captured and crystallized in it. Twenty years were to pass before the American boy could know the full significance of the French novelist. When he did know, however, he published an essay, in 1876, "M. Flaubert's Theory," in which a certain passage turns one's thought abruptly back to the time when the critic first saw the name Gustave Flaubert. While ostensibly the passage presents Flaubert's theory as a novelist, it represents concisely Harry James's attitude toward life in 1856, the attitude with which he had been responding to Paris:

Human life, we may imagine his saying, is before all things a spectacle, an occupation and entertainment for the eyes. What our eyes show us is all that we are sure of; so with this we will at any rate begin. As this is infinitely curious and entertaining, if we know how to look at it, and as such looking consumes a great deal of time and space, it is very possible that with this also we may end. We admit nevertheless that there is something else, beneath and behind, that belongs to the realm of vagueness and uncertainty, and into this we must occasionally dip. It crops up sometimes irrepressibly, and of course we do not positively count it out. On the whole we will leave it to take care of itself and let it come off as it may.[45]

NOTES

1. Hugo lived in the Place des Vosges from 1832 to 1848. What is now the Hugo Museum has been well marked by both French history and literature. Dumas used it as the home of the sinister Milady in *The Three Guardsmen,* making use especially of his personal knowledge of the back entrance that still leads toward the Rue Saint-Antoine by way of the Impasse Guéménee. "Actual use of it was made during the street fighting of the 1848 Revolution by National Guardsmen, who, bound from the Rue Saint-Antoine to head off the soldiers of Louis-Philippe in the square beyond, invaded Hugo's apartment. The story is told that the leader of the band found some written sheets on the table, and read them aloud to his followers. It was the manuscript of *Les Misérables,* just begun, but not finished until sixteen years later." Arthur Bartlett Maurice, *The Paris of the Novelists,* New York, Doubleday, Page & Company, 1919, 20.

2. *A Small Boy and Others*, 325, 326.
3. *Ibid.*, 330-332.
4. The James property at #58 West Fourteenth Street, New York City, was leased by Henry James, Sr., from Joel Stevens, November 15, 1847. These premises were bought by Mr. James from George J. Rogers on April 30, 1851, and sold by him to Eliza H. Greene on November 26, 1865. The James family, therefore, owned the house for ten years after leaving it in 1855, for their travels abroad. For details of the exchange of this property consult *Index of Conveyances Recorded in the Office of the Register of the City and County of New York, New York,* McSpedon and Baker, 1857-1865.
5. MS. letter from Mrs. Henry James, Sr., to Catherine Barber James of Albany, August 25, 1856, Houghton Library, Harvard University.
6. *A Small Boy and Others*, 335, 336.
7. Mrs. Christopher Pearse Cranch, who was then living in Paris and whose husband, the celebrated Unitarian minister and member of the Transcendentalist movement, had contributed poems to *The Dial, The Western Messenger,* and other magazines, in a vein sympathetic to the ideals of Emerson and Henry James, Sr.; Cranch later translated the *Aeneid* (1875), and became known as a painter.
8. Perry, *op. cit.,* I, 122-124.
9. Comte Fleury, *Memoirs of the Empress Eugénie,* New York, D. Appleton & Co., 1920, 98.
10. Emile Zola was not in Paris at this time. He arrived in Paris in February, 1858, and lived with his mother at #63 Rue Monsieur le Prince, the street which Daudet described vividly in *Les Rois en Exil* as the home of Elysée Méraut. Even Balzac did not achieve such minute study of Paris, its networks of streets and boulevards, as did Zola in his history of the Rougon-Macquart family.
11. *A Small Boy and Others*, 332, 333.
12. *Ibid.*, 334.
13. *Ibid.*, 364, 365.
14. *Ibid.*, 365, 366.
15. *Ibid.*, 367-369.
16. *Ibid.*, 378.
17. *Ibid.*, 378, 379.
18. *Ibid.*, 338, 339.
19. *A Handbook for Visitors to Paris,* London, John Murray, 1864, 179.
20. Léon Cogniet (1794-1881) had been a pupil of Pierre-March Guérin (1774-1833); in the 'Fifties Cogniet was enjoying the height of his reputation as a teacher and artist.
21. Thomas Couture (1815-1879) exhibited his *Romans of the Decadence* in 1847 and effected a reform, "putting the official art of France on a modern and practical basis. Couture felt strongly the lack of painter-like quality in David and even in Ingres. He loved succinct and colorful brush-work, and sought it in the suspected

Romantics, in Hals, and in Velasquez. He substituted for the gospel of the thrilling contour that of the exquisitely painted bit—*le morceau bien peint.* . . . In the great picture *The Romans of the Decadence,* painted in 1847, he established himself beyond cavil as a classicist, and nothing he did thereafter could forfeit this reputation." F. J. Mather, Jr., *Modern Painting,* New York, Henry Holt and Company, 1927, 117, 118.

22. *A Small Boy and Others,* 340, 341, 342. Couture's painting, *The Falconer,* was done in 1855. One critic states: "All the modern talk of structural planes, the dogma of the square touch, the cult of the *morceau bien fait,* derive from Couture. What counts in this art is to multiply brilliantly painted surfaces . . . Couture in his pictures, in his teaching and in his books, turns over and over the problem of fine painting, seeking to solve it by recipes. Directly or indirectly most of that painting to which journalism inevitably affixes the adjective brilliant has proceeded from him. Mather, *op. cit.,* 120. Another critic writes that Couture's appeal is "rather emotional than either dramatic or aesthetic; unconsciously, Couture was inclined to realism; consciously, he was a grandiose classicist." S. C. Kaines Smith, *An Outline of Modern Painting in Europe and America,* New York, William Morrow & Company, 1931.

23. Eugène Delacroix (1799-1866) appeared for the first time in the Salon of Paris in 1822 with his *La Barque du Dante;* two years later his *Massacre at Scio* aroused intense indignation among artists of the older school, one of whom called it a massacre of all academic rules, of all traditions. His *Liberty Leading the People,* 1830, caught and personified the French spirit toward liberty and democracy.

24. *A Small Boy and Others,* 344. Paul Delaroche (1797-1886) was much given to historical paintings called by one critic "the wearisome historical puppet shows" that indicate "how puerile a thing romanticism without romance can become." S. C. Kaines Smith, *op. cit.,* 6. In an essay on Delacroix, Charles Baudelaire states: "The only man whose name could evoke harsh words from his aristocratic lips was Paul Delaroche. He found no excuse for the latter's works, and he had an indelible memory of the way he had suffered from Delaroche's dirty and bitter painting—*done with ink and shoe-polish,* as Theophile Gautier once said." Charles Baudelaire, *Eugène Delacroix, His Life and His Work,* New York, Lear Publishers, 1947, 78.

25. *A Small Boy and Others,* 344, 345. Among the most celebrated of historical paintings by Delaroche are: *Death of Queen Elizabeth,* which created a sensation in 1829; *Cromwell by the Coffin of Charles I; Sons of Edward; Lady Jane Grey;* and *Assassination of the Duc de Guise.* One critic states: "Delaroche . . . was slyly trespassing on the ground of his dreaded contemporary, Delacroix. Only when Delacroix served his history hot and raw and concentrated, Delaroche served his diluted, cooled, as it were safely pickled in facile domestic

tears. He was a fair portraitist, and a narrowly intelligent teacher. He had the shrewdness to depart both from the publicism of David and from the isolated aestheticism of Ingres, in favor of an anecdotal and sentimental art eminently suited to the *nouveaux riches* of the Orleanist régime." Mather, *op. cit.,* 107.

26. Alexandre Decamps (1803-1860) was noted as a master colorist of Oriental scenes, but more emotional than Delacroix; he shared with Paul Huet the first French adventures into the realm of naturalistic landscape, the search for such scenes bringing him into contact with Oriental subjects, dominated by sunlight.

27. *A Small Boy and Others,* 345, 346.

28. *Ibid.,* 350. Jean - Louis - André - Théodore Géricault (1791 - 1824) created a sensation with his *Raft of the Medusa,* exhibited in the Paris Salon of 1819 and in London in 1820. The rigid classicists of the time were shocked by the picture's terrible realism "that un-flinching record of despair and agony and death, of contorted figures and livid flesh on the tragic raft of the lost frigate," for which he had made studies of the dead and dying in the hospitals of Paris so that no aspect of the realistic might escape him. S. C. Kaines Smith, *op. cit.,* 5. The painting strongly influenced Delacroix in such works as the *Massacre at Scio.* Baron Pierre-Narcisse Guérin (1774-1833) was a pupil of Regnault who inspired his taste for the antique. In addition to the *Burial of Atala,* Guérin was noted for his *Phaedra Accusing Hippolyta before Theseus;* Pierre-Paul Prud'hon (1758-1823) did the decoration of the Laocoon Gallery in the Louvre in 1799, but is remembered principally for his portraits and such works as *Psyché Sleeping;* Jacques-Louis David (1748-1825) was cele-brated for his fine series of portraits and magnificent historical scenes, many of which dealt with Roman subjects, such as *Oath of the Horatii, Rape of the Sabines,* etc.; the portrait by Madame Vigée-Lebrun (1755-1842) is found in the Salle Daru of the Louvre and is noted for its "look of sensibility."

29. *A Small Boy and Others,* 352. Paolo Veronese (1528-1588), succes-sor to Tintoretto, was the Venetian master who came at the very crest of the Renaissance; his brilliance of color and elaborateness of sub-ject, plus his grandeur of scale swept his work to realms of great splendor and extravagance. Notable especially are such vast canvasses as *Supper at Cana of Galilee* and *The Supper at the House of Simon, the Pharisee, Susannah and the Elders* and *Christ Carrying the Cross;* Bartolomé-Esteban Murillo (1616-1682), celebrated Spanish painter, reflected the Church faith of the people at the time of Velazquez who expressed the court. "A religious painter largely, though doing some *genre* subjects like his beggar-boy groups, he sought for religious fervor and found, only too often, sentimentality. His madonnas are usually after the Carlo Dolci pattern, though never so excessive in

sentiment . . . he became misty, veiled in light and effeminate in outline, though still holding grace." John C. Van Dyke, *History of Painting,* New York, Longmans, Green, and Co., 1901, 182. The work referred to, by Leonardo da Vinci (1452-1519), is, of course, his *La Gioconda,* or *Mona Lisa.*

30. *A Small Boy and Others,* 354.

31. Rachel (Elizabeth Felix) (1821-1858), daughter of a poor Jewish peddler, was born in Switzerland and after a childhood of acting in the provinces and small theatres made her debut at the Théatre Français on June 12, 1838, as Camille in Corneille's *Horace;* she was especially acclaimed in Racine's *Bajazet,* but in *Phedre,* on January 21, 1843, won her greatest success; she toured America in 1855, but with small success.

32. Mlle. Mars (1779-1847), was a member of the Comédie Française from 1795-1839, playing over one hundred and nine roles, principally ingenue parts; she retired from the stage in 1841.

33. Mlle. George (Marguerita Josephine Weimer), 1787-1867, left the theatre in 1849, returning for an occasional season and maintaining her reputation to the end.

34. Virginie Déjazet (1797-1875), was Rachel's teacher and patron to Sardou, acting several of his plays in a house she took in 1859, calling it the Théatre-Déjazet. "The dramas written for Déjazet by M. Sardou were the only new plays in which the sexagenarian actress was successful; and their success drew their author from his obscurity, and proved his possession of the dramatic faculty." Brander Matthews, *French Dramatists of the 19th Century,* New York, Charles Scribner's Sons, 1905, 174.

35. Cirque d'Été was near the Rond-Point on the Champs-Élysées, holding performances every evening (including Sunday, usually a gala day), from April to October, beginning at six o'clock; Cirque d'Hiver was on the Boulevard des Filles-du-Calvaire, giving performances every evening from November to May; Cirque de l'Impératrice was another popular amusement center, a short distance up the Champs-Elysées, "A large and very prettily fitted-up circus, in which excellent equestrian and gymnastic performances are given during the summer . . . affording a very agreeable way of spending one's evening after the promenade. Seats, 1 fr. and 2 frs." *A Handbook for Visitors to Paris,* London, John Murray, 1864, 234, 325.

36. *Ibid.* In describing the theatres this handbook states: "In the centre of the pit, occupying the best places may often be seen from 20 to 50 shabbily dressed men, seated in a compact body, and easily distinguished by the simultaneous movement of their hands. These are the *claque,* a hired and horny-handed body under a regular leader, paid to attend and applaud by signal; and perhaps the strongest illustration of the habitual submission of the French to dictation." Henry James, Jr., heard Gustave Flaubert declare that such elements,

in addition to the alien and polyglot "barbarian presence, in stalls and boxes," caused the ruin of the French theatre "through the assumption of judgeship by a bench to whom the very values of the speech of author and actor were virtually closed, or at the best uncertain." *A Small Boy and Others,* 356.

37. *A Small Boy and Others,* 355.
38. Madame de Girardin was a successful *femme de lettres française* whose plays were enjoying popularity at this time: *C'est la faute du mari* (1851), *Lady Tartufe* (1853), *La Joie fait peur* (1854), and *Le Chapeau d'un horloger* (1855); Mme. Chéri (1824-1861) was a star of the Gymnase during the 'Forties, especially in such roles as Clarisse Harlowe, Philiberte, and Diane de Lys; Victoria-Lafontaine made her debut at the Gymnase in 1857 under the name of Victoria, later marrying Louis Marie-Henrie Lafontaine. In 1857 she was the young ingenue, having been born about 1840.
39. Francois Ponsard (1814-1867) made a great success in 1843 with *Lucréce,* followed by *L'Honneur et l'Argent,* 1853, dealing with commercialism in the society of the day; *Charlotte Corday,* 1850, *Ulysse,* 1852, and *La Bourse,* 1856, gained him a wide public.
40. Mlle. Fargeuil (1819-1896) made her debut at the Opéra-Comique, but upon the failure of her voice entered vaudeville in 1836, achieving success at the Gymnase in the 'Forties and at the Vaudeville in the 'Fifties.
41. *A Small Boy and Others,* 358.
42. *Ibid.,* 359. Sardou's *Patrie* was first produced at the Ambigu on March 18, 1869. It was a historical drama, laid in the Netherlands and proved to be one of Sardou's finest plays. It was appropriately dedicated to John Lothrop Motley, whose *Rise of the Dutch Republic* (3 vols., 1856), followed by the *History of the United Netherlands* (4 vols., 1860, 1867), had supplied a wealth of material and general interest.
43. *A Small Boy and Others,* 361, 362.
44. In the preface which James wrote for the 1902 edition of *Madame Bovary,* he gives an account of his discovering an installment of the novel in the *Revue de Paris.* The first installment appeared in the October 1856 issue of the magazine.
45. Henry James, "M. Flaubert's Theory," *French Poets and Novelists,* as quoted by F. O. Matthiessen, *op. cit.,* 570, 571.

Chapter Nine

New Dimensions

"This experience was . . . the marked limit of my state of being a small boy."

In *The Newcomes,* when Arthur Pendennis arrives at the address of Colonel Newcome in the *haute ville* of Boulogne, no one is at home—not even a servant. At the suggestion of a neighbor, Pendennis turns from the quiet, grass-grown street toward the ramparts of the Upper Town, where the old gentleman and Thomas Newcome the younger were to be found every pleasant day. He "strolled along by those pretty old walks and bastions, under the pleasant trees which shadow them, and the gray old gabled houses from which you look down upon the gay new city, and the busy port, and the piers stretching into the shining sea, dotted with a hundred white sails or black smoking steamers, and bounded by the friendly lines of the bright English shore. There are few places where young children may play, and ruminating old age repose more pleasantly than on those peaceful rampart gardens." [1] The Boulogne in which the James family arrived in the early summer of 1857 was identical with that of Thackeray's novel. Unlike the Newcomes and the formidable "campaigner," Mrs. Mackenzie, however, they took accommodations in the "gay new town" with its straight, well-built streets and modern shops, many of which displayed English signs, offered "English spoken," and radiated a substantial English atmosphere. The city of about 35,000 then contained over 2,000 English residents and played host each year to hundreds in addition, since transportation from Folkstone to Boulogne was at that time the quickest route from London to Paris.

In the mid-Nineteenth century the city was the chief fishingport in France, as well as a busy industrial center; but its location made it also a popular and gay summer resort. The blending of the old and the new, the drab with the colorful, gave it an interesting character; yet, in comparison with Paris it suffered, in the eyes of the three older James boys, in every respect but that of its situation. These young boulevardiers of Paris found little in the provincial delights of Boulogne-sur-Mer after they had exhausted its meager wealth of historical and architectual charms. For a brief summer visit, however, there were definite attractions. The excellent bathing at the *plage,* with the Etablissement des Bains, its Gardens and handsome Casino, the evening promenades along the Jetée de l'Est, extending 650 yards into the sea, the brisk walks up the inclines to the rather poor statue of Napoleon I, or along the shore to the Roman beacon tower built under Caligula in 40 A. D.—all these diversions the children enjoyed during the bright summer days. The very atmosphere was delightful in its intense brightness, its clearness through which the colors struck one with exciting force— the blue and red *douaniers* and soldiers standing out sharply on the wharfs and piers, about which, in nervous, quick movements, small ugly men in cerulean blouses prepared their nets and fishing boats. Through the smokeless air, stretching along the water's edge were pink and yellow houses; at white-fronted cafés with bright blue letters, glistening mirrors, and marble-topped tables, white-aproned waiters, grasping huge long-handled coffeepots, poured steaming *café noire* for comfortably seated French habitués and English tourists.

Most fascinating for the visitors were the fisherfolk who had for many years built up a strong tradition, as well as a thriving business, which they carried on daily with their boats of every size and shape, their huge nets, and quaint costumes. Les Boulonnaises, scurrying about with their folded kerchiefs and their crisp cap-frills, their short striped petticoats, their tightly-drawn stockings, and their little clicking sabots captured the eye and imagination of Harry, who never tired of watching their ceaseless activities. These fishermen and their wives gave young Henry James his first taste of the charms of the provinces.[2] He was later to realize, as he states in *A Little Tour in France,* that people are too apt to think that France is Paris. Certainly he thought that in 1857; but he was this year to become vaguely unsatisfied with the belief that the "epitome of civilization which stretches from the Arc de Triomphe to the Gymnase theatre" was all that France had to offer. Boulogne very humbly suggested that there were many good things in the *doux pays de France,* of which he had got no hint during the previous months. France may be Paris, he thought, but Paris is not France.

Boulogne-sur-Mer, so called to distinguish it from Boulogne-sur-Seine near Paris, the Bononia or Gessoriacum of the Romans, is divided into the *haute ville,* or old town, on the heights to the east, and the much larger *basse ville,* or lower town including the harbor. In the 'Fifties it was classed with Marseilles, Le Havre, and Bordeaux among the first seaports of France. Visitors naturally preferred to stay in this modern section with its many restaurants, hotels, and shops, reflecting a certain degree of English comfort set off by French taste. The principal thoroughfares were the Rue Victor-Hugo and its continuation, the Rue Nationale; the Rue Adolphe Thiers, beginning at the Place Dalton, and the Grande Rue, ascending to the *haute ville.* The Jameses took accommodations on the Rue Neuve Chausée, also in the business district but still in part a residential street. The apartment was "the most spacious and pompous Europe had yet treated us to," with attractive balconies projecting over the lively scene on which the building fronted. It was owned by one M. Prosper Sauvage who had inherited it as evidence of "family," a quite modestly local, but ambitious family, dwelling *entre court et jardin* to the rear of the Jameses. The children were divided between the attractions of the front balconies and the domestic drama offered daily by M. Sauvage, his *femme,* and overflowing offspring in the extension across the inner court.

Harry, following the precedent he had established in Paris of walking more frequently by himself than in company with his brothers, began to explore the social scene which at the port was more lively than elsewhere. The seafaring and fisherfolk were the real strength of the place, he soon felt. In contrast to the mid-Victorian dowdiness of the English visitors, "the tanned and trussed and kerchiefed, the active and productive women" radiated a wholesomeness and "at every step and by their every instinct of appearance the perfect lesson of taste." These were genuine people doing their honest work, "so bravely stripped below and so perfectly enveloped above as the deep-wading, far-striding, shrimp-netting, crab-gathering matrons or maidens who played, waist-high, with the tides. . . . " Harry, with an already highly sharpened sense of observation was vividly impressed by these women, each in "varied essentials of fluted coif and folded kerchief and sober short and tense, dark, displayed stocking and clicking wooden slippers, to say nothing of long gold ear-drop or solid short-hung pectoral cross, with a respect for the rigour of convention that had the beauty of self-respect." [3]

Deeply etched on his mind, too, was "the old Thackerayan side" of the picture at the motley, sunny, breezy, bustling port. "The scene bristled, as I look back at it, with images from *Men's Wives,* from the society of Mr. Deuceace and that of fifty other figures of the same creation, with Bareacreses and Rawdon Crawleys and of course with Mrs. Macks, with Roseys of a more or less crumpled freshness and blighted bloom, with battered and bent, though doubtless never quite so fine, Colonel Newcomes not less; with more reminders in short than I can now gather in. Of those forms of the seedy, the subtly sinister, the vainly 'genteel,' the generally damaged and desperate, and in particular the invincibly impudent, all the marks, I feel sure, were stronger and straighter than such as we meet in generally like cases under our present levelling light. Such anointed and whiskered and eked-out, such brazen, bluffing, swaggering gentlemen, such floridly repaired ladies, their mates, all looking as hard as they could as if they were there for mere harmless amusement——it was as good, among them, as just *being* Arthur Pendennis to know so well, or at least to guess so fearfully, who and what they might be. They were floated on the tide of the manners then prevailing, I judge, with a rich processionaly effect that so many of our own grand lapses . . . leave no material for; so that the living note of Boulogne was really, on a more sustained view, the opposition between a native race the most happily tempered, the most becomingly seasoned and salted and self-dependent, and a shifting colony . . . inimitably at odds with any active freshness." [4]

In such an acute awareness of contrasts, in such an intuitive sense of values, Harry James was almost consciously sowing the seeds, during these unaccompanied walks, taken with a "luxury of freedom," that would sprout into that great harvest of the international novel. As an individual and as an artist his mind reacted, from these boyhood years throughout his long career, to the social forces lying behind the mores of peoples, the ethical significance underneath folkways, customs and conventions, the emotions which ultimately he found at the core of social relationships. The year in London had given him a concentrated experience of observing and assimilating the strata of English life which came within his perception; the year in Paris had offered a similar schooling in relation to various degrees of Parisian life and contributed in large measure, thereby, to the growth of his aesthetic sensibilities. But now in Boulogne, for the first time Harry James saw these two peoples mingling against a backdrop of such a watering place as he was later to use as a setting for several stories. *The Four Meetings* takes place at Havre, with Miss Caroline Spencer working out her little tragedy in an environment not unlike Boulogne; in *The Middle Years,* poor Dencombe meets his pathetic fate at Bournemouth, a similar resort directly across the Channel. The atmosphere, the types of people, the coastal setting, the whole milieu, "the living note of Boulogne," young Henry James was taking in with all the avidity of his fourteen years.

Upon the peaceful, respectable social scene at Boulogne during the summer of 1857 there broke a lurid note, a notorious poisoning case centered around one Madeleine Smith. The scandal stirred astounding interest, even in the rarefied atmosphere of the perfectly appointed salons at #20 Rue Neuve Chausée. " . . . I remember perfectly her trial during its actuality, and how it used to come to us

every day in the *Times,* at Boulogne, where I was then with my
parents, and how they followed and discussed it in suspense and how
I can still see the queer look of 'not proven,' seen for the first time,
on the printed page of the newspaper. I stand again with it, on the
summer afternoon—a boy of 14—in the open window over the Rue
Neuve Chausée where I read it. . . . " [5] But of the forces lying
behind such an episode Harry James knew little then, nor even, perhaps, in later years. Such notes sounded with crashing discords upon
the calm serenity of the James home, a serenity seldom disturbed
by social evils of any sort.

A new experience in what might be called broader education
awaited the three oldest boys, as the elder James arranged for them
to attend the College Imperial, "a deeply democratic institution
from which no small son even of the most soapless home could possibly know exclusion." It was situated toward the top of the rather
steep Grande Rue leading to the *haute ville* with its ancient citadel
dating from the 13th century and its singularly ugly cathedral then
under construction. Harry's attendance, which was suddenly cut short
after the first few weeks, had a dismal effect in general and left two
impressions in particular. The students were mostly sons of local
tradesmen, artisans, and fisherfolk, mixed together with a few English
lads, "predominately *internes* and uniformed, blue-jacketed and brass-
buttoned." One of these "foreigners" from across the Channel was
to stand apart forever in Harry's mind: "Vivid still to me is the summer morning on which, in the wide court . . . a brownish black-eyed
youth, of about my own degree of youthfulness, mentioned to me
with an air that comes back as that of the liveliest informational resource the outbreak, just heard of, of an awful Mutiny in India, where
his military parents . . . were in mortal danger of their lives; so that
news of their having been killed would perhaps be already on the
way. . . . Why I should have thought him almost Indian of stamp
and hue because his English parents were of the so general Indian
peril is more than I can say; yet I have his exotic and above all his
bold, his imaginably even 'bad,' young face, finely unacquainted with
law, before me at this hour quite undimmed—announcing as I conceived it, and quite as a shock, any awful adventure one would, as

well as something that I must even at the time have vaguely taken
as the play of the 'passions.' " [6]

Already sharply attuned to the potential drama in any social situation, Harry James's imagination set up crosscurrents of domestic
tragedy, created a play of "passions" about the obscure English boy,
so that he remembered the incident during the next half century. It
is interesting to note that at fourteen, as in later years, his imagination played vividly around the social element and not around the
historical. The Mutiny in India, an historical event of some proportion, weighed not the slightest in his thoughts which were immediately overbalanced by the schoolmate's tragic plight. It has been
said that history was in James "a felt objective residue," that he was
contemporary to an extreme. "He took his tradition entirely on its
face value; yet because he knew so much must have been behind that
face, he actually felt more continuity, more unity, than had ever
been really there. In that feeling lay the intensity of his sense of
history. He lacked historical imagination because his mind lacked
historical content; he had never been inside any history but his
own. . . . " [7] In Geneva, in London, in Paris, and in Boulogne,
history lay all around young Henry James, and as "a felt objective
residue" it came to him. He seldom went to it or projected himself
into it. Under Hawthorne's influence, he used an historical setting in
"The Romance of Certain Old Clothes," 1868, early in his career;
also, at the very end of his life, in the unfinished novel, *The Sense of
the Past,* 1917, he sends Ralph Pendrel back to 1820 but has him
released from the Regency era to return to his own time. For the
most part, however, all of his fiction is laid in the contemporary
scene, for he "described what he saw, and he created what lay under
what he saw." [8]

The other young schoolmate at the College Imperial who impressed
Harry in the summer of 1857 was one who was to make increasingly
greater impressions as the years passed. He was Benoît Constant
Coquelin, elder son of a Boulogne baker whose trade the boy was
originally intended to follow.[9] M. Coquelin's pastry shop, the princi-

pal one in town, the James boys well knew, especially for its criss-crossed apple tarts and melting *babas*. The boys envied Constant his home life, permeated as it was with such delectable aromas, for the sniffing of which his upward tilting nose seemed peculiarly well adapted. This same nose, in later years, was to give the then cele-brated French comedian a unique insight into the role of Cyrano, one of his greatest pieces of acting. "Coquelin is personally most present to me, in the form of that hour, by the value, as we were to learn to put it, of this nose, the fine assurance and impudence of which fairly made it a trumpet for promises; yet in spite of that, the very gage, as it were, of his long career as the most interesting and many-sided comedian, or at least most unsurpassed dramatic *diseur* of his time, I failed to doubt that, with the rich recesses of the parental industry for his background, his subtlest identity was in his privilege, or perhaps even in his expertest trick, of helping himself well." [10] These two boys alone, Coquelin and the English military orphan, took on definite and significant shape in "the dull precinct" of the College, from the confines of which Harry happily escaped on Sundays for long, aimless walks, or for visits to the *musée de province* on the Grande Rue. Among its ethnographical and historical col-lections, some Egyptian antiquities, and modest picture gallery Harry would roam, feeling that in comparison with the Louvre and the Luxembourg, Boulogne's musée was as bleak and unrelieved as the gray ramparts and the bare citadel of the *haute ville*. These excur-sions added little, he felt, to his "small loose handful of the seed of culture." The one bright spot, in this respect, was the public library, with its 55,000 volumes and interesting manuscripts, but also Merri-dew's English Library, like the English bookstore on Broadway in the New York years, offered real solace for empty hours.

The comfortable situation in which the family was established in mid-summer, with the older boys in the College and the younger children cared for by a new governess, the elder James describes in a letter to Grandmother James, now seventy-five years old and in ill health:

BOULOGNE-SUR-MER
20 RUE NEUVE CHAUSEE
JULY 23, 1857

MY DEAR MOTHER,

I have been away for a week in England, seeing to the issue of a little book of mine (*Christianity the Logic of Creation,* 1857), or I should have written before to express my concern at hearing of your recent attack. Of all persons one would say that your habits were the last to invite paralysis, and I would have been sure that the attack could not be lasting, even if Libby had not relieved us from all fear upon the subject. Of course at your time of life one may expect symptoms of decline more or less urgent, but I have somehow a fixed persuasion that you will never be laid aside from the activity you like, and which has so long blessed every one about you. It is an inexpressible comfort to me that Howard (James) is so attentive upon you, and that you are realizing his cordial sympathy and affection in this crisis. I would gladly go home myself if there were any need. But I have no doubt that you will perfectly rally from this assault, and be able to pour me out many a cup of tea yet. I am myself ill, though I don't know why I should be. Nausea every morning, and a great sense of debility every day, are my symptoms. But I suppose I am too sedentary.

The children are doing excellently. They go—the three eldest—to the College Imperial, and the two younger have their governess in the house. We shall remain here until October. What then, I cannot now foresee. We left Lydia Mason and family behind us in Paris, where I see they are having sufficiently hot weather. They are a nice amiable family and our children had a good deal of intercourse with them, which they now miss. . . . Mary and Aunt Kate and all the children give me messages of love for you, dear Ma, and I myself send you cordial heaps.

Ever faithfully yours,

H. J.[11]

Alice James, in a note made over thirty years later, reveals a significant side light on Harry's unique originality and intellectual development in the summer of 1857. Her governess, Marie Boningue, successor to Mlle. Danse of Paris, came from the outskirts of Boulogne, where her parents had a *campagne*. In response to a cordial invitation from Madame Boningue, the James family, all except William who must have begged off, climbed into a large, shabby *calèche* and drove out to the country. After a hearty meal the children were turned into the garden to play, a sandy, or rather dusty expanse, Alice remembered, with nothing in it "but two or three scrubby apple trees from one of which hung a swing. As time went on, Wilky and Bob disappeared, not to my grief, and the Boningues'. Harry was sitting in the swing and I came up and stood near by, as the sun began to slant over the desolate expanse, as the dreary hours (with that endlessness which they have for infancy) passed, when Harry suddenly exclaimed: 'This might certainly be called pleasure under difficulties!' The stir of my whole being in response to the exquisite, original form of this remark almost makes my heart beat now with the sisterly pride which was then awakened, and it came to me in a flash—the higher nature of this appeal to the mind as compared to the rudimentary solicitations which usually produced my childish explosions of laughter, and I can also feel distinctly the sense of self-satisfaction in that I could not only perceive but appreciate this subtlety, as if I had acquired a new sense, a sense whereby to measure intellectual things, wit as distinguished from giggling, for example." [12] Alice James, then only nine, was herself not unendowed with that quickness of mind, that sensitivity to wit, which her fourteen-year-old brother Harry so effortlessly turned over for her discovery. This early appreciation gradually developed in Alice on through the years so that her friendship and love for Harry was to become the most enjoyable part of her rather pathetic life.

The illness which ultimately made Alice an invalid, which plagued William for most of his youth and young manhood, which kept the elder James constantly concerned, and which, in the case of Harry, approached nearly unto death in 1857, seemed to be almost a family trait. It is the subject in part of nearly every letter in the family papers and must be considered in any study of the children. In June, 1855, at the time of the very rough crossing from New York to Liverpool, Harry had had an attack of fever which did not completely leave him until some time after arriving at Geneva. Suddenly at Boulogne, in August of 1857, the boy was stricken again, this time with a very pronounced case of typhoid. For eight weeks he was confined to bed utterly unable to rally to any treatment, often being in a delirious state and so weak that at times there seemed little hope of his recovery. Through letters to Grandmother James, we have rather detailed accounts of the whole experience which Harry himself came to see as a turning point in his life. His father wrote:

> BOULOGNE-SUR-MER
> 20 RUE NEUVE CHAUSEE
> SEPTEMBER 10, 1857

MY DEAR MOTHER,

I am happy to inform you that Harry goes on very well, on the whole. He has occasional breakdowns; for example he had a restless feverish night last night and was quite poorly this morning; but these things are only transient effects of a little too stimulating food, or something of that sort, and do not argue, according to the physicians, any permanent disaster. He is quite himself again in mind, and longs very much to be able to eat something. But the Doctors say that he must be kept still very low for some time, and I presume they are right.

We are otherwise all very well, and, I hope we may remain so. I think we shall give up our German journey entirely. I found on investigation that living would not be as cheap as I had expected in those countries, and the schools, with the exception of the advantages they furnish in regard to acquiring the German language, are no better than elsewhere. I have no doubt from all I can gather, that our own schools are, with the above exception, much superior to the European schools. I think that if Mary were quite well this fall, we might get home before the setting in of winter; but she needs a little consideration, and we shall probably not return till spring or summer.

Give our love to all at home, Howard and the girls, Aunt Charlotte and the children, Lily and Nelly and Bob, and believe me, my dear Mother,

> Ever faithfully yours,
>
> H. J.[13]

Direct to us, care of Baring Brothers, Ld., London.

The London bankers' address was given, not because of any plans to cross the Channel that autumn, but because there were, in fact, no plans, or definite addresses to offer. Serious thought had been given to the idea of travelling through the German section of Europe but it never took on more than a vague character as Harry's serious illness made any travelling quite unwise until he had regained strength. Consequently, as long as possible the family remained in

Boulogne and from the same address in October the elder James again wrote:

BOULOGNE, OCTOBER 15, 1857

MY DEAR MOTHER,

Harry, I am thankful to say, is doing very well, having had but one serious pull-back. He went day before yesterday for the first time into the chamber adjoining his own, and is now gaining strength every day, eating heartily and drinking a little porter. He is excessively thin and appears to have grown by his eight weeks' confinement to his bed, a half-head taller. He was extremely sick for a few weeks, and we trembled more than once for the issue. We found an excellent homeopathic physician, an Irishman by the name of Maconbrey, in the place, and we think his judgment has been mighty serviceable to Harry. We have concluded to return to Paris for the winter, as Harry is too feeble to cross the Channel for some time yet, and we are obliged to give up our apartment here. We have taken an apartment in the Rue Montaigne, No. 26, Faubourg St. Honoré where the girls will please henceforth direct their letters.

The other children are very well, and doing very well in their studies. We congratulate ourselves every day upon having brought them away from New York where, having no place to amuse themselves but the street, they were sure to be degraded in manners and characters by the contact of vicious associates. Willy is very devoted to scientific pursuits, and I hope will turn out a most respectable scholar. He has been attending the College Imperial here all summer, and one of his professors told me the other day "that he was an admirable student, and that all the advantages of a first-rate scientific education which Paris affords ought to be accorded him." He is, however, much dearer to my heart for his moral worth than for his intellectual. I never knew a child of so much principle, and at the same time of a perfectly generous and conciliatory demeanour towards his younger brothers, always disposed to help them and never to oppress.

Harry is not so fond of study, properly so-called, as of reading. He is a devourer of libraries, and an immense writer of novels and dramas. He has considerable talent as a writer, but I am at a loss to know whether he will ever accomplish much. Wilky is more heart than head, but has a talent for language, and speaks French they say with a perfect accent. They all speak very fluently indeed but Wilky and Bob (who is very clever and promising, having ten times the go-ahead of all the rest) are particularly forward in it. Alice also speaks very well, and I presume that this winter will greatly accomplish them.

Mary and Aunt Kate have had a very busy time as you may suppose with Harry, especially Aunt Kate, whose qualities as a nurse shone forth with unequalled lustre. Mary is somewhat unwell for a few days past . . . but I am in hopes will soon be as bright as usual. They both desire a great deal of love to you all.

I am sorry to find from Libby's letter that your arm (Remainder of letter is missing).[14]

Willy, then well over sixteen, was experiencing his first serious, regular schooling and responding to it with eagerness and promise, as his father implied. His interest in science seemed to be replacing an earlier interest in art, but the possibilities of a career as an artist were merely dormant, as the events of the following years were to prove. Harry, going on fifteen and forced more than ever into a very inactive life, turned instinctively to writing. In 1857, a certain new sense of things came over him so that within himself he felt a very tangible growth, not only physically but in terms of his inner self. In time, under normal conditions, these developments would probably have taken place in the boy unperceived; but the impact of the malignant typhus, the strain of the prolonged convalescence, the seeing of all this "as through a glass darkly," greatly intensified for him the putting off of the child and the taking on of the youth. "This experience was to become when I had emerged from it the great reminiscence or circumstance of old Boulogne for me, and I was to regard it, with much intelligence, I should have maintained, as the marked limit of my state of being a small boy. I took on, when I had decently, and all the more because I had so retardedly, recovered, the sense of being a boy of other dimensions somehow altogether, and even with a new dimension introduced and acquired; a dimension that I was eventually to think of as a stretch in the direction of essential change or of living straight into a part of myself previously quite unvisited and now made accessible as by the sharp forcing of a closed door." [15]

While the forcing open of this inner door was most certainly for him a sharp experience, the process of entering in upon the new chambers of consciousness, stretching out in a blurred vision to all sorts of new dimensions, was to be a very slow and uncertain advance.

The process hardly ever ceased developing in him; hence both as a man and as a literary artist his growth and maturity came slowly. There was no apparent change at all during the remaining eight months of Europe before the return to America, and Harry lived through this period languidly, his health being so poor that his responses even to Paris were in no way fruitful. He merely went along with the family, playing a more minor role than usual and getting used to the strange changes which had taken place during the summer and early autumn.

By the third week in October the Jameses were living at #26 Rue Montaigne in accommodations so expensive that the parents never would have taken them had they had any warning of the seriousness of the depression which had settled like a cloud over the family fortunes. Ever since the enactment of the Tariff of 1857, on March 3rd, economic and financial conditions had grown steadily worse. In August, 1857, a large insurance and trust company failed in Ohio, having heavy liabilities to Eastern institutions. This started a panic in New York, followed by a suspension of specie payments. Railroads playing an important part in the developing of the west went into bankruptcy, including the Illinois Central, the New York and Erie, and the Michigan Central. Such holdings came alarmingly near the core of the James' interests and by October Henry James, Sr., in Paris, felt for the first time the terror of great insecurity and uncertainty over money matters. His large family, accustomed to living in great comfort, if not luxury, were utterly dependent upon his inheritance. He, in turn, now felt heavily dependent upon his brothers and sisters at home, who were more fully informed and in a better position to handle the situation and salvage as much as possible. They, too, could supply the money absolutely essential for the meeting of immediate obligations. To his half brother, Rev. William James, oldest of the large Albany family, he wrote:

26 RUE MONTAIGNE
PARIS, OCT. 28TH

MY DEAR WILLIAM,

I wrote to Ma yesterday saying all that recent events force us to feel of anxiety and apprehension, but I neglected to tell her to send all our letters to the care of Baring Brothers, London. We do not know how long we may be able to stay here, and Baring will always know where to find us. It is something new for us to feel anxious for the future, and I realize now the comfort of remembering the warm hearts at home who will not suffer us to lack anything which their necessities may spare. I wrote to Ma to ask you and Augustus (James) and Howard (James) to aid her to contribute as large a sum as you can, to be put to my credit at Samual G. Ward's in Boston, in order that we may escape the worst rigors of the crisis. We shall get home as soon as we can command the means, without any undue sacrifice of our present obligations. Was ever anything clearer than that these commercial disasters indicate the widest *social* disease in the community. The lack of the sentiment of brotherhood—the prevalence of self-seeking—this is the disease of the common mind as it is of the individual. . . . [16]

To Mrs. Samual G. Ward, within the following week he wrote:

> PARIS, 26 RUE MONTAIGNE
> FAUBOURG ST. HONORE
> NOVEMBER 2, 1857

MY DEAR ANNA,

I seize the earliest hour after getting settled in our new quarters to express my consternation that you should have been in Boulogne so many hours, and we none the wiser or better for the incident.

. . . That reminds me that we have been very nearly sent home by these dreadful commercial disasters on the other side. As it is I think we shall consult duty by retracing our steps to Boulogne, and passing the winter there. The difference between 300 francs per month rent, and 800 francs is not to be despised at such a time. Indeed at any time such a difference ought to have a great weight in favor of Boulogne, for it is a most agreeable place, with good schools, and a capital market, and a population much more manly, or rather more womanly (for it is of those remarkable fisherwomen that I speak particularly) than that of Paris. . . . [17]

By early December the plan to return to Boulogne was carried out and very happily so. A jointly-written letter, full of pertinent, at times shrewd, remarks, from both of the parents, to Grandmother James, presents an incomparable account of the family affairs now quite calm again after the distressing days in Paris:

BOULOGNE, 29 GRANDE RUE,
DECEMBER 24, 1857

MY DEAR MA,

You have already heard through Henry's letter about a fortnight since
to brother William, that we are settled down here for the winter. I cannot
begin to tell you, dear Ma, how great an effort this resolution to remain
here until spring has cost us—With Henry it is still a daily battle, so
strongly does he feel home pulling at his heart, that we sometimes suspect him of planning privately a winter trip in the *Adriatic*.

We have had no reason, however, to regret our decision for we are
living here most comfortably and *economically* and but for the absence
of congenial society, the society of home, have everything we can desire.
We have an excellent house, not so commodious or elegant as the one
we were in last summer, but most advantageously situated, commanding
the liveliest scene in the town, our little parlours being warmed and
enlivened by the earliest and latest rays of the sun. For this we pay
but 200 francs a month, or 150 francs if taken for six months.

The boys are back again at the College where the fee is only ten
francs a month. Alice has a daily governess who comes three hours a
day, and Harry being as Willy says "supposed to be too delicate to go to
College" has a teacher at home. The whole expense of the children's
education here including music and dancing does not exceed 40 dollars
a month. So you see it has been a decided stroke of economy for us to
remain here. The accounts we have of the state of business at home
begin to be more favorable. Robertson's (Walsh) last letter was really
almost cheering, not that he intimates any positive change or revival in
business but he seems to be experiencing so great relief from the wearing
perplexities, and fears from which he has been suffering the last few
weeks; and he presents so delightful a picture for economy, and the
responses of energy and efficiency that have been developed in wife and
daughters by the present emergency—that one feels rather inclined to
rejoice with him in the discovery of richer treasures than any he has
lost. . . .

MY DEAR MOTHER——Mary has been obliged to run off to prepare
Alice for dancing school and leaves me to seal the letter. I wish you all
a Merry Christmas, though it will be a fortnight before the wish reaches
you, and the chill winds of the Atlantic will stand a fair chance of evapo-
rating a portion of the warmth. We had half a mind to go over by the
next trip of the *Adriatic,* but Mary ciphers out such enormous impedi-
ments to our comfort in America, on our reduced income, that we are
content to remain where we are. Boulogne is about the most cheerful
place in France, prosperous in a business point of view, full of bustle,

picturesque in situation and costume. Living is much cheaper than in Paris, schooling quite as good if not better, and I fancy we shall do altogether very well. We keep only two servants, neither of whom has ever lived in Paris, and we are not in dread consequently of being cheated out of our eyeteeth. In fact one of them, who is an excellent cook, is an English woman, and it is an immense comfort to hear her going about the house murdering her native tongue. When she asks you whether you will have "heggs and bacon" for breakfast, or simple "muffins and 'oney," and whether you found your " 'am well cooked at yesterday's dinner," you are content to miss the French elegance in order to secure English honesty.

I wrote a long letter to Brother William the other day. Give our love to all hands at home, Howard, Augustus, the girls, Aunt Charlotte and the Temples, and believe me ever dear Ma,

Yours most faithfully,

H. J.[18]

The question of financial conditions and measures of economy, always mentioned to some degree in letters to Grandmother James, the question of the children's health, of their education, and the question of whether or not to return to America—these were the themes upon which the parents reported in an almost prescribed pattern; yet each letter has its distinct individuality, its shifting of emphasis or scene, its varying reflections of one or another member of the family, for the moment occupying the center of interest. In later years, letters centered around Wilky and Bob, or Alice with her repeated and prolonged medical treatments, but Willy and Harry, conspicuously important to them all at this time came in for the larger share of comment. With Harry's gradual recovery and the quiet routine of winter in Boulogne, little excitement stirred the family hearth, however, and the European years seemed definitely to be coming to a close.

The absence of congenial society, mentioned by Mrs. James, was felt even more keenly by Harry, upon their return from Paris to Boulogne, in that he was by circumstance forced to spend much of his time at home, being considered, as Willy mockingly observed, 'too delicate to go to the College.' In all probability Harry made no strenuous efforts to re-enter the classes along with the other

boys, since he was not a good student, did not enjoy the regimenta-
tion of time and ideas, and wanted as much freedom as possible for
his reading and his attempts at writing. These were, all in all, dreary
months, with "no society of any sort at home" and little to be found
in the town, except that of quaint, frowzy, little English ladies who
frequented the rampart gardens in "such mushroom hats, such extremely circular and bestriped scarlet petticoats, such perpetual tight
gauntlets, such explicit claims to long descent, which showed them
for everything that everyone else at Boulogne was not. These mid-
Victorian samples of a perfect consistency 'represented,' by my
measure, as hard as ever they could—and represented, of all things,
literature and history and society. The literature was that of the
three-volume novel, then, and for much after, enjoying its loosest
and serenest spread; for they separately and anxiously and awfully
'wrote'—and that must almost by itself have amounted in them to
all the history I evoked." [19]

While Willy, Wilky, and even now young Robertson attended the
College Imperial,[20] with only younger Alice under the care of the
governess, Mlle. Boningue, Harry spent three mornings a week receiving instructions at home from a tutor, M. Ansiot, who was a
mild man, even "a curiosity, a benignity, a futility. . . . " He was
a large person, "a form of bland porpoise, violently blowing in
an age not his own . . . having had to exchange deep water for
thin air." The range of studies was restricted, by sociable agreement,
to exploring literature, with very little demand made upon Harry
beyond the points of interest then to his liking. M. Ansiot, in fact,
"rested with a weight I scarce even felt—such easy terms he made,
without scruple, for both of us—on the cheerful innocence of my
barbarism; and though our mornings were short and subject, I think,
to quite drowsy lapses and other honest aridities, we did scumble
together, I make out, by the aid of the collected extracts from the
truly and academically great which formed his sole resource and which
he had, in a small portable and pocketed library rather greasily preserved, some patch of picture of a saving as distinguished from a
losing classicism. The point remains for me that when all was said—
and even with everything that might directly have counted unsaid—

he discharged for me such an office that I was to remain to this far-off hour in a state of possession of him that is the very opposite of a blank. . . . The blank he fills out crowds itself with a wealth of value, since I shouldn't without him have been able to claim, for whatever it may be worth, a tenth (at that let me handsomely put it), of my 'working' sense of the *vieux temps*. How can I allow then that we hadn't planted together, with a loose felicity, some of the seed of work?—even though the sprouting was so long put off." [21]

Three mornings a week with M. Ansiot left two mornings and every weekday afternoon, not to mention complete week-ends, free. When tired of indoor pursuits Harry had wonderfully empty hours in which to roam aimlessly about. When not observing the literary ladies perched like so many colorful birds in the rampart gardens of the *haute ville,* he strolled down to Merridew's English Library at the corner of the Port and Rue de l'Ecu. The general romance of Merridew's he had sampled early in the summer, but now, with no duties at the College and a bit bored by the general ennui of his convalescence, he found the shop both an escape and a support. "The place 'meant,' on these terms, to begin with, frank and licensed fiction . . . The blest novel in three volumes exercised through its form, to my sense, on grounds lying deeper for me to-day than my deepest sounding, an appeal that fairly made it do with me what it would. . . . I stand, as I used to stand, within the positively sancti-fied walls of the shop . . . and surrender to the vision of the shelves packed with their rich individual trinities. Why should it have af-fected me so that my choice, so difficult in such a dazzle, could only be for a trinity? I am unable fully to say—such a magic dwelt in the mere rich fact of the trio. When the novel of that age was 'bad,' as it so helplessly, so abjectly and prevailingly consented to be, the three volumes still did something for it, a something that was all strangely, not an aggravation of its case. When it was 'good' (our analysis, our terms of appreciation, had a simplicity that has lingered on) they made it copiously, opulently better; so that when, after the span of years, my relation with them became, from that of comparatively artless reader, and to the effect of a superior fondness and acuteness, that of complacent author, the tradition of infatuated youth still flung over them its mantle. . . . " [22]

He found himself hanging about the bookshop, when not actually in it, "through the apprehension that something vague and sweet— if I shouldn't indeed rather say something of infinite future point and application—would come of it. This is a reminiscence that nothing would induce me to verify, as for example, by a revisiting light; but it was going to be good for me, good, that is, for what I was pleased to regard as my intelligence or my imagination . . . that I *should* so have hung about." [23] The apprehension that something good would come of this infatuation with Merridew's and its mid-Victorian novels was as vague as was the elder James's estimation of Harry's considerable talent as a writer, his being at a loss to know whether the boy would ever accomplish much with his writing. Yet Harry had a "divination" that these uncertain literary fumblings at Boulogne were not without purpose, even promise; like the ministrations of M. Ansiot, they washed themselves over him and began "to spread for me, to immensity. . . ." They were, in fact, the beginnings of that new dimension, stretching in the direction of an essential change, a living straight into a new part of his being and they helped greatly to make that new part accessible.

The contribution which the reading of these three-volume novels made to the development of his critical sense is specifically evident in some of his later writing. Their looseness of form, the overflow of content, the stringing out endlessly in installment after installment in current periodicals, then bulging profusely in the three volumes as collected novels—as "bad" as these aspects were, they "did" something strangely beneficial not only for the fiction but for young Henry James. This wide range of "good" and "bad" contemporary English fiction provided a background against which the novels of Turgenev, of Flaubert, Zola, and others of the French school were to stand out in vivid relief for him in subsequent years. In "The Art of Fiction," some twenty-five years later, James touches on this contrast, indicating as he does so a sustained sympathy for the English form then fast losing ground in the face of modern fiction: "Only a short time ago it might have been supposed that the English novel was not what the French call *discutable*. It had no air of having a theory, a conviction, a consciousness of itself behind it—of being the expression of an artistic faith, the result of choice and comparison. I do not say it was necessarily the worse for that: it would take much more courage than I possess to intimate that the form of the novel as Dickens and Thackeray (for instance) saw it had any taint of incompleteness. It was, however, *naif* . . . and evidently if it be destined to suffer in any way for having lost its *naiveté* it has now an idea of making sure of the corresponding advantages." In 1857-1858 Harry's deep response reflected no more choice or comparison than did the novels themselves; his taste and critical sense were then not far removed from those of the literary ladies who spun so many of these Victorian narratives. The whole question of *form*, of *reality*, of *experience* would be brought into play, and experience to Henry James the novelist was to be "an immense sensibility, a kind of huge spider-web of the finest silken threads suspended in the chamber of consciousness, and catching every airborne particle in its tissue"; it was to be "the very atmosphere of the mind." At Boulogne he was merely on the threshold of such a chamber, barely conscious of the vast gossamer web which his mind was to weave so finely in the years to come.

NOTES

1. William Makepeace Thackeray, *The Newcomes*, London, Bradbury and Evans, 1855, II, 308.
2. An old French account of Boulogne-sur-Mer reads in part: " . . . C'est enfin, et de beaucoup, le plus important de nos ports de pêche: 300 bateaux, 4,000 marins en dépendent, et c'est un spectacle bien curieux que l'arrivée à quai de la flottille de pêche. Les femmes de pêcheurs attendent leurs hommes, en jupe courte, petits sabots de bois, fichu croisé, larges anneaux d'or aux oreilles, coiffes pimpantes. A peine à quai, le poisson à grandes pelletées, à pleines corbeilles est jeté sur les charrettes qui l'emportent à la gare, aux ateliers de salaison ou aux fabriques de conserves. Même pendant l'absence du mari, la Boulonnaise ne reste pas inactive: elle promene sur le sable de la côte son large filet qui fouille les flaques, s'insinue dans les recoins des rocs et ramasse au passage crabes, crevettes et coquillages.

Ou bien, au faubourg de Capécure comme au quartier de la Beurrière, elle raccommode les grands filets qui enguirlandent les humbles maisons des pêcheurs." Ernest Granger, *Les Merveilles de La France, Le Pays, Les Monuments, Les Habitants,* Paris, Hachette, n. d.

3. *A Small Boy and Others,* 411.

4. *Ibid.,* 407, 408.

5. *The Letters of Henry James,* II, 374.

6. *A Small Boy and Others,* 402, 403, 404. The Mutiny in India was the result of the annexation of the province of Oudh, by the British in 1856, the province which furnished the Bengal army with most of its high caste recruits. The caste prejudices were thereby aroused and the Indians turned savagely against their English officers, in the notorious Mutiny in 1857. The wildly fanatic outbreaks compelled the British to retaliate so that the whole affair grew to shocking proportions and resulted in the death of a large number of English military people and natives. Sir Alfred Lyall, *The Rise and Expansion of the British Domain in India,* London, John Murray, 1920, 331.

7. Robert P. Blackmur, "Henry James," *Literary History of the United States,* New York, the Macmillan Company, 1948, II, 1047.

8. *Ibid.,* 1039.

9. Benoit Constant Coquelin (1841-1909), the French actor, known as Coquelin *ainé,* was born at Boulogne-sur-Mer on January 28, 1841 and was, therefore, the same age as William James and about two years older than Henry, Jr. Instead of becoming an apprentice to his father in the family bakery, he entered Regnier's class at the Conservatoire in 1859 and within a year won first prize for comedy, making his debut at the Comédie Française, December 7, 1860, as the comic valet, Gros-René, in Moliere's *Dépit Amoureux.* He later toured America with Sarah Bernhardt and was celebrated for his playing of Figaro and Cyrano.

10. *A Small Boy and Others,* 404, 405.

11. MS. letter from Henry James, Sr., to Catherine Barber James, July 23, 1857, Houghton Library, Harvard University.

12. *Alice James, Her Brothers, Her Journal,* 1934, 166, 167.

13. MS. letter from Henry James, Sr., to Catherine Barber James, September 10, 1857, Houghton Library, Harvard University. Percy Lubbock states, in *The Letters of Henry James,* I, 5: "During the second visit to Boulogne Henry was laid low by the very serious attack of typhus that descends on the last page of *A Small Boy.*" The illness occurred in August, 1857, during the first stay in Boulogne.

14. MS. letter from Henry James, Sr., to Catherine Barber James, October 15, 1857, Houghton Library, Harvard University. Parts of this letter have been published in several books, notably in R. B. Perry, *op. cit.,* I, 184, and F. O. Matthiessen, *op. cit.,* 87.

15. *A Small Boy and Others,* 398.

16. MS. letter from Henry James, Sr., to Rev. William James, October 28, 1857, Houghton Library, Harvard University.
17. MS. letter from Henry James, Sr., to Anna Barker Ward, October 28, (1857), Houghton Library, Harvard University.
18. MS. letter from Mary Walsh James and Henry James, Sr., to Catherine Barber James, December 24, 1857, Houghton Library, Harvard University.
19. *A Small Boy and Others,* 411, 412.
20. Forty years later, Robertson James wrote: " . . . and then Boulogne-sur-Mer and the College Municipale and its stone vaulted ceiling where Wilkie and I went and failed to take prizes. But the day when the Mayor of the City distributed these I do remember, and somehow I think that tho' it was not a prize we both had souvenirs or a reward of some kind—for I recall a beautiful book with gold figures. But around the Mayor who stood on a platform with great civic splendor and officials in uniform, I see yet the fortunate scholars ascend the steps of his throne, kneel at his feet and receive crowns or rosettes, or some symbol of merit which *we* did not get. The luck began to break early!" MS. letter from Robertson James to Alice H. James, February 24, 1898, Houghton Library, Harvard University. Published in part by R. B. Perry, *op. cit.,* I, 184, 185.
21. *A Small Boy and Others,* 417, 418.
22. *Ibid.,* 413, 414.
23. *Ibid.,* 414, 415.

Book III

1858-1870

Chapter Ten

Newport Horizon

"If culture, as I hold, is a matter of attitude quite as much as of opportunity . . . there couldn't have been better conditions for its operating drop by drop."

Having left the small boy forever behind him in Boulogne, young Henry James arrived in Newport in July, 1858, deeply conscious of the beginning of his youth. Twelve highly significant years were to pass, during this transformation from childhood to maturity, before he reached the end of his youth, marked for him by the death of Minny Temple in March, 1870. The Newport years, interrupted by one last year of educational experiments in Geneva and Bonn, prepared the way for the Cambridge period of Harvard, the *Atlantic,* and William Dean Howells. These influences, in turn, completed most of his literary apprenticeship. Thus slowly, in an unusually prolonged youth and early manhood, Henry James advanced toward his maturity as an individual and the unfoldment of his career as an artist.

The continual, varied stimulation of European travel and study between 1855 and 1858 had supplied the boy with a wealth of impressions. These he had accumulated through his extraordinary gifts of observation and sensitivity. With such cultural and intellectual forces pouring upon him in Geneva, London, Paris, and Boulogne, the child had not yet matured enough to discover how profoundly his development was being determined by their influence upon his peculiar nature. At Newport, his adolescent mind entered upon a period of self-analysis which explored the reaches of his imagination and the powerful effects his "sense of Europe" had had upon it. Intensifying this self-awareness, always acute in him, was the natural physical change of these years. The shyness and hesitancy which had tended to set him apart from other boys now appeared more pronounced. Instinctively gregarious and unendingly interested in people as he was, he became, after the illness at Boulogne and during this Newport year, more introspective than ever. Even in the midst of the happy family circle, what he most wanted was to be left alone, to think things out for himself. Newport provided ideal conditions for just such searching and contemplation.

The relationship between his desire to write and his changing state of mind became very pronounced, and the working together of these aspects began, he felt, "in so incalculably personal a manner, that no chemical analysis shall recover it. . . . Culture," he wrote years later, "is a matter of the form and substance of the vessel carried to the fountain no less than of the water-supply itself. . . . " The distilled waters of the Newport scene proved perfect refreshment for the youth whose thirst for the heady wines of Europe had, for the moment, been gratified.

To all outward appearance young Henry James was, like Newport itself, in a state of suspended animation. But, also like the town, his physical inertia and apathy concealed potentialities of which no one then dreamed. Consequently, though at first a bit disconcerted by the abrupt change from the European scene, he felt deeply at home. Newport in pre-Civil War days was quite unlike the fabulous, fashionable resort it became later in the century. The ostentatiously wealthy watering-place of the Vanderbilts and Astors would have held no attraction for the Jameses. In the mid-Nineteenth century, the famous old Rhode Island seaport was at low ebb compared either with later decades or with its flourishing history of the previous century. After the War of 1812, in which Newport played a notable part, the community settled into a kind of decayed dignity, never going too far into decline but showing little of its old spirit. In *The Red Rover,* James Fenimore Cooper observes: "No one who is familiar with the bustle and activity of an American commercial town would recognize, in the response which now reigns in the ancient mart of Rhode Island, a place that, in its day, has been ranked among the most important ports along the whole line of our extended coast. . . . Enjoying the four great requisites of a safe and commodious haven—a placid basin, an outer harbor, and a convenient roadstead, with a clear offing—Newport appeared to the eye of our European ancestors designed to shelter fleets and to nurse a race of hardy and expert seamen." [1] Such a purpose it had fulfilled in the great slave trade and in its shipping of rum, of horses, of wool, and haddock, of sugar, molasses, and indigo. Other purposes too it had filled, as a haven for those seeking religious freedom, from Roger Williams to Isaac Touro; in peace and war Newport had played stirring parts, as host to Bishop Berkeley with his utopian dreams of founding a college in the New World, and to General Washington, paying tribute to Count de Rochambeau in the old Vernon House at Clarke and Mary Streets. William Ellery Channing, Commodore Decatur, and Oliver Hazard Perry, all Newport sons, shed honor upon her name; but from 1815 to 1840 neither town nor citizen attracted notice and the community of a mere 6,000 became the genteel retreat of quiet Southern families and discriminating Northerners. With the construction of the Ocean House and the Atlantic House in 1840, Newport enjoyed a brief renaissance, but by 1858 when the James family arrived it was once again a sleepy seaport, resting on the glories of former days.

The circumstances which brought about the establishing of the Jameses at Newport resulted from several problems involved in their return from Europe. The family income, reduced by the Panic of 1857, while still adequate for comfortable living, was comparatively restricted; Harry's serious illness and slow convalescence necessitated a milder climate than that of New York or Albany; the Fourteenth Street house, though still in the family's possession, held no attraction because of the undesirable social changes which New York

was rapidly undergoing in the Fifties; ageing Grandmother James and
close relatives in Albany made the old Pearl Street house a natural
center of affections, but educational and cultural opportunities there
were far too limited. At Newport, however, Edmund and Mary
Tweedy strongly urged the elder James to join them, for they too had
returned from years of European wanderings and had found this
quiet, unpretentious resort in perfect keeping with their conservative tastes, and above all, blessed with an almost Mediterranean climate. The connections between the two families were based not
only upon years of intimate friendship but also on actual family
relations.

Mrs. Edmund Tweedy, "Aunt Mary," as she was affectionately
known to all the Temples and Jameses, had been Mary Temple, sister
of Robert Emmet Temple who had married the elder James's sister,
Catherine Margaret James. Both Robert Temple and his wife died
in 1854, leaving two sons and four daughters. The Tweedies, bereft
of their own young children, took their nieces, who were also Henry
James, Sr.'s, nieces, to Newport, bringing them up as their daughters.
In the summer of 1858, Catherine, or Kitty, was fifteen, just the age
of her cousin Harry James; Mary, or Minny, the second daughter, who
was "to count, and in more lives than can now be named, to an
extraordinary degree," particularly in the life of young Henry James,
was two years younger; Ellen was eight, two years younger than her
cousin Alice James; the youngest girl, Henrietta, was only five.
Robert, or Bob, Temple, who was then a young man of eighteen,
had been shipped off from Albany, soon after the death of his
parents, to a school in Scotland, returning "tall and goodlooking and
easy . . . " while William, or Will, Temple, two years younger than
his brother, was being educated in schools at home. Both boys appeared frequently on the Newport scene so that all six Temples
developed a very happy friendship with their five James cousins,
reviving and enlarging the earlier associations in Albany and New
York. The desirability of this companionship influenced considerably the James parents so that the whole question of a place of
residence was soon determined. Leaving Willy, Harry, and Wilky
with Grandmother James in Albany, the Jameses took the two

younger children, Robertson and Alice, to investigate the Newport possibilities. What they found there and the delight with which they responded to their friends' enthusiastic encouragement toward a decision settled the question, and Newport became their home.[2]

Fresh from three years in Europe with the stimulation of London, the excitement of Paris, the charm and color of Boulogne still vivid in their memories, the Jameses approached Newport with a very distinct sense of detachment. Had they been returning to New York the conditions would not have been so markedly different from their experiences abroad, for at least New York was intensely astir with its busy harbor, its teeming, sprawling waterfront, its prosperous and noisy markets and streets, filled with rude reminders that the days of Father Knickerbocker had gone forever. Because of these very reasons, in fact, the Jameses sailed into Newport harbor, curious, a little amused, but quite certain that they were going to be happy there. The town rose gently from the water to the great hotels along the highest part of the island, between the harbor and the sea, and was composed of a collection of houses devoid of beauty. There were two or three parallel streets with smaller cross streets; there was no *haute ville* with impressive ramparts nor *basse ville* with picturesque fisherfolk and pink and white houses. Boulogne had at least the distinction of a pronounced local color; Newport, on first sight, seemed to have no color at all. Among the old, weather-beaten houses, however, could be detected the dignified aspect of a statelier mansion, very respectable but sadly decayed; there too was the spacious town square, leading gently up to the Old State House whose architectural beauty struck Harry as remarkably fine. One was reminded of London by the spire of Trinity Church, with its eighteenth century lines and that indefinable air of venerable age. As the boat moved slowly into position, the long reaches of docks appeared obviously fallen into disuse, worn, dilapidated, utterly neglected except for a section near the edge of the town, off which a few small yachts and nondescript vessels idled listlessly. The air of quiet decay settled pleasantly upon the entire scene, arousing the imagination and curiosity. Newport was certainly not exciting, but it might be very delightful. Indeed, it was different from anything the Jameses had

yet seen; they agreed with the travelogue description which concluded
that like "Salem in Massachusetts, and Portsmouth in New Hampshire, Newport had seen its best days." [3]

The dinginess of the weather-beaten houses and the general depressing appearance of the town at the time the James family first
knew it remained in their thoughts for years to come. Eighteen years
later, in 1876, while on a short visit there with the Tweedies, William wrote to his brother Harry: "Newport as to its villas, and
all that, is most repulsive to me. I really didn't know how little
charm and how much shabbiness there was about the place. There
are not more than three or four houses out of the whole lot that are
not offensive, in some way, externally." [4] Again, much later, in 1904,
when the Newport of their youth was almost completely gone, William observed to his brother that the architecture of the town was
"more huddled, discordant, cheap, ugly and contemptible" than he
had ever seen it. By the turn of the century the grotesque grandeur
of the Victorian gingerbread castles and veranda-swept summer hotels
had added a grossly discordant note to the humbler scene of the
simple but unattractive cottages of the Fifties; at no time did the
Jameses think of Newport as a place of architectural beauty. Its
charm, which was indeed great, was found in other things, principally
in the climate and the rough beauty of the coast line contrasting with
the gentle roll of ground and the picturesque bluffs jutting up between the untouched beaches.

To what extent Harry James participated in the boating, fishing,
swimming, and riding with his brothers and friends is a question.
Never a robust child, he was still not completely recovered from his
illness at Boulogne and in all probability took advantage of his
semi-invalidism to indulge himself in his literary pursuits. A vast,
new field of reading was opening to him in this period of adjust-
ments and his more mature point of view impelled him toward fresh
attempts at writing, most of which he kept strictly from all other eyes.
This year at Newport, though outwardly so uneventful and serene,
ushered young Henry James into the beginning of his lifelong consideration of the art of fiction. While forced to keep his ideas mostly
to himself, and wisely so in view of the teasing, tormenting brothers

who never let pass a single opportunity for good-natured bantering
about his writing, Harry advanced quietly with his literary interests.
An invaluable account of Harry and his brothers at this time was
given to Percy Lubbock by Thomas Sergeant Perry[5] in some reminiscences of his early acquaintance with the Jameses:

The first time I saw the James boys (writes Mr. Perry) was at the
end of June or early in July in 1858, shortly after their arrival in
Newport for a year's stay. This year of their life is not recorded by
H. J. in his *Notes of a Son and Brother*, or rather its memories are
crowded into the chronicle of the longer stay of the family in America,
beginning with 1860. Mr. Duncan Pell, who knew Mr. James the
father, told his son and me that we ought to call on the boys; and we
did, but they were out. A day or two later we called again and found
them in. We all went together to the Pells' house and spent the
evening in simple joys.
    I have often thought that the three brothers shewed that evening
some of their characteristic qualities. I remember walking with Wilky
hanging on my arm, talking to me as if he had found an old friend
after long absence. When we got to the house and the rest of us
were chattering, H. J. sat on the window-seat reading Leslie's *Life of
Constable* with a certain air of remoteness. William was full of merriment and we were soon playing a simple and childish game. In
A Small Boy and Others H. J. speaks of Wilky's "successful sociability,
his instinct for intercourse, his genius for making friends," and these
amiable traits shewed themselves that evening as clearly as his brother's
jollity. Very soon afterwards H. J. with his two brothers entered the
school where I was studying, that of the Rev. W. C. Leverett, who is
mentioned in the *Notes*. I recall H. J. as an uninterested scholar. Part
of one day in a week was devoted to declaiming eloquent pieces from
Sargent's Standard Speaker, and I have not forgotten his amusement at
seeing in the *Manual of English Literature* that we were studying, in
the half page devoted to Mrs. Browning, that she had married R.
Browning, "himself no mean poet." This compact information gave
him great delight, for we were reading Browning. It was then too
that he read for the first time *The Vicar of Wakefield* and with great
pleasure.
    It was at that time that we began to take long walks together almost every
afternoon along the Cliffs, over the beaches to the Paradise Rocks, to
the Point, or inland, wherever it might be. A thousand scrappy recollections of the strolls still remain, fragments of talk, visions of the
place. Thus it was near the Lily Pond that we long discussed Fourier's

plan for regenerating the world. Harry had heard his father describe
the great reformer's proposal to establish universal happiness, and like
a good son he tried to carry the good news further. At another time,
he fell under the influence of Ruskin; he devoted himself to the conscientious copying of a leaf and very faithfully drew a little rock that
jutted above the surface of the Lily Pond. These artistic gropings, and
those in Hunt's studio where he copied casts, were not his main interest.
His chief interest was literature. We read the English magazines and
reviews and the *Revue des Deux Mondes* with rapture. We fished in
various waters, and I well remember when W. J. brought home a volume
of Schopenhauer and showed us with delight the ugly mug of the
philosopher and read us amusing specimens of his delightful pessimism.
It was W. J. too who told us about Renan one cool evening of February
when the twilight lingers till after six. H. J. in his books speaks without enthusiasm of his school studies, but he and I read at Mr. Leverett's
school a very fair amount of Latin literature. Like Shakespeare he had
less Greek.[6]

The friendship between Henry James and Thomas Sergeant Perry,
begun so pleasantly at Newport in July, 1858, continued for over
fifty years, until the two men were the sole surviving members of
the youthful Newport group. Perry, the "superexcellent and all-
reading, all-engulfing friend of those days," was as consecrated to
the love of long walks, of long talks, and endless reading as was
Harry, and the communion of interests and temperaments laid immediate groundwork for their happy relationship. Two years
younger than Harry and much less travelled, Perry was in some ways
more mature, even more widely read than his new-found friend so
that the assets and liabilities of the boys complemented one another.
Willy James, too, found much delight in Sarg Perry, though the
difference in ages at that time prevented the much closer bond of
interests which developed ten years later, when the two young men
were studying in Germany. Willy then spoke of Perry's "true
modesty, and unreserved kind feeling . . . his humor and enthusiasm," qualities which were increasingly treasured as William found
so many acquaintances cold-blooded, egotistical, and conceited. Of
such traits T. S. Perry was "sweetly free." The three boys, often
joined by Wilky and Duncan Pell, explored the coves, beaches, cliffs,
and fields which then lay untouched, "untrodden, unsuspected, prac-

tically all inviolate," on every side. "We knew then," Harry recalled, "that no such range of airs would ever again be played for
us on but two or three silver strings. They were but two or three—
the sea so often as the isles of Greece, the mildly but perpetually
embayed promontories of mossy rocks and wasted thankless pasture,
bathed in a refinement of radiance and a sweetness of solitude which
amounted in themselves to the highest 'finish.' " [7] They felt that the
whole region was theirs alone, a vast region it seemed to them as it
stretched away "to the low horizon's furthest rim."

When these carefree, idyllic summer weeks came to an end, the
James boys entered the Berkeley Institute, Classical and Commercial
School, designed apparently, with all due respect to the good Bishop,
to attract the more practical as well as the academic clientele, much
in the manner of Mr. Jenks' institute of learning on Broadway in
earlier years. The school was founded in 1855 at #10 Washington
Square under the direction of Reverend Asa Dalton whose brother-in-
law, the Reverend William C. Leverett, had become the principal by
1858. The Reverend Leverett was at the same time assistant rector
of Trinity Church, "in which throbbed, from long before the Revolution . . . the proud episcopal heart of Newport." He was well qualified for both positions, having graduated from Harvard College in
1852 with honors in the Ancient Classics, going on for a post-
graduate course in Greek and Hebrew, and being ordained in the
Protestant Episcopal Church in 1857.[8]

Like M. Roediger of Geneva, the Reverend Leverett was an
amiable person, but unfortunately insignificant in appearance and
ineffectual as a teacher. Jim Mackaye, who, along with Sarg Perry,
Duncan Pell, and the James boys, was a student at Berkeley Institute, recalled him as "a little suit of clothes, stuffed out—a
small Napoleon, in miniature. He would say to us boys, at our
desks: 'The class may lay aside their books,' and then he'd proceed
to 'show off' his own oratory." [9] The students were then required to
speak pieces, an exercise that must have given small pleasure to
Harry James with his hesitant speech. The whole atmosphere of the
school, in the stuffy old house on Washington Square, was far from
inspiring; in fact, Harry was reminded of the Institute Vergnès with

its steep, cold, dusty wooden staircase and bare rooms with "young gentlemen" packed closely together, silhouetted against the gritty, depressing background. It is small wonder that Harry, never very much attracted to regular academic procedures, was remembered by T. S. Perry as "an uninterested scholar," although, as his friend recalled, they covered a substantial amount of Latin and the conventional areas of English literature. The social aspects of the school were hardly more stimulating than the intellectual, although several schoolmates, in addition to Perry and Duncan Pell, were distinguished in various ways. Among them were Ned Deacon, Edward Parker Deacon, of Boston, whose daughter later became the Duchess of Marlborough; James K. Lawrence, son of the Governor of Rhode Island; George Peabody Wetmore, who later served as U. S. Senator from Rhode Island; Louis and Henry Tiffany, from the well known Southern family of Baltimore; and Wheaton King of the Vernon-King family in Newport.

Of particular interest for Willy James was the companionship of James Morrison Steele Mackaye, who became the celebrated actor and playwright of the Eighties, for Jim, as he was then called, expressed great enthusiasm for art, a subject in which both Willy and Harry were increasingly interested. But Mackaye's desire to study art had then reached such serious proportions that in October, 1858, he sailed for Paris, just as his friendship with the Jameses had given promise of many happy Newport days. It was Jim Mackaye, however, who aroused in Willy especially a desire to study with William Morris Hunt, who had settled in Newport in 1855.[10] Although it was not until their return from Europe in 1860 that Willy and Harry became actual students in Hunt's studio on Church Street, they formed the habit of frequenting the atelier and sketching a bit during the winter of 1858-1859. These overtures to art were to have serious influence on both boys, directly upon William who, within a year, turned to painting as a possible life's work and indirectly upon Harry whose ultimate theory of the art of fiction included such a basic affinity between painting and literature.

The sudden arrival at William Hunt's studio of John La Farge had a more immediate influence upon them both. Early in the summer of

1859, Sarg Perry, Harry James, Wheaton King, Duncan Pell, and one or two others of their group were strolling along the cliffs, returning from one of their usual outings, when Willy James came running toward them. Bursting with enthusiasm, he blurted out: "There's a new fellow come to Hunt's class. He knows everything. He has read everything. He has seen everything—paints everything. He's a marvel!" When T. S. Perry asked how old he was Willy replied: "Well, he may be sixteen, and he may be seventy." [11]

There was little exaggeration in Willy James's first account of John La Farge, as the entire group soon discovered. The exciting young artist, seven or eight years older than the James boys, offered a background of tradition and experience which far outshone theirs, as cosmopolitan as that had been. Born in old St. John's Park, far downtown in New York, of cultivated French parents who were the center of a colony of aristocratic *émigrés* of the French Revolution, the child enjoyed unusual advantages from earliest years. In the early Forties the family moved to Washington Place, not far from the house in which Harry James was born in 1843. The La Farge home was one of comfort, if not of luxury, and John's childhood was spent among books, paintings, good music, and cultivated people. His grandfather, Binsse de St. Victor, a miniature painter of some talent, gave him drawing lessons, to which the child showed little response. His interest in art was not apparent for several years; it began during his first trip abroad in 1856, when he arrived in Paris to visit family relations. There he met such men as Théophile Gautier, Charles Blanc, and Puvis de Chavannes. Edward May, the American painter, interested the boy in painting and introduced him to his teacher, Couture, who accepted him as a member of his atelier. Couture, astonished at La Farge's talent, urged him toward a career, but he returned to New York, studied law and occupied himself with clubs, friends, social duties, maintaining merely a dilettante's interest in art and literature. La Farge happened to meet William Morris Hunt, just returning from a long residence in France and bubbling over with enthusiasm for the French school of Millet and Couture. So strong was Hunt's feeling about the modern French painters and so encouraging was he about La Farge's efforts that he persuaded the

young New Yorker to close his law books and settle down in Newport under Hunt's instruction.[12] This scant account of the young
man's background the James boys soon discovered, but of the wealth
of his culture and the extent of his talent they were to learn infinitely
more.

Early in October, 1859, the James family left Newport for another
year in Europe, but during the summer months between the time of
La Farge's arrival and their departure, Harry James responded deeply
and often to the fascination of this unusual new force in his development. "La Farge was of the type—the 'European,' and this gave him
an authority for me that it verily took the length of years to under-
mine. . . . I find it difficult, even under the appeal to me of the
attempt, to tell how he was to count in my earliest culture. . . .
The case was that La Farge swam into our ingenuous ken as the
figure of figures, and that such an agent, on a stage so unpeopled
and before a scene so unpainted, became salient and vivid almost in
spite of himself. The figure was at a premium, and fit for any glass
case that its vivacity should allow to enclose it—wherein it might be
surrounded by wondering, admiring and often quite inevitably mis-
conceiving observers. It was not that these two weren't agents in
their way, agents in some especial good cause without the furtherance
of which we never should have done at all; but they were by the
very fact specialized and stiffened, committed to their one attitude,
the immediately profitable, and incapable of that play of gesture in
which we recognize representation. A representative, a rounded
figure, however, is as to none of its relations definable or announce-
able beforehand; we only know it, for good or for ill, but with something of the throb of elation always, when we see it, and then it in
general sufficiently accounts for itself. . . .

"It was as a man of the world that, for all his youth, La Farge
rose or, still better, bowed, before us, his inclinations or obeisance,
his considerations of address being such as we had never seen . . .
This was what most immediately and most iridescently showed, the
truth being all the while that the character took on in him particular
values without which it often enough, though then much more grossly,
flourishes. It was by these enrichments of curiosity, of taste and

genius, that he became the personality, as we nowadays say, that I have noted—the full freshness of all of which was to play but through his younger time, or at least through our younger apprehension. He was so 'intellectual'—that was the flower; it crowned his being personally so finished and launched. The wealth of his cultivation, the variety of his initiations, the inveteracy of his forms, the degree of his *empressement* (this in itself, I repeat, a revelation) made him, with those elements of the dandy and the cavalier to which he struck us as so picturesquely sacrificing, a cluster of bright promises, a rare original and, though not at all a direct model for simpler folk, as we then could but feel ourselves, an embodiment of the gospel of esthetics. Those more resounding forms that our age was to see this gospel take on were then still to come, but I was to owe them in the later time not half the thrill that the La Farge of the prime could set in motion. He was really an artistic, an aesthetic nature of wondrous homogeneity; one was to have known in the future many an unfolding that went with a larger ease and a shrewder economy, but never to have seen a subtler mind or a more generously wasteful passion, in other words a sincerer one, addressed to the problems of the designer and painter." [13]

The sixteen-year-old youth who was to become such a distinguished designer and painter in words sat utterly enraptured at the feet of this fantasy, this personification of the "sense of Europe" combined with "the gospel of esthetics." During the warm summer days Harry would sit respectfully to one side of the tense, keen, carefully working artist either near a studio window or more frequently outdoors. Nothing could draw young James away. Sarg, Duncan, and the others, even Willy, preferred, after a while, a swim at "Second Beach," as they called Sachuset, swimming like veritable Sandwich Islanders, but Harry remained at his post. The boys' animated talks on Browning, on Ruskin, on beauty, on nature—as exciting as they sometimes were, while drying off in the sun—could not compare with the words of wisdom or the strokes of genius by which La Farge held Harry enraptured. "I see him at this hour again as that bright apparition; see him, jacketed in black velvet or clad from top to toe in old-time elegances of cool white and leaning much forward with his protuber-

ant and over-glazed, his doubting yet all-seizing vision, dandle along
the shining Newport sands in far-away summer sunsets on a charming chestnut mare whose light legs and fine head and great sweep
of tail showed the Arab strain. . . .

"So, at any rate, he was there, and there to stay—intensely
among us but somehow not withal *of* us; his being a Catholic, and
apparently a 'real' one in spite of so many other omniscences, making
perhaps by itself the greatest difference. He had been through a
Catholic college in Maryland, the name of which, though I am not
assured of it now, exhaled a sort of educational elegance; but where
and when he had so miraculously laid up his store of reading and
achieved his universal saturation was what we longest kept asking
ourselves. Many of these depths I couldn't pretend to sound, but it
was immediate and appreciable that he revealed to us Browning for
instance; and this, oddly enough, long after *Men and Women* had
begun (from our Paris time on, if I remember) to lie upon our
parents' book-table. *They* had not divined in us as yet an aptitude
for that author; whose appeal indeed John reinforced to our eyes by
the reproduction of a beautiful series of illustrative drawings, two
or three of which he was never to surpass—any more than he was
to complete his highly distinguished plan for the full set, not the
least faded of his hundred dreams. Most of all he revealed to us
Balzac; having so much to tell me of what was within that formidably-
plated door, in which he all expertly and insidiously played the key,
that to re-read even after long years the introductory pages of
Eugénie Grandet, breathlessly seized and earnestly absorbed under his
instruction, is to see my initiator's youthful face, so irregular but so
refined, look out at me between the lines as through blurred prison
bars." [14]

These very early artistic gropings under La Farge's stimulation
were mere fumblings, in Harry's awakening to the wide world of
aesthetics, compared with the progress he was to make upon returning
from Bonn a year later. Although, as T. S. Perry observed, Harry's
chief interest then, as it was always to be, was literature, the lines
of demarcation between literature and art were but vaguely drawn; and
John La Farge seemed to blend confusingly into a figure of both

realms. The *Revue des Deux Mondes,* which the boys were just beginning to read with appreciation, represented to Harry the very world of La Farge. "Out of the safe rich home of the *Revue,* which opened away into the vastness of visions, he practically stepped, and into it, with all his ease, he mysteriously returned again." Closed up safely within the pink and very "European"-looking covers of the French periodical, John La Farge was to remain for Harry, stepping out again and with greater significance in the autumn of 1860.

There had been nothing permanent about this residence in Newport, as far as the elder James was concerned, for it had been to a large degree a question of expedience. Having published *Christianity the Logic of Creation,* in 1857, he had relaxed during the following year, quietly contemplating the beginnings of his next major work, *Substance and Shadow,* not to be completed until 1863. The delightful rest and pleasant activities in Newport had, for a year, been most enjoyable and beneficial, but in the spring of 1859 Henry James, Sr., made it clear that he was seriously considering a return to Europe. Boston and Cambridge, Emerson, John Dwight, Alcott and others of the Saturday Club group had been stimulating to him on occasional visits there from Newport, but like all genuine religionists and philosophical thinkers he depended but little upon friends or places for his inspiration. It did not matter greatly, in fact, where the elder James was, as far as his own work was concerned, but it mattered greatly to him that his children should be in the place which would best contribute to their development and well-being. As early as September, 1858, only three months after the family's arrival, he wrote to his friend and banker, Samual G. Ward of Boston, that they were remaining in Newport for the winter, where the village life "for a few months will be good discipline for us all, and set us up famously for Europe in the Spring." He then expressed, in a paragraph of that metaphysical haze through which he often seemed not to distinguish between substance and shadow, his belief that the growing tendency, on the part of Americans, to travel in Europe was the prelude to the millennium predicted by the combined philosophies of Swedenbourg and Fourier: "What sets all the world travelling now-a-days is the need of satisfying in some degree the quickened sentiments of the race, by throwing off the limitations, once so rigid, of men's nativity, and rising into the fellowship of all people and knowledge and tongues. It is curious to see how many and how singular are the missionaries this Divine enterprise equips; persons whom *a priori* (or fifty years ago) you would never think of seeing move all their days from their own chimney corners, now trans (partly illegible) Europe, Darby and Joan together, knowing no language but American, putting up with inconveniences the most unbelievable, mounting to *sixièmes* and *septièmes* in order to go to bed, elbowed by police and snubbed by customs' officers, yet bearing all and rejoicing under all precisely as if they were so many ancient Pauls at Ephesus. It is beautiful to see this new born contentment welling up in the soul, and gives one hopes of immense things to come."[15]

When one considers the tremendous turmoil of the Civil War, alarmingly approaching on every side in America, the "immense things to come," seem as utterly removed from the cold realm of facts as was his own metaphysical detachment from the practical aspects of life. An idealist in the highest sense of the word, Henry James, Sr., was concerned always not with natural society but with society in "the redeemed form of man." Stephen Pearl Andrews, the reformer who entered into a debate with James on free love, a few years earlier, aptly described his opponent's great weakness. While paying tribute to James's spiritual qualities and intellectual powers, Andrews pointed out his inability to make practical application of his religious and social theories; he saw James as one who "tended powerfully toward metaphysical subtleties and spiritual entities, until he is completely off the solid earth, and loses all knowledge of practical things." He placed James in "the school of seers and prophets . . . a mere *jet d'eau* of aspiration, reaching a higher elevation at some points than almost any other man, but breaking into spray and impalpable mist, glittering in the sun, and descending to earth with no weight or mechanical force to effect any great end." [16] Although such a statement is an exaggeration, it explains in part the fact that the elder James failed to bring his utopian concepts into concrete relation with immediate human problems, that he failed to establish a satisfactory framework for the educational ideals he so constantly adhered to on behalf of his children.

One of his unusual ideas, not metaphysical but in a sense as impractical as his general beliefs on education, is that they should not follow the conventional procedure of going to college. One of his earliest statements to this effect occurs in a letter to Mrs. Francis G. Shaw, mother of Robert Gould Shaw, written in July, 1859, when he speaks of considering a return to Geneva, "for you know we are anxiously thinking of embarking for that educational paradise. We can't get a house in Cambridge, and are disposed to think it would not be the place for us in all respects if we could. Besides, I am not looking forward to giving my boys a college course, our desire after Cambridge having been prompted by the wish to get my oldest boy in the Scientific School. But we *may* not go, as our minds are still undetermined." [17]

His objections to the idea of college were ultimately overruled after the return to Newport, just as his hopes of curing Harry of the habit of excessive novel-reading by placing him at the Institute Rochette in Geneva to study science and mathematics, were to be defeated during their stay at that "educational paradise." Whether these plans succeeded or failed, whether the family went abroad or remained in America, however, the elder James was constantly sustained, as he told Mrs. Shaw in this letter, by the one *"fixed mind,"* the basic metaphysical principle that they were all "absolute creatures of God," cared for, guided, animated every moment by Him, and upon this spiritual understanding James rested the weight of his unimpeachable faith.

By the end of the summer he wrote again to Samual Ward of their European plans, but far more definitely. Dated from Newport, September 18, 1859, the letter states: "I have grown so discouraged about the education of my children here, and dread so their inevitable habits of extravagance and insubordination, which appear to be the characteristics of American youth, that I have come to the conclusion to retrace my steps to Europe, and keep them there a few years longer. My wife is completely of the same mind and though we feel on many accounts that we are making personal sacrifices in this step, the advantages to the children are so clear that we cannot conscientiously hesitate. I am a good patriot, but my patriotism is even livelier on the other side of the water. At all accounts, I am quite sure that my main object in life, which is to do justice to my children, will be so promoted by our return to Europe, as to make all my lesser activities and obligations easily fulfilled." [18]

The effect of the decision to leave Newport, both upon the James children and their friends, was a mixture of delight and regret. To Harry, whose "sense of Europe" had been greatly revived by John La Farge, the plans were more exciting than had been those of 1855. To Willy too, with a deeply rooted and rapidly growing interest in painting, Europe offered very desirable prospects, although his parents had definitely in mind the hope of diverting his interest in art to a pursuit of scientific study, as the year was to prove. In both youths, however, there were genuine pangs of regret that they would leave behind a group of friends and companions to whom they had become deeply attached, the first circle of friends their own age which circumstances had permitted them to cultivate. It would indeed not be easy to part with Sarg Perry, John La Farge, Duncan Pell, and Jim Mackaye who had returned from Paris just a few weeks before. Seventy years later, Thomas Sergeant Perry, then the only surviving member of those Newport times, recounted to Percy Mackaye, son of the late celebrated actor and playwright, Steele Mackaye, who had always been "Jim" to the Jameses, the sad scene of their departure: "October 3, 1859, is a date that revives for me the early memory of a poignant sorrow, for on that night Harry and Willie James were going away to Europe, and I was in the depths of a boyish despair. So also was Jim Mackaye, your father, who went down with me to the boat to bid our comrades goodbye. All of us were intimate friends, schoolmates and neighbors. We didn't differentiate our ages; we were all too interested in ideas. Our companionship was a keen mutual delight, and our parting was a rather solemn occasion. When Jim and I walked back together through the night, up Bull Street to Kay— where Colonel Mackaye's house, with the Gothic roofs and little tower, stood near a rustic lane with stables—I remember tarrying outside with Jim, talking affectionately of our friends, the Jameses,

who were to sail from New York for Havre, in the *S. S. Vanderbilt,*
on October 8th. There we talked on a good while, out of our
hearts, till at last Jim turned in the path to his home and I went
away through the lane." [19]

NOTES

1. Less than twenty years after the founding of Newport in the 1640s,
   shipping had become a major enterprise. "By 1675, the island
   farms, which have the best soil in the State, were furnishing ex-
   ports for the middle and southern Colonies, the West Indies and
   Europe. Wool was sent to France in exchange for linen; horses,
   beef, pork, butter, cheese, and flour went to the Barbados for sugar,
   molasses, and indigo; and codfish, haddock, and mackeral were
   exported to the West Indies and southern Europe in exchange for
   salt, rice, and wines." *Rhode Island,* American Guide Series, Boston,
   Houghton Mifflin Company, 1937, 202.

2. As brief as the separation from the boys was to be, it brought forth
   from thirteen-year-old Wilky a letter dated from Albany, July 1,
   1858, which reflects the precociousness, the affection, the sensitivity,
   and humor which was to characterize so much of the correspondence
   between these remarkable children and their devoted parents: "How
   I miss you, particularly at this present moment as all the house
   has sallied forth to see 'The Albany Rural Cemetery' and left Grandma
   and me to sympathise with each other at home, but we don't though
   at-all, for Grandma is fast asleep and I am wide awake, striving to
   write a nice filial letter—but alas! I suppose by this time you are at
   New Port and enjoying yourselves very much. We have had a delightful change in the weather, and on the whole are enjoying ourselves a great deal. All the news I can tell you is that Mr. Alcott has
   done something and if Uncle Howard (James) was home I could
   tell you what he did do. I must now conclude with hands full
   of love to the young party and heaps of the same to the old party.
   I remain dear F. and M., Your affectionate son, G. W. James. P. S.
   Brethren W(illy) and H(arry) and all the family send their love
   to the chicks, the rooster, and the hen." MS. letter from Garth
   Wilkinson James to Henry James, Sr., July 1, 1858, Houghton
   Library, Harvard University.

3. "Newport—Historical and Social," *Harper's New Monthly Magazine,*
   vol. IX (Aug., 1854), 289, 290. The Old State House, at the
   head of Washington Square, was built in 1739, to house the General Assembly, but was also used for public meetings, religious, and
   social functions. From the second-floor balcony, above which is the
   celebrated gilded pineapple in the pediment over the window, official
   proclamations were read of the death of George II, the ascendency of

George III, and the acceptance of the Declaration of Independence. The Synagogue and Cemetery on Touro Street are monuments to the distinguished Jewish colony, established in the 17th century and continuing until the early 19th. Of Dutch extraction, the earliest Jewish group obtained a deed for a burial-ground in 1677, and the Synagogue was dedicated in 1763. Trinity (Episcopal) Church dated from 1724, being completed in 1726 and later used by Bishop Berkeley who preached from its three-deck pulpit, the top of which is reached by a winding staircase that brings the preacher almost on a level with the galleries running around three sides of the structure. See *Rhode Island,* American Guide Series, 198-232.

4. *The Letters of William James,* I, 184: He continues in this letter: "I have been staying at the Tweedies with Mrs. Chapman, and James Sturgis and his wife, and enjoying extremely, not the conversation indoors, but the lonely lying on the grass on the cliffs at Lily Pond, and four or five hours yesterday at the Dumplings, feeling the moving air and the gentle living sea. There is a purity and mildness about the elements here which purges the soul of one. . . . I go the day after tomorrow (Monday) with the Tweedies to New York, assist at Henrietta Temple's wedding on Tuesday, and then pass on to the Centennial (in Philadelphia) for a few days. I suppose it will be pretty tiresome, but I want to see the English pictures, which they say are a good show. . . . " Their cousin Henrietta Temple married Leslie Pell-Clarke of Newport on June 6, 1876, at Christ Church, Pelham, New York. Leslie Pell-Clarke was the son of Duncan Campbell Pell, Lieutenant Governor of Rhode Island and brother of Duncan Archibald Pell, schoolmate and companion of the James boys at Newport.

5. Thomas Sergeant Perry (1845-1928) was one of the first friends of the James boys during their Newport years and the friendship extended over many decades; he was in Germany for a time in 1867 with William James when both young men were abroad studying; Perry returned to Harvard, having graduated in 1866, as a tutor in French and German, later becoming a member of *The North American Review* staff and of the Department of English at Harvard. In his critical writings he early showed interest in realism and through his admiration for Turgenev influenced young Henry James and William Dean Howells in their theory of the novel.

6. Quoted by Percy Lubbock, *The Letters of Henry James,* I, 6-8. Duncan Archibald Pell (1840-1874) was the son of Duncan Campbell Pell, Lieutenant Governor of Rhode Island. One year older than Willy James and nearly three years older than Harry, he was, along with Thomas Sergeant Perry, their constant companion during the Newport years. At nineteen he enlisted as a private in Company "A" of the First Rhode Island Regiment and was in the Battle of Bull Run, served as aide-de-camp to General Burnside, and was captured

near Warrenton, spending two months in Libby Prison. He was considered "one of the handsomest men of his day." He died young.
On January 23, 1874, Mrs. Henry James, Sr., wrote to her son William, "Father is writing and will tell you about Duncan Pell's death."

7. *Notes of a Son and Brother,* 107.

8. Information secured from the Harvard Archives, Harvard University.

9. Percy Mackaye, *op. cit.,* I, 76, 77.

10. William Morris Hunt (1824-1879), after studying with Millet in
Paris, returned to the United States in 1855 as one of the American
interpreters of the new French school. In 1856 from Newport, he
wrote to his mother: "I think the advantage of the right kind of
society, climate, and geographical position make this the most suitable
place for us to choose as a residence. I have bought a house here
. . . on the opposite side of the street from Mr. King's place, just
opposite the old Jew burying-ground—an old-fashioned, bluish-gray
house placed back in the yard some distance from the road, with
several trees about it." The house now forms part of the Hill Top
Inn in Newport. See Martha A. S. Shannon, *Boston Days of Wm.
Morris Hunt,* Boston, Marshall Jones Company, 1923, 43.

11. Percy Mackaye, *op. cit.,* 65.

12. John La Farge (1835-1910), artist and author, became one of Henry
Adam's closest friends, going to Japan and the South Seas with him
in 1886, bringing back some excellent watercolors and paintings.
His mural decorations for Trinity Church, Boston, established his
fame and brought him many commissions, the Minnesota State
capital being one of the best known. In relation to his Newport
years, the Art Association there in 1913 held an exhibition in the
old Church Street Studio and Miss Theodora Watson, another of
Hunt's students, was present. "She seemed troubled to find that
the entrance through the paved court was used rather than the small
door on the other side. 'When I worked here with Hunt, we always
came in through this door,' Miss Watson declared. 'My easel stood
here, and John La Farge's there. Henry and William James were on
the other side.' " Shannon, *op. cit.,* 47.

13. *Notes of a Son and Brother,* 88-91.

14. *Ibid.,* 92, 93. Like the admiring youth at his feet, John La Farge
was to go on to brilliant success and in not an unlike way, " . . .
a man of broad culture and a scholar, La Farge, as time went by,
developed his personality among European intellectuals. His training might have been known as 'hit or miss,' yet he profited by an
eclectic foundation and held to what he was taught. . . . La Farge
possessed all manner of tastes and the widest possible range as an
artist. He admired Japanese prints. He lectured. He wrote. He
studied old masters. Far earlier than anyone else he believed in the
Pre-Raphaelites." Homer Saint-Gaudens, *The American Artist and
His Times,* New York, Dodd, Mead, & Co., 1941, 153.

15. MS. letter from Henry James, Sr., to Samual Gray Ward, September 27, 1858, Houghton Library, Harvard University.
16. See Matthiessen, *op. cit.*, 12-14. Stephen Pearl Andrews (1812-1886) was a reformer interested in various radical movements, including the liberation of the slaves by purchase. His basic religious and economic free thinking is presented in his book, *The Science of Society*, a book that is quite as utopian as anything written by Henry James, Sr.
17. R. B. Perry, *op. cit.*, I, 186.
18. MS. letter from Henry James, Sr., to Samual Gray Ward, September 18, 1859, Houghton Library, Harvard University.
19. Percy Mackaye, *op. cit.*, I, 75, 76.

Chapter Eleven

Swiss and German Discipline

"Impressions . . . were naught without a backing, a stout stiff hard-grained underside that would hold them together. . . ."

Frederick Winterbourne, whose expanding consciousness affords the pattern of *Daisy Miller,* arrives in Vevey from Geneva, impressed by the visions of Newport and Saratoga that the Swiss resort evoked. The "grand" hotels with innumerable balconies and multicolored flags flying from pointed roofs remind him of the Ocean House or Congress Hall. Distinctly European features he observes at the Trois Couronnes, in Vevey, however: " . . . neat German waiters, who look like secretaries of legation; Russian princesses sitting in the garden; little Polish boys walking about, held by the hand, with their governors; a view of the sunny crest of the Dent du Midi and the picturesque towers of the Castle of Chillon." In the background, glittering in the brilliant sunlight, the less expensive pensions are arrayed, their names inscribed in German-looking lettering on pink or yellow walls; each has a well-kept garden, in which the rustic summerhouse commands a superb view of the "First of Lakes," as Voltaire called it.

At Geneva, forty miles down the Lake by one of the picturesque steamers, Winterbourne had spent a good portion of his twenty-seven years, "studying," as his friends vaguely stated. Placed in school there as a boy, he later attended the College, lingering on during subsequent years, held by the magic which caused Americans sometimes to live too long in Europe. In 1859, young Henry James was only sixteen; he had never been to Vevey nor seen Saratoga, but he was in many ways a potential Winterbourne. The details with which he later sketched the setting of *Daisy Miller* were acquired in abundance during his boyhood experiences in Geneva.

After eleven days of bad weather, the James family arrived in Le Havre on October 20, 1859 from the steamship *Vanderbilt*. A brief day's visit offered enough picturesque scenes to provide "The Four Meetings" with fine local color some years later. Stopping only two days in Paris, they travelled on to Geneva, making the entire trip by train, the railroad having been opened over the Jura the previous year. On October 25th, only five days after landing, they were established at the Hotel de l'Ecu, finding no apartment to suit their needs. For young Henry this was an agreeable arrangement as he took delight in observing the flow of guests, not so many English and Americans as might be expected, but enough probably to supply prototypes of Mrs. Costello, rude little Randolph, and Daisy herself, that "child of nature and of freedom . . . the most prosperous child of my invention."

In contrast to the uncertainty and indecision about schools in 1855, arrangements were now made within a very few days. In a full letter to Thomas Sergeant Perry of Newport, Henry, Jr., wrote an account of the family's experience since leaving New York, giving specific information on the arrangements for schooling. The letter is dated Nov. 18, 1859, and he speaks of having been in school for three weeks; thus very little time was lost: "We arrived here in good season for the opening of the schools. & we boys are disposed of as follows: Wilkie & Robbie are installed at boarding school out in the country. They've a very nice place, capital play ground and provisions for fun out of doors; their teacher M. Maquelin is a very good man, and Americans and English are in the minority which is very rare here in Geneva. Willie goes to the Courses of the Academy which he finds to suit him exactly. I have become a member of the school of M. Rochette, which thus far I have no cause to regret;

I have to work harder than I have ever done before, the school-hours being from 8 A. M. to 5 P. M. with but an hour's intermission. Hitherto I have had to study all evening, and on my holidays which are Thursday afternoon and Sunday and have therefore no time of my own at all. But I shall be soon able to have most of the evenings free, as I have caught up with my class, which was a couple of weeks ahead of me and have given up one study for which I had no time. There are twenty scholars who attend as I do from eight to five, and several who only come for certain classes, and leave as soon as they are over. The school is intended for preparing such boys as wish to be engineers, architects, machinists, 'and the like' for other higher schools, and I am the only one who is not destined for either of the useful arts or sciences, although I am I hope for the art of being useful in some way. I get on there nevertheless very well." [1]

The reasons for his being in a school which specialized in sciences were never clear to him, either while attending it or decades later when he reminisced about it. With genial amusement he then looked back upon himself as having "been so disposed of under a flattering misconception of my aptitudes that leaves me to-day even more wonderstruck than at that immediate season of distress." Actually his parents had no illusions about his aptitudes, but they had developed, during the previous year in Newport, a deep concern over his indulgence in reading fiction and in William's strong attraction toward painting as a possible career. This return to Geneva, in 1859, was taken as a remedial step for both sons, and the severity of young Henry's "season of distress" at M. Rochette's school was not unknown by his mother and father. Lenient as they were, they felt that it would be "good" for him to struggle with subjects demanding the discipline and perseverance he so reluctantly gave to such things. Recalling the severe demands, he wrote: "I so feared and abhorred mathematics that the simplest arithmetical operation had always found and kept me helpless and blank—the dire discipline of the years bringing no relief whatever to my state; and mathematics unmitigated were at the Institution Rochette the air we breathed." [2] To Sarg Perry, at the time, he made no mention of "awful little M. Galopin, that dispenser of the paralysing chalk," who summoned him to the terrifying blackboard to solve a problem, nor M. Verchère, with whom he "worried out Vigil and Tite-Live." Boylike, he kept up a brave front, but he remembered it all for years as "mere darkness, waste and anguish."

There were bright moments, however—going with Willie to "the Junction," where the Rhone and Arve meet, or along the borders of the Lake, also occasionally to see the younger brothers at Champel. But the school predominates in his letters. To Perry he wrote again, on January 26, 1860:

" . . . Perhaps you would like to know about my school. The building is wholly unlike that of the Berkeley Institute. It is a dilapidated old stone house in the most triste quarter of town. Scarcely a soul passes it all day, and I do not remember to have seen a wheeled vehicle of any kind near it since I've been there. Beside it is the prison and opposite the Cathedral of St. Peter, in which Calvin used to preach. It seems to me that none but the most harmless and meekest men are incarcerated in the former building. While at my lesson in a class room which looks out on the door, I have once in a while seen an offender brought up to his doom. He marches along with handcuffs on his wrists (sic), followed by a gendarme in 'spick & span' uniform. The gendarme knocks on the door, which is opened by some internal spring, shoves in his charge, the door closes, the gendarme retraces his steps. What happens after the prisoner is inside I don't know, but as the only officer I have ever seen about the prison is a diminutive little porter with a most benign countenance, I am inclined to think that the most inoffensive are sent to him to deal with. . . . " [3]

While the old prison has been removed from its ancient site behind the Cathedral, the same sort of procedure might be observed today at the gate of the Prison de St. Antoine, not far away, on the other side of the Bourg de Four. The quiet dignity, the ordered life, and beauty of the city lend even to the stern arm of the law a certain picturesqueness which suggests the scene and action of light opera. The grim facade of #7 Rue de l'Evéché (#105 a century ago), occupied by the Institution Rochette in 1859, does have an ominous look, however, which supports Henry James's darker memories of it, recorded in Notes of A Son and Brother. From the "hard-grained underside" of his recollections, the elderly novelist saw the school as "—the dark, the dreary Institution, squeezed into a tall, dim, stony-faced and stony-hearted house at the very top of the Cité and directly in the rear of the Cathedral, portions of the apse of which seem to me to have straggled above or protruded toward it, with other odd extraneous masses than itself pressing still nearer. This simplification, quite luxuriously for my young mind, was to mere mean blackness of an old-world sordid order. I recognized *rich* blackness in other connections, but this was somehow of a harsh tradition and a tragic economy; sordid and strong was what I had from the first felt the place, though urging myself always to rub off history from its stones . . . " [4] This sense of responsibility was a primary impetus in him; being partly moral and partly aesthetic, it made him feel that somehow, such queer crooked streets and cobblestone alleys, twisting through the oldest parts of Geneva did something "to the imagination and the taste."

Concerning his companions in the first-year courses, there were four young men, about his age, of whom he wrote to Perry: "Two of them are Genevese, one is Russian and the other an Englishman. He is the only one with whom I have been able to become the least bit friendly. He seems to be a nice sort of fellow, but as he is only an externe I do not see much of him. Of one of the Genevese I think I may say I never saw a more uninteresting individual, and of the other Genevese and the Russian that I have often seen more interesting. None of the other fellows have shown the least desire to make friends." [5] This European reserve, so different from the camaraderie of the Newport school, was particularly acute in Geneva. The elder James noted it as did William, who complained in 1903 to his Swiss colleague, Theodore Flournoy: "Never inside a private house, and only after three months or more familiar enough with other students to be admitted to Zofingue" [6] (a student society of the Academy).

With typical alertness to social order, Henry James behaved toward his Genevese schoolmates with what he later called "bourgeois circumspection," recognizing a condition which is still extant in Geneva: "The dread in the Genevese of having definitely to 'know' strangers and thereby be at costs for any sort of hospitality to them comes back to me as written clear; not less than their being of two sorts or societies, sons of the townspeople pure and simple and sons of the local aristocracy perched in certain of the fine old houses of the Cité and enjoying a background of sturdily-seated lakeside villas and deeply umbrageous campagnes. I remember thinking the difference of type, complexion and general *allure* between these groups more marked, to all the senses, than any 'social distinction' I had yet encountered." [7] While the Institution Rochette was not destined to play a large part in Henry James's education, the social order surrounding it contributed to his sharpening awareness of basic values in European culture. "I couldn't," he confessed, "seeing and feeling these things, really believe I had picked up nothing."

Perhaps the most pleasant and impressive part of this Geneva sojourn was the course in French literature which young Henry James took under Charles Töpffer, son of the celebrated Swiss writer, Rudolphe Töpffer. He had studied sculpturing in Paris, achieving distinction there and doing in his native city such pieces as the bust of his father, now in Töpffer Square. In 1859, when teaching at M. Rochette's, Charles Töpffer was twenty-seven, charming in manner, enthusiastic about French life, and full of entertaining stories about student days in Paris. His young American admirer was to remember gratefully the hours spent with this kindred spirit who offered him the "breath of culture as I modestly aspired to culture."

With M. Toeppfer I was almost happy; with each of these instructors my hour was unshared, my exploits unwitnessed, by others; but M. Toeppfer became a friend, shewed himself a *causeur*, brightened our lesson with memories of his time in Paris. . . . He had haunted the parterre of the Théatre Francais, and when we read Racine his vision of Rachel, whom he had seen there as often as possible, revived; he was able to say at moments how she had spoken and moved, and I recall in particular his telling me that on her entrance as Phèdre, borne down, in her languorous passion, by the weight of her royal robes— "Que ces vains ornements, que ces voiles me pèsent!"—the long lapse of time before she spoke and while she sank upon a seat filled itself extraordinarily with her visible woe. But where he most gave me comfort was in bringing home to me that the house commemorated, immortalized, as we call it, in the first of his father's Nouvelles Genevoises, *La Bibliothèque de mon Oncle,* was none other than the structure facing us where we sat and which so impinged and leaned on the cathedral walls that he had but to indicate to me certain points from the window of our room to reconstitute thrillingly the scenery, the drollery, the whimsical action of the tale. There was a demonstration I could feel important, votary and victim of the "scene," the scene and the "atmosphere" only, that I had been formed to. That I called interesting lore—called it so at least to myself, though feeling it at the same time of course so little *directly* producible. . . . There abode in me, I may add, a sense that on any subject that did appeal and that so found me ready—such subjects being indeed as yet vague, but immensely suggestive of number—I should have grasped the confident chalk, welcomed the very biggest piece, not in the least have feared the blackboard. They were inscribed, alas for me, in no recognized course.[8]

Young Henry James's education had always been and would continue to be a series of impressions, picked up without organized form or order, taken in in exact proportion to his responsiveness to them. There was no hope of conforming to recognized procedures, to prescribed curricula, to conventional patterns. Furthermore, failure to do so did not, in this case, constitute the "obscure and deeply hushed failure" that he later pronounced upon his withdrawing from M. Rochette's. After five months of disciplining study, he was considerably eased by a new arrangement. At the end of the spring vacation, he was allowed by his parents to drop all subjects at the Institution except German, French, and Latin, and was permitted by the Academy to sit in on a number of courses, some being attended by William and others to which he was attracted. The spring months in Geneva came as a concurrent blessing, after the cold dampness and the frequent "bise." He didn't object so strongly to the dancing lessons twice a week and decided that he liked Geneva "best of all" the cities he had been in. " . . . it has no Galleries or Museums," he wrote Perry, "or Churches but it is nevertheless very interesting. Such dingy old streets and courts and alleys, black with age some of them are, steep and dirty, such quaint old houses, high and sombre are very picturesque." [9] Thus he was again more or less free to take up his avocation of the flâneur, an employment which had much greater importance to his development than could then be realized. To Henry James's creative mind, the best training and greatest challenge would always be the transforming of impressions of life into new substance. This process culminated in the higher process of his art. It was to become an absolute for him, as Percy Lubbock states, "that the work of the imagination was the highest and most honourable calling conceivable, being indeed nothing less than the actual creation of life out of the void." The dark interlude in the grim school behind St. Pierre Cathedral came as close to being a void as did any part of his education. The remaining months in Geneva during 1860 led him back in the direction of his natural inclination, though indeed as a somewhat wiser and chastened young man.

Each morning, after the Academy's doors reopened in April, Henry and William left the Hotel de l'Ecu for their lectures, going up to the Grand' Rue by way of the steep incline of the Rue de la Tour Boël. These were happy days. "My whole impression now," he recalled, "with my self-respect re-established, was of something exquisite: I was put to the proof about nothing; I deeply enjoyed the confidence shown in my taste, not to say in my honour, and I sat out lecture after lecture as I might have sat out drama, alternate tragedy and comedy, beautifully performed—the professor in each case figuring the hero, and the undergraduates, much more numerous, though not in general maturer than those of the Institution, where I had been, to my perception, every one's junior, partaking in an odd fashion of the nature at once of troupe and spectators. The scientific subjects, in a large suggestive way, figured tragedy, I seemed to feel, and I pushed this form to the point of my following, for conscience's sake, though not with the last regularity, lurid demonstrations, as they affected me, on anatomy and physiology; these in turn leading to my earnest view, at the Medical School, of the dissection of a *magnifique gendarme*—which ordeal brought me to a stand." [10]

There is little evidence either in letters written from Geneva then or in recollections written decades later that young Henry James's attendance at the Academy, from April to July in 1860, added perceptibly to his intellectual or literary development. He did recall attending the "conferences" of the celebrated Professor Frederic Amiel[11] occasionally, that "mild grave oracle of the shrine." But this period of luxuriating through the lecture-halls and corridors of what later became the University of Geneva was to remain with

him merely as a "confounding blur of light." In his room at the
Hotel de l'Ecu, however, he was carrying on secret literary efforts,
shared with no one, apparently. In May, Wilkie wrote to Perry from
the Pensionnat Maquelin: "Willy & Harry have been getting along
very well indeed this last winter. Harry has become an author I
believe, for he keeps his door locked all day long, & a little while
ago, I got a peep in his room, and saw some poetical looking manuscripts lying on the table, & himself looking in a most author-like
way." From the time of his earliest scribblings in the New York
days, young Henry had taken much teasing from the brothers and
not until the family was settled at Newport during the Civil War
were his ambitions to write taken seriously.

He must have found the family gatherings at the Hotel l'Ecu on
Sunday afternoons somewhat trying and wisely kept his door locked.
Alice, the adored young sister delighted in these occasions, however,
with all four boys together, hanging over the balconies on the Rhone
side of the Hotel. Wilkie and Bobby entertained them all with caustic
comments about their boarding school life. How much truth there
may have been in their flamboyant accounts it was hard to tell.
The elder James joined in the fun, with all the vigor and humor
of this strong personality. How they missed him whenever he took
a brief trip, as he occasionally did, to Paris and London! The following letter from Wilky, who was then fourteen, overflows with the
love and affection which constantly enclosed the family:

GENEVA, DEC., 1859

MY DEAR FATHER,

We arrived a little while ago from school and have already read your
welcome letters that have made one feel very sympathetic for you, but
still I cannot help smiling at the easy, graceful and homesick style in
which they flow. . . . How do you find Paris and London? I would
give a great deal to be there with you, to be arm and arm with you
in Regent's Street or St. John's Wood. But I suppose those sweet days
have passed and that we are now not to depend so much upon the
pleasures that unity or friendship can afford, because we are growing
older and must prepare to harden ourselves to deny ourselves the mere
affections, so that in the world to come we may have peace and as
much of these pleasures as we like. Enough of this, however. . . .

How are the Wilkinsons? Give them all my love, and tell Mrs. Wilkinson how glad I was to receive her letter, or something agreeable that would touch her sentimentally (you know what I mean).

Father, you cannot imagine how much we miss you, and what a blank space your absence makes in this house. Even away off at school I feel it. I have a sort of unprotected feeling (not physically so, but mentally)—I feel as if there was something missing—but I have no doubt it does an immense deal of good to both sides to have occasionally these little separations. We received five letters after you left, one of them from La Farge, who gives us four pages of nothing else but Newport gossip and Newport this and thats. . . .

Willie interrupts me here and wants me to go into the parlor with him to hear him deliver a little sonnate on Alice which he has just composed and which he means to perform with much gusto. I will tell you its success when it is finished. . . . Song went off very well, and excited a good deal of laughter among the audience assembled.

As I have exhausted all my news, and as bedtime is approaching and as my eyes are gradually closing, even so must this letter which is meant to tell you how much we love you, how much we miss you, and how much we would give for you to be back under the roof of this hotel. Good-bye, dear Papa. Ever your affectionate son,

G. W. JAMES[12]

In a letter equally playful, gay, and affectionate, written by eighteen-year-old William to his father on one of those empty weekends, Mrs. James is described as being able to "do nothing but sit and cry for you. She refuses to associate with us and has one side of the room to herself. She and the Aunt (Kate) are now in the Aunt's room. Wilky and Bobby, at home for the day, are at church. It is a hard grey day. H(enry) is telling a story to Louis Osborne, and I will try to make a sketch of them. There has been a terrible bise; the two *Cornhill Magazines* have come. Mrs. Thomas has been too sick to be at dinner, and we have seen something of some most extraordinary English people." [13] Enclosed in the original letter was "some very beautiful poetry" written as usual in honor of Alice, which "loses a great deal by not being sung," although Alice, it is noted, "took it very cooly."

Mrs. Thomas was a handsome American widow, originally from New York but later of the American colony centered on the Avenue

Gabriel in Paris. Her children were attending M. Haccius's establishment, rival to M. Roediger's pension which the James boys had attended in 1855. The Osbornes were also American expatriates, who
had placed their sons at Pensionnat Maquelin, while the father
travelled in the east. Harry recalled that not long after Willy made
the sketch of him telling Louis Osborne a story, the family received
word of the father's death in the Holy Land. Similar to Harry's
reaction in Boulogne to the young English lad who awaited news
of his parents' death in India were his intense observations of M.
and Madame Maquelin's arrival at the Hôtel de l'Ecu, bearing the
sad news in a letter just come. Harry, holding young Louis on
his knee, did not at all envy the Maquelins their mission and
felt deeply for poor, "helpless, little listening Louis," whose dramatic
situation hovered for years in Harry's mind.

The "most extraordinary English people" were to be remembered
vaguely as speaking with the James parents, rather condescendingly,
about the recent novel, *Adam Bede,* by a new author, George Eliot.
The elder James had enthusiastically lent his copy of the novel to the
English couple, thinking they would greatly enjoy this first effort
of their fellow countryman. The Anglo-American currents of contrast, so much a part of Harry James's later life, were distinctly
felt by him in this incident at Geneva. "I catch again the echo
of their consternation on receiving it back with the remark that
all attempt at an interest in such people, village carpenters and
Methodists, had proved vain—for that style of Anglo-Saxon; together with that of my own excited wonder about such other people,
those of the style in question, those somehow prodigiously presented
by so rare a delicacy, so proud a taste, and made thus so irradiate a
strange historic light. It *referred* them, and to a social order, making
life more interesting and more various; even while our clear democratic air, that of our little family circle, quivered as with the mon-
strosity. It might, this note that made us, in the parlance of today,
sit up, fairly have opened to me that great and up to then unsuspected door of the world from which the general collection of mon-
strosities, its existence suddenly brought home to us, would doubtless
stretch grandly away." [14]

Concurrently with his first knowledge of the name George Eliot, came to Harry James the sense of sharp Anglo-Saxon class consciousness, the question of social strata, of lines of demarcation which went deeper than he could then possibly comprehend. He was to meet George Eliot twice, to become one of her most ardent admirers and followers, just as he was to meet in infinite variety the Anglo-Saxon nature in all the complexities of its highly developed social order. Of these things, however, he was hardly aware at Geneva, in 1860.

William James's tendency in later years to discount his educational experiences in Geneva was based on his regret over the lack of discipline his career as a philosopher and psychologist demanded. By contrast, young Henry James vicariously profited from William's Geneva activities, coming out ultimately with far more useful material. This is seen, for example, in his minute account of William's participation in the Swiss student's society, Zofingue, which shows the extraordinary observation and sensitivity his mind had already developed. In a letter to Perry written on May 13, 1860, he relates: "Not long since Willie joined a society of Students the 'Société des Lofingues' (sic) which exists all over Switzerland. A few weeks ago they held one of their annual fêtes, and as any member can invite a friend I went to it along with Willie. It took place at the village of *Moudon*, about three quarters of a day's journey from Geneva, and 12 miles back of Lausanne. Drinking, smoking big German pipes and singing were the chief elements of the fun. It lasted three days. On the first night there was a grand concert given to the townsfolk by the students at the town hall, the like of which they had probably never seen. The second day there was a splendid banquet to which the mayor and alderman were invited, and a lot of clergymen also. The latter had nothing of their calling about them but their white neck-ties for they drank as hard, sung as loud and gave as many toasts and jolly speeches as the most uproarious student—*medical* student, even there. On the same night took place the ceremony of the Landsvater which originated, I think, in the German Universities, but which this society has adopted. I cannot well make you understand what sort of an affair it is. It is a kind of oath of allegiance to their country & of brotherhood among themselves accompanied

by a great swilling down of beer, of grasping of hands, of clashing
of rapiers, and of glorious deep-mouthed German singing. Half the
students were roaming in drunken ardour through the town and
through the halls of the inns that night seeking whom they might
devour. Willie, a German fellow, and I myself did not get scarcely
a wink of sleep till near morning because of the constant attacks upon
the door of the bed room which we three shared together." [15]

On one other occasion William took Henry along to a student
gathering, somewhat different from the beer-drinking encampment
in Vaud. The Swiss *Jeunesse* in 1860 were greatly aroused by the
political events involving the territory neighboring on the Canton of
Geneva. To Perry, Henry wrote that March, "I suppose you have
heard even in your uncivilized parts about the annexation of Savoy
to France. It has just taken place and the Swiss are in an 'awful wax'
about it, as there is danger of their being compromised by it. I don't
suppose there will be any fighting on the subject although Switzerland *has* begun to marshall her troops. During yesterday (March
26th) and today these streets have filled with soldiers." [16] Concerning one of these demonstrations, he wrote in his reminiscences: that
it was held in a huge tent where a banquet was going on and "out
of a sea of agitated and vociferous young heads, sprang passionate
protests and toasts and vows and declaimed verses, a storm of local
patriotism, though a flurry happily short-lived." [17]

In addition to such outings together, William and Henry had a
strong common interest at this time in their respective intellectual developments. They read and discussed much current literature, English
mostly, and discussed their ideas at great length. In Newport they
had begun to read the *Revue des Deux Mondes.* Now at Geneva
other such "vales of Arcady" were opening out before them in the
earliest numbers of *The Cornhill Magazine,* mentioned in William's
letter to their father. The arrival of each orange-covered copy from
London took on a lively importance, shared intensely by the reading
aloud of the most outstanding items, and coveted individually by the
young literati. "Is anything like that thrill possible to-day—for a submerged and blinded and deafened generation, a generation so
smothered in quantity and number the discrimination, under the

gasp, has neither air to breathe nor room to turn around? Has any like circumstance now conceivably the value, to the charmed attention, so far as anything worth naming attention, or any charm for it, is anywhere left, of the fact that Trollope's *Framley Parsonage* there began?—let alone the still other fact that the *Roundabout Papers* did and that Thackeray thus appeared to us to guarantee personally, intimately, with a present audibility that was as the accent of good company, the new relation with him and with others of company not much worse, as they then seemed, that such a medium could establish. To speak of these things, in truth, however, is to feel the advantage of being able to live back into the time of the more sovereign periodical appearances much of a compensation for any reduced prospect of living forward. For these appearances, these strong time-marks in such stretches of production as that of Dickens, that of Thackeray, that of George Eliot, had in the first place simply a genial weight and force, a direct importance, and in the second a command of the permeable air and the collective sensibility, with which nothing since has begun to deserve comparison. They were enrichments of life, they were *large* arrivals, these particular re-newals of supply—to which, frankly, I am moved to add, the early Cornhill giving me pretext, even the frequent examples of Anthony Trollope's fine middle period, looked at in the light of old af-fection and that of his great heavy shovelfuls of testimony to con-stituted English matters; a testimony of course looser and thinner than Balzac's to *his* range of facts, but charged with something of the big Balzac authority. These various, let alone numerous, deeper-toned strokes of the great Victorian clock were so many steps in the march of our age, besides being so many notes, full and far-reverber-ating, of our having high company to keep—high, I mean, to cover all the ground, in the sense of the genial pitch of it." [18]

The genial note on which the discipline of Henry's Geneva school-ing thus ended was made even pleasanter by a trip on foot with Wil-liam to Interlaken via Chamonix. For inexperienced walkers this trip, even with guides and occasionally the use of a donkey, was a serious affair. How deeply Henry was impressed can be seen in the detailed letters he wrote to Sarg Perry. Their staying over night with

the good fathers of the hospice at St. Bernard was the really unforgettable event of the expedition. Their hosts and the magnificent
dogs, the great Alpine wastes and vast stretches of deep snow made
vivid pictures in their memories. Henry noted in particular the night
spent "on a mattress and pillow which were apparently stuffed with
damp sand."

The last stages of the trip presented the spectacle of going over
the Gemmi pass: "From Loèche you see nothing but a vast towering
surface of vertical rock—naked and rugged. You cannot believe it
possible that you can pass over it for no trace of a path can be dis-
cerned. And indeed the path is most curious. It is very narrow (5
feet at the widest and generally about 3) very steep and winds in
such zigzags, that is turns from right to left, that you never see
whence you've come or whither you are going. In one place (so says
the guide book, the spot escaped my notice) a plumb-line may be
dropped over the precepice down a distance of 1600 ft. without any
abuttement to interfere. On the plateau on the summit we had for
a little over an hour of snow, and were down on the other side in
seven hours from the time we started. That same evening we reached
Interlaken where we found all the 'folks' except Robby whom at that
young gent's own earnest solicitation father left at school in Geneva.
. . ." [19]

In going on to Bonn, the next stop in their educational wanderings, the Jameses were postponing the decision to return to the States,
though even the boys were beginning to question the family's prolonged expatriation. In contemplating the summer, and perhaps the
winter, in Germany, Henry told Perry in his first letter from Bonn,
on July 18th, that William had decided he wanted to study painting at
Newport with William Morris Hunt. So serious was the intention
that it was being considered by the family as the first definite cause
for returning to America. In explaining this to his Newport correspondent, Henry continues: "Besides that, I think that if we are to
live in America it is about time we boys should take up our abode
there; and more I see of this estrangement of American youngsters
from the land of our birth, the less I believe in it. It should also be

the land of their breeding. I cannot devote my whole letter to this because I have so much more to say." [20]

This statement represents a genuine attitude on the part of young Henry James to strengthen his American bonds and heritage, actually to be an American in the full sense of the term. This desire he was to struggle with for the next ten years, until the death of Minnie Temple put an end to his youth. Between 1860 and 1870, he made the strongest efforts he was ever to make to be an American and to write American fiction. But the interlude at Bonn was still an ordeal to be gone through before returning to native land and hopes. En route from Interlaken to Bonn, via Wiesbaden and Frankfort, young Henry James thought on these things, and the longer he endured the German mind, tongue, and atmosphere that summer, the stronger he believed that America was really the land of promise for himself and his literary ambitions.

The elder James, profiting by the Geneva experience, decided again to separate the boys. William, he felt, should be established alone to concentrate on his German and think through this idea of studying art. He was, therefore, hopefully installed in the tutorial household of one Herr Stromberg; Harry and Wilky were placed together in a similar establishment, the home of Herr Doctor Humpert at #390 Bonngasse; Alice and their parents, after seeing the three oldest boys comfortably settled in Bonn, went to Paris with Aunt Kate for the summer. In this manner the family were more widely scattered than they had ever been before and the older boys' educational current drifted into German culture and the German language for the first time.

In 1860 Bonn was a very delightful city indeed. The birth-place of Beethoven and the poet Arndt, who died just six months before the James came to the city, Bonn is beautifully situated on the Rhine in full view of the Siebengebirge, or Seven Mountains. The pleasant villas with their gardens on the river, situated on the Coblenzer-Strasse, the shady promenades of the Hofgarten, the Poppelsdorfer Allée, and the view from the Alte Zoll, contributed to the charms which attracted a large colony of English people each season. The Beethoven House, at #20 Bonngasse, was not very far from Herr

Doctor Humpert's home. Further along toward the Hofgarten, near the fine Medieval towers of the Münster, whose nave and transept dated from the 12th century, was the University, occupying the south side of the town. Originally the Electoral Palace, it dated from the late 17th century but did not become the University until 1818. To the James boys the most impressive part of Bonn and its surroundings was the Drachenfels, a mountain about a thousand feet high, which arises abruptly from the river. Romantically perched on its summit are the remains of the Castle of Drachenfels, below which, legend states, is a cave, the den of the dragon slain by Siegfried and made immortal by Richard Wagner. Through the groves up the sides of the Drachenfels, the boys often wandered, or upon the Rhine Wharf which stretched along the river, with the famous Rhine Bridge, usually considered the most beautiful in the Rhineland, spanning the river in three graceful arches. Utterly different from Geneva or Boulogne, London or Paris, Bonn gave William, young Henry, and Wilkinson much to observe in a milieu that was more foreign to their tastes and training than anything else Europe had offered. Upon Harry this milieu had the strongest effect.

Bowing doggedly under the "determined strict servitude to German," Harry felt as though "the black shadow of the Ecole Préparatoire" had once again fallen across his path. The atmosphere of the guttery Bonngasse during those summer weeks was close and stale; even more so were the heavy rooms of the Humpert house, lightened somewhat by the presence of the Herr Doctor, a professor at the Bonn Gymnasium, who tutored Wilky and Harry for a period each day. More in keeping with the heaviness of the general air were the Frau Doctorin and her elderly, scowling sister, Fraülein Stamm, who made Harry think of Hepzibah Pyncheon in *The House of Seven Gables*. The ancient spinster was forever wiping green hock-glasses and holding them up in the meagre light; or she was laboriously setting out long-necked bottles, with chalky cakes, in preparation for refreshment in the front section of the long general eating-and-living room. This great, stuffy chamber stretching from street to court between two high dark walls received light dimly from each end, with various shades of illumination faintly suggested

here and there from polished touches of elegance or the gleaming
necks of bottles and rims of glasses. "I recall how oppressively
in that apartment, how congestedly, as in some cage of which the
wires had been papered over, I felt housed and disconnected; I
scarce then, I think knew what the matter was, but it could only
have been that in all those summer weeks, to the best of my belief,
no window was ever once opened. Still, there was the scene, the
thick, the much-mixed chiaroscuro through which the two ladies of
the family emerged from an exiguous retreat just off the middle
zone, where the four or five of us, seated with our nutcracker-faced
pastor, conveyed the food to our mouths with a confidence mainly
borrowed from the play of his own deep-plunging knife; and then
the forward, the festal extension, the privilege of occasionally
lingering in which, or of returning to it from renewed refreshment,
was a recognition both of our general minding of our business upstairs—left as we were to thumb our Flügel's *Dictionary* by the hour
so long as we invoked no other oracle. Our drowsy Doctor invited
no such approach; he smiled upon us as if unseen forefingers of
great force had been inserted for the widening of his mouth at the
corners, and I had the sense of his not quite knowing what to make
of our being so very gently barbaric, or rather so informally civilised;
he safely housed and quite rankly fed us, guided us to country walks
and to the swimming-baths by the Rhineside, introduced us to fruit-
gardens where, on payment of the scantest tribute, we were suffered
to consume off-hand bushels of cherries, plums, and pears; suffered
us to ascend the Drachenfels and to partake of coffee at Rolandseck
and in other friendly open-air situations; but flung his gothic shadow
as little as possible over my so passive page at least, and took our
rate of acquisition savingly for granted." [21]

Once outside the Humperts' house things were not so bad, so
that often Harry would get up early, walk through the unawakened
town out into the open country, particularly in the neighborhood of
the surrounding hills, perhaps the Venusberg, long, low, and strong,
with the dews heavy on the foliage, and glistening on the ruins
of an occasional old cloister. After watching the sunshine stir to
life the scene before him, Harry would conscientiously return to

his quarters and bend double over Schiller's *Thirty Years' War* in a strenuous spirit, altering from time to time with Goethe's *Wahlverwandtschaften,* till late in the warm afternoon. German prose he found much harder than the verse, less related to "life," characteristically German in its complicated heaviness. Yet both prose and verse he pounded at, in honest obligation to his parents' wish and with some sense of guilt still lingering from his failure in the sciences at Geneva. Laying aside the German volumes, Harry would take a half day off, crossing over the Rhine by the funicular ferry, a little way up from Beuel, directly opposite to Bonn. There, on one day especially remembered, strolling through the long vistas of the beeches and poplars, like gothic allées rustling above him, Harry caught the spirit of the German countryside, communed with it, responded to it, listened to its voice, which seemed to say to him: "We are German woods, we are German woods—which makes us very wonderful, do you know? and unlike any others: don't you feel the spell of the very sound of us and of the beautiful words, 'Old German woods, old German woods,' even if you can't tell why?" He couldn't tell why, though he heard the call and responded to the magic; yet he felt that somehow, through its mystically gothic powers, the woods, the whole Rhineland itself, was administering with peculiar directness to his culture. Now, seventeen years old and more aware of the reasons for his being in Europe, Harry was culture conscious, far more so than he had ever been. John La Farge at Newport had had much to do with his being out for culture at every turn, and it seemed in Bonn, oddly enough, to come at him "with the most absurd conciliatory rush. . . . The beauty was in truth that everything was a source, giving me, by the charmingest breach of logic, more than it at all appeared to hold; which was exactly what had not been the case at the Institution Rochette, where things had appeared, or at least had pretended, to hold so much more than they gave. The oddity was that about us now everything—everything but the murmur of the German woods and the great flow and magic name of the Rhine—was more ugly than beautiful, tended in fact to say at every turn: 'you shall suffer, yes, indeed you *are* doing so (stick up for your right to!) in your sense of form; which however is quite compatible with culture, is really one of the finest parts of it, and may decidedly prove to you that you're getting it.' " [22]

Had young Henry James's aesthetic tendencies impelled him toward the strong romantic traditions of the nineteenth century, instead of toward the new realism of the twentieth, these voices of the German woods, the mythical and legendary matter of the Rhineland which Wagner was at that time transposing into immortal music, might have quickened his creative ability. Even so, he was stirred, as he had been at Geneva under different forces, to an intellectual self-consciousness, an awareness that he was forming his mind. "To feel a unity, a character and a tone in one's impressions, to feel them related and all harmoniously coloured, that *was* positively to face the aesthetic, the creative, even, quite wondrously, the critical life," and almost on the spot, he felt, to become an author. From earliest childhood he had stored away an infinite number of sensations, impressions which suddenly began, it seemed, "to scratch quite audibly at the door of liberation, of extension, of projection; what they were *of* one more or less knew, but what they were *for* was the question that began to stir, though one was still to be a long time at a loss directly to answer it." [23] As real as this creative urge was, the forces needed to bring it into play were not at his command. There was the rub, "the dark difficulty," preventing the connection between the impulse and its fruition. Impressions were not only all right, they "were the dearest things in the world," but in and of themselves they were not enough. "This failure then to take one's stand in the connection could but come from the troubled view that they were naught without a backing, a stout stiff hard-grained underside that would hold them together and of which the terrible name was simply science, otherwise learning, and learning exclusively by books." The "uninterested scholar" of Newport was beginning, at Geneva and Bonn, to see the relationship between life and learning, between literature and life; and "a stout stiff hard-grained underside" to his storehouse of impressions was slowly taking form.

Never in his profoundest contemplations had it occurred to him that impressions themselves might be science, might be learning. On the contrary, he had come to believe "that life and knowledge were simply mutual opposites, one inconsistent with the other," and when "knowledge impinged upon life, pushed against here, as it were, and drove her to the wall, it was all right, and such was knowledge's way and title." On the other hand when life played the same tricks with knowledge, nothing but shame and failure could accrue for "the ruder, even if lighter, party." Gradually he was to perceive that neither was of the least use to him without the other; but in the meantime the conflict continued in his thinking with a dramatic force which made the discipline of study and the joys of observing life intensely interesting. In thinking his way through this dilemma, Henry James was to evolve a basic concept in his theory of literature. In 1884, in "The Art of Fiction," he stated: "The power to guess the unseen from the seen, to trace the implication of things, to judge the whole piece by the pattern, the condition of feeling life in general so completely that you are well on your way to knowing any particular corner of it—this cluster of gifts may almost be said to constitute experience, and they occur in country and in town, and in the most differing stages of education. If experience consists of impressions, it may be said that impressions *are* experience, just as (have we not seen it?) they are the very air we breathe." The first seventeen years of young Henry James's life were constituted almost completely of such experience, as were to be the remaining stages of his education. One might say, in this respect, what James himself said of Flaubert's *Madame Bovary,* "that here the theory seems to have been invented after the fact. The author began to describe because he had laid up a great fund of disinterested observations; he had been looking at things for years, for his own edification, in that particular way." Nothing could be more true of the relationship between Henry James's early years and his development as a literary artist.

Not all of the boys' time was given over to the heavy demands of their German studies in Bonn. From their parents in Paris they received, among other lighter reading matter, *Once A Week,* a current periodical which brought with it George Meredith, Charles Reade, J. E. Millais, George du Maurier and other happy voices from the Anglo-Saxon world. When not rioting on the supreme German classics, Harry was given over to installments of *Evan Harrington,* or Charles Reade's *A Good Fight,* "the assured little prelude to *The Cloister and the Hearth.*" Copies of the magazine the boys took along with them on most of their outings together, accounts of which were given in a profusion of letters to their parents and Aunt Kate, always with special mention to Alice. These letters reveal not only a detailed description of their daily duties and pleasures but a great deal about the boys themselves.

BONN, SUNDAY
AUGUST 12th (1860)

MY DEAREST PARENTS,

I began to write to you the other day, but had not time to finish, and thought that I had better wait till Sunday when I would have plenty of time and more to tell you. The delay has not been caused by any lack of affection I can assure you, for I have thought of you every hour since you have been gone.

Wilky and Harry have both written. I suppose you have got their letters, and we have received Father's letter, Nelly's, and the *Once a Weeks.* Your hearts, I know, would have been melted if you had had a view of us this morning. I went directly after breakfast for the boys and though Harry had an "iron stomach-ache" as he called it we went together on that low wooded hill which Aunt Kate could see from her window and walked until dinner time, Harry being part of the time in great pain. In one part we found a platform with a stone bench commanding a view of the whole valley. We were rather tired and so we sat down upon it, Harry and Wilky each with a *Once a Week,* while I tried to draw the valley in my pocket book. We wondered what our beloved parents were doing at that moment (½ past 11) and thought that you must all have been in the parlor, Alice, the widow, with her eyes fixed on her novel, eating some rich fruit which father has just brought in for her from the Palais Royal, and lovely Mother and Aunt Kate in armchairs with their hands crossed in front of them listening to Father who is walking up and down speaking of the superiority of America to these countries, and how much better that we should go home—and we wished, oh how we wished, we could have been with you to partake of the fruit and join in the conversation. However, there are only three weeks more and then we rush to your arms. With a heavy sigh we got up from the seat and went on, but in a way so fraternal, presenting such a sweet picture of brotherly unitedness and affection that it would have done anyone good to have seen us. And so it is every day in our shorter walks and talks.

Nothing new has happened since you left. Mrs. Stromberg has gone to Ems for a few weeks, so that there is more quiet at our house. The German gets on slowly, very marked improvement in talking I have noticed. I have not studied so hard last week as before and prevent Harry from working his eyes out which he seems on the whole rather less inclined to do than when you left. I am going to read as much as I can the rest of the time. It seems to be a mere process of soaking, requiring no mental effort, but only time and steady patience. Wilky has just come upon me. He says he is sensibly improving in German. Harry says he wakes up every day from his lethargy to wish he was in Paris, instead of availing himself of the little time he has here; he ought to be ashamed (!) Harry has not touched the *Once a Week* until today!!! The weather has been ever the same, quite cold with rain every day, though the rain has been in shorter showers than before, and the sun shows himself more. All the better for the month of September, I suppose. I think we shall go to Cologne some day next week, not Sunday so that Stromberg and rest may not come.

My room is very comfortable now that I have got used to it and got a pair of slippers of green plush heavy and strong enough to last all my life and then be worn by my children. My bed is all right and it will please Aunt Kate to hear that I have had two FLEAS (my first) which have bitten my skin off of me nearly. Now I can sympathise with her sufferings, which I never rightly respected before. The Zof-fingian photograph has come. I had hard work to get it out of the post office. It is perfectly laughable, though a better picture than I expected. They have given me a moustache big enough to furnish three horse guards. Tell Nelly that her letter was an unexpected pleasure, and I will answer it if I can get time. How long does she expect to stay abroad? Tell us something about her. Who is this Doctor Adams? the man she is engaged to? She tells me to address my letter for her to Munroe, care of Dr. Adams. Ask her if I shall still address her as Miss James. She hopes to meet me. Tell her it would of course be painful, but I think I could do it if the Doctor were not present. However as I do not know her real relation to him perhaps it would not be proper to communicate these messages. So use your discretion.

I suppose you are enjoying the fat of everything in Paris. What is this Hotel des 3 Empereurs? Does it stand opposite the Hôtel du Louvre on the other side of the Place du Palais-Royal? We should all like to be there very much, although we ought to be thankful for our comforts here. Fine plums are now 50 for a groschen. The sweet lovely delicious little grey-eyed Alice must be locked up alone on the day after the receipt of this with paper and envelope to write a letter unassisted, uncorrected, and unpunctuated to her loving brothers who would send her novels and plums if they could. Please all of you write every day, you cannot do so too often. We will write as often as we can. Wilky sends oceans of love to all and if Harry were here he would do the same. What a blessing it is to have such parents, such a lovely Mother, and dear Aunt Kate and magnificent Father and delicious Alice! Ever your affectionate Son, Nephew, and Brother,

WILLIAM JAMES[24]

On the following Sunday William again wrote a long letter to his parents, part of which is devoted to a visit with his brothers, having had dinner with them and the Humpert family. He describes Harry and Wilky as living "on the fat of the land, though they do not seem as sensible of their advantages as they should be. As I was led to expect nothing of the kind, I was surprised at the sumptuousness of the dinner, rich beef, sausages, pigeons, capital vegetables and soup, all cooked just right and the most delicious cherry pie, with two bottles of costly Rhine wine in honour of the day. The Doctor was as cordial as usual and the two old ladies perfect characters for Dickens. They have been so shut out from the world and have been melting together so long by the kitchen fire that the minds of both have become confounded into one, and they seem to constitute a sort of two-bodied individual. I never saw anything more curious than the way in which they sit mumbling together at the end of the table, each using simultaneously the same exclamation if anything said at our end strikes their ears. The boys say they always speak together using the same words or else one beginning a phrase, the other ending it. It is a singular life." Harry, William reports, was studying a good deal, but adds that the family need not be apprehensive about him. "There has been no renewal of the stomach aches that I am aware of,

and he looks fatter and fresher than when you left. He and Wilky
appear to get on very harmoniously together. They enliven themselves occasionally by very good-natured brotherly trials of strength
in their bedroom, when study has made them dull and sleepy. In
these, sometimes one, sometimes the other is victor." Harry, then
seventeen and fully recovered from the typhoid fever at Boulogne,
was in better health than he had been for some time, although occasional stomach disorders, from which he suffered severely for
the next few years, caused some distress and interfered with his
activities. Wilky, always robust and full of spirits, was a good companion for Harry, being far less intellectual in his interests than
William and much more apt to engage Harry in a bit of boyish
rough-and-tumble, something Harry needed very much. In this same
letter William describes morning calls from his two brothers and
visits he made to their room, sometimes before Wilky had awakened.
He would stumble out of bed, feeling guilty that he had overslept
and call to Harry, who was already hard at work, "Why did not you
stop me?" When they couldn't persuade Harry to leave his books,
William and Wilky would take a few hours off to visit Rolandseck,
the three-hundred-and-fifty foot elevation on the opposite bank of
the Rhine from the towering Drachenfels. The ruined tower of
Rolandseck, a few arches still standing, was a picturesque setting
from which to view the magnificent panorama up and down the
river. Having had their full of the scenery, Willy and Wilky would
have a furious race down to the station, often to find themselves a
second or two late. They would then take a boat and row across to
Bonn, enjoying themselves extremely for "1 thl., 10 sgr." Willy
noted. Arriving home to find Harry still hard at his studies, the
boys resolved to force him into some strenuous exercise. "We are
going to put Harry through a slashing big walk daily," stated Willy
and also decided to do something about Harry's wardrobe, "His
old white Lordet clothes began to look so shockingly grimy that we
have at last induced him to take them to be cleaned. He clung to
them with such affection that it was no easy matter." [25] Regular
reports were made concerning the progress in German, couched always in profusions of love, good wishes, and longing for the family

reunion; extraordinary letters in many respects these boys wrote, especially William.

In such general family letters William did not include the very serious question of his career, a subject he had been debating within himself for many months and about which he had hesitated to speak to his father. Shortly after arriving at Bonn he had expressed his conviction that he wished to become an artist and therefore did not think it wise to continue his scientific studies. Henry James, Sr., was not at all prepared for the shock of this announcement, and though always the most sympathetic and lenient of fathers he required the rest of the summer to adjust himself to his oldest son's decision. In letters to Edmund Tweedy the elder James reveals his disturbed state of mind and indicates his natural tendency to reconcile himself to the needs and wishes of his children over and above his personal desires and plans for them:

BONN, JULY 18 (1860)

MY DEAR OLD TWEEDIUS,

. . . Have you any commands for Newport? I ask because it is our intention to return in the *Adriatic* of September 11th. We have come to this resolve rather hurriedly, but we do not feel unadvisedly. We came on here to put the boys in German families for the summer, and take them in winter to Frankfurt or some similar place. But we had hardly reached here before Willy took an opportunity to say to me—what it seems he had been long wanting to say but found it difficult to come to scratch—that he felt the vocation of a painter so strongly that he did not think it worth my while to expend any more time or money on his scientific education! I confess I was greatly startled by the annunciation, and not a little grieved, for I had always counted upon a scientific career for Willy, and I hope the day may even yet come when my calculations may be realized in this regard. But as it was I had nothing to do but to submit; and as our motive to stay in Europe was chiefly derived from the imagined needs of his education, so now we are glad enough to turn homeward, and let him begin at once with Mr. Hunt. The welfare of the other youngsters will, however, be as much consulted by this manoeuvre, I am persuaded, as Willy's. They are none of them cut out for intellectual labours, and they are getting to an age, Harry and Wilky especially, when the heart craves a little wider expansion than is furnished it by the domestic affections.

They want friends among their own sex, and sweethearts in the other; and my hope for their own salvation, temporal and spiritual, is that they may "go it strong" in both lines when they get home. Early marriages are thought very bad as a prudential step here in Europe, but an immense deal of imprudence may yet be transacted in America with the happiest social and individual consequence. . . . Love to all and believe me, ever faithfully yours,

H. J.[26]

Nearly a week later, also from Bonn where the Jameses remained a few days after getting the three boys established, the elder James further clarified the situation to the Tweedies, who were travelling in Scotland:

BONN, JULY 24 (1860)

MY DEAR OLD TWEEDIUS,

I assure you that your solicitude lest we should be returning too soon, though grateful to our hearts, is quite superfluous to our heads. And if you could project yourself in any degree into my consciousness, you would read our title to go so clear, that you would yourself be the first "to bid adieu to every fear, and wipe your weeping eyes." We left those "mansions in the skies" the last time, experimentally. We were not sure where we had best settle ourselves down at home: we found difficulties of an apparently insuperable character in the way of getting furnished lodgings near Boston. Newport did not give the boys what they required exactly, and we didn't relish their separation from us. Willy especially felt, we thought, a little too much attraction to painting—as I suppose, from the contiguity to Mr. Hunt; let us break that up, we said, at all events. I hoped that his career would be a scientific one, as I thought and still think that the true bent of his genius was towards the acquisition of knowledge: and to give up this hope without a struggle, and allow him to tumble down into a mere painter, was impossible. Let us go abroad then, we said, and bring him into contact with books and teachers. It is indispensable for him, and it *may* be useful to the other boys. Well, we have tried the experiment. Willy refuses to give up his predilection for painting without a fuller trial: the other boys have been all along perfectly starved on their social side, and not the least bettered on their intellectual. As you say, German might do good to Bob and Wilkie, provided they could *apply* it when they get home. But they would have to wait long years possibly before they could get situations in which they would carry away with them, and in the meantime they would be losing all their arithmetical and general school culture which is vastly better imparted in our schools than in any we have found here. One chief disappointment also on this side of the water has been in regard to Alice, who intellectually, socially, and physically has been at a great disadvantage compared with home. But to make a long story short: as our chief inducement to stay here was the idea of promoting Willy's scientific culture and aspiration: as in regards to the other children we saw no reason to prefer this side of the Atlantic to the other for a single day; so we look upon Willy's strong desire to return to Mr. Hunt as a Providential indication to change our plans, and go where the spirit and the flesh alike draw us. I am very glad we came abroad this last time: we should otherwise always have had a misgiving that something was to be found here better for the boys than at home. As it is we go home profoundly persuaded that no wilder hallucination exists, at least in reference to boys who are destined to grow up into American men. America is "the lost Paradise restored" to boys and girls both, and it is only our own paltry cowardice and absurd ducking to old world conventionalities that hinder our realizing it as such at once. . . . Love me and mine as we love thee and thine. Ever dear old fellow-soldier, yours,

H. J.[27]

The impact of William's decision to become a painter obviously shocked the elder James into a very practical evaluation of his whole concept of the education he was seeking for his children. His opposition to art was stronger than his feeling about almost any other realm of interest, in terms of a career. Art, he felt, was frivolous, irresponsible, narrow, vain, and inferior to either the dignity and glory of religion or the seriousness and usefulness of science. William could not have made a more severe demand upon his father's indulgence. In answering his father's objections, William stated in part: "I do not see why a man's spiritual culture should not go on independently of his aesthetic activity, why the power which an artist feels in himself should tempt him to forget what he is, any more than the power felt by Cuvier or Fourier would tempt them to do the same. Why should not a given susceptibility of religious development be found bound up in a mind whose predominant tendencies are artistic, as well as in one largely intellectual, granting, even, that the former be much the most elementary, the least dignified and useful? My experience amounts to very little, but it is all I have to go upon; and I am sure that far from feeling myself degraded by my intercourse with art, I continually receive from it spiritual impressions the intensest and purest I know." [28] The concern for his children's spiritual welfare was ever the basic thought in the father's mind and was, of course, at the bottom of his concern for William's inclinations. The challenge, the conflict, which the situation brought into play seemed to bring Henry James, Sr., down out of the clouds of religious and social idealism, landing him squarely on his feet. The jolt was sudden and the repercussions many. Never before had he been forced to face such an issue concerning his children and consequently he had had no previous necessity to evaluate things in such immediate, cold terms. His conclusions, as stated to Edmund Tweedy, are surprisingly clear and decisive: he had been suffering from a wild hallucination that Europe, not America, was "the lost Paradise restored" for the education of boys and girls alike; he had been under the power of this illusion through an unadmitted tendency to bow before old world conventionalities and culture; he was now ready to return to America free from such illusions and convinced that in their native land his children would enjoy a better education and fuller development than Europe had to offer them. Furthermore, in spite of William's present desire to study with Mr. Hunt at Newport, the father believed, and rightly so, that ultimately his oldest son would turn to the scientific career, "the true bent of his genius," and that by trying out the idea at Newport William would become free to turn to his true calling. Just five years earlier, on sailing out of New York harbor, Henry James, Sr. had had some momentary misgivings of Europe's promise and a belated realization that America was the golden land. He was now, in the summer of 1860, perfectly sure of what he believed and willingly and permanently left Europe behind him.

It is interesting to observe that in these letters to Edmund Tweedy no mention is made of Harry. The dilemma revolved about William. Wilky and Bob are discussed in terms of the practical application of their knowledge of German. Alice is considered in relation to her intellectual, social, and physical well-being, but

Harry seems not to be considered and is referred to most indirectly
and vaguely. William, Wilky, Bob, and even Alice were all destined
to grow up and reside in America; Harry was not. What seemed to
be a wild hallucination in the father's mind on behalf of the other
children proved to be for Harry the most profitable and beneficial
reality. Of this fact neither Harry nor his father, in 1860, could have
had the slightest realization. Actually, the very uncertainty and in-
tangibleness of Harry's future career left him quite out of the family
problem at this time, and with characteristic detachment he quietly
continued to work out his own salvation.

With September 11th set as the sailing date, the Jameses arranged
for a family reunion in Paris on the 1st, the three oldest boys coming
down from Bonn and young Bobby arriving from Geneva. Ten days
in Paris offered an exciting prospect for them all, particularly Harry to
whom, by this time, Paris seemed more wonderful than ever. Still,
during the last week in August, the Rhineland held out strong attractions too, particularly Cologne, which the boys decided to visit
before leaving. Wilky, unable to wait a few days to tell his parents
about it, wrote on Monday evening after returning from the
cathedral town earlier than the others. Willy, he states, "is so enchanted with the cathedral that I think he would stay there all night
if Harry and I would let him." A proposed trip to Strasbourg was
cancelled, on the grounds, as Willy explained, "that the expense
would be greater than the receipt, and the other boys cared little
about going." Harry later regretted this, especially as their train
passed through the city which they saw "as a mild monster behind
bars . . . above chimneys, housetops and fortifications." To add to
the excitement of these last few days, letters arrived from Newport,
one to Wilky from Oliver B. Perry telling that his brother T. S.
Perry, "Sarg," had graduated from William C. Leverett's school,
"recited a 'Greekoration,' and took leave of his brother students.
. . . " Other letters, to Willy and Harry, from Wm. Hunt and John
La Farge expressed much joy and eagerness to have the Jameses
back in Newport. On top of these exciting thoughts the Humpert
family became sentimentally German over the boys' departure, as
Harry wrote to his parents: "The Doctor entertained thoughts of

accompanying us to America but his lady gave symptoms of such dread and horror at the idea that he has relinquished it. She and Miss Stamm seem to think that it is the exception in going to America not to be drowned and assurances to the contrary are received with uplifted eyes and hands and raised eyes, and incredulous 'Ahs!' and 'Ohs,' and pious ejaculations. I wish we could take Madame Humpert to America with us to cook. She is by far the best one I ever saw. I wish you could come on and take a few lessons from her; I shall bring you a lot of receipts by which I shall expect you to profit next winter. I shall look for a *marked improvement* in the cooking department." [29]

Harry's luke warm feelings about Bonn grew even less warm as the time for leaving approached. He expresses amazement to his mother that Willy and Wilky could find so much to write about so often, "for what they can find to say about Bonn to fill so many pages is to me inconceivable." On Saturday, September 1st, very early in the morning, the three boys began the long, tiring journey to Paris. Harry especially looked forward to the rapture "of the Parisian idea of bed after the rude German conception, our sore discipline for so many weeks." The most impressive thing about the fifteen-hour trip was the fact that the boys shared a compartment with the *gens* of a noble French family, a pair of footmen and a lady's maid, "types of servile impudence taking its ease, who chattered by the hour for our wonderstruck ears, treating them to their first echo of the strange underworld, the sustaining vulgarity, of existences classified as 'great.' They opened vistas, and I remember how when, much later, I came to consider the designed picture, first in Edmond About and then in Alphonse Daudet, of fifty features symptomatic of the social pace at which the glittering regime hurried to its end, there came back to me the breath of this sidewind of the frenzied dance that we had caught during those numerous and so far from edifying hours in our fine old deep-seated compartment." [30]

French society was at that moment of the Empire, moving more or less *en masse* upon Homburg and Baden-Baden, and when Madame la Marquise, "young and good-natured and pretty without beauty" looked in upon her dependents, young Henry James imagined he was taking in "the scented air of the Tuileries" which he was so soon to see again. The breath of Empress Eugenie's court, caught so intimately en route from Bonn to Paris, Harry was never to forget; and in Paris, as the old-world hours were dragging dreadfully to a close for him, he slipped out often "to hang, from the balcony of our quatrieme . . . over that Place du Palais Royal and up against that sculptured and storied facade of the New Louvre which seemed to me then to represent, in its strength, the capacity and chiselled rim of some such potent vivifying cup as it might have been given us, under a happier arrangement, to taste now in its fulness and with a braver sense for it."

In retrospect, the whole year at Geneva and Bonn, seemed too, in a sense, much like a cup, filled with a draught at times bitter, yet again almost sweet. On thinking it over, Harry concluded that he had "*tasted* German, to the great and delightful quickening of my imagination." The quickening, of course, could not compare with that which he had experienced in London or Paris, and which he was, nine years later, to know upon going over the Alps into Italy for the first time. Already he had begun to wonder about Italy, "far more than I was constitutionally capable of wondering about Germany. It was enough for me at Bonn that I felt no lack of appetite—had for the time all the illusion of being on my way to something; to something, I mean, with which the taste of German might somehow *directly* mix itself." He thought, rather pleasantly now, of the drowsy afternoons at Bonn, perusing Goethe's *Hermann und Dorothea* with Herr Humpert, or of reading Racine's *Phèdre* with M. Töpffer in the heavy twilight of the room behind the cathedral at Geneva. Indeed, he had been in the dark shadow of the Institute Rochette and under the brow of the towering Drachenfels, but the experience was not without refreshment, without a discipline which had strengthened and held together his impressions.

NOTES

1. As quoted by Virginia Harlow, *Thomas Sergeant Perry,* Durham, N. C., Duke University Press, 1950, 240. The Pensionnat Maquelin, to which the two youngest boys were sent, occupied building, part of which today are used by the Ligue des Sociétés de la Croix-Rouge and part by the Hotel Beau Séjour, in the Champel section of Geneva. The school was founded at Orbe, Switzerland, in 1822 by Jean Francois Henri Venel who moved it to Champel in 1831, continuing as director until his death in 1855. The school prospered, having among its pupils at one time Prince Louis Napoleon, later Napoleon III. Upon the death of M. Venel, it was directed by Paul Louis Maquelin, senior professor of the faculty. An account of the school is found in Edmond Barde, *Anciennes Maisons de Campagne Genevoises,* Geneva, 1937, 95.

2. *Notes of a Son and Brother,* 3.

3. As quoted by Harlow, *op. cit.,* 242.

4. *Notes of A Son and Brother,* 6.

5. Quoted by Harlow, *op. cit.,* 243.

6. *The Letters of William James,* II, 187.

7. *Notes of A Son and Brother,* 6.

8. *Ibid.,* 7-10. Rudolphe Töpffer (1799-1846) was one of Geneva's most distinguished citizens. He achieved considerable success with his Geneva novels: *Le presbytere* (1839), *Nouvelles et mélanges* (1840), *La bibliothèque de mon oncle* (1843), and several others. Of his tramps through the Alps he wrote *Voyages en Zigzag* (1848), cleverly illustrated by himself. In 1832 he was appointed professor of aesthetics at the Academy of Geneva where he continued until his death. It was said of him: "Töpffer a écrit dans un français un peu archäique des contes d'une charmante fantaisie, où il unit avec bonhomie l'ironie et la morale, la gaieté et le sentiment, la rêverie et l'humour." *Nouveau Larousse,* VII, 131.

9. Letter to Thomas Sergeant Perry, dated from Geneva, March 26, 1860, as quoted in Harlow, *op. cit.,* 245.

10. *Notes of A Son and Brother,* 11-12.

11. Henri-Frederic Amiel (1821-1881), Swiss writer, philosopher, and critic, after studying in Berlin, was appointed professor of aesthetics at the Academy of Geneva in 1849. In 1854, he became professor of moral philosophy. His major work, *Journal Intime,* 2 vols. (1882-1884), after obtaining a European success was translated into English by Mrs. Humphry Ward and highly praised by Matthew Arnold. An essay on Amiel appears in Paul Bourget's *Nouveaux essais de psycho-*

logie contemporaine, Paris, 1885. Amiel's *Journal* has also been translated by Van Wyck Brooks, New York, Macmillan Company, 1935.

12. R. B. Perry, *op. cit.,* I, 187, 188.
13. *Notes of A Son and Brother,* 18.
14. *Ibid.,* 19.
15. As quoted by Harlow, *op. cit.,* 247-248.
16. *Ibid.,* 246.
17. *Notes of A Son and Brother,* 15-16.
18. *Ibid.,* 20-22.
19. As quoted in Harlow, *op. cit.,* 254.
20. *Ibid.,* 252.
21. *Notes of A Son and Brother,* 30, 31. Snatches of such activities occur in letters from the boys to their parents in Paris. Harry wrote: "On Sunday Wilkie and I went to Rolandseck with the Humperts. . . . There were about 800 people there, all bent upon the same pleasure as ourselves, and among them was an American lady who shone with the beauty of an angel among the 700 hideous German women." A few days later Wilky wrote: "Harry and Willy took a walk this afternoon to a fruit garden, where plums, cherries, gooseberries and currants were abundant. After half an hour's work on Harry's part, he left Willy finishing merely the plums, the cherry and gooseberry course to come later. I sincerely hope he has got home safely. Harry says he was so enchanted that he (Willie) thought that Harry was a great fool to leave so soon." It is small wonder that in his next filial letter Harry said: "I don't know what is the matter with me, but I have not been able to study for a few days past so well as I had hitherto done." MS. letter from Henry James, Jr., and from Wilkinson James, to Henry James, Sr., August, 1860, Houghton Library, Harvard University.
22. *Notes of A Son and Brother,* 31, 32.
23. *Ibid.,* 25.
24. MS. letter from William James to Henry James, Sr., August 12, 1860, Houghton Library, Harvard University. Parts of this letter were published by R. B. Perry, *op. cit.,* I, 194-196; also in Matthiessen, *op. cit.,* 91, 92. In *Notes of A Son and Brother* (43, 44), Henry James printed an altered version of this letter which reveals the extent of his literary license in using the original manuscript of William's letter. The Zoffingian picture was taken in connection with the students' "Société de Zoffingue" in Geneva. Nelly James was an Albany cousin.
25. MS. letter from William James to his parents, August 19, 1860, Houghton Library, Harvard University. Most of this letter has been published by Perry, *op. cit.,* I, 195, 196.
26. R. B. Perry, *op. cit.,* I, 191, 192.

27. MS. letter from Henry James, Sr., to Edmund Tweedy, July 24 (1860), also published in part by Perry, *op. cit.*, I, 192, 193. In the closing paragraph of this letter the elder James speaks of their seeing Madame Ristori play *Mary Stuart* there in Bonn and of his finding little pleasure in her "sanguinary beak, the lurid bloated eye of menace, and the relentless talons." Harry was quite entranced by Ristori and was to see her play the same part in America several years later, still with anything but agreement with his father's reactions to her. See *Notes of A Son and Brother*, 41, 42.

28. Perry, *op. cit.*, I, 199.

29. MS. letter from Henry James, Jr., to his parents, August 27, 1860, Houghton Library, Harvard University. Harry includes a comment on his youngest brother: "We have not heard from Bobby for a long time; his last communication was merely an official announcement of his intention to enter a dry-goods store on his return to New York where he would receive a comfortable salary of from $500 to $1,000." In *Notes of a Son and Brother* (36-39) is an account of a trip over the Alps which Robertson took during the summer of 1860 with M. Maquelin and the boys from the Pensionnat, related by Bob in a delightful letter to Harry in Bonn.

30. *Notes of a Son and Brother*, 55.

Chapter Twelve

Repatriation

"(It was) clear to me in the light thus kindled that my American consciousness had hitherto been . . . singularly starved."

On July 26, 1915, after forty years of English residence, Henry James became naturalized as a British subject. Thus, within a few months of his death, he settled once and for all the question of his allegiance. This final act in the long drama of his Anglo-American relations, precipitated as it was by the First World War, was the culmination of his singular fate, that of being a man without a country. It might well be said that the first scene in which his patriotic feelings were challenged was set against the background of the Civil War, for the firing on Fort Sumter in April, 1861, startled him into an abrupt realization that his sense of Europe and his feeling for America were already in sharp conflict. For the next half century he was in a peculiar sense a homeless man, looked upon as a foreigner in England, while he seemed to relinquish his citizenship in the United States. He was determined not to lay down his American birthright, though not residing in America. At the bottom of this dilemma was the love of his native land, the essence of his "inalienably American soul," as William Dean Howells wrote, "for American was what James remained through all the perversities of his expatriation, and his adoration of foreign conditions and forms. . . . " [1] In 1914, when war broke out, and in the following months, when all Anglo-Saxon civilization was threatened by the on-slaught of German forces, it was intolerable to Henry James that the United States did not at once join in support of the cause of the Allies, a cause to which he was passionately devoted. As an English friend, one who knew him intimately, has stated: "If he had lived to see America join the Allies he would have had the deepest joy of his life; and perhaps it is worth mentioning that his relations with the American Embassy in London had never been so close and friendly as they became during those last months." [2] Much of the strength of such an enduring bond of affection for his native land can be traced back to the Civil War period, in which he made the strongest efforts to establish himself at home.

Inextricably entwined within the fabric of Henry James's loyal-ties was his sense of renunciation, a sense which upon study assumes the importance of a philosophy. Woven in and out of his life, from the small, hesitant boy to the successful, international novelist, it appears and reappears, again and again, sometimes conspicuously as in giving up his citizenship, but more often in obscure, subtle acts and attitudes that are not at all apparent. To a considerable extent this philosophy of renunciation was a basic element in much of his fiction; it stems, as do many of his novels and short stories, from the whole record of his boyhood and youth. It was a faith in and an obedience to an inner law, to a social conscience growing up within him at each turn of his personal experience. Isabel Archer, Lambert Strether, Milly Theale, and Christopher Newman, for example, express in varying degrees this fundamental thesis. Indirectly connected with the faith of the elder James, that of the Christian dogma developed in terms of Swedenborg and Fourier, the novelist's special sense of renunciation replaces the Christian consciousness of guilt by the consciousness of worth. In this ideal-ism, the soul renounces, not that it may be chastened and tempered by suffering, but that it simply may live up to itself. In *The Portrait of a Lady,* upon the death of Ralph Touchette and in the face of her affection for Casper Goodwood, Isabel gives up the possibilities of escape from the circumstances of her marriage; under the dictates of her conscience and out of her sense of duty toward Pansy, she returns to Italy, to Gilbert Osmond and a home devoid of happiness. In so doing, she is living up to her social conscience, in the face of immense odds, exhibiting a magnanimity quite in proportion to the fineness of her character. In the "Preface" to this novel James comments on the moral sense of a work of art in relation to the amount of felt life concerned in producing it: "The question comes back thus, obviously, to the kind and the degree of the artist's prime sensibility, which is the soil out of which his subject springs. The quality and capacity of that soil, its ability to 'grow' with due freshness and straightness any vision of life, represents, strongly or weakly, the projected morality." As an artist, Henry James's prime sensibility was comprised of the infinite responses to the social scene in a highly ordered society whose consciousness of worth was its impelling moral force, obedience to which not infrequently brought into play the sense of renunciation portrayed in Isabel Archer.

In less complex circumstances but constructed on the same theme, Christopher Newman in *The American* wanders into Notre Dame, stunned by Madame de Cintré's retreat into the house of the Carmelites. As Newman contemplates his revenge upon the Bellegardes, the author observes: "Whether it was Christian charity or mere human weakness of will—what it was, in the background of his spirit—I don't pretend to say; but Newman's last thought was that of course he would let the Bellegardes go. If he had spoken it aloud he would have said that he didn't want to hurt them. He quite failed, of a sudden, to recognize the fact of his having cultivated any such link with them. It was a link for them perhaps, their having so hurt *him*; but that side of it was now not his affair. At last he got up and came out of the darkening church; not with the elastic step of a man who has won a victory or taken a resolve—rather to the quiet measure of a discreet escape, of a retreat with appearances preserved." To do the decent thing, as James saw the story, was to behave in the most interesting manner, and this Newman does. After arriving at his just vindication, he withdraws from the triumphant injuring of the Bellegardes, sacrificing the inclination on behalf of his higher moral sense. "All he would have at the end," James observed, "would be therefore just the moral convenience, indeed the moral necessity, of his practical, but quite unappreciated magnanimity." [3]

Again and again James turned over this endlessly applicable concept of giving up, never twice in exactly the same way, but always related to the idea of renunciation. It is concisely expressed in *The Ambassadors* when Strether explains: "That, you see, is my only logic. Not, out of the whole affair, to have got anything for myself." In the background of Henry James's spirit lay the core of such moral necessity, an intrinsic trait in his character, as it was in his fiction. This ethical background has been explained as the basis of his Americanism. "Was not James in all this traceably a product of that mystical New England spirit represented so strongly in his Swedenborgian father and his religio-philosophical brother? James may have been as expatriated an American as you will; his stories laid at home may be particularly thin and wanting in quality. But his most typical characters are, with few exceptions, Americans; and while the background is European, the psychology is Anglo-Saxon, and what is more, Anglo-Saxon of Concord and Cambridge, Mass. What 'foreigner' could be expected really to appreciate the character of Milly Theale or Maggie Verver, of Lambert Strether or even of little Maisie? . . . He may not be American as Mark Twain or Benjamin Franklin or Edgar Lee Masters are American, but he is American as Emerson and Thoreau and Hawthorne are." [4] It was during this Civil War decade of repatriation that young Henry James developed this American spirit, faintly in Newport at first but strongly in the Cambridge years.

Throughout boyhood and youth, temperamentally and by force of circumstances, he was often required to withdraw from situations, to establish a series of discreet escapes, of retreats with appearances preserved. He did so, however, not so much in a sense of expediency or defeat as in accord with a sense of adjustment to values. These criteria were based upon the religious and social convictions of his father, even though the understanding between the philosopher and the novelist was never more than a triumph over "divergent temperaments." [5] The son's "moral neutrality," or "aesthetic morality," as it is called, was developed in the overflow of the father's exuberant moralism, in addition to which was his own innate tendency to be a detached observer. From the earliest years he had stood back, passively, fascinated by people and their relationships; gradually he came to judge them according to a code of ethics based, more and more, upon breeding and aristocratic *niceness,* rather than directly upon the Decalogue. Yet, underneath the accretions of social patterns lay the cornerstone of Christian idealism and upon such a foundation he established his best characters. While it may be true that in proportion to his development as an artist he became more absorbed with art than with life, he regarded art as a means of conveying life as he knew it, and the connection between his writing and his own life remained as constant in his advanced years as it was in his youth.

At the kindergarten in Albany, at schools and with tutors in New York, he early learned where he stood in relation to William and the other children. Set apart by illness, at first in Geneva and later in Boulogne, he was forced to give up his place; he withdrew, for example, from the Institute Rochette and the Law School at Harvard. To an ordinary person such a chain of discouraging events might have led to profound and far-reaching despondency, to feelings of inferiority; yet, in Harry's case, such were not the results. Counterbalancing his being set aside were two factors: his innately kind and generous nature, and an intuitive realization of his artistic potentialities. As a result, his attitude toward others, even when only a small boy, was not one of self-effacement or disparagement but of spontaneous consideration for others—in the case of his family, of love. Toward Willy, with whom he had grown up almost as a twin, such feelings were constantly manifested through the years, tested repeatedly by their drifting widely apart as they went forward in their very different careers. But from the start it was possible for Harry to keep his balance, for, in addition to the affection that gave such warmth and sympathy, he had the security of the growing realization of his own worth, of those peculiar talents in which he vaguely but deeply believed. As the years passed and

Harry was increasingly required to give up what might have seemed the expected achievement or experience, the idea of living up to himself and his own concepts became more apparent. Even back in the New York years he had had "divinations" that things would count for him, that the endless taking in of impressions and of responding to all he observed would culminate in tangible evidences of his gifts. The sense of new dimensions growing out of the Boulogne experience, of sharpening of directions coming from the discipline at Geneva and Bonn gave added strength to his quiet convictions. Upon returning to Newport, in Hunt's studio, in the shadow of the Civil War, at Harvard, and through his friendship with Minny Temple, he had greater cause, between 1860 and 1864, than he had ever had before, to practice his philosophy of renunciation; and through it he would arrive at some realization of his youthful literary ambitions.

Closely related to this phase of his development was the impact of repatriation. The experience of Europe had carried with it the effect of detachment, an effect which ultimately proved to be "without an absolute remedy" for young Henry James. Yet, for a decade he was to make the most sincere and consistent efforts to reconcile himself to America. Newport offered the basis of reconciliation at a time when the habit of taking America for granted had been broken. After the European years, Newport figured as "comparatively remedial," as a compromise between his sense of Europe and his parents' firm decision to leave the foreign scene forever behind them. Neither Mr. nor Mrs. James was ever to go abroad again, spending the remaining years of life in Newport, Boston, and Cambridge. Wilky and Bob settled in Florida after the Civil War, then drifted out to the Middle West, never going back to Europe. William had a year in Germany, studying and seeking better health, and frequently went to Europe in later years, but actually he never again resided abroad. Alice, too, remained in America, except for a brief trip with Aunt Kate and the last few years of her invalidism spent under Harry's care in London. The family, therefore, actually entered upon permanent and successful repatriation as they settled down in Newport in 1860. In the parents' minds there was no question about this, as there had been two years earlier. In the spring of 1858, upon returning to America for the first time since the departure from New York in 1855, Henry James, Sr., wrote to a friend that he was "going home to battle with prejudice." To another friend on the same day he expressed the hope "that it will not now be long before we shall all be re-united under those tonic skies of the great and free Western Republic." [6] Now, with the Civil War six months away, American skies were far from tonic, though the Newport scene was deceptively bright and welcoming.

After a "boisterous nasty passage" with everyone dismally sick except Bob and the elder James, they arrived in New York on Monday, September 24, 1860, on the *Adriatic,* stopping at the La Farge House before going on to Newport, a week later. The Jameses, after a brief stay at the Bellevue, began the task of moving into the Mackaye house at #13 Kay Street, at the corner of Bull, immediately next to the Hazard house which the Tweedies were to occupy upon their return.[7] The boys knew the house well from the previous year in Newport when Jim Mackaye, along with Sarg Perry, had been an intimate friend; the small tower, the Gothic roofs, the rustic lane, the stables and gardens all presented a comfortable, inviting picture and within a matter of hours the place had become their home. To Harry the choicest part of the establishment was forever to be a big, square closet, containing the very atmosphere of Europe, for "on the shelves and around the walls . . . the pink *Revues* sat with the air, row upon row, of a choir of breathing angels." Out of the covers of the *Revue des Deux Mondes* had first stepped John La Farge in Newport the year before, and from it again he now issued forth, he and the whole spirit of the Second Empire, sparkling with literary figures which La Farge and the *Revue* made very alive indeed. While in Europe Harry had found that his chin "had scarce risen to the level of that publication," but now, at the age of seventeen, filled with literary aspirations shared only with T. S. Perry, "he speedily shot up so as quite to bend down to it: it took its place therewith as the very headspring of culture." But before any peace and quiet were possible for such cultural pursuits, the high-spirited, younger boys had to be placed in school. Their father's experiments in education now centered on his two youngest sons, whom he soon escorted to Concord, Massachusetts, where they entered the rather unusual, co-educational school of Frank Sanborn. With the aid of a loan from Emerson, whose children he had been tutoring, as well as the prestige of such a name supporting him, Franklin Benjamin Sanborn, upon graduating from Harvard in 1855 and settling in Concord as a teacher, soon established his school. He was exactly the sort of teacher the elder James desired for Wilky and Bob in 1860; he was an Abolitionist leader, was arrested for refusing to testify concerning his aid to John Brown, was deeply interested in transcendentalism, and always active in all charity and humanitarian work of the community.[8] His strength and vigor were expressed in his appearance which suggested "a picturesque combination of d'Artagnan and Daniel Webster, with a dash of cowboy," appealing at sight to every child who entered his school.

The building was a small gray structure, about forty feet long and twenty feet wide, with a big stove in the center, three of the walls panelled with blackboards and the entrance wall fronted by the master's desk on a low dais. A central aisle divided the pupils, girls on one side, boys on the other, the desks accommodating two each. As might be expected, there were more boys than girls. Surrounding the schoolhouse, was the idyllic Concord community, offering picnics at Esterbrook Farm, bathing and skating at Walden Pond, regattas on the river below the old Red Bridge, overnight encampments on Monadnock Mountain, horseback riding parties, grand masquerades at the town hall, dances, and general fun at the Alcotts' lively home. Wilky and Bob enjoyed school life as they had never imagined it before. They were popular with their schoolmates, who remembered them as good-looking, open-hearted boys, putting on no airs about their foreign languages and foreign travels; they were, in fact, as "simple and hearty as sailors on leave." Hawthorne's son spoke of them as having the best of manners and "no unfortunate habits." Bob, he remembered, was robust and hilarious, "tough, tireless as hickory, great in the playground, not much of a scholar."

Wilky was "the glass of fashion and mould of form, but never the least clothes-conscious or la-de-da; good-natured to the marrow." [9]

The boys remained at Concord until enlisting in the army, Wilkinson in 1862 at the age of seventeen and Robertson in 1863, when Sanborn's school was closed. They both took commissions, Wilky as First Lieutenant and Adjutant in the 54th Massachusetts, under Robert Gould Shaw, and Bob in the 55th Massachusetts Militia.[10] From happy, carefree school boys, they were thrust into the manhood of war too abruptly. One wonders what effects the war, the school, and Sanborn might have had on Harry James, had he followed his younger brothers instead of remaining at Newport with William. The strong Concord milieu, so directly connected with Emersonian thought and far removed from European culture, might have given him even more of the New England spirit than he caught indirectly from Hawthorne, and through his father, from Emerson. On a visit to the boys, during their second year at Sanborn's, Harry was deeply impressed. In the break with Europe, he felt that even at Newport he "had landed somewhere in quite another world or at least on the sharp edge of one." To push further inland, to the rugged American scene of Concord, for example, struck him as a powerful possibility. "What straight solicitation *that* phase of the American scene could exert—more coercive to the imagination than any we were ever again, as Americans, to know. . . ."[11] Only as a transient, detached visitor did he know Concord, though the years at Cambridge were to be a great help in feeding his starved American consciousness.

Beginning in October, 1860, and continuing until the following spring, Harry, along with Willy, each day made faithful but futile efforts to paint in Hunt's studio, just across from the old Jewish Cemetery, in "an old-fashioned, bluish-gray house placed back in the yard some distance from the road, with several trees around it." The master, genuinely interested in Willy's promise of talent, kindly tolerated Harry's sitting unobtrusively on the outer edges of the small atelier and was, the boys felt, "one of the most original and delightful of men." To them he appeared to be more French than American, a French sculptor, perhaps, rather than a painter. Harry saw him as "all muscular spareness and brownness and absence of waste, all flagrant physiognomy, brave bony arch of handsome nose, upwardness of strong eyebrow and glare, almost, of eyes that both recognized and wondered, strained eyes that played over questions as if they were objects and objects as if they were questions, (he) might have stood, to the life, for Don Quixote, if we could associate with that hero a far-spreading beard already a little grizzled, and manner and range of gesture and broken form of discourse that was like a restless reference to a palette and that seemed to take for granted, all about, canvasses and models and charming amusing things. . . . " [12] Harry felt that Hunt could never have perched on Rosinante, and yet the Don Quixote figure persisted, even with the knight of La Mancha resorting to a spinning buggy behind a favorite trotter.

With Willy seriously competing with one or two of the less advanced students, though never presuming to reach the outer regions of John La Farge's realms, Harry sat in a small area devoted to plaster casts and simpler compositions on which he earnestly worked away the hours. As brief as the experience was, it left a significant impression upon him, quite aside from La Farge's urging him to turn wholeheartedly to his literary efforts and give up painting. That he was soon to do, not continuing at the studio for the full six months of Willy's apprenticeship.

In describing Hunt's atelier and his place in it, Harry observed: "Pupils at that time didn't flock to his gates—though they were to do so in Boston, during years, later on; an earnest lady or two, Boston precursors, hovered and flittered, but I remember for the rest (and I speak of a short period) no thoroughgoing élèves save John La Farge and my brother. I remember, for that matter, sitting quite in solitude in one of the grey cool rooms of the studio, which thus comes back to me as having several, and thinking that I really might get to copy casts rather well, and might in particular see myself congratulated on my sympathetic rendering of the sublime uplifted face of Michael Angelo's 'Captive' in the Louvre. I sat over this effort and a few others for long quiet hours, and seem to feel myself again aware, just to that tune, of how happy I ought to be.

No one disturbed me; the earnest workers were elsewhere; I had a chamber of the temple all to myself, with immortal forms and curves, with shadows beautiful and right, waiting there on blank-eyed faces for me to prove myself not helpless; and with two or three of Hunt's own fine things, examples of his work in France, transporting me at once and defying. . . . Frankly, intensely—that was the great thing—these were hours with Art, art definitely named, looking me full in the face and accepting my stare in return—no longer a tacit implication or a shy subterfuge, but a flagrant unattenuated aim. I had somehow come into the temple by the back door, the *porte d'honneur* opened on another side, and I could never have believed much at best in the length of my stay; but I was there, day by day, as much as any one had ever been, and with a sense of what it 'meant' to be there that the most accredited of pupils couldn't have surpassed; so that the situation to this extent really hummed with promise." [13]

One morning, expecting merely to continue sketching an acanthus leaf or one of the blank-faced casts, Henry entered the studio to find a startlingly new and difficult model. Gus Barker, one of the handsomest of the Albany cousins, was posing in the nude, perched on a pedestal, presenting the manly form of a Greek athlete. As Harry tried his hand at the advanced problem of drawing from life, his previous hopes of achieving something like aptitude and proficiency in the art collapsed with a crash. He was forced to recognize then and there that he might labor for months over plaster casts, even show improvement in that realm, without approaching the skill, the gift, required for reproducing the human figure. Especially discouraging to him was the apparent success that Willy was achieving, producing a sketch that "dazzled" Harry out of every presumption. He knew, as he had never known before, that nothing less than such ability constituted real drawing and "since our genial kinsman's perfect gymnastic figure meant living truth," he thought, "I should certainly best testify to the whole mystery by pocketing my pencil." [14] Willy's finished rendering of Gus Barker was so successful that it was preserved for many years, ever a reminder to Harry of this turning point in his own career in Hunt's studio. Another cousin, Kitty Temple, was done in oils by Willy, as well as by La Farge, whose sketch was naturally more mature and masterly, showing the charming seventeen-year-old girl in profile, sewing on a piece of fancy work, her handsome head and features strikingly set off against the dark dress and gray background. To such artistic altitudes Harry never dreamed of aspiring, so that by the spring of 1861 he had officially relinquished his regular place in the group.

Having suffered from no serious illusions about his ability to paint, Harry was neither humiliated nor depressed by his withdrawal. Willy's decision to give up a rather promising possibility of a career as a painter and La Farge's pronouncement to Harry that writing was really his calling gave reason for him to believe that the situation was not at all embarrassing. The current of fiction to which Harry now turned was a small stream indeed compared with the broad stretch ahead of him, yet during these Newport years it gathered substance and momentum. La Farge, "as referentially and unexhaustibly bookish" as he was charming and talented, plunged Harry "straight into the square and dense little formal garden of Mérimée," generously giving the younger man hours of "talk, talk as talk, for which no moment, no suspended step, was too odd and fleeting." In 1860, John La Farge married at Newport Margaret Perry, sister of Thomas Sergeant Perry, thus bringing into close bonds the artist's relationship with Henry James, Sarg Perry's best friend. In the intimacy of such friendship young Henry's literary efforts found more tender care and stricter confidence than he dared to seek in the bosom of his own family. This paradoxical situation was explained by Perry many years later, in his account of Harry as a hopeful young scribbler:

After his return to America in 1860, the question what he should do with his life became more urgent. Of course it was in literature that he took the greatest interest. One task that he set himself was translating Alfred de Musset's 'Lorenzaccio,' and into this version he introduced some scenes of his own. Exactly what they were I do not

recall, though I read them with an even keener interest than I did the
original text. He was continually writing stories, mainly of a romantic
kind. The heroes were for the most part villains, but they were white
as lambs by the side of the sophisticated heroines, who seemed to have
read all Balzac in the cradle and to be positively dripping with lurid
crimes. He began with these extravagant pictures of course in adoration
of the great master whom he so warmly admired.

H. J. seldom entrusted these early efforts to the criticism of his
family—they did not see all he wrote. They were too keen critics, too
sharp-witted, to be allowed to handle every essay of this budding talent.
Their judgments would have been too true, their comments would have
been too merciless; and hence, for sheer self-preservation, he hid a good
part of his work from them. Not that they were cruel, far from it.
Their frequent solitude in foreign parts, where they had no familiar
companions, had welded them together in a way that would have been
impossible in America, where each would have separate distractions of
his own. Their loneliness forced them to grow together most harmoniously, but their long exercise in literary criticism would have made
them possibly merciless judges of H. J.'s crude beginnings.[15]

Perry's observation of the James boys' training in literary criticism,
even in these early years, is of special significance in the case of
field of criticism. Young Henry James was primarily a critic, within four years from this return from Europe getting his start with
book reviews and an occasional story of no marked merit, showing
Harry, whose literary career, in spite of these crude attempts at
Balzacian treatment of extravagant romances, first took shape in the
signs of uncertainty in handling fiction. It was through his early
development as a critic that he entered into the realm of the novel
and short story, his talent for which was always based upon and
connected with his genius as a critic. As has aptly been noted:
"James's whole history is a process of clarification of thought, a story
of increasingly precise principles. He would never have been the
novelist he was without the schooling of the earlier criticism, and
without the novels he would never have been the critic he showed
himself to be in the *Prefaces*." [16] Between 1860 and 1864, the date
of his first published essay, some profound changes took place in his
development, changes which had much bearing upon his choice of
career and which account in no small degree for the peculiar nature

of that career. The most outstanding and far-reaching alteration resulted from an injury he received in the spring of 1860, "at the same
dark hour" of the Civil War.

In response to a fire alarm, the young men of Newport, including
Willy and Harry James, joined the volunteer firemen in fighting the
blaze. In order to pump water to a sufficient pressure, an antiquated
fire apparatus was used, requiring many pairs of arms on the cross-
bar handles on either side of the machine. In lending a hand to
this work, Harry became "jammed into the acute angle between
two high fences, where the rhythmic play of my arms, in tune with
that of several other pairs," put him under dire stress. He discovered, after about twenty minutes of excitement and effort, that
he had wrenched his back severely. For the next few days he was
confined to his bed, suffering from pain, experiencing distress and
fatigue from any exercise, or even normal walking. After several
weeks, when he showed little improvement, he went up to Boston
with his father to be examined by an eminent surgeon. The pronouncement was made that nothing serious was wrong—just a bad
sprain, apparently, which required much rest.

In spite of the rather light and casual diagnosis, Harry believed
from the first that the results would be of long duration; time
proved him to be correct, for "the effects were to draw themselves
out incalculably and intolerably." Furthermore, the condition was
followed by complications of chronic indigestion and constipation,
relief from which he constantly sought at home and abroad for many
years. His brother William, oddly enough, suffered from the same
disorders, so that the brothers, during the next ten years or more,
seldom exchanged letters without discussing in some detail the various remedies tried. Among the family papers are innumerable letters between Willy and Harry which contain pages of accounts
and suggestions about cures, attempted or contemplated. Often, in
letters to the family in general, the brothers would include separate
notes about their ills, not wishing to burden their parents or
sister, especially, with unpleasant details. This sense of propriety
and modesty, particularly on Harry's part, which prevented open
discussion of such personal matters, even with his family, has been

grossly misunderstood and erroneously interpreted by scholars who
have not, apparently, read the wealth of material available.[17] Consequently, several biographers have implied that as a result of his
accident at Newport in 1860, Henry James was sexually impotent,
supporting the claim on the evidence that he never married and that
certain of his stories treat the question of sex in a way which
might indicate something other than a normal concern with the subject. There is absolutely nothing in James's own account in *Notes of
a Son and Brother* or in either the published or unpublished letters
among the James family papers to justify such an assumption. There
is, however, abundant evidence to support the contention that the
injury was to his back and that for the rest of his life he was never
free from its effects upon his health.[18]

Perhaps one of the most serious aspects of the result of this injury
and the consequent weakness and ill health it brought to young
Henry James was the influence it had upon his relationship with
Minny Temple. In a letter to William, expressing his shock and
grief over her death in March, 1870, he stated: "Among the sad
reflections that her death provokes for me, there is no sadder than
this view of the gradual change and reversal of our relations: I
slowly crawling from weakness and inaction and suffering into
strength and health and hope: she sinking out of brightness and
youth into decline and death. . . . She never knew how sick and disordered a creature I was and I always felt that she knew me at my
worst. I always looked forward with a certain eagerness to the day
when I should have regained my natural lead, and one (sic) (our)
friendship on my part, at least, might become more active and
masculine." [19]

The friendship began in the very earliest years in Albany and
New York, when the large group of cousins centering about Grandmother James's house on North Pearl Street, overflowed into "the
other house, the house of . . . the various brood presided over by
my father's second sister, Catherine James, who had married at a
very early age Captain Robert Temple, U. S. A.," among whose
children was Mary, "radiant and rare." Born on December 7, 1845,
Mary Temple was two and a half years younger than Harry. The

scraps of holidays that the James children spent in Albany and those their Temple cousins spent in the Fourteenth Street house in New York prior to 1855 had brought Mary, or Minny as she was affectionately called, and Harry into early companionship. In 1858, when the James family returned from Europe for a year at Newport, Minny, then only only thirteen, had again appeared on the scene, a charming, lively, delicate child whose vivacity and wit were exceedingly pleasing. In 1860, the Jameses were again back from Europe but the Edmund Tweedys were still abroad; upon their return, the four Temple girls, Katherine, Mary, Ellen, and Henriette, orphaned several years earlier, came to live permanently with Aunt Mary Tweedy.[20] With this happy arrangement, Harry then about eighteen and Minny sixteen, began the active years of their friendship which increased in closeness for the rest of her short life and remained in his consciousness long decades afterward. She was to become the prototype for two of his greatest characterizations, Isabel Archer in *The Portrait of a Lady*, and Milly Theale in *The Wings of a Dove*.[21]

An inspiration from the beginning, she came into full bloom during these Civil War years at Newport, on looking back to which Harry saw her aglow with life, shining with a "lustre, an essence that preserves her still, more than half a century (sic) from the date of her death, in a memory or two where many a relic once sacred has comparatively yielded to time. Most of those who knew and loved, I was going to say adored, her have also yielded—which is a reason the more why thus much of her, faint echo from too far off though it prove, should be tenderly saved. If I have spoken of the elements and presences round about us that 'counted,' Mary Temple was to count, and in more lives than can now be named, to an extraordinary degree; count as a young and shining apparition, a creature who owed to the charm of her every aspect (her aspects were so many!) and the originality, vivacity, audacity, generosity, of her spirit, an indescribable grace and weight—if one might impute weight to a being so imponderable in common scales. Whatever other values on our scene might, as I have hinted, appear to fail, she was one of the first order, in the sense of the immediacy of the impression she produced, and produced altogether as by the play of her own light spontaneity and curiosity—not, that is, as through a sense of such a pressure and such a motive, or through a care for them, in others. 'Natural' to an effect of perfect felicity that we were never to see surpassed is what I have already praised all the Albany *cousinage* of those years for being; but in none of the company was the note so clear as in this rarest, though at the same time symptomatically or ominously palest, flower of the stem; who was natural at more points and about more things, with a greater range of freedom and ease and reach of horizon than any of the others dreamed of. They had that way, delightfully, with the small, after all, and the common matters—while she had it with those too, but with the great and rare ones over and above; so that she was to remain for us the very figure and image of a felt interest in life, an interest as magnanimously far-spread, or as familiarly and exquisitely fixed, as her splendid shifting sensibility, moral, personal, nervous, and having at once such noble flights and such touchingly discouraged drops, such graces of indifference and inconsequence, might at any moment determine. She was really to remain, for our appreciation, the supreme case of a taste for life as life, as personal living; of an endlessly active and yet somehow a careless, an illusionless, a sublimely forewarned curiosity about it: something that made her, slim and fair and quick, all straightness and charming tossed head, with long light and yet almost sliding steps and a large light postponing, renouncing laugh, the very muse or amateur priestess or rash speculation. To express her in the mere terms of her restless young mind, one felt from the first, was to place her, by a perversion of the truth, under the shadow of female 'earnestness'—for which she was much too unliteral and too ironic; so that, superlatively personal and yet as independent, as 'off' into higher spaces, at a touch, as all the breadth of her sympathy and her courage could send her, she made it impossible to say whether she was just the most moving of maidens or a disengaged and dancing flame of thought. No one to come after her could easily seem to show either a quick inward life or a brave, or even a bright, outward, either a consistent contempt for social squalors or a very marked genius for moral reac-

tions. She had in her brief passage the enthusiasm of humanity—
more, assuredly, than any charming girl who ever circled, and would
fain have continued to circle, round a ballroom. This kept her indeed
for a time more interested in the individual, the immediate human,
than in the race or the social order at large; but that, on the other
hand, made her ever so restlessly, or quite inappeasably, 'psychologic.'
The psychology of others, in her shadow—I mean their general resort
to it—could only for a long time seem weak and flat and dim, above
all not at all amusing. She burned herself out; she died at twenty-
four." [22]

To Henry James there was "no one to come after her," but
the realization of this fact did not take form until he received
the report of her death; only then did he fully grasp the extent to
which she stood out to him against the immediate social order of
Newport and Cambridge, and, as years went on, against the social
order at large. In the early Sixties when Harry's injury placed him
in a condition of semi-invalidism and before Minny had begun to
decline in the advancing stages of consumption, he was indeed at an
embarrassing disadvantage in their friendship. On the other hand,
Minny, as he wrote later, had many admirers, for, "Every one was
supposed, I believe, to be more or less in love with her. . . . " She
expressed more and more during these few scant years of her life
that inimitable charm and wit and grace which captivated such young
men as Sarg Perry, John Gray, Oliver Wendell Holmes, Jr., and
Willy, as well as Harry James. Yet, as will be shown, during the
last year or two of her life, as Harry found himself in his career
and gradually regained his health, his friendship with Minny took on
the strength and promise he had desired earlier. In 1870 he wrote
of her to his brother: "I cared more to please her perhaps than she
ever cared to be pleased. Looking back upon the past half-dozen
years, it seems as if she *represented,* in a manner, in my life, several
of the elements or phases of life at large—her own sex, to begin
with, but even more *Youth,* with which owing to my invalidism,
I always felt in rather indirect relation." [23] Thus, as in so many
other aspects of his experience in the first three decades of his life,
he was forced to stand aside, to give up the active for a more pas-

sive participation in a situation which was of considerable significance to him.

During the spring vacation from the Sanborn school in 1861,
Wilky and Bob brought Edward Emerson home to Newport for a
visit. Just a year younger than Harry, he was as much drawn to the
two older brothers as he was to the younger ones, but Henry James,
Sr., completely captivated the boy. In the center of this "most interesting, brilliant, original, and affectionate" family life stood the elder
James. "He was of medium height, limped along on his wooden
leg with some activity, but his mind and wit were most active and
his temperament sympathetic. His face reminded one at once of the
representations of Socrates, with the bald head, short nose, eyes
humorous yet kindly (but spectacled), and beard of moderate dimensions; and, like Socrates, he delighted in starting a theme to
argue with his companions to its conclusion—seemingly surprising.
For he was not only a humorist, but master of the superlative; and,
after a little almost stuttering hesitation, he, like his sons after
him, would bring out an adjective or adverb or appellation that
would startle the literal-minded, but he, with no malice, chose to
attach other than the usual significations to the word, and this
might lead him to illuminating discussion. Notable examples of this
entertaining habit (edifying, if understood) occur in his writings." [24]
The vitality and spontaneity of the father could best be seen in
action at the dining table when all the family and guests were
gathered together. For anyone not prepared for the rapidity and
exuberance of the conversation which leapt around and across the
board, a meal with the Jameses was indeed an experience. Young
Edward, accustomed to the propriety and dignity of the Emerson
home in Concord, found himself overwhelmed by the clash of wit and
brilliance of repartee to which he was submitted during this visit.
Wilky, he remembered, "would say something and be instantly cor-
rected or disputed by the little cock-sparrow Bob, the youngest, but
good-naturedly defend his statement, and then Henry (Junior) would
emerge from his silence in defence of Wilky. Then Bob would be
more impertinently insistent, and Mr. James would advance as
Moderator, and William, the eldest, join in. The voice of the Modera-

or presently would be drowned by the combatants and he soon came
lown vigorously into the arena, and when, in the excited argument,
he dinner-knives might not be absent from eagerly gesticulating
ands, dear Mrs. James, more conventional, but bright as well as
notherly, would look at me, laughingly reassuring, saying, 'Don't be
listurbed, Edward; they won't stab each other. This is usual when the
oys come home.' And the quiet little sister ate her dinner, smiling,
lose to the combatants. Mr. James considered this debate, within
ounds, excellent for the boys. In their speech, singularly mature
nd picturesque, as well as vehement, the Gaelic (Irish) element in
heir descent always showed. Even if they blundered, they saved
hemselves by wit." [25] Mr. Emerson well knew the James spirit
nd wit and was always amused by it, so that his son's account of
is visit at Newport did not surprise the Concord sage at all. Alice
ames, in her journal, relates an anecdote which illustrates the point.
Mr. George Bradford had opened a school at Newport which Alice
was attending at this time. He was visiting the Emersons one day
vhen Wilky James was also a guest there. In the conversation
Mr. Emerson said to Mr. Bradford: "And what sort of girl is
Alice?" "She has a highly moral nature," replied Mr. Bradford;
whereupon in great amusement Mr. Emerson exclaimed, "How in
he world does her father get on with her." [26]

In addition to the excitement and entertainment on Kay Street,
Edward was introduced to many of the James family's interesting
friends, among whom were the Tweedy family with the four Temple
sisters making a lively and delightful household for a visit from
he James children and their guest. Over in Lawton's Valley was
Julia Ward Howe and her family, the daughters being a strong at-
raction, especially to the intensely sociable and affable Wilky.[27]
George Henry Calver, translator of Goethe and follower of Fourier's
ocial philosophy, Charles L. Brooks, clergyman and German scholar,
nd Henry T. Tuckerman, 'a genial and graceful poet of the Artless
Age . . . with a certain deafness and a glossy wig and a portly presence and the reputation . . . of the most practised and desired of
liners-out," were some of Newport's distinguished characters and
friends of the Jameses. Of them all, other than Mr. James himself,

Edward Emerson was most impressed by William Hunt, toward whos
studio the boys naturally drifted, to see the master, La Farge, an
others. "While I was there," Edward always remembered, "Hur
came in and cordially asked me, boy as I was, to his studio upstair
There he showed me, to my great delight, the first studies for hi
wonderful 'Anahits,' or 'Flight of Night,' which years later adorne
the Capitol of Albany. He also showed me the charming lithograph
from his paintings, such as the 'Hurdy-Gurdy Boy' and the 'Girl a
the Fountain.' He gave me copies of these and more. Hunt, in hi
charming way, seemed to know no age in persons who were intereste
in beautiful things." [28] Harry too was most impressed by Hunt'
Girl at the Fountain, "with her back presented while she fills he
bucket at the spout in the wall, against which she leans with a ter
sion of young muscle, a general expression of back, beneath her dres
and the pressure of her raised and extended bare arm and flattene
hand: this, to my imagination, could only become the prize of som
famous collection, the light of some museum. . . . " [29]

It was at the same time, the spring of 1861, however, that Harr
and, later Willy, gave up their work in Hunt's studio and wer
groping about for the next step in their eclectic education. Bot
boys, during the excited weeks which followed the firing on Fo
Sumter, unable to join up with the willing youths who straine
at the leash to be off to war, were thrown heavily upon themselve
Willy's admission that his insistence upon studying painting had bee
a mistake left little for him to do but follow his father's wis
that he study science. Whether it was to be natural science o
science in the broader sense of philosophy, he could not decide
even after entering the Lawrence Scientific School at Harvard tha
autumn. In changing from the chemistry department, in 1863, t
the Medical School from which he was graduated, and in accompany
ing Professor Agassiz on his Brazilian Expedition in 1865, Willia
followed a roundabout path to his ultimate career in psycholog
and philosophy.

Harry's problem was even more perplexing, aggravated as i
was by his injury and made vague by the lack of a practical mean
of utilizing his literary interests and efforts. He remained i

Newport, therefore, during Willy's first year at Harvard, regaining his strength slowly and reading widely in his enforced retirement. Harry here read all of Hawthorne's works and gained from them the hope that an artistic career was possible in America. Hawthorne's example was a great encouragement to him to attempt such a career himself, in spite of his constant uncertainty of his own ability.[30] Howells in Cambridge was to make him sure. In the meantime, the War, patriotism, the spirit of America had caught even Newport in a whirl of excitement with Henry James, Sr., being the orator of the day, on July 4, 1861. For weeks, the family was constantly aware of father's preparation for the address and the discussions frequently centered around the main thesis, the superiority of America over Europe. Soaring to almost spread-eagleish heights of patriotism at times, *The Social Significance of our Institutions,* as the speech was entitled, stated in impassioned tones: " . . . The letter kills, the spirit alone gives life; and it is exclusively to this undeniable spiritual difference between Europe and America, as organized and expressed in our constitutional policy, that all our formal differences are owing. Our very Constitution binds us, that is to say, the very breath of our political nostrils binds us, to disown all distinctions among men, to disregard persons, to disallow privilege the most established and sacred, to legislate only for the common good, no longer for those accidents of birth or wealth or culture which spiritually individualize man from his kind, but only for those great common features of social want and dependence which naturally unite him with his kind, and inexorably demand the organization of such unity. It is this immense constitutional life and inspiration we are under which not only separate us from Europe, but also perfectly explain by antagonism that rabid hostility which the South has always shown toward the admission of the North to a fair share of government patronage, and which now provokes her to the dirty and diabolic struggle she is making to give human slavery the sanction of God's appointment. . . . "[31] Entwining the religious, social, and patriotic threads of thought around the highly inflamed spirit of the moment, the elder James brought bursts of fervor from his listeners and even greater eruptions of enthusiasm from his family. The whole experience did much to impress upon young Henry the depths of American spirit stirred by the War.

At the end of that summer, when Willy went up to Harvard and the two younger brothers returned to Sanborn's school, Harry found more pleasure than ever in the companionship of T. S. Perry. He too was still "on the eve of entering Harvard," going up with Harry in the autumn of 1862 and graduating in the Class of '66. Harry remembered him affectionately as "an exemplary, at once, and a discouraging friend; he had let himself loose in the world of books, pressed and roamed through the most various literatures and the most voluminous authors, with a stride that, as it carried him beyond all view, left me dismayed and helpless at the edge of the forest, where I listened wistfully but unemulously to the far-off crash from within of his felled timber, the clearing of whole spaces or periods shelf by shelf or great tree by tree." [32] Almost as important to Harry, who was already sensitive to "every wind-borne particle of personal history," Perry's family heritage and tradition seemed highly in keeping with the accentuating of things American. He traced his descent back to Benjamin Franklin, whose brother had settled in Newport in 1726, upon running into trouble with the Boston fathers over *The New England Courant*. In moving to Rhode Island, he brought with him the first press to be used in that colony, printing on it *The Rhode Island Almanack* and the *Rhode Island Gazette*. His son, James Franklin, Jr., founded there the *Newport Mercury*, still an influential paper. Closer family connections were the two commodores, Oliver Hazard Perry, a national hero following his defeat of the British on Lake Erie in the War of 1812, and his brother, Matthew Calbraith Perry, who in 1854 negotiated a treaty with Japan, opening her ports to western trade. Such men had made American history and to their descendant Harry was accordingly drawn.

Sarg Perry, on the other hand was greatly attracted to the James family whose scintillating battles of wit and rollicking good times provided great entertainment, though Harry, he observed especially at this time, did not enter fully into the arena of conflict: "Mr. James, the father was getting out a somewhat abstruse book called *Sub-*

stance and Shadow, or *Morality and Religion in their Relation to Life*
(1863). W. J. amused himself and all the family by designing a
small cut to be put on the title page, representing a man beating a
dead horse. This will illustrate the joyous chaff that filled the
Jameses' house. There was no limit to it. There were always books
to tell about and laugh over, or to admire, and there was an abundance of good talk with no shadow of pedantry or priggishness.
H. J.'s spirits were never so high as those of the others. If they had
been, he still would have had but little chance in a conflict of
wits with them, on account of his slow speech, his halting choice
of words and phrases; but as a companion in our walks he was delightful. He had plenty of humour, as his books shew, and above
all he had a most affectionate heart. No one ever had more certain and more unobtrusive kindness than he. He had a certain air
of aloofness, but he was not indifferent to those who had no claim
upon him, and to his friends he was most tenderly devoted. Those
who knew him will not need to be assured of that." [33]

The question of college loomed increasingly large for Harry
during Willy's first year at Harvard. So interested was he in
the possibility that he went to Cambridge a few weeks after the term
began, staying with Willy from October 31st to November 4th and
enjoying immensely his first taste of American college life. Tom
Ward, Gus Barker, John Ropes, Charles Atkinson, Oliver Wendell
Holmes, Jr. and others of Willy's classmates and friends gave Harry
some idea of the stimulating and enjoyable companionship his
brother was cultivating in and about the Harvard Yard. Furthermore,
Willy's profuse and frequent letters, full of hilarious comments and
observations on his experiences, professors, courses, boarding-house
meals, and landlady continued to pour into Newport, carrying with
them much of the atmosphere of undergraduate life.[34] The letters
also reveal much about life at Newport, news about which Willy
constantly demanded, as for example in the one he wrote to Kitty
Temple in September, 1861, asking for full explanation of the report that Minny Temple had just cut her hair short like a boy's.[35]
Never could he receive enough news of family life nor send full
enough accounts of his love and longing for every member from his

parents down to Moses, the family horse. As the evidence increased that Harvard was providing Willy with a better educational experience, in terms of conventional curriculum and a prescribed procedure of study, than he had ever had before, the elder James's decided coolness toward sending his children to college began to wane. Harry believed that his father's ideas on the subject were unduly colored by his remorseful recollections of his own undergraduate days at Union College where his youthful deportment and indulgence had brought upon him the wrath of his father, old William James of Albany. Willy and Harry had paid a visit to Schenectady to see Union College a few years before, under the impulse on Willy's part that he might like to attend his father's alma mater. All enthusiasm declined, however, under their father's total lack of interest in the possibility; furthermore, he showed little more in their subsequent enthusiasms for Columbia or Yale, or Brown in Providence, not too far from Newport. Harvard was finally admitted as a possibility, particularly since the Albany cousins were there; but very gradually indeed, and with very little warmth of feeling did Henry James, Sr., send his second son off to Cambridge in the autumn of 1862.

Why Harry should have entered the Harvard Law School was always a mystery, even to himself, "a singularly alien member" of that department as he proved to be. On looking back on it, he thought of the step as "one of the oddest errands . . . I could possibly have undertaken." He was nineteen years old, in poor health, and had spent the previous year in a state of enforced inertia at the very time that the entire youth of the nation was stirring to abnormal activity. His father's consent to his joining Willy was given "in the most offhand and liberal manner," with little conviction, apparently, that the experience would prove to be anything more than of general cultural value. As barren as the year was to be for Harry in certain respects, it did give him a sense of doing something, of being somewhere purposefully, although, as he realized before withdrawing the following July, what he really wanted to be was "just *literary*." The unusual bustle and stir of this second year of the War electrified the air, even within the quiet of the Har-

vard Yard, yet the utter charm of the place Harry felt in every direction. The horsecar ride of three miles from the old Parker House,
across the Charles River and the long, lazy meadows stretching up
and down both sides of the quiet stream, brought Harry pleasantly
into Harvard Square, an irregular space formed by the junction of
three streets. There was the time-honored wooden pump, beyond
which a flight of granite steps led into the town post office. A bit
northward, along a tree-lined country road was Longfellow's stately
home, emerging from which the smiling, smartly clad, good-looking
poet, in his middle fifties, enjoying the popularity of his recently
published *Tales of a Wayside Inn,* strode toward the Square each
day. Further along was Lowell's house, withdrawn behind trees in
much the way of its master who did not particularly encourage callers,
though the Jameses were to know him well within the next few years.
As Harry accompanied Willy, now a sophomore and, as usual, in full
command of the situation, to their quarters, he felt very much the
freshman. Behind the wooden-fenced enclosure containing the dormi-
tories and administration building, he caught glimpses of the old
Yard with the tall, wide-branching elms;—in and out of the gate-
posts young collegians sauntered, nice looking fellows in wide
peg-top trousers, soft hats or caps, once in a while a 'beaver' sending forth black gleams. Hands in pockets, or toying with canes,
these well-mannered youths were certainly agreeable, gentlemanly,
in fact. Equally impressive were the rooms that Harry was now to
share, "quiet cloistered rooms . . . in the comparatively sequestered
Divinity Hall of that still virtually rustic age," given over mostly to
post-graduate students "of a Unitarian colour," and members of
Harvard's theological Faculty. The atmosphere, more than anything
else, settled over Harry with a power which he was never to forget,
providing, in fact, one of the strongest forces of his entire experience of repatriation.

Mr. Emerson and Concord had already represented to Harry the
potency of the New England spirit, but now, here at Harvard, he
sensed its impact upon the Newport and European backgrounds
from which his youth had stemmed. "The superstition or after-
taste of Europe had then neither left me nor hinted that it ever

might; yet I recall as a direct source of interest, to be desperately dealt with, and dealt with somehow to my inward advantage, the special force of the circumstance that I was now for the first time in presence of matters normally, entirely, consistently American, and that more particularly I found myself sniff up straight from the sources, such as they unmistakably were, the sense of that New England which had been to me till then but a name. This from the first instant was what I most took in, and quite apart from the question of what one was going to make of it, of whether one was going, in the simple formula, to like it, and of what would come, could the impression so triumph, of such monstrous assimilations. Clear to me in the light thus kindled that my American consciousness had hitherto been after all and in the best singularly starved, and that Newport for instance, during the couple of years, had fed it but with sips of an adulterated strain. Newport, with its operaglass turned forever across the sea—for Newport, or at least *our* Newport, even during the War, lived mainly, and quite visibly, by the opera-glass—was comparatively, and in its degree incurably, cosmopolite; and though on our first alighting there I had more or less successfully, as I fancied, invited the local historic sense to vibrate, it was at present left me to feel myself a poor uninitiated creature." [36]

His initiation was strongest, perhaps, at the boardinghouse where the two boys took their meals. Eating at hotels and pensions in vari- ous cities of Europe had hardly prepared Harry for the unique ex- perience of this *table d'hôte,* ruled over by "that gently fatuous Miss Upham something of whose angular grace and antique attitude" he had learned from Willy's letters the previous year. To Harry the *maison* Upham became a vivid translation into American terms of Balzac's Maison Vauquer, in *Le Père Goriot,* though the curiously sordid, even sinister scene of Balzac's story was utterly removed from the quiet dignity of the New England spinster's dining room on Kirkland Street. That was intensely, peculiarly American. Harry's introduction to the faculty was most deeply impressive under the professorial light of Francis James Child, whose *Observations on the Language of Chaucer* had just appeared and whose *English and Scottish Popular Ballads,* twenty years later, made such a monumental contribution to scholarship and literature. Fortunately for Willy and Harry, Professor Child took his morning meal at Miss Upham's board where he impressed the boys as much as he did in the classroom each day. Then head of Harvard's Department of English, Professor Child was a "delightful man, rounded character, passionate patriot, admirable talker, above all thorough humanist and humorist. He was the genial autocrat of that breakfast-table not only, but of our symposia otherwise timed, and as he comes back to me with the fresh and quite circular countenance of the time before the personal cares and complications of life had gravely thickened for him, his aspect *all* finely circular, with its close rings of the fairest hair, its golden rims of the largest glasses, its finished rotundity of figure and attitude, I see that *there* was the American spirit—since I was 'after' it—of a quality deeply inbred, beautifully adjusted to all extensions of knowledge and taste and to me, quite sublimely quickened by everything that was at the time so tremendously in question. . . . I was always just across from him, as my brother, beside whom I took my place, had been, and I remember well how vivid a clock-face it became to me; I found still, as in my younger time, matter enough everywhere for gaping, but greatest of all, I think, while that tense season lasted, was my wonder for the signs and portents, the quips and cranks, the wreathed smiles, or otherwise the candid obscurations, of our prime talker's presented visage." [37]

Theophilus Parsons and ex-Governor Washburn were two other members of the faculty who left indelible impressions upon Harry, particularly the former "whose rich, if slightly quavering, old accents were the first to fall upon my ear from the chair of instruction beneath a huge hot portrait of Daniel Webster . . . a vivid and curiously-composed person, an *illustrative* figure, as who should say—exactly with all the marks one might have wished him, marks of a social order, a general air, a whole history of things. . . . " The individual ways in which these men related to the dense American atmosphere behind them was of special importance to Harry to whom Cambridge and Boston were then "literally the American feast." "Theophilus Parsons, with his tone, his unction, his homage still to some ancient superstition, some standard of manners, reached back as to a state of provincialism rounded and compact, quite self-supporting, which gave it serenity and quality, something comparatively rich and urban; the good ex-Governor, on the other hand, of whom I think with singular tenderness, opened through every note of aspect and expression straight into those depths of rusticity which more and more unmistakably underlay the social order at large and out of which one felt it to have emerged in any degree but at scattered points. Where it did emerge, I seemed to see, it held itself as high as possible, conscious, panting a little, elate with the fact of having cleared its skirts, saved its life, consolidated its Boston." [38] The faculty, the lecture halls, the whole Cambridge scene was as "American, and above all as suffused with New England colour, however one might finally estimate that, as I could possibly have wished."

The falling of the curtain on Harry's Law School studies followed not long after his attempt, one day, to argue a case with a fellow student, under what seemed to him an awful glare of publicity, although the audience consisted merely of a few other students. Overly sensitive, he thought of the incident as "a black little memory," in which he quavered stammeringly away before his opponent. The hesitation in his speech and his general physical and nervous exhaustion hardly suited him for that sort of public exhibition. In fact even routine duties at this time, two years after his injury, called for little short of heroic efforts because of the "bodily over-strain that I only afterwards allowed myself dejectedly to measure. The mere sitting at attention for two or three hours—such attention as I achieved—was paid for by sorry pain. . . . " It is not surprising, therefore, that he gradually "let everything slide—everything but the mere act of rather difficultly living (by reason of my scant physical ease)," turning quite resignedly to general reading in the College Library and revived interests in his literary possibilities. His withdrawal from scientific studies in Geneva at the Institute Rochette had been abrupt. This academic retreat was slow and more graceful, though surrounding circumstances accentuated the action, as the Union Army was approaching those extremities of position which darkened the entire thought of the North. Further-

more, Wilky and Bob James had, by the spring of 1863, brought the
War home to the Jameses. Wilky, having received a severe foot
wound in the charge on Fort Wagner, was brought back to Newport for the slow and painful recovery. Bob fought in the siege of
Charleston and, like Wilky, was cited for bravery, though not
wounded. The battlefield contacts thus established by the two
youngest sons stirred the entire family with a patriotic fervor that
was never so aroused as it was on July 1, 1863, the day on which the
huge battle of Gettysburg began. Profoundly impressed by the
dramatic aspects and awful significance of this turning point of the
War, Harry never forgot the family group, "New York cousins and
all, who, in a Newport garden, restlessly strolling, sitting, neither daring quite to move nor quite to rest, quite to go in nor quite to stay out,
actually *listened* together, in their almost ignobly safe stillness, as to
the boom of faraway guns. This *was*, as it were, the War—the War
palpably in Pennsylvania. . . . " [39] In the previous August, at Portsmouth Grove, a short sail up the Island from Newport, Harry had
witnessed a vast gathering of invalid and convalescent troops, the
panoramic sweep of which struck him with profound emotion. The
wounded men symbolized to him the endless sacrifice and noble
devotion which lay behind the whole national cataclysm. Nothing in
Europe had ever moved him to such feeling. He caught in a moment
that spirit of the American soldier, which corresponded very closely,
he found "with the tender elegiac tone in which Walt Whitman was
later on so admirably to commemorate him." As the Battle of Gettysburg prolonged itself through those first three momentous days of
July, 1863, young Henry James knew that his repatriation was established. On the eve of the First World War, fifty years later, the
image of the Newport garden and the spirit with which he had been
so stirred were still vividly before him, and he wrote, in retrospect:
"I was getting furiously American, in the big sense I invoked,
through this felt growth of an ability to reach out westward, south-
ward, anywhere, everywhere, on that apprehension of finding myself
but patriotically charmed. Thus there dawned upon me the grand
possibility that, charm for charm, the American, the assumed, the
postulated, would, in the particular case of its really acting,

count double; whereas the European paid for being less precarious by being also less miraculous. . . . It was as if one's sense of 'Europe,' sufficiently sure of itself to risk the strategic retreat, had backed away on tiptoe. . . . " [40]

NOTES

1. William Dean Howells, *Life in Letters of William Dean Howells,* ed. Mildred Howells, Garden City, N. Y., Doubleday, Doran, 1928, II, 394.

2. Percy Lubbock, *op. cit.,* II, 381. The anguish of James's feelings at this time is suggested in a letter he wrote to Mrs. Thomas Sergeant Perry, dated from London on September 7, 1915: "My ci-devant country, moreover, is not by any means, my dear Lilla, as 'proud of me' as *that* comes to! I assure you that she isn't. I have received during these last years, in various odd straggling ways, superabundant testimony to her refusal to cultivate any such damnable vice! Of course that matter of her position on all these and like questions, her great doctrine that to invite scores and scores of millions of aliens to naturalize themselves with *her* is in the highest degree exemplary and edifying, while any such proceedings on the part of one of her own children elsewhere deserves but single reprobation—of course that fine discrepancy is too obvious to waste words on! Let me assure you (for your verses help me to feel it) that if you yourself, at the end of long and intimate establishment here, had wanted to attest the attachment which the huge 'new fact,' the national exposure on such a scale as had never been dreamt of in the world before, would have laid unappeaseably on your soul, you would absolutely (after straining your eyes and ears across the sea, for a year, all in vain), have found no other way that met your case." John T. Morse, Jr., *Thomas Sergeant Perry,* Boston, Houghton Mifflin Co., 1929, 53.

3. Henry James, *The Art of the Novel,* ed. Richard P. Blackmur, New York, Charles Scribner's Sons, 1934, 22.

4. Joseph Warren Beach, *The Method of Henry James,* New Haven, Yale University Press, 1918, 143, 144.

5. Austin Warren, *op. cit.,* 152. In commenting on the beauty of the understanding between James and his father, Warren continues: "Henry was an artist; his father, a philosopher. Persons, and the relations they sustained to one another, were Henry's subject; the father rejected persons in favor of the universally human. Henry described and analysed a disappearing society; his father prophesied a Society to come. Henry turned for his criterion to the aristocrat, subtle in his sense of values; his father, to the man on the street,

who possessed no self-conscious individuality to interpose between his fellow and God. One found his Shekinah in the drawing room; the other, in the horse car."

6. MS. letter, Henry James, Sr., to Fanny Macdaniel, May 13, 1858, Houghton Library, Harvard University.

7. Jim Mackaye's sister, Sadie Mackaye, recorded in her diary for October 10, 1860: "The summer has been passed at Newport, in our Kay Street cottage, and here we are back in New York. Jim and I came on together earlier than expected, as Father rented our house in Newport to the Jameses for the winter. . . . " Percy Mackaye, *op. cit.,* I, 82. The Jameses occupied the house for two years.

8. Julian Hawthorne, who was a fellow student under Sanborn, along with Edward Emerson, Wilky and Bob James, recalled their teacher as "a tall, wiry, long-limbed young scholar with brilliant eyes looking keenly beneath a great shock of black hair; a quick, kindly, humorous smile brightening over his thin, fresh-hued face and finely moulded features, expressive at once of passion and self-control. He walked with long steps and with a slight bending of the shoulders, as if in modest deprecation of his own unusual stature." *The Memoirs of Julian Hawthorne,* ed. Edith Garrigues Hawthorne, New York, The Macmillan Co., 1928, 77.

9. *Ibid.,* Julian Hawthorne's account continues: "These two were perfectly delightful characters, though, of course, unknown outside their circle of personal friends. Robust Bob was full of fun and pranks and audacities, but in all a perfect gentleman, in purpose and practice. He was hugely popular in the school. But Wilkie was incomparable; besides being the best dressed boy in school, and in manners and talk the most engaging, his good humor was inexhaustible. He was of middle height, broad-shouldered and symmetrical, with a good head, well set, and a smiling countenance. Peg-top trousers were in fashion then; Wilkie's were the widest and most enviable. He was sixteen years old when he came to us, but he appeared older by two or three years, being self-possessed and having the bearing of a man of the world. In the company of ladies he was entirely at ease, and devoted; they all loved him."

10. Wilkinson James was wounded in the charge on Fort Wagner, in which Colonel Shaw was killed. Henry James, Sr., in writing to a friend concerning Wilky, commented: "We all feel profoundly for the Shaws. Wilky was by him when he fell, but had no time to ask him anything. He supposes the wound to have been instantly fatal, from his never having been seen again." MS. letter, Henry James, Sr., to Samual Gray Ward, August 1, 1863, Houghton Library, Harvard University.

11. *Notes of a Son and Brother,* 221. For a discussion of Concord and the Sanborn school see *ibid.,* 125 ff.; also, R. B. Perry, *op. cit.,* I, 90-92, and Burr, *op. cit.,* 305 (note error in date of the James

boys' entrance into Sanborn's school), and Matthiessen, *op. cit.,* 95, 96.

12. *Notes of a Son and Brother,* 83, 84.

13. *Ibid.,* 79, 80. One of the Boston lady-pupils of William Hunt at this time was Miss Theodora Watson, who, in 1913 at an exhibition held in the old Church Street Studio, recalled vividly the arrangements of chairs and easels, indicating where La Farge and the two James boys had worked. (See above, Chapter X, note 12). William Hunt, after studying in Rome and Düsseldorf, went to Paris to work under Couture, being that master's favorite for five years. He then spent three years studying with Jean François Millet and other Barbizon painters such as Diaz. In 1855 he returned to the United States, settling at Newport for eight years before going on to Boston for the rest of his career. A teacher of wide influence, William Hunt is said to have been the first American master to admit women students into his classes. See Homer Saint-Gaudens, *op. cit.,* 130, 131.

14. *Notes of a Son and Brother,* 96. Augustus Barker, son of William H. Barker of New York City and Jeanette James, sister of Henry James, Sr., was born at Albany on April 24, 1842. He died near Kelly's Ford, Mount Holly Church, Virginia in the Civil War, September 18, 1863, as a captain. From Harvard, in 1861, he enlisted in the New York Cavalry, was stricken with typhoid fever, taken home and recuperated, after which he returned to his regiment; he was captured and taken to Libby prison. His father was a brother to Mrs. Samual Gray Ward of Boston, whose husband was the elder James's banker and friend.

15. Quoted by Percy Lubbock, *op. cit.,* I, 8, 9.

16. Laurence Barrett, "Young Henry James, Critic," *American Literature,* vol. XX, January, 1949, 400.

17. Typical of Harry's letters to his brother is the following excerpt written from Malvern, England, nine years after his accident at Newport: "The place is unfortunately built up and down hill and whenever one goes out it is always (to some degree) a perpendicular trudge—which for a man with my trouble is a circumstance to be regretted. You get tired before you have been out half long enough. But (strange as it may appear) it was not precisely for my back that I came. I have been, I assure you, vastly well satisfied with my progress in that respect (Here my letter becomes *private* and unfit for the family circle.) It was to obtain relief and redress against my infernal constipation that I sought these precincts. Strange to say, however, that the manner of my London life rather fostered it. Changes of air and of habits gave me vast appetite and my custom of dining almost habitually with the Nortons on rather a faint stomach contributed to stuff me out considerably. I have no fear but that with time and *steadily* continued habits of temperate eating I shall obtain

a sufficient regularity. The only thing is to tide over the trying period of getting into these habits." MS. letter, Henry James, Jr., to William James, April 8, 1869, Houghton Library, Harvard University. Two years earlier, while studying in Berlin, William wrote to Harry: "I have been trying blisters on my back and they do undeniable good. Get a number about the size of a 25 cents piece, or of a copper cent. Apply one every night on alternate sides of the spine over the diseased muscle. . . . Try a dozen in this way at first, then wait two weeks and try a half-dozen more, and so on. If the blistering is done too *continuously* it loses its effect. . . . I think it does good; the ice (treatment) is too powerful—the parts can't react against it. . . . " MS. letter, William James to Henry James, Jr., December 26, 1867, Houghton Library, Harvard University.

18. For a characteristic treatment of the psychological interpretation of the injury see Stephen Spender, *The Destructive Element,* London, Jonathan Cape, 1935, 36 ff. William Dean Howells always remembered the young Henry James as ill, stating that Percy Lubbock, in his introduction to *The Letters of Henry James,* did not sufficiently take into account the causes for James's exile, the most important of which is that "he was a sick man who was less a sufferer in Europe than in America." Howells also, in speaking of his early friendship with James in Cambridge in the late Sixties, says: " . . . he ate nothing then or ever, except the biscuit he crumbled in his pocket and fed himself after the prescription of a famous doctor then prevalent among people of indigestion. He was a constant sufferer, tacit and explicit, and it was a form of escape from this misery for him to talk of what he was writing. . . . " Edmund Gosse, upon reminiscing about a party in the late summer of 1886 at the home of Frank Millet, outside London, in company with James, Edwin Abbey, John Singer Sargent, Alfred Parsons and himself, recalled: "Almost every afternoon he took a walk with me, rarely with Sargent, never with the sedentary rest, for Henry was inclined to saunter. He had not wholly recovered from that weakness of the muscles of his back which had so long troubled him, and I suppose that this was the cause of a curious stiffness in his progress, which proceeded rather slowly. He had certain preferences, in particular for the level road through the green landscape. . . . " Quoted by Lubbock, *op. cit.,* I, 89.

19. Quoted by Matthiessen, *op. cit.,* 260, 261.

20. See above, Chapter X, 278.

21. *Letters of William James,* I, 36.

22. *Notes of a Son and Brother,* 76-79

23. Quoted by Matthiessen, *op. cit.,* 260.

24. Edward Emerson, *The Early Days of the Saturday Club, 1855-70,* Boston, Houghton, Mifflin Co., 1918, 327, 328.

25. *Ibid.*

26. Burr, *op. cit.,* 218, 219.

27. Mrs. Howe's daughter Maud wrote in her reminiscences: "The James boys, Willie, Wilkie, Harry and Bobby (not to be confused with the bandits!) are faint figures in the earliest memories of Lawton's Valley. Companions of my elder sisters, I regarded them as 'Olympians.' I knew their father better—the elder Henry—my mother's crony; a strongly built man with keen eyes, gray beard, ruddy face, and an ivory-headed cane with which he tapped his way down the flight of stone steps that led to the valley where mother received his visits. The cadence of the waterfall comes back to me with snatches of talk I could not understand, concerning their favorite philosophers, Spinoza, Kant, and Hegel." Maud Howe Elliott, *This Was My Newport,* Cambridge, The Mythology Company, 1944, 85.

28. Edward Emerson, *op. cit.,* 476.

29. *Notes of a Son and Brother,* 80, 81.

30. C. Hartley Grattan, *The Three Jameses, A Family of Minds,* New York, Longmans, Green and Co., 1932, 223.

31. Quoted by Matthiessen, *op. cit.,* 66.

32. *Notes of a Son and Brother,* 135, 136.

33. Quoted by Lubbock, *op. cit.,* I, 9. On June 14, 1863, Bronson Alcott recorded in his journal: "Henry James writes expressing his pleasure in Louisa's Sketches. He sends her his new book entitled *Substance and Shadow.* It is a bold criticism on the hollow faith of our times, and an attempt to place Swedenborg at the head of modern theologians. James is the only mind I know equal to an attempt of the sort, and is more deeply read in Swedenborg than any one I know. I am not ready to accept all his conclusions, though given in a commanding way and fortified by a fierce logic whose terms are irresistible. Still it appears to a subtler sense than his how fatal is the sophistry that underlies all his statements; and he deals error largely with his truth." Odell Shepard, ed. *The Journals of Bronson Alcott,* Boston, Little, Brown & Co., 1938, 356.

34. Many of these letters appear in Perry, *op. cit.,* vol. I, and *The Letters of William James,* vol. I.

35. He wrote of Minny's "fearful catastrophe" in his characteristic tone of exaggerated humor: "Do you know, Kitty,—now that it's all over, I don't see why I should not tell you,—I have often had flashes of horrid doubts about that girl. Occasionally I have caught a glance from her furtive eye, a glance so wild, so weird, so strange, that it has frozen the innermost marrow of my bones; and again the most sickening feeling has come over me as I have noticed fleeting shades of expression on her face, so short, but ah! so piercingly pregnant of the mysteries of mania—*unhuman,* ghoul-like, fiendish-cunning. Ah me! ah me! Now that my worst suspicions have proved true, I feel sad indeed. . . . " *Letters,* I, 38.

36. *Notes of a Son and brother*, 303, 304.
37. *Ibid.*, 320, 321.
38. *Ibid.*, 350.
39. *Ibid.*, 311.
40. *Ibid.*, 367, 368, 331.

Chapter Thirteen

The Birth of a Realist

"I formally addressed myself . . . to the profession of literature . . ."

In the beginning of their long friendship, William Dean Howells and young Henry James formed the habit of walking together about Cambridge, to the Botanical Gardens, strolling "in the sun on the edge of a hotbed of violets," or through the woods of Shady Hill, sometimes up the avenue of trees toward the Norton mansion. The warm Indian summer days, in the autumn of 1866, brilliant with the foliage in the height of its color, took them often along the road to Fresh Pond, "in those days a wandering space of woods and water where people skated in winter and boated in summer." The recently appointed Assistant Editor of the *Atlantic Monthly* found the promising young writer, six years his junior, an ideal companion, for he talked with surprising acuteness of methods of fiction, of contemporary French and English writers, sometimes speaking modestly but eagerly of his own budding efforts. Gradually they learned each other's story: that of the provincial boy from Martin's Ferry, Ohio, writing his way from Columbus to New York and Boston, from the *Ohio State Journal* to the *Nation* and the *Atlantic,* and that of the cosmopolitan youth from New York, London, Paris, and Newport who had written comparatively little that had as yet reached the printed page. Their nocturnal rambles were pleasantest, pressing firmly upon memory, especially one which took them "to the wooded quadrangle, now long since doubtless vanished into forgotten formlessness where James resentfully identified a much-windowed very plain mansion, the house where he lodged when an unwilling student of the Harvard Law-school." [1] Resentful though he may have become, Harry had found Winthrop Square a most welcome retreat, a "contracted nook," in the winter of 1862-1863, upon despairing of law, letting everything slide, and deciding to be "just literary."

Henry James, Sr., then frequently in Boston to see about the printing of *Substance and Shadow,* quite understood this desire for quiet independence, having never taken the Law School experiment seriously. Accordingly, Willy was settled in new rooms on Mt. Auburn Street, near Hilliard, carrying on his second year of scientific studies, while Harry established himself in comfortable quarters on Winthrop Square. True, the black horse hair sofa was hard, but in general the accommodations were not uncongenial to Harry's tastes and purposes. The house was old, "with everything in its slanting and gaping and creaking, but with humble antique 'points' and a dignity in its decay. . . . " Above all there was a deep recess or alcove thrusting out from one side of the living room, with a large window commanding an admirable view across the marshes of the Charles River; inside there was a fine old secretary-desk, before which one could sit and at least dream of calling forth the muse of prose fiction, elusive creature that she was. "I but lose myself in the recovered sense of what it richly 'meant' to me just to *have* a place where I could so handsomely receive her, where I could remark with complacency that the distant horizon, an horizon long since rudely obliterated, was not, after all, too humble to be blue, purple, tawny, changeable in short, everything an horizon should be. . . . " [2]

The sky line and cloud formations were inspiringly reminiscent of the English and Boulognese scenes of a few years earlier, adding to "the atmosphere of literary composition as the act had begun to glimmer for me." The sudden rupture with the empty form of bringing home sheepskin volumes from the Law School Library created a delicious sense of playing hooky, a feeling he

had not infrequently enjoyed before. Resorting to Gore Hall exclusively for his reading matter was like basking in the literary
sun, for "the College library, with its sparse bristle of aspiring
granite, stood open to far more enchanted distances than any
represented by the leathery walls, with never a breach amid their
labelled and numbered blocks," of the legal chambers. As if to
prolong the pleasure of breaking with law, Harry continued his
regular attendance at lectures, never once missing those in the fore-
noon at Dane Hall; he delighted in this incongruous faithfulness,
understanding less and less of what the lectures were about, letting
his thoughts spread out in ever widening circles of general culture,
swimming happily into the ken of Sainte-Beuve, among other literary
company from Gore Hall.

The "absurd little boxing-match" within him continued on through
the entire spring term of 1863, long after Harry had actually given
up the sponge.[3] But his presence in the lecture hall, below the
portrait of Daniel Webster, had little to do with law, was not even
vaguely associated with whatever Professor Theophilus Parsons
might be saying from the chair of instruction. But character was
all over the place, as were interesting individuals who captured
Harry's thought, richly affected as it had always been by the idea
of how people looked, a much more fascinating chain of association
than what they taught or were being taught. "The question of how
people looked, and of how their look counted for a thousand relations, had arisen before me too early and kept me company too long
for me not to have made a fight over it, from the very shame of
appearing at all likely to give it up, had some fleeting delusion led me
to cast a slur upon it. It would do, I was already sure, half the
work of carrying me through life, and where was better proof of all
it would have to give than just in the fact it was then and there
doing? It worked for appreciation . . . and on the day, in short, when
one should cease to live in large measure by one's eyes (with the
imagination of course all the while waiting on this) one would have
taken the longest step towards not living at all. My companions—
however scantly indeed they were to become such—were subject to
my so practising in a degree which represented well-nigh the whole

of my relation with them, small reciprocity for them as there may have been in it; since vision, and nothing but vision, was from the beginning to end the fruit of my situation among them. There was not one of them as to whom it didn't matter that he 'looked,' by my fancy of him, thus or so; the key to this disposition of the accents being for me to such an extent that, as I have said, I was with all intensity taking in New England and that I knew no better *immediate* way than to take it in by my senses." [4] This, to Henry James, was, as he later pronounced in "The Art of Fiction," *experience,* and he already had become, as he admonishes the novice to be, in that same essay, "one of the people on whom nothing is lost!"

There is no evidence that the muse of prose fiction yielded to the seduction of the Winthrop Square rooms, but Harry took his independence there in a romantic mood, dramatizing himself a bit, perhaps, setting the stage for his becoming a writer. Apparently he achieved nothing more than a "mere loose observational play" of ideas and impressions, important in that they lasted on to the end of his career and constituted for him his initial step in the literary life: "I formally addressed myself under the protection, not to say the inspiration, of Winthrop Square to the profession of literature, though nothing would induce me now to name the periodical on whose protracted silence I had thus begun to hang with my own treasures of reserve to match it." [5] The future realist began with a definitely romantic bent and with a sense of romance that was relatively weak, indeed; only through his early writing as a critic did he free himself from the false lead and, under Howells, Norton, Fields, and other sympathetic publishers and friends, find himself. The only piece to which he confessed the muse had touched him was a letter to Miss Maggie Mitchell, whose performance of *Fanchon the Cricket,* a translation of George Sand's *La Petite Fadette,* at the Howard Athenaeum in Boston had moved him to express to her the full force of his overwhelming admiration. The graceful person, not unimpressed by her unknown admirer across the Charles River, responded by sending him "a little printed copy of the play, a scant pamphlet of 'acting edition' humility, addressed in a hand which assumed a romantic cast as soon as I had bethought myself of finding for it a happy precedent in that of Pendennis's Miss Fotheringgay." [6]

Going to Boston from Cambridge to the theatre via the horse cars was as rugged an experience as bounding over the London cobblestone streets in a family cab six years earlier; but what one braved in trying to get back to Winthrop Square after the theatre demanded an uncanny appetite for theatrical entertainment. This young Henry James had already developed, and feasted upon Boston's meager offerings, most distinguished by such figures as Miss Maggie Mitchell, and Miss Kate Bateman, one of the famous Bateman "children," the Jameses had so admired in New York a decade earlier.[7] In sending his epistle to Miss Mitchell and in youthfully awaiting some special acknowledgment, Harry felt that he had joined "the bright band of the fondly hoping and fearfully doubting who count the days after the despatch of manuscripts." It was to be nearly two years later, however, before anything from his pen reached publication and the long months of uncertainty, of ill health, of change and adjustment, of doubts and frustration, made a discouraging approach to the awe-inspiring *Atlantic* and *North American Review*. Few writers of distinction have had a longer road to success, even after more rapid initiations, since Henry James's path, for a period of more than a decade, was "strewn with the remains of feeble and abortive experiment." [8] In July, 1863, upon joining Willy in returning to Newport, all he asked was the faintest hope of producing something that someone might publish.

In the late spring of 1862, when the lease on the Mackaye house was expiring and could not be renewed, Henry James, Sr., bought a house, adding a story to it, purchasing furniture, pictures, and the endless accessories of a permanent home. Newport seemed then the most desirable community in which to settle, although the War, the connections with Harvard, and Harry's literary learnings soon proved Boston and Cambridge better suited to the changing interests of the family.[9] In September 1863, after the tenseness of the war-torn summer, Harry remained at home when Willy returned to Harvard for his third year. In response to questionings from his parents Willy wrote from Cambridge: " . . . To answer the weighty questions which you propound: I am glad to leave Newport because I am tired of the place itself, and because of the reason which you have very well expressed in your letter, the necessity of the whole family being near the arena of the future activity of us young men. I recommend Cambridge on account of its own pleasantness (though I don't wish to be invidious toward Brookline, Longwood, and other places) and because of its economy if I or Harry continue to study here much longer . . . I am convinced that somewhere in this neighborhood is the place for us to rest. These matters have been a good deal on my mind lately, and I am very glad to get the chance of pouring them into yours. As for the other boys, I don't know. And that idle and useless young female, Alice, too, whom we shall have to feed and clothe! . . . Cambridge is all right for business in Boston. Living in Boston or Brookline, etc. would be as expensive as Newport if Harry or I stayed here, for we could not easily go home every day." [10] Within a few months, in the spring of 1864, the Jameses moved from Newport to a house at #13 Ashburton Place in Boston. Mrs. James was thus nearer Willy; Mr. James was closer to the Saturday Club, to which he had recently been elected,[11] and Harry James was within walking distance of the office of Charles Eliot Norton, who was to become the symbol of a "positive consecration to letters."

While Harry knocked about Boston and Cambridge, forming independent relations, two or three of them proving of momentous importance to him subsequently, the elder James moved into floodtides of intellectual currents. Mrs. James T. Fields, wife of the editor of the *Atlantic Monthly* and hostess to one of Boston's prominent literary *salons,* found Henry James, Sr., a great addition within her circle. In her diary she recorded many passages of his conversations about John Sterling, Carlyle, Emerson, and Swedenborg, delighting in James's report that Carlyle had found Bronson Alcott "a terrible old bore." Alcott, upon dining with the Jameses, found his host a more fierce talker than Carlyle had proved: "He talks freely of our priests and scholars, complains of their subserviency and disloyalty to the hour. Even Emerson and Phillips fall short of his mark. James has a trenchant wit, deals damaging blows on all sides, hates pedants, priests, and fine folks with a refreshing passion. I respect his sincerity and wish his thought the largest audience. Brave, benevolent, earnest, he would break the heads of not a few of the popular idols by his formidable fist, to clear the temples for the purer worship." [12]

Ten days later, on December 30, 1864, Alcott was in the large Boston audience at the Lyceum when the elder James read his lecture on Carlyle: "My wife enjoys it greatly, the hearty manner of the lecturer and the anecdotes are so exceedingly characteristic and witty, his estimate of the man's genius and influence so discriminating and just. A heartless intelligence worshipping force, he intimates, and incapable of apprehending moral excellence . . . tells his anecdotes of more than one interview with the terrific talker with great good humor and naiveté, giving his broad Scotch accent as well as his words and sentiments. Everybody enjoyed his lecture—Emerson even more, perhaps, than any." [13]

Julia Ward Howe, who was also in the audience at the Lyceum, remembered the lecture with equal delight, considering Mr. James "a dear man . . . a great addition to the thought-power current in Boston society." She described him as having reasonably good features, observing that "his countenance fairly glowed with amiability, geniality, and good-will." James rather shocked Mrs. Howe, as he did many of the most broad-minded of people. Speaking one Sunday in the Church of the Disciples in Boston he said "that the moral law and the Christian Church were the meanest of inventions. He intended by this phrase to express his sense of the exalted moral and religious obligation of the human mind, the dignity of which ought to transcend the prescriptions of the Decalogue and the discipline of the church . . . His views of the Divine are highly anthropomorphic, and I remember that he said among other things (in a private conversation), 'My dear Madame, God is working all the time in his shirt-sleeves with all his might.' " [14] James's concept of God was as far removed from the anthropomorphic as was that of Emerson or Thoreau; such misunderstandings of his statements, coming back to him, would supply unmerciful fun at the dinner table, often at the expense

of some of Boston's most noted and respected people. When Willy
and Harry had been small boys in the Fourteenth Street house in
New York, they grew up amid their father's brilliant merriment,
penetrating wit, and roars of hearty laughter. At Newport, Edward Emerson, T. S. Perry, and other visitors responded fully, often
in astonishment, to the scintillating repartee which crackled like
electric current. Now, in staid Boston, the same *esprit* prevailed,
with even an intensification of intellectual give-and-take, since the
two oldest sons were coming into their maturity, enjoying more
than ever their father's stimulating mind. Edwin Lawrence Godkin,
who founded the *Nation* in 1865 and later edited the New York
Evening Post, visited the Jameses in Boston and was highly entertained by the abandon with which discussions and arguments were
conducted. Harry James, he remembered, then "a youth of nineteen
or twenty, was just beginning to try his literary wings. There could
not be a more entertaining treat than a dinner at the James home,
when the young people were at home. They were full of stories
of the oddest kind, and discussed questions of morals or taste or
literature with a vociferous vigor so great as sometimes to lead the
young men to leave their seats and gesticulate on the floor. I remember, in some of these heated discussions, it was not unusual for
the sons to invoke curses on their parents, one of which was that
'his mashed potatoes might always have lumps in them!' " [15]
   In his room on the third floor front of #13 Ashburton Place,
during many days and nights between the spring of 1864 and the
autumn of 1866, young Henry James began very serious apprenticeship of his craft. His memory of that time later moved back upon it
"as through an apartment hung with garlands and lights. . . . "
Never was the image to leave his mind of "the very greenbacks, to
the total value of twelve dollars, into which I had changed the cheque
representing my first earned wage." He had earned it, it seemed,
with an extraordinary ease on the very table where the greenbacks
were spread out before him. Other greenbacks followed, often
rather greasy ones, with an agitation and thrill known only to
young authors, but never did he recapture the sheer bliss of this
first honorarium. The initial experience came about as a result

of his setting out one fine morning to Shady Hill in Cambridge. "I had addressed in trembling hope my first fond attempt at literary criticism to Charles Eliot Norton, who had lately, and with the highest, brightest competence, come to the rescue of the *North American Review,* submerged in a stale tradition and gasping for life, and he had not only published it in his very next number—the interval for me of breathless brevity—but had expressed the liveliest further hospitality, the gage of which was thus at once his welcome to me at home. I was to grow fond of regarding as a positive consecration to letters that half-hour in the long library at Shady Hill, where the winter sunshine touched serene book-shelves and arrayed pictures, the whole embrowned composition of objects in my view, with I knew not what golden light of promise, what assurance of things to come: there was to be nothing exactly like it later on—the conditions of perfect rightness for a certain fresh felicity, certain decisive pressures of the spring, *can* occur, it would seem, but once. This was on the other hand the beginning of so many intentions that it mattered little if the particular occasion was not repeated; for what did I do again and again, through all the years, but handle in plenty what I might have called the small change of it." [16]

In the *North American Review* for October, 1864, appeared young Henry James's first published article, an unsigned review of Nassau W. Senior's *Essays on Fiction.* With this beginning, Mr. Norton's hospitality extended to more than twenty reviews within the next five years. James T. Fields of the *Atlantic Monthly* and Edwin L. Godkin of the *Nation,* both friends of the James family, also offered their columns for reviews and stories, the first of which, *The Story of a Year,* appeared in The *Atlantic* for March, 1865. With The *Galaxy* taking a review and several short stories, James not only addressed himself to the profession of literature but entered it prolifically, with over seventy critical articles and reviews and fourteen short stories published between 1864 and the close of 1870, the year which marks the end of his youth.[17] A careful reading of the short stories sheds interesting light upon the author's slow development out of the shallows of weak romance into the strong currents and depths of his mature realism. The stories indicate, furthermore, the sincerity with which he attempted to establish himself at home, for, with one exception, they are all set in America, mostly in the Civil War period and in New England.

Henry James was just twenty-two in March, 1865, when *The Story of a Year* appeared, barely past the adolescent years when romance and realism blurred together in the reflected light of Hawthorne on one side and Balzac and Flaubert on the other. His natural approach to literature was critical and scientific, as his work as a critic reveals, even in the beginning of his career; but his youthful experiences, his early environment and foreign training inclined him toward the romantic, and in this vein the first stories were written. The discrepancy between the acumen with which he detected the "fatal gifts of fluency" expressed by the feminine writers, particularly Mrs. Stowe and the American school of the feminine Fifties, still strong in fiction, and the weakness of his own romantic short stories is simply the difference between precept and practice. The critical essays from the same pen which wrote *The Story of a Year, A Landscape Painter, A Day of Days,* and other fumbling attempts, pronounced strong, even harsh judgment upon the very type of fiction he was then producing.[18] Nearly a decade was to pass before he wrote his way into a technical skill which approached the strength and clarity of his critical sense.

Very little, if any, of such technical ability is evidenced in *The Story of a Year,* the thread of which is so thin and poorly spun that it barely holds together. Elizabeth Crowe, a shallow girl, as we are several times directly told, becomes engaged to John Ford, a strong-principled, young college graduate, on the eve of his departure for war in the spring of 1863. She is a well-meaning, simple, pretty girl, untutored and not intelligent enough to be cleverly designing nor strong enough to remain true to her betrothed. In a neighboring town, on a visit encouraged by Mrs. Ford not without reason, Lizzie has a harmless flirtation which leads to a proposal from Robert Bruce, an admirable and earnest suitor. Having learned, rather melodramatically, from a newspaper list of casualties that John is seriously wounded, she is torn between her sense of loyalty to him

and her attraction to Bruce. During the weeks Mrs. Ford is in
Virginia nursing her son, poor Lizzie is tormented to the point of
accepting Bruce when news comes that John is dying. But John rallies
and is brought home to die, creating a denouement, including a
scene between Lizzie and John, which leaves the reader wondering
to what low ebb public taste had fallen and how young James could
continue to turn out the penetrating analyses of fiction his book reviews contain. Yet, without pressing the point, certain germs of the
later fiction, as well as some close connections with the author's immediate life and thought, can be found in the story.

In such lines as "I trust I shall not be held to a minute description
of our dear Lizzie's person and costume," "I have no intention of
following Lieutenant Ford to the seat of war," or "I cannot describe these things," the author begs off from the expected description. Partly not equal to it, but more because he believed that true
description is derived from a study and exposition of human nature,
James strikes a compromise and attempts to plumb the shallows of
Lizzie's mind. This, however, he fails to do and the character
analysis falls away as badly as does the action. None of the characters
breathes or has his being from real life, though Ford suggests it.
In speaking to Lizzie about the possibility of being lost in battle, he
echoes the elder James's impatience with humbug and sentimentality:
"If by chance I'm taken out of the world, I want you to beware of
that tawdry sentiment which enjoins you to be 'constant to my memory.' My memory be hanged! Remember me at my best,—that is,
fullest of the desire of humility. Don't inflict me on people." Furthermore, he suffers from no illusions about the war and his part in
it: "I expect to see a vast deal of shabbiness and baseness and
turmoil, and in the midst of it all I'm sure the inspiration of
patriotism will sometimes fail." In such passages is heard the note
of realism, though faintly, which rings more strongly in one or two
other early tales. To a slight degree, in the relations between Lizzie
and Mrs. Ford, more than between John and Lizzie, perhaps, the
author promises some of the subsequent interplay of human relationships that so distinguishes his realism. For example, in shifting the
burden of her distress over John's wounds to Mrs. Ford, who im-

mediately goes to him, James comments on the girl: "Like most
weak persons, she was glad to step out of the current of life, now
that it had begun to quicken into action. In emergencies, such persons are tacitly counted out; and they as tacitly consent to the arrangement. Even to the sensitive spirit there is a certain meditative rapture
in standing on the quiet shore (beside the ruminating cattle), and
watching the hurrying, eddying flood, which makes up for the loss of
dignity." Here, indeed, young Henry James knew whereof he spoke.
Wilky's experience of being wounded at Fort Wagner and being
brought home for a prolonged convalescence had given him first-
hand material for Ford's far more tragic case. But only his own
inner life as a "sensitive spirit," detached, passive, and meditative, enabled him to suggest, though he but suggests it, the sympathy and
understanding for Elizabeth Crowe that he later expressed in his
study of Maggie Tulliver or the child Maisie Farange.

The spring of 1865 brought with it epoch-making events, stirring
the huge national consciousness and penetrating deeply into that of
the young writer on Ashburton Place. Grant's success and Lee's
surrender sent the sharpest vibrations in every direction, but the
greatest upheaval had been wrought in Harry's mind the previous
spring by the death of Hawthorne, dear to the heart of the Jameses:
"Ashburton Place resounds for me with a wild cry, rocks as from a
convulsed breast, on that early morning of our news of Lincoln's
death by murder; and, in a different order, but also darkening the
early day, there associates itself with my cherished chamber of
application the fact that of a sudden, and while we were always
and as much as ever awaiting him, Hawthorne was dead. What I
have called the fusion strikes me as indeed beyond any rendering
when I think of the peculiar assault on my private consciousness of
that news: I sit once more, half-dressed, late of a summer morning
and in a bedimmed light which is somehow at once that of dear old
green American shutters drawn to against openest windows and that
of a moral shadow projected as with violence—I sit on my belated
bed, I say, and yield to the pang that made me positively and loyally
cry. . . . To tell at all adequately why the pang was fine would
nevertheless too closely involve my going back . . . on the whole rich

interpenetration. I fondly felt it in those days invaluable that I had during certain last and otherwise rather blank months at Newport taken in for the first time and at one straight draught the full sweet sense of our one fine romancer's work—for sweet it then above all seemed to me; and I remember well how, while the process day after day drew itself admirably out. I found the actual exquisite taste of it, the strain of the revelation, justify up to the notch whatever had been weak in my delay. This prolonged hanging off from true knowledge had been the more odd, so that I couldn't have explained it, I felt, through the fact that *The Wonder Book* and *Twice-Told Tales* had helped to enchant our childhood; the consequence at any rate seemed happy, since without it, very measurably, the sudden sense of recognition would have been less uplifting a wave. The joy of the recognition was to know at the time no lapse— was in fact through the years never to know one, and this by some rare action of a principle or a sentiment . . . that placed the *Seven Gables*, the *Blithedale Romance* and the story of Donatello and Miriam (the accepted title of which I dislike to use, not the 'marble' but very particularly the human Faun being throughout in question) somewhere on a shelf unvisited by harsh inquiry. . . . His work was all charged with a *tone,* a full and rare tone of prose, and . . . this made for it an extraordinary value in an air in which absolutely nobody's else was or has shown since any aptitude for being. And the tone had been, in its beauty—for me at least—ever so appreciably American; which proved to what a use American matter could be put by an American hand: a consummation involving, it appeared, the happiest moral. For the moral was that an American could be an artist, one of the finest, without 'going outside' about it, as I liked to say; quite in fact as if Hawthorne had become one just by being American *enough,* by the felicity of how the artist in him missed nothing, suspected nothing, that the ambient air didn't affect him as containing. Thus he was at once so clear and so entire— clear without thinness, for he might have seemed underfed, it was his danger; and entire without heterogeneity, which might, with less luck and to the discredit of our sufficing manners, have had to be his help." [19]

Whether or not young Henry James was American enough to become the artist he wished to be was a question these few years of
apprenticeship would decide. Hawthorne was an inspiration in this
respect and Howells was soon to cheer Harry on "with a sympathy
that was in itself an inspiration." The next two stories, however,
not in the Hawthorne vein and written before meeting Howells,
leaned heavily upon the author's own resources. *A Landscape
Painter*, in The *Atlantic Monthly* for February, 1866, is cast in
diary form which entails a minimum of action, freeing the author
for the character study that already was becoming the stronger
interest. Action had never been a part of the detached, observing
young author's life and it was to play a very minor role in his
fiction. Locksley, the central character with $100,000 a year, is re-
covering from a love affair, broken off when he discovered the
mercenary interests of the young lady. He seeks a quiet seaside
retreat to paint and to play the role of the poor artist. In the
introductory framework used to establish the diary device, the author,
a friend to Locksley, suggests Newport. While the obscure little
fishing cove finally decided upon is far removed from the Rhode
Island resort, it is obvious that James makes good use of his
Newport days in describing the rocky shore, the rolling fields sweeping up from the water, the sky effects and general atmosphere.
The few backdrop passages employed carry with them an authentic
ring not achieved in *The Story of a Year*. Finding no satisfactory
accommodations at the "abominable little tavern," Locksley arranges
to stay with a retired sea captain and his daughter, a music mistress.
Esther Blunt becomes increasingly interesting to Locksley and to the
reader, though she never becomes a clear image beyond the general
statements concerning her face and figure, which offer "a tolerable
catalogue, but no picture," as the author quite agrees. While nursing Locksley through a fever, Esther, though innately reserved and
"a woman of character," succumbs to curiosity and reads the artist's
diary, thus discovering that he is wealthy. With an excellent sense
of the situation Esther carries forward her intentions so that Locksley proposes and is accepted; thus the romantic element is concluded,
but the story continues in a minor key. Worried because he has

deceived her about his wealth, Locksley decides on the first day of the honeymoon to show her the diary as a means of breaking the news gently. She astonishes him by stating bluntly that she has already read the diary because she suspected him. When he calls her action that of a false woman, she replies in the closing lines of the story: "A false woman? No,—simply of a woman. I am a woman, Sir. . . . Come, *you* be a man!" In the first flush of attraction to her, Locksley had summed up, in his diary, his impressions: "There you are, Miss Blunt, at full length,—emphatically the portrait of a lady." Isabel Archer, much later, was to sit for such a portrait, but Esther is no more than she claimed to be, a woman, and a rather designing one at that. While his heroine has a slightly foreign tone, a watering down, perhaps, of Thackeray's scheming women or the unscrupulous heroines of French literature, the story comes out better than its predecessor. It is apparent that James was analysing his characters and that with the device of the diary, restricting as it was in a sense, he managed better what he wanted to say.

A Day of Days, his other story in 1866, carries forward the experiments he tried in *A Landscape Painter,* having more analysis and less action, being reduced almost to no action at all. The situation is simply reversed, the central character now being a wealthy young girl, with "a very pretty little fortune," who develops with unconvincing rapidity a deep love for a poor young man, Thomas Ludlow, calling briefly at her brother's country place before leaving for Europe. Infatuated with him and bored with society, Adela Moore seeks a proposal from him and under pressure of her intentions he withdraws. The improbable episode is not made real by James's analysis of Adela, though he stakes all on this attempt to create the character as true to human nature. In this, as in the two previous stories, the time is contemporary, the setting vaguely in New England, and the characters mostly people of wealth. Romantic tales though they were, it is evident that the author was studying people, trying to portray them in relation to certain basic truths about human nature. His progress was painfully slow at first, for he unwisely strayed beyond the realm of people he knew. As has been said, he "was not content to treat Adela, or Locksley, as

they should have been treated, in their own setting, coming into connection with people of their own class, but he took them out of it,
imagined people of a lower class, and brought the two awkwardly
and stiffly together with a result that neither seems true to human
nature." [20] After finding himself in fiction, in the European setting
particularly, he created characters mostly within the circumference
of his knowledge, having then learned that his talent did not extend
to the lower orders about whom he knew so little.

While there was no end to the steady flow of criticism from his
pen, the fiction was slow and thin. One story in 1865 and two
the next year, although not a bad showing, did not balance well
against almost thirty articles on such writers as Trollope, Arnold,
Louisa M. Alcott, Walt Whitman, Dickens, Swinburne, Charles
Kingsley, Hugo, and above all George Eliot. The high point in the
mid-summer of 1866 was the arrival of *Felix Holt,* coming at a time
when he found no help for his fiction problem in such novelists
as Henry Sedley, Mrs. Gaskell, or Mrs. Craik. The Jameses had
read *Adam Bede* in Geneva with great pleasure and enthusiasm which
increased with *The Mill on the Floss, Silas Marner,* and even with
Romola, but *Felix Holt* appeared now upon the critical scene where
the best that English, French, and American writers had to offer
was testing James's metal. What brought him close to the work
of George Eliot was a basic resemblance to his own tendencies.
Her plots were artificial, even clumsy; the conduct of her story
slow; her style diffused. On these points he knew himself to be
weaker than the admired English novelist, but like her he hoped
to compensate for these defects by a firm and rather elaborate
delineation of individual character, by developing "that extensive
human sympathy, that easy understanding of character at large,
that familiarity with man, from which a novelist borrows his real
inspiration. . . . " Even more helpful was the observation that her
treatment of the lower classes was far more successful than of the
remote upper classes, as in *Felix Holt;* the moral then was to
observe with the keenest penetration the people one knew, the class
he represented and understood. This was the great lesson from which
James profited much, for it brought him more in line with the peculiar

nature of his talent. Staying within his own boundaries, studying, probing, analysing, and depicting human consciousness and character, he moved slowly from romance in proportion as he found the essence of reality, of "actuality," as Howells called it.

But there was need of thinking these things through, of talking them out with an intelligent, understanding companion. Willy had always met such a need, and he was back from Brazil, but deep in his studies at the Harvard Medical School, preoccupied with work and with the large circle of stimulating fellows, Holmes above all.[21] Quite alone, then, Harry was struggling through to solid ground as a young critic and struggling even more desperately to get down on paper the fiction which he felt instinctively he had to write. With Wilky and Bob James he had never had the intellectual communion that Willy naturally supplied; furthermore, at the end of the War the younger brothers had obtained a plantation in Florida, trying to run it by Negro labor, backed financially, of course, by their father; here they worked desperately to make a success of it, holding out until 1870 when the plantation had to be abandoned. Alice, who had suffered a kind of nervous breakdown in Newport, which made her a semi-invalid for the rest of her life, was in New York for special treatment. Henry James, Sr., was busy with his lectures, already making preliminary sketches of his major work, *The Secret of Swedenborg,* published in 1869. Harry was, therefore, very much on his own, for the family had always so "hung together that this replete organ could not go on helping itself" when the various members were so scattered. Separated though they were, the Jameses kept alive the affection and genuine interest their closely bound lives had always known. Alice, many years later, came across a letter from Willy to Wilky, after the Brazilian trip in the spring of 1866, stating: "Harry, I think much improved; he is a noble fellow, so true, so delicate and honorable . . . and Alice has got to be quite a nice girl. . . . "[22] In March, Willy wrote to Tom Ward, expressing a desire to visit him in New York, explaining however that the "family spends six months at Swampscott from the first of May on," and inviting Tom to visit them there during Willy's vacation from Harvard. Sarg Perry,

Henry Bowditch, Charles Peirce, John Ropes, John Gray, Chauncey Wright, and Wendell Holmes represented the Harvard friends whom Willy constantly brought home and who did much to enliven the rather depleted family group. Kitty and Minny Temple too stopped by for brief visits, greatly enjoying the young college men, John Gray and Wendell Holmes especially, and greatly admired by them all.[23] Life was far from dull, indeed, though it was not always conducive to the literary act, as Harry called it.

In looking back on these particular years in Boston, Harry thought of them in a constant hum: "I literally came and went, I had never practised such coming and going; I went in particular, during summer weeks, and even if carrying my general difficulty with me, to the White Mountains of New Hampshire, with some repetition, and again and again back to Newport, on visits to John La Farge and to the Edmund Tweedys (their house almost a second summer home to us); to say nothing of winter attempts, a little weak, but still more or less achieved, upon New York—which city was rapidly taking on the capital quality, the large worldly sense that dear old London and dear old Paris . . . didn't grudge it . . . but Boston itself could easily rule, in default even of New York, when to 'go,' in particular, was an act of such easy virtue. To go from Ashburton Place was to go verily round the corner not less than further afield; to go to Athenaeum, to the Museum, to a certain door of importances, in fact of immensities, defiant of vulgar notation, in Charles Street, at the opposite end from Beacon. . . . The fruit of golden youth is all and always golden—it touches to gold what it gathers; this was so the essence of the case that in the first place everything was in some degree an adventure." [24]

An interview with Mr. Norton or Mr. Fields was the highest type of adventure in Boston, but a visit with the Tweedy family, the Temple girls, and John La Farge at Newport was "absurdly, insistently romantic," for Newport was changing. The comparatively untouched isle of the Jameses' return from Europe, six years before, was stirred by the shock of public affairs and private enterprise into "the most 'evolved' material civilization our American world could then show," epitomized in the daily *corso* or processional drive of the fashionable life along the Avenue. The opposing camp, to which the Jameses traditionally belonged, looked with "noble scorn" upon the "round of pleasures," especially during the years "while Rome was burning," as Aunt Mary Tweedy remarked to Julia Ward Howe and the ladies of Lawton's Valley. Young Henry James, however, in the detached quiet of Samuel Gridley Howe's peaceful garden, a good drive's length from the seaward quarter, contemplated with much pleasure and profit the fashionables, the elegant ladies, the mustachio'd men, the "braver bonhomie of the social aspect at large." The Newport of pre-Civil War days was giving way to that of his novelette of the following decade, *An International Episode,* in which Mrs. Westgate and Bessie Alden could entertain Lord Lambeth and Percy Beaumont with all the *éclat* of a Continental watering place.[25]

In the summer of 1866, the resort reminded Harry of certain old French towns where "it was possible to distinguish invidiously the Ville from the Cité. The Point was our *cité,* the primal aboriginal Newport—which, striking us on a first acquaintance as not other than dilapidated, might well have been 'restored' quite as M. Viollet-le-Duc was even then restoring Carcassonne; and this all the more because our elder Newport, the only seat of history, had a dismantled grassy fort or archaic citadel that dozed over the waterside and that might . . . be smartly waked up. The waterside, which was that of the inner bay, the ample reach toward Providence, so much more susceptible of quality than the extravagant open sea, the 'old houses,' the old elms, the old Quaker faces at the small-paned old windows, the appointedness of the scene for the literary and artistic people, who, by our fond constructive theory, lodged and boarded with the Quakers, always thrifty these, for the sake of all the sweetness and quaintness, for the sake above all somehow of *our* hungry felicity of view, by which I mean mine and that of a trusty friend or two, T. S. Perry in especial—those attributes, meeting a want, as the phrase is, of the decent imagination, made us perhaps overdramatise the sphere of the clever people, but made them at least also, when they unmistakably hovered, affect us as truly the finest touches in the picture." [26]

Sarg Perry, enjoying a few months' vacation between graduation from Harvard and studying in Berlin, along with Willy James the next year, joined Harry and the Temple girls in the Newport fun, centered mostly in their own set within the *cité,* but venturing also into the *ville,* brilliantly smart with the glitter and glamor of "the rich and guileless." The contrast between the solid group of "the old clever people," mostly all Bostonians, except a few New Yorkers "who might have been mistaken for such,—never indeed by Bostonians themselves, but only by other New Yorkers," and "the clever old ones" of the Avenue position afforded Harry his first opportunity to study the finer shades and subtle strata in the great social world. Study them he did, "through the purple haze or golden dust of supercilious parades."

At the close of the summer of 1866, which Harry had divided between being with the family at Swampscott and visiting friends in New York, Boston, and Newport, the Jameses settled in a house on Quincy Street in Cambridge, immediately behind the Harvard Yard. It was a large, roomy house (later converted into the Colonial Club and now a part of the University buildings), well suited to the full life soon flowing through its hospitable rooms. Willy had begun his courses in the Harvard Medical School after returning from Brazil in the spring, and brought home from classes interesting new friends and acquaintances.

In addition, social activities began to consume an almost disproportionate amount of time and thought. Willy complained in a letter to Alice "we have had nothing but invitations (6) in 3 or 4 days," and described Harry as at the moment attending "a tea-squall in favor of Miss Haggerty," at the Misses Ashburner's home. The Temple sisters, sometimes accompanied by Ellen Van Buren or one of the other Albany cousins, began making visits of a week or two, causing thereby much activity in the way of dinners, theatre parties, or outings along the Charles River. As enjoyable as this Cambridge life proved to be, Harry, now the earnest young man of letters, took his work very seriously. "I am divided," he wrote many years afterwards, "between the shame on the one hand of claiming them, these concocted 'short stories,' that they played so great a part, and a downright admiring tenderness on the other for their holding up their stiff little heads in such a bustle of life and traffic of affairs." [27] In the midst of his feeble beginnings as a fictionist, distracted by social intrusions, and never free from the weakness of back or from the indigestion which troubled him for years, Harry found a new companion in William Dean Howells, whose friendship was to mean more in his literary apprenticeship than any connection young Henry James had ever made.

Neither Howells nor James, in later years, could remember the circumstance of their first meeting. To the twenty-nine-year-old assistant editor of The *Atlantic Monthly,* it seemed that suddenly they were always meeting, "at his father's house and at mine, but in the kind Cambridge streets rather than in those kind Cambridge houses which it seems to me I frequented more than he. We seem to have been presently always together, reading our stuff to each other; his stuff which we both hoped might make itself into matter for The *Atlantic Monthly,* then mostly left to my editing by my senior editor Mr. Fields." [28]

Just exactly in what way and to what extent the successful writer from Ohio specifically influenced his new-found literary friend is still a question. Since they lived so closely together in the small Cambridge community there was no occasion for an exchange of letters between them in these early years. There is evidence only of their having talked endlessly with each other, meeting more or less regularly, two or three times a week, discussing always their literary interests and efforts. At that time Howells himself had not arrived at a clear concept of his realism and apparently encouraged James to write romances more than anything, yet, he certainly came to understand the unique realism that James began writing in the first period of his maturity, after these Cambridge years of apprenticeship were ended. In the November *Century* for 1882, Howells published an article on Henry James, making some reflections on Dickens and Thackeray, which were badly misunderstood in England, though the essay reveals that William Dean Howells had a thorough understanding of Henry James and the kind of fiction he was then writing. Two paragraphs in particular make this clear:

"It is a little odd, by the way, that in all the printed talk about James—and there has been no end of it—his power of engaging your preference for certain of his people has been so little commented on. Perhaps it is because he makes no obvious appeal for them; but one likes such men as Lord Warburton, Newman, Valentine, the artistic broker in *The Europeans,* and Ralph Touchett, and such women as Isabel, Clair Belgarde, Mrs. Tristram and certain others, with a thoroughness that is one of the best testimonies to their vitality. This comes about through their own qualities, and is not affected by insinuation or by downright *petting,* such as we find in Dickens nearly always, and in Thackeray too often.

"The art of fiction has, in fact, become a finer art in our day than it was with Dickens and Thackeray. We could not suffer the confidential attitude of the latter now, or the mannerisms of the former, any more than we could endure the prolixity of Richardson or the coarseness of Fielding. These great men are of the past—they and their methods and interests; even Trollope and Reade are not of the present. The new school derives from Hawthorne and George Eliot rather than any others; but it studies human nature much more in its wonted aspects, and finds its ethical and dramatic examples in the operation of lighter but not less vital motives. The moving accident is certainly not its trade; and it prefers to avoid all manner of dire catastrophes. It is largely influenced by French fiction in form, but it is the realism of Daudet rather than the realism of Zola that prevails with it, and it has a soul of its own which is above recording the rather brutish pursuit of a woman by a man which seems to be the chief end of the French novelist." [29]

The rise of realism in America is usually dated as beginning in 1870, and Howells's first novel, *Their Wedding Journey,* in 1872, pronounced his basic idea in the exclamation: "Ah! poor Real Life, which I love, can I make others share the delight I find in thy foolish and insipid face?" Between the travel sketches, resulting from his four years in Venice as American Consul, and his first novels, Howells was thinking his way through to a theoretical basis, talking freely and fully with young Henry James, from the beginning of their friendship, in 1866. His *Century* article, in 1882, contained a clear statement of his understanding of realism, especially as it related to James. By 1891, in *Criticism and Fiction,* Howells declared: "The time is coming, I hope, when each new author, each new artist, will be considered, not in his proportion to any other author or artist, but in his relation to the human nature, known to us all, which it is his privilege, his high duty, to interpret." Twenty-five years earlier, he and young Henry James were thinking and talking their respective ways toward realism and undoubtedly influenced each other profoundly; yet it is difficult to show the specific ways in which each aided the other. Howells was several years older than James, "but I was much his junior," he later wrote, "in the art we both adored." He was not so well read in the contemporary French writers, but in his editorial position on The *Atlantic* his critical and writing experience was broader, and above all, the position gave him the opportunity of publishing whatever he and young Henry James agreed was good enough. For this sympathetic understanding and generous assistance James was always grateful. In an open letter from London, on February 19, 1912, read at the dinner given in New York, celebrating Howells's seventy-fifth birthday, Henry James stated:

" . . . My debt to you began well-nigh half a century ago, in the most personal way possible, and then kept growing and growing with your own admirable growth—but always rooted in the early intimate benefit. This benefit was that you held out your open editorial hand to me at the time I began to write—and I allude especially to the summer of 1866— with a frankness and sweetness of hospitality that was really the making of me, the making of the confidence that required help and sympathy and that I should otherwise, I think, have strayed and stumbled about a long time without acquiring. You showed me the way and opened me the door; you wrote to me, and confessed yourself struck with me— I have never forgotten the beautiful thrill of *that.* You published me at once—and paid me, above all, with a dazzling promptitude; magnificently, I felt, and so that nothing since has ever quite come up to it. More than this even, you cheered me on with a sympathy that was itself an inspiration. I mean that you talked to me and listened to me— ever so patiently and genially and suggestively conversed and consorted with me. This won me to you irresistibly and made you the most interesting person I knew—lost as I was in the charming sense that my best friend was an editor, and an almost insatiable editor, and that such a delicious being as that was a kind of property of my own. Yet how didn't that interest still quicken and spread when I became aware that— with such attention as you could spare from us, for I recognized my fellow beneficiaries—you had started to cultivate *your* great garden as well; the tract of virgin soil that, beginning as a cluster of bright, fresh, sunny, and savoury patches, close about the house, as it were, was to become that vast goodly pleasaunce of art and observation, of appreciation and creation, in which you have laboured, without a break or a lapse, to this day, and in which you have grown so grand a show of— well, really of everything. . . ." [30]

The wisdom of Howells's discernment of James's potential talents is a question, in that he poured almost complete approval upon all of the stories James wrote, though in the light of time all but one or two of the first thirteen of them were very poor things indeed. Furthermore, he encouraged his friend to write romances for The *Atlantic,* being himself at this time strongly inclined toward romanticism, as he explains in *My Literary Passions.* James, inwardly inclined toward Balzac, followed Howells's request that he adhere closely to Hawthorne, writing thereby *The Romance of Certain Old Clothes;* yet, James was at the same time producing more realistic stories for The *Galaxy.*[31] Even with them, Howells was quite taken; but more especially, of course, with those which passed through his own hands for The *Atlantic.*

Beginning with the first manuscript from young Henry James that James T. Fields asked Howells to consider, he expressed immediate approval, telling the senior editor that he would take not only that, but "all the stories you can get from the writer." [32] Even more attracted was he to the young man himself, a cosmopolitan, fluent in French, conversant with European art and literature, already well travelled, utterly unprovincial in all respects. He wrote Clarence Stedman of their talks, " . . . young Henry James and I had a famous one last evening, two or three hours long, in which we settled the true principles of literary art. He is a very earnest fellow, and I think extremely gifted—gifted enough to do better than any one has yet done toward making us a real American novel. We have in reserve from him a story for the *Atlantic,* which I'm sure you'll

like." [33] *My Friend Bingham,* Harry's fourth story, appeared in
The *Atlantic* for March, 1867, and was followed in the June-August
issues by his fifth, *Poor Richard.* These two stories, and nine
critical essays for The *Nation* and The *North American Review*
comprise his writing for that year. Compared with the six stories
and seventeen articles of 1868, he was, apparently, doing more
thinking than writing, as he partly suggested by declining an
offer to publish again in The *Galaxy.*[34]

There was also, at this time, the question of health, for along
with his brother Willy, Harry was suffering severely from chronic
indigestion and physical exhaustion, as Howells records in his recollections of their early friendship: "Our walks were by day and by
night but our sessions in my little house were twice or thrice by
night a week and on Sunday were always after our simple family
supper where he joined us only in spirit, for he ate nothing then or
ever, except the biscuit he crumbled in his pocket and fed himself
after the prescription of a famous doctor then prevalent among people
of indigestion. He was a constant sufferer, tacit and explicit, and
it was a form of escape from this misery for him to talk of what
he was writing, with the young pair whom he frequented. . . ." [35]

My Friend Bingham was written and completed, however, before
Harry had formed his intimate connections with Howells and his
wife, who listened and responded so enthusiastically to their charming, urbane young guest in the small parlor "by the light of our kero-
sene globe-lamp." It borders on the melodramatic in the main
episode, the accidental killing of the small son of an impoverished
widow, by a wealthy man whose remorse combined with her pity
brings about, rather unconvincingly, their love affair. More in the
vein of George Sand than George Eliot, the story presumably is one
of passion, but the narrative framework in which it is cast creates an
indirectness which sacrifices the intensity that might otherwise
have been achieved.

The author, as in *A Landscape Painter,* poses as a friend of
George Bingham, a device that James was to use repeatedly, "that
of a cordial observer." As such, he explains to the reader, "it
was impossible that, even with the best will in the world, I should

fathom the emotions of the actors." Yet, the observer is the one to vouch for the characters; to add the touch of reality which would, he hoped, make them authentic. As in the case of the diary device, this narrative framework was a kind of crutch on which the author might lean when the responsibility of handling the story proved too much for him. Yet, in certain passages which sound an autobiographical note, James achieves a tone of authority that helps to carry the contrivance: "Towards the close of summer, in my twenty-eighth year, I went down to the seaside to rest from a long term of work, and to enjoy, after several years of separation, a *tête-à-tête* with an intimate friend. My friend had just arrived from Europe, and we had agreed to spend my vacation together by the side of the sounding sea, and within easy reach of the city." Swampscott, an hour's train ride up the North Shore from Boston, rather than Newport, offered the locale. Sarg Perry, Jim Mackaye, Willy, and Harry himself blended from fact into fiction in George Bingham, "just back from Europe," having come into "a handsome property" at twenty-three, and his young friend, twenty-seven, equally travelled and cultivated.

Because they "were genuine friends," Bingham confesses that he "had been in love, and had been cruelly jilted (the converse of the landscape painter's experience), but had now grown able to view the matter with much of the impartial spirit of those French critics whose works were his favorite reading." Talking and strolling by the sea, the friends carry guns and shoot an occasional bird which their dog retrieves. Bingham, on seeing a large gull settle on a crag above the water's edge, raises his gun and fires, just as a young child, previously observed with his mother, appears near the bird. The ensuing scene with the mother, the funeral, the return to the city, all these narrative elements move more freely and effectively than the action in any earlier story. The gradual recovery of Mrs. Hicks from the shock of her child's death is presented indirectly, for "these matters are too delicate to be put into words."

The remainder of the story is its failure, for the love which evolves from this tragic incident contains no warmth or force that the reader can feel. However, Mrs. Hicks, the same substantial type woman as Esther Blunt, takes on more interesting aspects: "It was obvious that she had been a woman of plain associations: her allusions were to homely facts, and her manner direct and unstudied; and yet, in spite of these limitations, it was equally obvious that she was a person to be neither patronized, dazzled, nor deluded. O the satisfaction which, in the course of that quiet dialogue, I took in this sweet infallibility! How it effaced her loneliness and poverty, and added dignity to her youth and beauty! It made her potentially, a woman of the world." Such a woman "of plain associations" was not the type in whom James later found his heroines. A woman of the world, potentially or otherwise, needed for him to have the breadth and depth of a European background, and the meagerness of the American scene one feels strongly in Mrs. Hicks, Esther Blunt, Adela Moore, and Lizzie Crowe. As earnestly as he struggled during these five Cambridge years toward catching the native spirit and milieu, he was working at a disadvantage, as his fiction after 1870 proved.

In a very affectionate, brotherly letter to Alice in New York, Harry wrote of his social and literary activities, on February 3, 1867: " . . . Father and Mother reached home safely on Wednesday evening, and the first thing father did on entering the library was to exclaim with religious fervour, 'Good heavens! What a wonderful place this is!' But although glad to be back, I think they enjoyed themselves much in New York. . . . I am told that the wildest excitement prevails in New York about my literary *efforts*. Have patience yet awhile—a slight romance from my facile pen is to appear in the next *Atlantic* and another either in April or May. I know not—Did you read in the last *Atlantic* a thing called 'Lago Maggiore.' 'Tis by a Mr. Howells who lives here, and is a very nice gentleman. If you haven't read it, do so; for it is very good. Do you read Dr. Holmes's book? . . . " [36] The "slight romance" was *My Friend Bingham*, and the other, not so slight, was *Poor Richard*. Running in three parts during June, July and August in *The Atlantic*, this was the most ambitious story Harry had produced. Willy, who had left for Germany in April to study and improve his health, wrote enthusiastically from Teplitz on March 4, 1868: "So far I think 'Poor Richard' the best of your stories because there is warmth in the material, and I should have read it and enjoyed it very much indeed had I met it anywhere." He stated bluntly, however, that he found all of Harry's stories too *thin,* "even 'P(oor) R(ichard),' relatively to its length. . . . " [37]

Howells remembered years later that the manuscript for *Poor Richard* was the first of James's to be decided upon by him in his capacity as assistant editor, and he was highly pleased with it; James himself always thought of it as "the most presuming as yet of my fictional bids." There can be no question that the story far outdistances the four previous ones. In the first place, it is told directly, as though the author no longer had need of the diary device, or of assuming the point of view of a minor character. Furthermore, it is as free and uncurbed in its substance and expression as *My Friend Bingham* was restrained and halting.

The opening scene presents Gertrude Whittaker and Richard Clare, with description reduced to a minimum and the characters revealed through heated conversation which establishes the narrative quickly. She is a young woman of twenty-four, whose father had recently left her a great fortune. She lives alone, except for an elderly companion, a distant relation, who barely enters the situation at all. Like James's other homespun heroines of the period, she is "country-bred, and homely-featured," with "neither the tastes nor the manners of a fine lady." Being robust and active, warm hearted and capable, she manages her country place well, and is, at the moment, attempting to control the aroused feelings of Richard, a dissolute country lad quite passionately in love with her. With strength and tact she puts him off, offering her friendship on condition that he give up drinking and manage his neighboring farm properly, though she gives him no hope of marriage.

The time is the early years of the Civil War, and both Captain Severn and Major Lutterell are paying court to Gertrude, having not yet been called to duty. All three suitors have some possibilities. She inclines toward Severn, poor and proud, though Lutterell is at times equally attractive until his true character is finally revealed.

Richard is least favored as the three move into an interesting situation at dinner with Gertrude. In the scene after dinner in the garden,
Gertrude observes her gentlemen with shrewdness and plays her part
among them with definite finesse. The author here shows, perhaps
for the first time with any sustained powers, his growing ability to
appreciate and present the more delicate shades of human reactions
between people bound together in a situation calling for sensitive
understanding and treatment. A week following the dinner, Richard
calls as Severn is leaving, and senses quickly that between Gertrude
and the Captain there has grown a serious bond of attraction. Like
an unruly boy, he presumes upon her and is sent off to sulk and
become ill at his neglected farm. When Gertrude learns of his
condition she calls on him, finding him greatly improved and
hard at work, trying to be the man she wants him to be. More
than ever impressed by him she tells herself, "This is not romance.
. . . it's reality." Richard, sensing her approval, sees her as an en-
chantress, but, the author states, "her spell was a steady one; it
sprang not from her beauty, her wit, her figure,—it sprang from her
character." Again the reader wishes he did not have to be told so,
that Gertrude herself would express this power as she is portrayed from incident to incident; particularly does the reader wish
it in this story, for Gertrude comes close to achieving three dimensions.

The narrative takes an abrupt turn of interest when Richard
and Lutterell meet Severn, who comes to say farewell to Gertrude,
as they are riding away from her home. In an impetuous moment
of jealousy, Richard affirms that Gertrude is not at home and
Lutterell makes no effort to correct the statement; thus the Captain
goes off to battle to be killed, leaving Gertrude under the impression that he did not care enough even to bid her good-bye. The
guilty conscience suffered by Richard and the incriminating silent
consent by the Major throw the two remaining suitors in a strained
situation which is resolved by Richard's confessing to Gertrude,
causing her to break her engagement to Lutterell. The Major withdraws, quite logically taking no revenge, later marrying a Philadelphia heiress with "seventy thousand a year." Gertrude Whit-

taker breaks up her home and goes abroad, living mostly in Florence. Richard, after earning a captaincy in the War, returns briefly to his home, then goes vaguely off to St. Louis.

Poor Richard is significant, though not intrinsically valuable for its literary merits, for it shows the joining forces of young Henry James's own life and his contemporary reading. No proto-types can be suggested for the three suitors or for Gertrude, but the rich, independent, marriageable heiress was not an unusual person in the social circles of the Jameses, and the slight touches of the Civil War parallel his indirect knowledge obtained through his younger brothers. Gus Barker, of the Albany cousinage, was shot by guerillas, as was Edmund Severn. The comparable situations, however, between the author's life and the incidents in the story are few, for he was leaning less heavily on devices and personal experience; thus he consequently wrote a more effective bit of fiction. The situation of Gertrude and her suitors, among them a farmer lad, is more in the vein of George Sand than out of Harry's life, yet he localized the story in America by the Yankee terms and characters set against the Civil War. Particularly related to George Sand are, "the analysis of love by the author, the long discussions about it, often in the nature of soliloquies or asides, by the characters. . . . "[38] Though *Poor Richard* must be grouped in the category of the pre-vious tales, it is more promising in its better handling of action and situation and in its evidence of the author's growing tendency to analyze his characters in terms of human nature.

In August, 1867, upon receiving another manuscript from his friend James, Howells wrote to Charles Eliot Norton: "I see the Jameses rather frequently. They are all in town. Harry James has written us another story, which I think admirable; but I do not feel sure of the public any longer, since the *Nation* could not see the merit of *Poor Richard*. It appeared to me that there was remarkable strength in the last scenes of that story; and I cannot doubt that James has every element of success in fiction. But I suspect that he must in a great degree create his audience. In the meantime I rather despise existing readers." [39]

With Willy in Germany, Bob and Wilky in Florida, and Alice in New York, the Jameses consisted of Harry and his parents who remained in Cambridge, under the circumstances, giving up the usual months at the shore. Harry was glad of the quiet. Late in May, John La Farge paid a short visit;[40] Wendell Holmes went off to Maine for salmon fishing; and Harry and Willy exchanged letters on their problems of health. Sarg Perry was in Paris, shortly to join Willy in Berlin. The letters from Germany contain frequent references to poor health, aggravated by a strained back which Willy had been suffering from for several months. Mrs. James and Aunt Kate Walsh believed that he had injured his back while helping to move things into the Cambridge house in the autumn of 1866; he felt, however, that the trouble was more related to his chronic nervous exhaustion and indigestion. It is strange that both brothers should have been so afflicted. Their mutual problem of remedies and cures, tried for years at home and abroad, was actually one of the bonds of sympathy and affection between them.[41] Willy's year in Germany, though in many ways beneficial, did very little to improve his condition. Upon returning to Cambridge in November, 1868, he entered upon another year of invalidism, during which Harry left for Europe in an equally futile attempt to find some relief. But in the meantime Harry struck a vein of inspiration in his fiction, producing critical essays and reviews with equal success.

The Story of a Masterpiece, in The *Galaxy* for January and February, 1868, was presented as the principal item of content, its first page being flanked by a full page illustration from Gaston Fay as a frontispiece.[42] Potentially quite interesting, the story is disappointing in its failure to sustain interest, its shifting of the point of view, and in a certain looseness of construction, which breaks in parts under a long retrospect of action previous to the first scene. It is an account of the development of jealousy on the part of John Lennox, a wealthy widower, toward Marian Everett of New York, whom he meets during a six weeks' visit at Newport. Through an artist, also met at Newport, Lennox becomes interested in a portrait painter, Baxter, who, time proves, has been in love with Marian in Europe not long before. Attracted by a picture which bares striking likeness to his fianceé, Lennox asks Baxter to do another portrait, for which Marian graciously consents to sit. The final portrait confirms Lennox's fears and suspicions, though he goes through with the marriage like a true gentleman of 1868, after, however, slashing the portrait in shreds on the night before his wedding. Had James more wisely given less detail and space to the Swiss romance of the painter and Marian, keeping Lennox more definitely as the central figure throughout, much would have been gained in the story's construction and effectiveness. The ending, which is not a bad one, might have been stronger had James not been persuaded by his editor to make the marriage a certainty, for he had originally intended that Marian's wedding to Lennox be merely implied.[43] It is obvious that James was here experimenting in artistry, carrying on the analytical tendency of his previous work, but leaning more upon explanation, rather than implication, to establish his points.

John Lennox's stay at Newport and Marian Everett's romance in Switzerland stem, of course, from Harry's appreciation of those localities. Miss Everett, who spends much time with cousins at Newport, suggests a composite of the Temple sisters, though she proves far too lacking in depth to be a projection of any of them. Lennox's attraction to the artist Gilbert, "for whose talent and conversation he had conceived a strong relish," is reminiscent of the Jameses' devotion to William Hunt; likewise, Gilbert's finding of the talented young Baxter parallels Hunt's taking John La Farge as his protégé. Gilbert's love of Browning, calling the first portrait "My Last Duchess," had similar connection with Newport days when Harry, Willy, Sarg Perry, and Duncan Pell read the poet by the hour and John La Farge painted his famous Browning sketches. Such fictionized autobiographical touches James used to advantage, getting from them sufficient strength of documentation to support weaker passages. He was striving for much the sort of thing in his fiction that Baxter presumably achieved in his portrait of Marian, excellent in its execution of objectivity, but even more powerful in the inner truth it brought out. Lennox, struck by this and alarmed by the levity, the horrid blankness of the portrait's eyes, therein realizes the true nature of the woman he is to marry, for Baxter "had painted with something more than knowledge—with imagination, with feeling. He had almost *composed;* and his composition had embraced the truth." When the artist says: "I'm sorry for what's disagreeable; but I meant it all to be real. I go in for reality; you must have seen that," Lennox complains: "But you can be real without being brutal—without attempting, as one may say, to be actual." James was to find, in his next story, that by giving up the contemporary scene and dealing with figures in eighteenth-century New England in the Hawthorne sense of romance, he was to produce that sense of actuality which his feeble efforts in realism had not as yet achieved.

The Romance of Certain Old Clothes appeared in The *Atlantic* in February, 1868, and deals with the theme of jealousy between two sisters. The elder girl, Viola, loses their suitor, Arthur Lloyd, to young Perdita. He comes to Massachusetts from an English university, about twenty years before the Revolution, with their brother upon his return from studies and travel in England and on the Continent. The potential tragedy between the girls is nicely suggested in the restrained consideration they display toward each other during the months of uncertain courtship. "The only apparent change in their habits was that they had less to say to each other. It was impossible to talk about Mr. Lloyd, and it was ridiculous to talk about anything else." They were occupied with sewing, pressing out their muslins, and contriving washes and ointments and cosmetics, "like the ladies in the household of the Vicar of Wakefield." Viola bears up magnificently about Perdita's wedding, though there is an intense scene between them when the bride discovers, just before leaving on the honeymoon, that Viola is trying on the wedding gown. James does not make too much of this foreshadowing and succeeds in giving it a light enough tone to keep it merely a natural incident. What is not so natural is the too rapid decline and death of Perdita after one year of marriage and the birth of her daughter; yet, in terms of sheer narrative, the episode is plausible as is the marriage of the widower to Viola. The story comes to strong effects when Viola goes up to the attic to her sister's great chest of clothes which Lloyd has sworn to Perdita on her deathbed will be kept for their daughter. As he searches for his wife in the twilight of the June evening and reaches the top of the stairs, Lloyd finds her dead on her knees, having fallen backward from a kneeling position over the opened chest. On her face is the terror of something more than death: "Her lips were parted in entreaty, in dismay, in agony; and on her bloodless brow and cheeks there glowed the marks of ten hideous wounds from two vengeful ghostly hands."

The study of character after the manner of Hawthorne maintains a clear balance between the sisters; their natural jealousy and the supernatural revenge of Perdita on her sister for violating her property carrying all the more weight because James does not attempt to explain. The explanatory type fiction, which had marked the previous stories, here has given way in the freedom he enjoyed by going into a past age, thus becoming less dependent on props and more on creative ability. The brief, compact account of the setting, the characters, the situation, and action shows definite progress in the author's grasp on the narrative.

Howells wrote enthusiastically of it to Norton, and Willy James was inspired by it to give his brother some sound, constructive criticism. In Germany he received copies of *The Story of a Masterpiece* and *The Romance of Certain Old Clothes* in the same mail, reading them at once and basing his reactions on a comparison between them: "Both stories show a certain neatness and airy grace of touch which is characteristic of your productions (I suppose you want to hear in an unvarnished manner what is exactly the impression they make on me). And both show a greater suppleness and freedom of movement in the composition; although the first was unsympathetic to me from being one of those male *vs.* female subjects you have so often treated, and besides there was something cold about it, a want of heartiness or unction. It seems to me that a story must have rare picturesque elements of some sort, or much action, to compensate for the absence of heartiness, and the elements of yours were those of everyday life. It can also escape by the exceeding 'keen'ness of its analysis and thoroughness of its treatment, as in some of

Balzac's (but even there the result is disagreeable, if valuable);
but in yours the moral action was very lightly touched, and rather
indicated than exhibited. I fancy this rather dainty and disdain-
ful treatment of yours comes from a wholesome dread of being sloppy
and gushing and over-abounding in power of expression, like the
most of your rivals in the *Atlantic* . . . and that is excellent, in
fact it is the instinct of truth against humbug and twaddle, and
when it governs the treatment of a rich material it produces first
class works. But the material in your stories (except *Poor Richard*)
has been *thin,* . . . so that they give a certain impression of the
author clinging to his gentlemanliness though all else be lost,
and dying happy provided it be *sans déroger.* That, to be sure,
is expressed rather violently, but you may understand what I
mean . . . The story of 'Old Clothes' is in a different tone from
any of yours, seems to have been written with the mind more unbent
and careless, is very pleasantly done, but is, as the *Nation* said,
'trifling' for you. . . . " [44]

More than anyone else, Willy James knew intimately the peculiar
gifts of his brother Henry, as this "unvarnished" criticism clearly
indicates, and he sensed the basic weaknesses of this early fiction
in its absence of heartiness, a trait quite foreign to Harry's talent;
he saw the need of some compensating factors, "rare picturesque
elements," or "much action," neither of which had yet been pronounced. His suggestion that Harry compensate for the lack of
virility "by the exceeding 'keen'ness of" analysis and thoroughness
of treatment was actually what the young author was endeavoring
to do; it was, furthermore, to become the greatest of his forces.
Close to the truth was the comment that these stories gave the
impression "of the author clinging to his gentlemanliness though
all else be lost," for never did Henry James during half a century
of writing lapse from this position. What neither Willy nor Harry
then realized was that by this very gentlemanliness, this fastidious
sense of things, combined with an increasingly penetrating insight
into human nature, would young Henry James become a great novelist.

Early in April, having left Berlin for Dresden, Willy was suddenly filled with remorse over the candidness with which he had
criticized Harry's stories, writing most sympathetically to him:
"I am very glad to hear from you, my dear Harry, that you are
doing well; the news of your sudden backsliding in the winter
was very painful to me. You have no idea how my sympathy with you
has increased since I have had the same. I am glad you can go
out so much. Keep it up. I wrote you from Teplitz a long letter
relative to your writing. Exactly what, escapes me in the ardor
of composition. I cannot now remember, but I have the impression
I assumed a rather law-giving tone. I hope it did not hurt you in
any way, or mislead you as to the opinion I may have of you as a
whole, for I feel as if you were one of the two or three sole intellectual and moral companions I have. If you could have known
how I have ached at times to have you by and hear your opinion on
different matters or see how things would strike you, you would
not think I thought lightly of the evolution of your mind. But
I have no doubt you understood rightly all I may have said." [45]
Indeed, Willy was one of the few people from whom Harry could
take unvarnished criticism and profit by it, though the four remaining
stories of 1868 do not give evidence that he received much help
either from his brother or any other source.

A Most Extraordinary Case, appearing in The Atlantic for April
1868, carries on the theme of jealousy, treated in the two previous
stories, but is set in a contemporary, post-war scene, on an estate
up the Hudson River from New York. A wealthy widow takes
her husband's nephew under her care upon finding him penniless
and in ill health in New York, recovering from his wounds. Her
charming niece, who is her companion, and the family physician
are the only other characters in the plot. The nephew and the
doctor almost unconsciously become rival suitors, the doctor ultimately winning Miss Hofmann's hand and young Mason pining away
to death. The plot, what little of it exists, James utterly neglected
in his excessive analyzing of the characters. After establishing
Ferdinand Mason in his aunt's country house, the author places
the young man and Dr. Knight in repeated situations wherein they

spend hours outdoing each other in mental fencing about Mason's
health or Miss Hofmann's beauty and character. There is little if
any artistry of form and not enough substance to the plot or characters to justify the lengthy exploratory analysis in which the reader
becomes impatient if not lost.

The one interesting aspect of this story is James's acutely sympathetic portrayal of Ferdinand Mason's position as an invalid.
Harry's "backsliding" and repeated failures to find relief from his
own illness and infirmities here supplied a significant insight into the
relation between Mason and Miss Hofmann. His own relationship
with Minny Temple, about which he was to write so freely to his
Mother and brother Willy upon learning of Minny's death in 1870,
is noticeably parallel to the description he gives of the sick young man,
the "extraordinary case." To advance the courtship, he wrote, Mason
"must be vigorous and elastic . . . must be able to forget his lungs
and his liver and his digestion." Because of his weakness of health,
Mason held his tongue. "He would have suffered anything rather
than reveal his emotions, or allow them to come accidentally to
Miss Hofmann's knowledge. He would cherish them in silence
until he should feel in all his sinews that he was himself again,
and then he would open his heart. Meanwhile he would be patient;
he would be the most irreproachable, the most austere, the most
significant of convalescents. He was as yet unfit to touch her,
to look at her, to speak to her. A man was not to go a wooing in
his dressing-gown and slippers."

In *A Most Extraordinary Case* it is the young man who goes into a
decline while the girl moves onward into the fullness of life; in what
Henry James called "the lost romance of my youth," it was Minny
Temple whose life was consumed with illness while young Henry
James recovered, though slowly, to live on through the decades a
rich, though lonely, life. As unsatisfactory as the story is and as inferior as it is to the others, Willy wrote at length about it in what
amounts to a compensation for his previous and more unfavorable
criticism; he takes the opportunity, however, to compare *A Most
Extraordinary Case* with one or two of the other tales in a effort to
arrive at some better understanding of what Harry is trying to do.[46]

Harry, himself, however, would have had difficulty in being perfectly clear on the matter, for in *De Grey: A Romance,* in The *Atlantic* for July, 1868, he turns to the supernatural again, but not in the tradition of Hawthorne, unfortunately.

The story is laid in New York City about 1820 and deals, rather wildly, with the effect of the supernatural upon successive generations of the De Grey family. The curse, from which no woman loved by a De Grey can escape, is not badly established through the projection of the theme back into the origins of the curse in an eighteenth century member of the family. Father Herbert, the cultured, learned Catholic priest who reveals the secret curse to Margaret Aldis upon learning of Paul De Grey's fatal love for her, is well done, giving a plausibility to the belief in the supernatural power, his religion substantiating the mysterious element in it. The rather melodramatic death of Paul in his fall from a horse and Margaret's madness resulting from the shock and grief are the weakest part of the story. Father Herbert's resigned acceptance of the tragedy is justified by his complete belief in the power of the curse; and his love for Paul, whom he has tutored and tended for twenty years, is simply made deeper in this fulfillment of the handwriting on the wall, a predestination devoutly believed in. Mrs. De Grey supplies a sufficiently effective mother, detached enough not to interfere with the carrying out of the ominous power suggested throughout the story. The curse provides the story with more form than had been achieved in *A Most Extraordinary Case,* but the reader senses a lack of control on the author's part, almost as though he had got the evil power started and found it not fully at his command, whirling as it does out of his imagination rather than from his mind. *De Grey* is clearly an improvisation emanating from a mood, a spell; it is, therefore, not the sort of tale James was really interested in and must be classed as another experiment, probably under the influence of his study of George Sand and quite different from the realistic story in which he really found himself.[47]

In The *Galaxy* for June, a month before *De Grey* appeared in The *Atlantic,* James published *A Problem* in which an artistic at-

tempt for form is based upon the rather flimsy device of some
fortunes told at the beginning and fulfilled in the end. The framework thus established encouraged the author to go too deeply into
the analysis of his characters, David and Emma, from their honeymoon, through the violent jealousy, the birth and death of their
child, and their ultimate reunion. The prediction of their future,
of the child's death and their second marriage, offered by a
gypsy Indian, permeates the young couple's thinking. So intrigued
is the author by the psychological complications herein established
that he neglects to create an atmosphere about or sympathy for
his characters; there is no pathos even in the most poignant situations about the child, for the whole story is chilled in the cool
over-analysing of the minds at the expense of the hearts. James's
struggle between romance and realism is clearly working itself out
in stories he never afterwards cared to acknowledge.

Osborne's Revenge, the last story of 1868, appeared in The
Galaxy for July. Dealing again with the theme of revenge, almost
overworked in four previous stories of that year, it treats realistically
Osborne's determination to punish the girl who has, in his opinion,
been the cause of his friend's suicide. Robert Graham, who has
"a charming literary talent, and plenty of leisure," staying at a
mineral springs resort in New York state, falls madly in love with
rather plain Henriette Congreve, living there with a married sister.
Philip Osborne, a busy New York lawyer and an intimate friend,
hears of the situation and its injurious effects on Graham whose
love, apparently, is not returned. He persuades him to come to
New York and then sends him off on a vague business mission to
St. Paul, Minnesota.

The reader rather wonders how the author will handle the mid-
West locale but is abruptly informed that Graham dies within a
few days at his own hand, having sent brief notes off to Osborne and
Miss Congreve in anticipation of his act. At the very beginning of
the story, therefore, this character with a nice literary talent and
much leisure time is shortly dispensed with, but not before the
reader sees him as "an insignificant, lounging invalid, who, in
general company, talked in monosyllables, in a weak voice, and

gave himself the airs of one whom nature had endowed with the right to be fastidious, without ever having done a stroke of work." Obviously facts are here made into fiction and James has turned once more to his actual knowledge, of himself, his friends, and the places within his own experience, for Miss Congreve and Osborne soon meet in Newport where the revenge is now put into practice. Their meeting occurs when he rescues her five-year-old nephew from the rising tide, a situation reminiscent of *My Friend Bingham*. The subsequent affair between Osborne and the young lady is strengthened by several good dramatic touches, such as Miss Congreve's tearing up Osborne's letter from Graham without reading it, just as she had destroyed the note Graham had written her. We realize then, as Osborne soon does, that she did not know the death was from suicide.

The ending of the story is grossly disappointing and inadequate. After several expository pages in which the action slows to a complete stop, Osborne, who has found Miss Congreve unusually attractive and consequently a difficult subject for revenge, discovers that she is engaged to another man, has been for some time and never cared for Robert Graham. She had never given him the least encouragement and certainly did not jilt him. Thus, there has never been any cause for Osborne's revenge; and the ending is so divorced from the beginning, the impelling force so deceiving, that the reader feels that he has been definitely tricked. In the other stories James had been straightforward, if laborious at times; here the annoying twist of the *donné,* added to which is much clogged analysis, resulting in the bad ending, leaves the reader little short of exasperated. The story is not made probable enough to be realistic, yet it is not imaginative enough to be romantic.

It is very clear, therefore, that young Henry James had just about reached the end of his endurance in his twisting and turning over the conflicting forces within him, in trying to arrive at a fiction which did justice to his possibilities. Furthermore, it is apparent that the American scene had afforded him very little opportunity to make use of all the formative years of travel and study in Europe, of bringing into play the deeply rooted "sense of

Europe" that had for nearly a decade been kept far under the surface of this thought and feeling. The next year and a half of experience saw him move unfalteringly from *A Light Man* to *Gabrielle
de Bergerac,* from *Travelling Companions* to *A Passionate Pilgrim,*
from romance to realism as he moved from America to Europe.
And in this last period of his youth, the final stage of his apprenticeship, he crystallized his basic concepts of the fiction he was
to write.

In his "Preface" to *The American* he states clearly what he had
tried so desperately to understand between 1865 and 1870: "The
real represents to my perception the things we cannot possibly *not*
know, sooner or later, in one way or another; it being one of the
accidents of our hampered state, and one of the incidents of their
quantity and number, that particular instances have not yet come
our way. The romantic stands, on the other hand, for the things
that, with all the facilities in the world, all the wealth and all the
courage and all the wit and all the adventure, we never *can* directly
know; the things that can reach us only through the beautiful cir-
cuit and subterfuge of our thought and our desire." [48]

In going abroad in 1869, young Henry James was to throw off
his hampered sense and to arrive at a detached state in which he
could see clearly that his fiction must be based upon his perception
of those things which he could "not possibly *not* know, sooner or
later, in one way or another"; he then learned too that such things
for him were to be found in Europe, not in America.

NOTES

1. Mildred Howells, ed., *Life in Letters of William Dean Howells,*
   II, 399.
2. *Notes of a Son and Brother,* 343.
3. According to the official records of the Registrar's Office of the
   Harvard Law School, Henry James, Jr., of Newport, Rhode Island,
   entered on September 2, 1862, and remained two terms, leaving on
   July 10, 1863.
4. *Notes of a Son and Brother,* 349, 350.
5. *Ibid.,* 358.

6. *Ibid.*, 357. Julia Margaret Mitchell (1832-1918) first appeared in *The Soldier's Daughter* at Burton's Theatre in New York in 1851, later achieving great success in the role of Oliver Twist and in light comedies such as *The French Spy.* In 1860 she introduced the role of Fanchon, which was a brilliant success; she later played in *Jane Eyre*, and *Elsa*, "but *Fanchon* was her chef d'oeuvre and endeared her to the public for many years." Coad and Mims, *op. cit.*, 191.

7. Kate Bateman (1842-1917), widely known with her sisters in the Fifties as precocious impersonators of Richard III and other adult characters, at the age of twenty played in New York as Juliet and Lady Macbeth. Augustin Daly had Mosenthal's *Deborah* translated for her into *Leah the Forsaken*, first produced at the Howard Athenaeum in Boston, December 8, 1862, with Kate Bateman in the title role, opening at Niblo's Garden in New York in January, 1863; it enjoyed a great success in both cities. See Arthur Hobson Quinn, *A History of the American Drama, From the Civil War to the Present Day,* New York, Harper & Brothers, 1827, 9.

8. Joseph Warren Beach, *The Method of Henry James,* New Haven, Yale University Press, 1918, 165.

9. In a letter to his brother Howard, the elder James wrote from Newport on April 12, 1862: " . . . I have been buying a house here, and putting a new storey upon it. I shall naturally need furniture and pictures, etc. . . . I have established my financial reputation afresh by buying a house at half its worth. I shiver to think how soon I may be elected a director, and next President of the Newport Bank . . . I shall live and die the friend and crony of Duncan C. Pell . . . Mary is as busy as she can be getting the house ready. We shall get in it by the 1st of June, I hope, and I expect a visit from you and Jane in the summer." MS. letter, Henry James, Sr., to Howard James, April 12, 1862, Houghton Library, Harvard University.

10. *Letters of William James,* I, 46, 47.

11. "Mr. James was the only man chosen into the Club in 1863, when he was on the point of moving to Cambridge." Edward W. Emerson, *op. cit.*, 330. His name had been connected with the Club from its very beginnings, however, for Samual Gray Ward wrote to Ralph Waldo Emerson on October 5, 1849: "I should be delighted with your plan of a circle, if it can be brought about . . . Cabot Bangs, and William (Henry) Channing are the men I should seek, and Henry James of New York, if he were here, as he used to talk of coming . . . He is an exansive, expanding companion and would remove to Boston to attend a good club a single night." *Ibid.*, 8. James, Sr., first appeared as a guest at a Club dinner on January 26, 1861, writing a letter in brilliant superlatives afterward to Emerson, giving vivid impressions of Hawthorne, Channing, and others he met there.

12. *The Journals of Bronson Alcott,* 368.

13. *Ibid.*, 368. On September 15, 1864, Henry James, Sr. wrote to Park Godwin, Bryant's son-in-law and assistant, on the New York *Evening Post,* asking him to arrange for James to give his Carlyle lecture in New York, informing him that he was scheduled to give it in Albany on January 5, 1865. He adds, "We have left Newport and settled down here for the remainder of our lives. Physically one regrets Newport, but morally one has no regrets . . . " MS. letter, Henry James, Sr., to Park Godwin, New York Public Library Collection of James Papers. Mrs. James T. Fields recorded in her diary on February 19, 1864, that Henry James, Sr., was in Boston, looking for "a furnished house tor a year in Boston until his departure." M. A. De Wolfe Howe, *Memories of a Hostess,* Boston, The Atlantic Monthly Press, 1922, 74. There is no evidence that the James family had any intention of going abroad, as Mrs. Fields implies. The elder James was, in fact, desirous of establishing a permanent home and did not leave America again.

14. Julia Ward Howe, *Reminiscences,* 1819-1899, Boston, Houghton Mifflin, 1899, 323 f.

15. Rollo Ogden, ed., *Life and Letters of Edwin Lawrence Godkin,* New York, The Macmillan Company, 1907, II, 118.

16. *Notes of a Son and Brother,* 405, 406.

17. For a list of contributions to periodicals consult LeRoy Phillips, *A Bibliography of the Writings of Henry James,* New York, Coward: McCann, 1930. The *North American Review,* founded in Boston in 1815 and designed on the order of its English contemporaries, was at first a quarterly and later a monthly periodical. Charles Eliot Norton (1827-1908), editor from 1864 to 1868, was also a founder and co-editor of the *Nation,* established in New York in 1865 with Edwin L. Godkin (1831-1902) as co-editor in charge. The *Galaxy,* 1866-1878, another New York literary magazine, was intended to counteract the supposed provincialism of the *Atlantic.* Samuel Clemens (1835-1910) was one of its noted contributors. Being financially unsuccessful at the end of twelve years, it failed and its subscription list was sold to the *Atlantic.*

18. In the second critical article James published, for example, an unsigned review of Harriet Elizabeth Prescott's *Azarian: An Episode,* in The *North American Review* for January, 1865, he stated: "The fine writing in which *Azarian* abounds is the cheapest writing of the day. Every magazine story bears traces of it. It is so widely adopted, because to a person of clever fancy there is no kind of writing that is so easy—so easy, we mean, considering the effect produced. Of course, it is much easier to write in a style which necessitates no looking out for words: but such a style makes comparatively little impression. The manner in question is easy because the writer recognizes no standard of truth or accuracy by which his performances may be measured. He does not transcribe facts—facts must be counted,

measured, weighed, which takes far too much trouble. He does not patiently study the nature and appearance of a thing until he has won from it the confession of that absolute appreciable quality, the correct statement of which is alone true description; he does not commit himself to statements, for these are dangerous things; he does not, in short, extract; he affixes."

19. *Notes of a Son and Brother*, 407-409, 411. Lincoln was shot by John Wilkes Booth on April 14, 1865, and died the following morning. Hawthorne died on May 19, 1864. Concerning his funeral, Dr. Holmes wrote in his journal: "On the 24th of May we carried Hawthorne through the blossoming orchards of Concord, and laid him down under a group of pines, on a hillside, overlooking historic fields. All the way from the village church to the grave the birds kept up a perpetual melody. The sun shone brightly, and the air was sweet and pleasant, as if death had never entered the world. Longfellow and Emerson, Channing and Hoar, Agassiz and Lowell, Greene and Whipple, Alcott and Clarke, Holmes and Hillard, and other friends whom he loved, walked slowly by his side that beautiful spring morning." Quoted by Edward Emerson, *op. cit.*, 345, 346.

20. Cornelia Pulsifer Kelley, *The Early Development of Henry James*, Urbana, Illinois, The University of Illinois Press, 1930, 58.

21. To Tom Ward, W. J. wrote: "The only fellow here I care anything about is Holmes, who is on the whole a first-rate article, and one which improves by wear. He is perhaps too exclusively intellectual, but sees things so easily and clearly and talks so admirably that it's a treat to be with him. T. S. Perry is also flourishing in health and spirits. Ed(ward) Emerson I have not yet seen. I made the acquaintance the other day of Miss Fanny Dixwell of Cambridge (the eldest), do you know her: She is decidedly A1 and (so far) the best girl I have known." *Letters of William James*, I, 75, 76. Fanny Dixwell became Mrs. Oliver Wendell Holmes, Jr., in 1872.

22. Quoted by Burr, *op. cit.*, 150. Late in December, 1865, Colonel Mackaye's wife, Jim Mackaye's step-mother, Maria Ellery Mackaye, wrote Jim in Paris, thanking him for the Christmas box of drawings he had sent from his art studies, telling him news of the Jameses: "We have been to hear Henry James lecture on Carlyle. Harry James has written a story for the *Atlantic* called 'The Painter's Journal!' (*A Landscape Painter*). Wilkie is at home, and talks of going into a mercantile house. Willie is expected soon home from Brazil. I suppose you know that Mr. La Farge had an attack of paralysis in the autumn and that it will be years before he can paint again. . . . " Quoted by Percy Mackaye, *op. cit.*, I, 121.

23. From Boston on March 27, 1866, William James wrote to Tom Ward: "I spent the first month of my return in nothing but 'social intercourse,' having the two Temple girls and Elly Van Buren in the house for a fortnight, and being obliged to escort them about to

parties, etc. nearly every night. The consequences were a falling in love with every girl I met. . . . " *Letters of William James*, I, 74.

24. *Notes of a Son and Brother*, 413, 414.

25. "Following the Civil War the social life of Newport, which had been rather simple and restrained for more than a half century, suddenly expanded and became much more sophisticated. The city gradually lost much of its southern clientéle and became the summer playground for wealthy northern families. The gay set of the period 1865-1880 owed much to Mrs. Nicholas Beach, Mrs. August Belmont, and Ward McAllister, who were for many years untiring in their efforts in promoting the amusements for the summer visitors. Mrs. Beach inaugurated dancing receptions, Mrs. Belmont elaborate dinners, and Mr. McAllister started breakfasts and picnics on a scale never before attempted. The latter were planned with great care. Music, flowers, and food were provided, so when the guests arrived they had nothing to do but enjoy themselves. For many years these picnics were well attended, and when enthusiasm waned, Mr. McAllister gave cotillion dinners at his farm. . . . Another form of entertainment was the aquatic picnics, which were held at the yacht club station and sometimes on one of the yachts anchored in the bay." *Rhode Island*, American Guide Series, 212.

26. *Notes of a Son and Brother*, 423, 424.

27. *Ibid.*, 436.

28. *Life in Letters of William Dean Howells*, II, 397.

29. Quoted in *Life in Letters of William Dean Howells*, I, 327, 328; published originally in The *Century Magazine*, 3 n.s., vol. 25, (November 1882), 25 ff.

30. *Letters of Henry James*, II, 221, 222.

31. Concerning *The Day of Days*, published in The *Galaxy* on June 15, 1866, James expressed uncertainty on the title and the ending, writing to the editor: " . . . I have at your request added 5 m.s. pages (as far as I could) to my story. I agree with you, on reflection, that it will be better for them and I enclose them herewith, Truly yours, Henry James, Jr., P. S. Suppose (if it is not too late to make a change) you call the story *Tom Ludlow's Letters* instead of the actual title. Isn't it a better name? H. J., Jr." MS. letter from Henry James, Jr., to C. W. Church, May 21, 1866, Collection of James Papers, New York City Public Library, New York.

32. William Dean Howells, "Henry James, Jr.," *Century*, 3 n. s. (November 1882), 25. Howells adds: "One is much surer of one's judgment at twenty-nine than, say, at forty-five; but if this was a mistake of mine I am not yet old enough to regret it."

33. *Life in Letters*, I, 116. On December 25, 1866, Mrs. James wrote to her daughter Alice: "Harry's story has been pushed out, much to Mr. Field's annoyance, by *Catherine Morne* (Miss Palfrey's story) which was accepted with the understanding that it was to be only in

three parts. It now turns out to be thrice that length or more; and as it is very dull Mr. Fields has requested Miss Palfrey to close it at once; but she declines to do so—so Harry has got to wait some months longer. He seems very indifferent about it." MS. letter from Mrs. Henry James, Sr., to Alice James, December 25, 1866, Houghton Library, Harvard University. The story was quite probably *My Friend Bingham,* his first to appear in 1867.

34. From Swampscott on October 9, 1866, young James wrote to the editor of The *Galaxy:* "My dear Sir: I received your letter some days ago, but the accumulation of a number of letters upon my hands has prevented my answering it earlier. I am surprised that you should be disappointed at not hearing from me, insomuch as I had endeavoured to be very explicit in my last note—written to you in the beginning of the summer—as to my inability to write anything for The *Galaxy* at present. I am compelled, with regret, to repeat this assurance. My literary labour at the present moment is almost null and I do not hope to add to it for some time to come. I should otherwise be very glad to do my best in your service. I am very glad to hear of the prosperity of The *Galaxy* and with my best wishes for its continuance, I remain, Yours very truly, Henry James, Jr." MS. letter from Henry James, Jr., to C. W. Church, October 9, 1866, Collection of James Papers, New York City Library, New York.

35. William Dean Howells, *Life in Letters,* II, 398.

36. MS. letter from Henry James, Jr. to Alice James, February 3, 1867, Houghton Library, Harvard University. William Dean Howells' article, "Forza Maggiore," appeared in The *Atlantic,* February, 1867; Oliver Wendell Holmes, Sr., published his novel *The Guardian Angel,* in 1867; it is probably the book here mentioned.

37. Quoted by Perry, *op. cit.,* I, 264. In a previous letter some few weeks earlier, Willy had written to Harry: "I was much pleased the other day by receiving from Fraulein Bornemann some old *Atlantic* Monthlies, in which I found parts II, and III, of your *Poor Richard.* I found it good, much beyond my expectation, story, character, and way of telling, excellent in fact. And hardly a trace of that too diffuse explanation of the successive psychological steps which I remember attacking you for when you read it to me." MS. letter from William James to Henry James, Jr., February 12, 1868, Houghton Library, Harvard University.

38. Kelley, *op. cit.,* 71.

39. William Dean Howells, *Life in Letters,* I, 117, 118.

40. Mrs. James wrote to her oldest son: "La Farge is staying here. He looks badly and says that he had quite a break down after getting back to Newport. He ascribed it to the cold rainy weather, but perhaps he had worked too hard in New York. He had a photograph of a sketch he has made—The Wolf Charmer—with him; it is a

very striking picture. Father took him yesterday to the Club dinner where he met several people whom he wanted to see, and had, he said, a delightful time. I am most happy to see that he sits and reads, and exacts very little of Harry in the way of long talks." MS. letter from Mrs. Henry James, Sr., to William James, May 27, 1867, Houghton Library, Harvard University.

41. In a letter from Berlin to Oliver Wendell Holmes, Jr., Willy wrote: "Since I have been here I have admired Harry's pluck more and more. *Pain,* however intense, is light and life, compared to a condition where hibernation would be the ideal of conduct, and where your 'conscience,' in the form of an aspiration towards recovery, rebukes every tendency towards motion, excitement, or life as a culpable excess. The deadness of spirit thereby produced 'must be felt to be appreciated.' " *The Letters of William James,* I, 100.

42. Early in October, 1867, upon receiving no reply from Mr. Church of The *Galaxy* in response to the submitted story, Harry wrote in a contrite tone, compared with the declining of a request for something the previous summer: "I sent you a fortnight ago a letter and a *MS* in different packages. As I have received no answer as yet, I am afraid one or the other has miscarried—if not both, or perhaps your answer has gone astray. If the *MS* has reached you— a story with my name ascribed—I beg you will let me know at your earliest convenience. Truly yours, Henry James, Jr." MS letter from Henry James, Jr., to C. W. Church, Collection of James Papers, New York City Public Library, New York.

43. In response to Mr. Church's acknowledgment of his letter and manuscript, James wrote: "My dear Sir: I received your note and the enclosed cheque, for which many thanks. I am sorry the story is not a little shorter but I am very glad that you are to print it all at once. [The story appeared in two installments, the additional ending making it too long for one issue.] As for adding a paragraph I should strongly object to it. It doesn't seem to me necessary. Silence on the subject will prove to the reader, I think, that the marriage *did* come off. I have little fear that the reader will miss a positive statement to that effect and the story closes in a more dramatic manner, to my apprehension, just as I left it. Yours most truly, H. James, Jr. P. S. Let me reiterate my request that I may see a proof. This I should particularly like to do. H. J., Jr." MS. letter from Henry James, Jr., to C. W. Church, October 23, 1867, Collection of James Papers, New York City Public Library, New York.

44. Perry, *op. cit.,* I, 263, 264.

45. MS. letter from William James to Henry James, Jr., April 5, 1868, Houghton Library, Harvard University.

46. From Dresden he wrote: "My dear Harry, I am just in from the theatre and feel like dropping you a line to tell you I have got your

last *Atlantic* story (*Extraordinary Case*), and read it with much
satisfaction. It makes me think I may have partly misunderstood
your aim heretofore, and that one of the objects you have had in
view has been to give an impression like that we often get of people
in life: their orbits come out of space and lay themselves for a
short time along of ours, and then off they whirl again into the
unknown, leaving us with little more than an impression of their
reality and a feeling of baffled curiosity as to the mystery of the
beginning and end of their beings and of the intimate character of
that segment of it which we have seen. Am I right in guessing that
you had a conscious intention of this sort here? I think if so, you
have succeeded quite well with the girl, who gave me an impression
of having roots spreading somewhere beyond your pages, and not
failed with the men, though somehow they are thinner. Some expressions of feeling from the sick one did however 'fetch' and had to
me the mark of being drawn from experience. Of course the
average reader feels at the end as if he had had a practical joke
played upon him—and I myself after being let down so suddenly
from the pitch of curiosity excited by the title and the progress
of the narrative felt rather as if you'd gone off sticking your thumb
to your nose at my feelings. I chuckled fiendishly at the [not legible]
—but soon justified it on esthetic principles. You seem to acknowledge that you can't exhaust any character's feelings or thoughts
by an articulate displaying of them. You shrink from the attempt to
drag them all reeking and dripping and raw upon the stage, which
most writers make and fail in. You expressly restrict yourself accordingly to showing a few external acts and speeches, and by the
magic of your art making the reader *feel* of these the existence of a
great body of being of which these are casual features. You wish to
suggest a mysterious fullness, which you do not lead the reader
through. It seems to me this is a very legitimate method and has
a great effect when it succeeds (I only think at the moment of
Mérimée as an example—I read a story of his, *Arseré Guillot* last
summer that struck me much by it.) Only it must succeed. The
gushing system is better to fail in, since that admits of a warmth of
feeling and generally of intention that may reconcile the reader.
I think in much of your previous productions you have failed through
selecting characters uninteresting *per se*, and secondly in not indicating enough of them to make them stand out mysteriously. (I except
from all this *Poor Richard* which seems to belong to another type)
e.g. The husband in your old clothes story, both the husband and the
painter and the old lady in your masterpiece story under the first
head. Your young women seem to me all along to have been done
in a very clean manner—they feel like women to me, and have always
that atmosphere of loveliness and unapproachability which the
civilized woman wears into the world without seeming any the less
fleshly for it. This last one, although she is indicated by so few

touches seems to me to stand out vividly. I think a few plastically conceived situations help this effect very much: *e.g.* where she smiles and takes a bite from her cake (Great oaks from little acorns grow!) Your style grows easier, firmer and more concise as you go on writing. The tendency to return on an idea and over-refine it becomes obsolete —you hit it, the first lick now. The face of the whole story is bright and sparkling—no dead places, and on the whole the skepticism and as some people would say impudence implied in your giving a story which is no story at all is not only a rather *gentlemanly* thing, but has a deep justification in nature, for we know the beginning and the end of nothing. Still, while granting you success here, I must say that I think the thorough and passionate conception of a story is the highest, as of course you think yourself. I haste to send you these remarks as I fancy in my previous ones I got exaggerating in the unfavorable sense." MS. letter from William James to Henry James, Jr., April 13, 1868, Houghton Library, Harvard University. Published in part, as was the letter of April 5, 1868, by R. B. Perry, *op. cit.,* I, 270, 271.

47. For a discussion of the probable influence of George Sand on this and one or two of James's other stories of this period see Kelley, *op. cit.,* 80-91.

48. Henry James, *The Art of the Novel,* 31, 32.

Chapter Fourteen

The End of Youth

" . . . youth is an army, the whole battalion of our faculties and our freshness, our passions and our illusions, on a considerably reluctant march into the enemy's country. . . ."

The story of young Henry James comes to a close in 1870 with certain events which determined, to a large measure, the remainder of his life. In later years, he liked to think of his youth as a book in several volumes, "with a volume here and there closing, as something in the clap of its cover may assure us, while another remains either completely agape or kept open by a fond finger thrust in between the leaves."[1] The most personal volume, that dealing with Minny Temple, had "its pages very gravely pressed together" by her death on March 8, 1870, bringing to an end so much that was dear to him in the early years of Albany, New York, and Newport that it, above all, "was to mark the end of his youth. . . ."[2] A companion volume, in which Minny's life was written down in a hundred different connections, held the record of these inimitable Jameses, Henry, Sr., Mary Walsh James, Willy and Harry, Wilky and Bob, Alice, and the indispensable Aunt Kate. A decade of family history was still to be added, but only as a mere last installment in which the chronicle of family unity and affection led off into other and divergent stories.[3] Very rarely

417

after 1870 was the entire family together again, and never could those happy, rollicking, carefree days be revived. In this shifting consciousness of gradual change, young Henry James was well aware that life was moving along, but there had been no decisive incidents, no explosive events to draw the lines of demarcation between youth and maturity. In his fiction, certainly, no mastery of the art had announced the close of his youthful efforts, though *Gabrielle de Bergerac* gave promise of better things to come. In his slender volume of literary efforts, Harry kept not a fond finger but rather an uncertain thumb, thrust in between the leaves as he waited hopefully for the next volume to be opened. There would be recorded the "agitations, explorations, initiations," of those months abroad which made 1869-1870 the *annus mirabilis* of young Henry James's life. In this last volume of his youth, so rich in the accounts of travel through England and Italy, the new theme of internationalism appeared, full of potentialities for the future fiction, exciting in its suggestions of contrasting cultures. In "the large library of life," here indeed were pages completely agape, pages on which the record of Minny Temple's death stood out in the boldest of type, pronouncing for Henry James an epitaph on youth.

At the beginning of March, 1870, about a year after Harry had come to say good-bye, Minny Temple was again at Pelham, visiting the Emmet family. Though her attacks of illness had been more frequent and prolonged so that her relatives and friends must have seen these last stages of consumption, she apparently had no realization that so few days remained. With characteristic buoyancy she wrote to a friend: "I feel the greatest longing for summer or spring; I should like it to be always spring for the rest of my life and to have all the people I care for always with me!" For the rest of Henry James's life, this charming, sparkling twenty-four-year-old girl remained the personification not only of spring, but of youth. Even as a very little girl living in Albany, or visiting the Jameses in New York, she possessed such originality and vivacity, such a mixture of audacity and kindness that Harry had from the first thought her the liveliest and most enjoyable of his many cousins.

At Newport in 1861, happily settled with Aunt Mary Tweedy, Minny, "radiant and rare," with the exquisite charm of being sixteen, suddenly appeared to the James boys as a shining young apparition. With indescribable grace and spontaneity, she was "slim and fair and quick, all straightness and charming tossed head," infinitely more attractive than they had remembered her. Within nine brief years she was to fade, "the palest flower of the stem," cutting off Harry's growing devotion to her so sharply that he never fully recovered from the shock of her death. From Malvern, England, when the news reached him he wrote to his mother in abject grief, trying to comprehend the awful fact, for Minny had been "such a breathing immortal reality that the mere statement of her death conveys little meaning; really to comprehend it I must wait—we must all wait—till time brings with it the poignant sense of loss and irremediable absence. I have been spending the morning letting the awakened swarm of old recollections and associations flow into my mind—almost *enjoying* the exquisite pain they provoke. Wherever I turn in all the recent years of my life I find Minny somehow present directly or indirectly—and with all that wonderful ethereal brightness of presence which was so peculiarly her own. And now to sit down to the idea of her *death!* As much as a human creature may, I fancy, she will survive in the unspeakably tender memory of her friends. . . . It is no surprise to me to find that I felt for her an affection as deep as the foundation of my being, for I always knew it." [4] In addition to the more than seventy pages devoted to her in his reminiscences, Henry James paid the greatest tribute to her memory by creating from it the very essence of Isabel Archer and Milly Theale. To trace the delicate, complex, deeply-rooted affection which grew up between young Henry James and Minny Temple is a task which only he could have undertaken. Yet, with the data extant in their letters and those of their mutual friends, it is possible to catch something of her rare spirit and his devotion to her. [5]

In Newport, during the Civil War years, Kitty, Minny, Ellen, and Henrietta Temple, together with the James boys and Sarg Perry, John La Farge, Duncan Pell, and others, comprised what Harry fondly called "our circle." He remembered the group as "forming a little world of easy and happy interchange, of unrestricted and yet all so instinctively sane and secure association and conversation, with all its liberties and delicacies, all its mirth and its earnestness protected and directed so much more from within than from without, that I ask myself, perhaps too fatuously, whether any such right conditions for the play of young intelligence and young friendship, the reading of Matthew Arnold and Browning, the discussion of a hundred human and personal things, the sense of the splendid American summer drawn out to its last generosity, survives to this complicated age." [6]

When Newport gave way to North Conway and Jefferson, New Hampshire, after the War, the group continued, strengthened by new friends from Harvard, particularly Oliver Wendell Holmes, Jr., who joined the Jameses and Temples for short summer holidays there. Minny's name was linked first with one young gallant, then another—young Holmes, or John Gray, Harry, or Arthur Sedgwick; this, Harry thought, was as it should be, for "everything that took place around her took place as if primarily in relation to her and in her interest. . . . She had beyond any equally young creature I have known a sense for verity of character and play of life in others, for their acting out of their force or their weakness, whatever either might be, at no matter what cost to herself; and it was this instinct that made her care so for life in general, just as it was her being thereby so engaged in that tangle that made her, as I have expressed it, ever the heroine of the scene." [7]

Rhode Island summers had drifted on into winters with very little change, but New Hampshire vacations came to an end, scattering the group, the young men mostly to Cambridge, the Temple sisters on regular visits in Philadelphia, New Rochelle, New York, and Newport. In January, 1867, they descended upon the Jameses in Quincy Street, so interestingly near the Harvard Yard, for one of their many encampments which called for a round of parties

that Harry found a serious hazard to his literary progress. Just then
he was working on *My Friend Bingham* and preliminary sketches
for *Poor Richard*, in addition to critical notes for The *Nation* and
essays for The *North American Review*. In this conflict between
the immediate social attractions and long-range literary endeavors,
Harry seldom hesitated to choose the latter. Thus he wrote to his
sister Alice, who was in New York for medical care: "I suppose
you know that the Temples are paying us a visit. A hundred times
a day they cry out how they miss you and then and there break out
afresh and we all sob and tear our hair out together. They are
having what I suppose they would call a 'quiet time,' their only
festival as yet having been a little party at the Childs', to which I
didn't go and where I believe they enjoyed themselves. Minny, as
you know, has abandoned her European journey and seems rather
glad to have done so." [8]

To the very end of her numbered days, Minny hoped to go
abroad, her last plan being to join Harry in Rome during the winter of 1869-1870. As it was, she had to content herself with the
limited travel and enjoyment her health permitted her at home.
These Cambridge visits, while comparatively unexciting, gave the
Temple girls much pleasure, especially the small dinners which
included such guests as Fanny Dixwell, Schuyler Van Rensselaer,
Anna Livermore, Arthur Sedgwick and his sister, Wendell Holmes
and others. One such affair, Harry noted, was "pretty slow," though
the girls didn't think so, finding John Gray more "lovely" than
ever. While Harry was never averse to these social events, he was
at this time placed at such disadvantage by his ill health, his preoccupation with his writing, and the competition of handsome
young men with the glory of war still about them, that he felt himself to be a comparatively undistinguished member among the
group. The shifting of attentions must have interested him considerably, however, as they interested Mrs. James, who observed the
little dramas sharply. To Alice she wrote of this particular visit of
the Temple girls: "Minny, I think, is quite disenchanted, and evidently looks at Holmes with very different eyes from what she did;
that is, she sees him as others do, talks of his thinness and ugliness

and pinchedness, as well as of his beautiful eyes—and seems to
see his egotism. Mr. Gray is as nice as ever, and seems to be quite
sweet on Kitty. The girls are very nice. Minny looks very thin and
not so pretty." [9]

So the circle of pleasant activities turned, with the cousins and
friends gradually moving into the last phases of those youthful relationships which already placed Newport days in a golden haze.
Increasingly concerned with problems of a young man of letters,
Harry quite willingly played a minor social role, joining parties
only so far as his writing would permit. In this way he got much
work done, whether the household happened to be alive with such
delightful distractions or in its normal, quiet state—with Alice
often in New York, Willy hard at work in the Medical College,
and the two younger boys off in Florida on their plantation. From
time to time Harry appeared at certain Cambridge events, such as
the Norton's evening for Charles Dickens on his visit to Boston
in 1867, being presented to the great author in the drawing room
after dinner when the lesser lights of Cambridge assembled in
Dickens's honor; Harry also attended Mrs. Agassiz's receptions or
the Misses Ashburner's teas, but for the most part he worked dili-
gently on his fiction and criticism. By the end of 1868 he achieved
a remarkable record, having in that year done more stories than he
had published during the previous three years, plus eighteen critical
articles and reviews.

On November 15, 1868, William Dean Howells wrote to
Charles Eliot Norton that "Harry James has just been here and left
the manuscript of a story which he read me a week ago—the best
thing, as I always say, that he has done yet. He seems in firmer
health than ever, and is full of works and purposes." [10] *Gabrielle
de Bergerac* was the story, and it did indeed prove, in several ways,
the best thing young Henry James had yet done; furthermore, it
marked the end of the first period of his fiction, bringing his
apprenticeship definitely to a close, shifting his center of interest
from the American to the European scene and, in terms of his literary life, also marking the end of his youth. One other story,
however, far inferior and dealing, as do the previous ones, with the

local setting, appeared, not in Howells's *Atlantic* but in The *Galaxy*
for July, 1869—*The Light Man*. Even for this meager little tale,
Howells expressed praise, being Harry's most constant and genuine
supporter, equalled in his boundless friendship and encouragement
only by Willy and the elder James.[11]

In a strained attempt to treat realistic analysis artistically, *The
Light Man* is constructed on a framework of the diary device, later
to be replaced by the use of travel notes in the European stories.
Jealousy is again the theme, now between two close friends who
are acting as secretary-companions to elderly, wealthy Mr. Sloane.
The old man's will and the possible inheritance of his estate are the
insidious forces which wreck the friendship of Theodore Lisle and
Maximus Austin. Action plays no part and suspense very little, even
at what is intended as the climax of the story, nor do the improbable characters ever seem real or plausible. The only interesting
elements deserving comment are the theme of patriotism to America
and the subject of unnatural love, each of which is slightly treated
and can be seen, perhaps, as faint foreshadowings of James's subsequent development of these topics. Mr. Sloane, having exhausted
his health and much of his wealth during youthful indulgences in
Europe, "began to feel certain natural filial longings for this dear
American mother of us all. They say the most hopeless truants and
triflers have come to it. . . . " In the same vein, Max Austin, upon
returning to America at the beginning of the story, finds himself
thrilled to be a "citizen of a great country, and for that matter of
a great city. I walked today some ten miles or so along Broadway,
and on the whole I don't blush for my native land. We're a capable race and a good looking, withal; and I don't see why we
shouldn't prosper as well as another."

In relation to the very delicate subject that James was later to
treat in *The Pupil* and *The Turn of the Screw* with all the finesse
and subtlety of his more mature style, Max protests to Theodore,
while discussing their broken friendship: "I never pretended to
love you. I don't understand the word, in the sense that you attach
to it. I don't understand the feeling between men. To me, love
means quite another thing. You give it a meaning of your own;

you enjoy the profit of your invention. . . ." Such subject matter, full of those potentialities of human relationship that was to become James's great forte, is barely suggested in *The Light Man,* but the story hints of his realization that it, like the American-*vs.*-Europe theme, had great promise.

Gabrielle de Bergerac, published in The *Atlantic Monthly,* July, August, and September, 1869, is quite a different matter. Howells and James had talked it over thoroughly, as they strolled in the Botanical Gardens, poking their canes in the gravelled walks. It deserts the contemporary American scene for pre-Revolutionary France; it turns from realism to romance, but in a different way from that which James had used in *The Romance of Certain Old Clothes.* As in the case of that eighteenth century story in a New England setting, this French tale succeeds not in its historic background but in the analysis of the characters, especially the heroine, and in the fine phrasing of its better prose. The romantic element in *Gabrielle de Bergerac* is well balanced with sufficient touches of realism to give it a substance and a charm that the previous romances had not contained.

Like the earlier stories, it is built upon a narrative framework in which one of Gabrielle's descendants, now an old man, relates the tale of lower French nobility shortly before the Revolution. Living in the small, neglected chateau in the provinces are the Baron de Bergerac, a proud man, taciturn in his poverty, the Baroness, sickly, unhappy, pining for the brilliant worldly life, and Gabrielle, the Baron's sister and aunt to the narrator, then a boy of nine. The family is joined by M. Coquelin, a student-adventurer who becomes tutor to the son. Also, there is a friend, M. le Vicomte de Treuil, a dashing young cavalier who brings the Baroness news of the great world and without much persuasion from de Bergerac seeks Gabrielle's hand, though she has no dowry. The poor girl, because she has no choice, consents to marry M. de Treuil upon his return from attending a wealthy, dying relation whose estate he will inherit. In the meantime, however, she finds herself deeply in love with Coquelin, who has loved her in humble silence since the day of his arrival. When the Vicomte comes to claim Gabrielle she refuses him, much to his grief and to her brother's intense anger. A terrific scene follows in M. Coquelin's lodge, not far from the chateau, which is climaxed by Gabrielle's escape with Coquelin. They marry, have three children, and die on the scaffold as Girondists in the Revolution, the reader is told. At no point in the romance do the action and plot exceed the limits of probability and in several scenes the realistic note lends a steadying force to the general imaginative tenor of the tale. James uses historic background material lightly but adequately, never becoming so involved in the description that the authenticity of the eighteenth century period is questioned by the reader; yet, he catches the spirit of the times and creates about the characters a French quality which gives them a charm none of his previous characters had expressed.

Prior to *Gabrielle de Bergerac,* James had shown little capacity for handling descriptive passages, yet, when Coquelin and Gabrielle, accompanied by her small nephew, spend a day visiting the ruins of a feudal castle at Fossy, the author succeeds in giving a delightful sketch of the crumbling towers and battered walls of the dilapidated fortress with its vast corridors and musty vaults. James obviously knew his Scott well and furthermore had actually climbed about similar ruins along the Rhine, during the summer at Bonn; thus the strain on his imagination was not great, and the castle holds firmly to its immense underwalls and dungeon pits as the three figures move about its keep and parapets. The excitement of the near tragedy which Coquelin experiences in mounting to one of the highest platforms of the castle ramparts is carried off with sufficient realism to keep the incident out of the thriller class; and the consequent confession of love which Gabrielle makes, under the emotional stress of Coquelin's danger, is both logical and artistic in execution.

This insight into and analysis of character James applies with equal success to M. Coquelin in his relationship with the future Baron de Bergerac. The many tutors which James had had, especially while living in Europe, afforded him a sensitive understanding of the connections between a tutor and his charge, and the reader feels that the author has complete control of the delicate intercourse between them. More important than any element of fiction in *Gabrielle de Bergerac,* however, is the pronounced superiority of James's style which characterizes the story. It is as if he had suddenly, in turning from the American scene to the rich fabric of the French milieu, freed himself from the forced tone, the awkwardness and heaviness of spirit and technique, which he could not seem to overcome. His instinctive attraction to France, the experiences in Paris and Boulogne, his whole "sense of Europe" came into play, giving the story so much more lightness, though firm and controlled, than any piece of fiction he had written; in this way especially does *Gabrielle de Bergerac* mark the end of his apprenticeship, although the story is by no means a proof that young Henry James had arrived at a mastery of his fiction. Howells, however, was unbounded in his praise of *Gabrielle de Bergerac,* seeing in it the gifts of the author's temperament and experience, which made James, he believed, "inveterately and intensely French." On the other hand, scholars find in this story more influence from the reading of George Sand than from his own creative ability and personal experience.[12] Scholarly theses, however, can be unduly academic. The story's success may quite probably be accounted for to some degree on both scores. In any case, its wide popularity and definite superiority over anything that had yet come from his pen indicate clearly that James had struck new ore when that of his native land seemed quite exhausted. In thus turning to Europe for his material, as he was soon to do extensively in his next period of fiction, young Henry James was approaching his maturity as an author.

There is very little evidence, in the family letters or records, that young Henry James was consumed with desire to go to Europe during the 'Sixties, as has been suggested. On the contrary, the thoroughness with which he worked in and with the American scene during this first period of literary productivity supports the contention that he was fully preoccupied in the effort to establish himself at home. Of the thirteen short stories written between 1865 and his departure for Europe in February, 1869, the first twelve deal directly with American settings, characters, and atmosphere, containing only the slightest, indirect allusions to Switzerland, France, or England. The last story of this first group, *Gabrielle de Bergerac,* is the only one which is wholly foreign, but even in that James introduced the American Revolution, in which M. Coquelin had fought with the French troops. The consistency with which James worked with his American materials in story after story indicates no consuming passion for Europe, though his critical writing was at the same time often devoted to contemporary French literature. Interestingly enough, of the fourteen stories he wrote between 1870 and 1875, all except four grew out of visits to Europe: six resulted from his Italian travels, two from his French tours, one out of his stay at Hamburg, and *A Passionate Pilgrim* the only one from his months in England. Obviously then, the second period of his fiction is as overwhelmingly European as the first is American, and, obviously too it was far more Continental than English. Between the two periods stands *Gabrielle de Bergerac,* significantly proving to be the most popular of any story he had yet written.[13]

After William James's return from a year in Germany, in the autumn of 1868, Henry's plans to go abroad began to take some form. Continued poor health, for which he found no relief, was a far more primary cause of his going than might be imagined, as the profusion of confidential letters he wrote home to Willy during the next year clearly proves. A second basic cause was the exhausting of his literary efforts at home. The concocted, belabored stories of his apprenticeship clearly did not flow freely from his pen under a full and spontaneous inspiration. By 1869 he had apparently scraped the bottom of the barrel and turned, as a result, to the possibilities of his dormant but strong sense of Europe. Almost before he fully realized it, his trip had begun, his farewells being climaxed by a brief but ever so portentous visit with Minny Temple at Pelham. It later appeared inconceivable to him that he was actually seeing her for the last time: "I was then to make in Europe no such stay as she had forecast ('a good many years')— I was away but for fifteen months; though I can well believe my appetite must have struck her as open to the boundless, and can easily be touched again by her generous thought of this as the right

compensatory thing for me. That indeed is what I mainly recall
of the hour spent with her—so unforgettable none the less in its
general value; our so beautifully agreeing that quite the same course
would be the right thing for *her* and that it was wholly detestable
that I should be voyaging off without her. But the precious question
and the bright aspect of her own still waiting chance made our talk
for the time all gaiety; it was, strangely enough, a laughing hour
altogether, coloured with the vision of the next winter in Rome,
where we should romantically meet: the appearance then being of
particular protective friends with Roman designs, under whose
wing she might happily travel. She had at that moment been for
many weeks as ill as will here have been shown; but such is the
priceless good faith of youth that we perfectly kept at bay together
the significance of this. I recall no mortal note—nothing but the
bright extravagance of her envy; and see her again, in the old-time
Pelham parlours, ever so erectly slight and so more than needfully,
so transparently fair (I fatuously took this for 'becoming'), glide
as swiftly, toss her head as characteristically, laugh to as free a dis-
closure of the handsome largeish teeth that made her mouth almost
the main fact of her face, as if no corner of the veil of the future had
been lifted. The house was quiet and spacious for the day, after
the manner of all American houses of that age at those hours, and
yet spoke of such a possible muster at need of generous, gregarious,
neighbouring, sympathising Emmets; in spite of which, withal, the
impression was to come back to me as of a child struggling with her
ignorance in a sort of pathless desert of the genial and the casual.
Three months before I returned to America the struggle had
ended." [14]

Though young Henry James's feelings for Europe had been more
dormant than pent-up during the nine years since the family's return
to Newport in 1860, his enthusiasm and anticipation increased with
great force as his ship approached Liverpool on February 28, 1869.
He landed on a Sunday, "a wet, black Sunday," to find himself in
a dilemma, torn between the excitement of seeing and feeling
England again and the depression of spirits which chronic homesickness placed over him, not unlike the thick, moist English fogs

that settled down upon Liverpool and London. Going directly from the ship to the Adelphi Hotel, he sat in the coffee room contemplating his acute mixture of emotions, taking in, however, "the homeliest notes of the impression, the damp and darksome light washed in from the steep, black, bricky street, the crackle of the strong draught of the British 'sea-coal' fire, much more confident of its function, I thought, than the fires I had left, the rustle of the thick, stiff, loudly unfolded and refolded *Times,* the incomparable truth to type of the waiter, truth to history, to literature, to Dickens, to Thackeray, positively to Smollett and to Hogarth, to every connection that could help me to appropriate him and his setting, an arrangement of things hanging together with a romantic rightness that had the force of a revelation." [15]

Travelling on to London on Monday, March 1st, he began immediately his endless walking about the great city, drinking in overwhelming amounts of exciting impressions; yet, from his quarters at No. 7 Half-Moon Street, Piccadilly, on Tuesday he wrote to Mrs. James: "My own dearest Mother, I have been debating with myself for the past half hour as to whether my being horribly homesick this evening is a reason for or against my scribbling these few lines, but passion, not reason, has settled the question, and here I am beating with my pen at this poor blank paper as grimly as my wretched infantile heart is thumping against my breast. What is the good of having a mother—and such a mother—unless to blurt out to her your passing follies and miseries? At all events, sitting here in this dreary London, between my fire and my candles, I must begin a letter, or else I shall begin to howl and drive the poor landlord to send out for a policeman. Yes, I confess it without stint or shame, I am homesick—abjectly, fatally homesick. Tomorrow, doubtless, I shall be better—the crisis will have passed, but meanwhile until bedtime, let me be my own dear mother's son." [16]

The crisis did pass, and the morrow did come, but therein was established a kind of pattern of thought and feeling, elated one moment, brimming with rich experiences, dejected the next, borne down by physical exhaustion and a sickening longing for family and friends, the homesickness almost of "a small boy." Of great assistance and consolation to him were the Nortons, who were spending some months in London and who took him under their protective and stimulating wing. Escorted by the younger Miss Norton, he was ushered into the thrilling presence of George Eliot; with the elder Nortons he dined with John Ruskin at Denmark Hall, and spent an inimitable evening of hospitality with William Morris, "in the medieval mise-en-scène of Queen Square." With Mrs. Norton he lunched at the table of Charles Darwin at Holwood. The rarest of all these glorious hours, however, was provided by Dante Gabriel Rossetti "in the vernal dusk of Queen's House, Chelsea." Coming as these privileged interviews did at the very turning point of his early career, they made an indelible impression upon his mind and whetted his innate appetite for the wealth of aesthetic and intellectual stimulation Europe held in store for him.

After two weeks in London, Henry wrote to William an assurance that he was proportioning his strength and excursions wisely: "I feel every day less and less fatigue. I made these long recitals of my adventures in my former letters only that you might appreciate how much I am able to do with impunity. You must not think of course that I am literally on the gallop from morning till night—far from it. . . . But I may say that I can do all that I care to—all I should care to if I were in perfect order. I wouldn't go in if I could for perpetual and promiscuous pleasure. It cheapens and vulgarizes enjoyment. But when a man is able to breakfast out, to spend a couple of hours at the British Museum, and then dine out and go to the play, and feel none the worse for it, he may cease to be oppressed by a sense of physical wretchedness." [17]

Breakfast with Hon. George Brodetick, son of Lord Middleton, dinner with the Nortons in honor of Frederic Harrison and Professor Beesley, the political economist, and an evening reception for John Morley of The *Fortnightly Review*—such was his typical day during these first few weeks. But the strain of such a life, as carefully as Harry was to conserve his strength, proved too much for him, so that on April 1st he left for Great Malvern in the hope of regaining his strength.[18] Just a year later, while again in retreat at Malvern, he was to receive word of Minny Temple's death.

The seriousness of young Henry James's ill health at this time has not been fully realized, for the letters he wrote to his brother William about his ailments are of such a nature as to be "*private and unfit for the family circle.*" They have not, therefore, been published and contain little of general interest besides the detailed account of the extreme suffering he endured from back-aches and constipation. The baths, the injections, the douches, and mechanical appliances with which he sought relief are almost unbelievable to the modern reader. Many of his letters to William contain six or seven closely written sheets of paper, devoted to minute descriptions of his frantic efforts to find a cure. Upon reading these unpublished letters, one realizes what fortitude he displayed in carrying through the travels that he did undertake and the extent to which his physical discomfort must have interfered with his enjoyment and appreciation of the places he visited and the people he met. Concerning the other portions of his long letters, not mentioning his ills, he wrote to his brother: "You mustn't let my letters bore you. Don't read them if you don't feel like it—but keep them nevertheless. They will serve me in the future as a series of notes or observations—the only ones I shall have written." [19] This conscious effort to record impressions of his travels was the beginning of his travelogue sketches for which he went to Europe in 1872.

Three weeks later, en route to London and the Continent, Harry stopped for a few days at Oxford, making notes that were later to be of much use to him in writing *A Passionate Pilgrim*. The wonderful charm of the University and town did not completely counterbalance his interest in and concern for home. Even in letters overflowing with enthusiastic accounts of what he saw he made urgent request that family and friends write him local news, especially Wendell Holmes and T. S. Perry. He was also concerned about the publication of his last two stories, writing to Willy: "Another piece of mine will appear in The *Galaxy*—probably very ill printed. . . . I am haunted with the impression that it contains an imperfect quotation of a Scripture text to the effect that out of the lips of babes and sucklings cometh knowledge. If there is such a text or anything like it, ask him (the elder James) to establish it; if not, suppress it." [20]

Young Henry James, apparently, was not so well versed in the Bible as one might expect of a son of his father. Oxford was far too interesting for one to worry there about scriptural texts, however, especially when poor health was not, for the moment, interfering with travel. Henry was feeling better than he had in months, he reported, "even after a week's hard sightseeing." Such interludes of freedom from discomfort and fatigue he had already learned to appreciate. After a few days in London and Paris, he arrived in Geneva in May, again struck by the magnificent beauty on all sides and touched by memories of childhood visits of a decade or so earlier. In June he joined the Nortons at Vevey, that charming Lake resort which he later used to such advantage in the opening scenes of *Daisy Miller*. In July, his pleasure in making a small Swiss tour by himself was greatly heightened by the splendid reports from home of the wide popularity which the first installment of *Gabrielle de Bergerac* had received,[21] but more especially by a letter from Minny Temple.

Writing from Newport on June 3, 1869, Minny thanked him profusely for his most welcome letter which reached her opportunely, for she had been very ill and needed the stimulation and distraction he had thus provided. Still quite innocent of the extremity of her condition, she gaily described plans for visiting the Emmets at Pelham and Harry's family in Cambridge, reporting on visitors at Newport such as John Gray and Henry James, Sr. Minny's yearning to see George Eliot was surpassed only by her desire to go to Rome for the winter, "by hook or by crook," if necessary. She envied Harry these very pleasures and the appealing way in which she expressed herself, though the news she sent was merely petty accounts of their circle, brought Harry down with one of his severe attacks of homesickness, even in the face of the glorious Alps and in expectation of first going over into Italy. Minny's words, "You mustn't be homesick," had exactly the opposite effect upon him, and had his health not then been unusually fine and his expectations hopeful of seeing Minny in Rome that winter, he might very well have turned toward

Liverpool. It is fortunate that he didn't, however, for the absolute intoxication with which he responded to the charm of Italy proved of very great importance in his development as a writer.

The question which puzzled him most, as he travelled leisurely in early September toward Rome by way of Venice, Brescia, and Florence was why his parents had not brought the family to Italy during the years they had spent in Europe. By comparison, he felt that neither England nor Switzerland, France nor Germany could be classed with Italy, with the wealth and beauty of these magnificent Italian cities. He wandered in absolute rapture among the antiquities, floated in solitary delight along the Grand Canal, or strolled with awe through the palatial Uffizi. He picked up chance acquaintances at Verona and Venice, and met Anna Vernon of Newport while in Florence; but principally he moved about alone, observing, absorbing, taking in impressions with a richness and fullness he had never been capable of doing on any previous trip.

As struck as his imagination was by the sheer beauty of the architecture, the sculpture, the paintings, and the cities themselves, what actually impressed him the most was the overwhelming contrast he felt in civilizations, the Italian, the English, the American. Not only were the outward manifestations of different cultures of tremendous interest to him, but even more so the basic characteristics which underlay these cultures. The extent to which young Henry James had already come to some fundamental concepts of his whole philosophy of internationalism out of which emanated some of the best of his fiction can be seen in a passage from a letter written to his mother from the Hôtel de l'Europe, Florence, on October 13, 1869: "Willy asked me in one of his recent letters for an 'opinion' of the English, which I haven't yet had time to give—tho' at times I have felt as if it were a theme on which I could write from a full mind. In fact, however, I have very little right to have any opinion on the matter. I've seen far too few specimens and those too superficially. The only thing I'm certain about is that I like them—like them heartily. W. asked if as individuals they 'kill' the individual American. To this I would say that the Englishmen I have met not only kill, but bury in unfathomable depths, the Americans I have met. A set of people less framed to provoke national self-complacency than the latter it would be hard to imagine. There is but one word to use in regard to them—vulgar, vulgar, vulgar. Their ignorance— their stingy, defiant, grudging attitude towards everything European —their perpetual reference of all things to some American standard or precedent which exists only in their own unscrupulous wind-bags —and then our unhappy poverty of voice, of speech and of physiognomy—these things glare at you hideously. On the other hand, we seem a people of *character,* we seem to have energy, capacity and intellectual stuff in ample measure. What I have pointed at as our vices are elements of the modern man with *culture* quite left out. It's the absolute and incredible lack of *culture* that strikes you in common travelling Americans. The pleasantness of the English, on the other side, comes in a great measure from the fact of their each having been dipped into the crucible, which gives them a sort of coating of comely varnish and colour. They have been smoothed and polished by mutual social attrition. They have manners and a language. We lack both, but particularly the latter. I have seen very 'nasty' Britons, certainly, but as a rule they are such as to cause your heart to warm to them. The women are at once better and worse than the men. Occasionally they are hard, flat, and greasy and dowdy to downright repulsiveness; but frequently they have a modest, matronly charm which is the perfection of womanishness and which makes Italian and Frenchwomen—and to a certain extent even our own—seem like a species of feverish highly-developed invalids. You see Englishmen, here in Italy, to a particularly good advantage. In the midst of these false and beautiful Italians they glow with the light of the great fact, that after all they love a bath-tub and they hate a lie." [22]

All the years of subsequent travel and residence abroad were to substantiate these impressions and conclusions arrived at in 1869-1870, and the ramifications in James's short stories and novels which can be traced back to these basic ideas are innumerable; they extend from *Travelling Companions* to *The Golden Bowl,* and behind his comprehension of them lay the twenty-six years of boyhood and youth, in Europe and America, which had so peculiarly prepared him for his career.

The one immediate literary result of this Italian tour, in terms of fiction, was *Travelling Companions,* published in The *Atlantic* for November and December, 1870, and written from notes after his return home. While this story occurred after what James felt was the actual end of his youth, it is so incidental to this experience and represents so clearly the changed currents of his fiction, that it bears some mention here. Using the narrator-hero device through which to project his travelogue material, for the story element is very slight indeed, he succeeds in writing a spontaneous, effortless, flowing style, free from the self-conscious adherence to form practiced earlier; in comparing this style with that of the American tales of the previous four years, one feels that James has arrived at a much happier medium of expression for subject matter far more in keeping with his real interests and talent. Furthermore, he is now treating characters principally from his own class, who express his way of thinking and with whom he is far more natural and effective than with the earlier, concocted characters.

Permeating the setting and the figures in it is the spirit of James's enthusiasm for Italy, the warmth and color of his immediate responses to all this glorious sightseeing. Echoing his words of comparison, expressed in the letters to his family, James has the narrator of *Travelling Companions* state: "In these dead cities of Verona, Mantua, Padua, how life had revelled and postured in its strength! How sentiment and passion have blossomed and flowered! How much of history had been performed! What a wealth of mortality had ripened and decayed! I have never elsewhere got so deep an impression of the social secrets of mankind. In England, even, in those verdure-stifled haunts of domestic peace which muffled the sounding chords of civilization, one has a fainter sense of the possible movement and fruition of individual character. Beyond a certain point you fancy it merged in the general medium of duty, business, and politics. In Italy, in spite of your knowledge of the strenuous public conscience which once inflamed these compact little

states, the unapplied, spontaneous moral life of society seems to have
been more active and more subtle." Such comments upon and comparison of foreign cultures James could not have written in Cambridge or Boston or Newport without the intense stimulation he
experienced from the exciting contacts which touched him on every
side from London to Rome; nor could they have been so acute had
he not had the storehouse of youthful impressions now so brightly
rekindled within him.

American society, as represented by Mr. Evans of *Travelling Companions,* was suddenly silhouetted against the Italian background,
and definitely not to advantage: "He was in many ways an excellent
representative American. Without taste, without culture or polish,
he nevertheless gave an impression of substance in character, keenness in perception and intensity in will, which effectively redeemed
him from vulgarity."

James's readers, from the very beginning of his international fiction,
were extremely oversensitive to such accusations on the score of
American lack of taste, of polish, of culture, as blatantly true as the
criticism was in the post-Civil War period of reconstruction. Remembering only the sting of being called vulgar, most of his readers
failed to note that he paid tribute to the American character, its
strength and power, its acuteness and perception. This, of course,
was the basic misunderstanding involved in the furor resulting later
from *Daisy Miller,* in which the corruption of European society is
exposed in contrast to Daisy's fineness of individuality, her clear
freshness of character, and charm of free manner—all of which
were so badly misinterpreted as mere evidence of her vulgarity.

The question of how much Henry James balanced the equation
between the raw material of American substance and the highly
wrought but fatal beauty of European civilization can be answered
only in terms of the full canon of his fiction devoted to the international theme. Nevertheless, the year 1870 found him at the close
of his youth, awestruck by the vast potentialities offered in this
theme of contrasted cultures. *Travelling Companions,* stemming
from the Italian journey, and *A Passionate Pilgrim,* begun that same
year as a result of his English impressions, are what James later

called mere "sops instinctively thrown to the international Cerberus formidably posted where I doubtless then didn't quite make him out, yet from whose capacity to loom larger and larger with the years there must already have sprung some chilling portent. Cerberus would have been, thus, to one's younger artistic conscience, the keeper of the international 'books'; the hovering disembodied critical spirit with a disengaged eye upon sneaking attempts to substitute the American romantic for the American real." [23] With such attempts Henry James was finding his first faint success.

Before leaving Florence for Rome and the remainder of his Italian tour, Harry was impelled to write a long letter to Minny Temple, one that he later rejoiced in having written, for it was the last she received from him before her death. At Malvern, the following March, he was struck by the irony of the circumstances which found him roaming through the magnificent old cities which Minny so longed to see at the very time that she was gradually declining, "softened and sweetened by suffering and sitting patient and yet expectant, so far away from the great world with which so many of her old dreams and impulses were associated. . . . " [24]

There was not, in Harry's mind, the faintest foreshadowing of Minny's imminent tragedy as he poured out to her profuse descriptions and accounts of Venice and Florence. At that very time Minny was visiting the Jameses in Cambridge where she impressed Willy as she had never impressed him before. The comment which he consequently made to Harry in a letter early in December takes on a peculiar significance, not only in terms of Minny herself, but in relation to the two brothers' feeling toward her: "Minny Temple was here for a week a fortnight since. She was delightful in all respects, and although very thin, very cheerful. I am conscious of having done her a good deal of injustice for some years past, in nourishing a sort of unsympathetic hostility to her. She is, after all, a most honest little phenomenon, and there is a true respectability in the courage with which she keeps 'true to her own instincts.' I mean it has a certain religious side with her. Moreover, she is more devoid of 'meanness,' of anything petty in her character than anyone I know, perhaps either male or female. *Je tiens a* telling you this, as I recollect last winter abusing her to you rather violently." [25]

On November 7, 1869, a month before William's letter, Minny wrote to Harry from Pelham where she had gone from the Jameses': "My darling Harry, I was at Cambridge last week when your letters came to your father and Willy, from Florence, giving an account of your health and spirits that went to my heart. To think that you should be ill and depressed so far away, just when I was congratulating myself that you, at all events, were well and happy, if nobody else was. Well, my dearest Harry, we all have our troubles in this world. I only hope that yours are counterbalanced by some true happiness, which Heaven sends most of us, through some means or other. I think the best comes through blind hanging on to some convictions, never mind what, that God has put deepest into our souls, and the comforting love of a few chosen friends, which comes to us 'all along of "said" hanging-on,' and because we have an eternal right to it, and not a mere arbitrary desire for it. Don't you think so?" [26] The courage she displayed, as Willy had observed, in sticking to the meagre convictions she had to hold on to was more than touching to young Henry James, who cherished this last letter, and the two others from her of a few months earlier, for the remaining decades of his long life.

The frustration and distress which Harry was experiencing in Florence was caused by financial worries as well as by ill health. As expenditures mounted to a figure quite beyond that estimated for the itinerary planned, he actually considered, even while still in Switzerland, giving up the Italian trip. Having confided in his mother how pressing his financial situation was, he was greatly relieved and assured by the characteristically loving support which was expressed by her in the return mail, urging him to enjoy to the fullest amount every opportunity at hand, regardless of expense.[27]

As reassuring as Mrs. James's letters were, Harry's conservative nature would not permit him the free indulgence of tastes and inclinations that Italy aroused in him, but he carried forward his plans economically, going on to Rome for a stay of several weeks. Moved beyond words by the colossal magnificence of St. Peter's, the moon-

lit grandeur of an evening in the Colosseum, or the majestic sweep
of Rome from the Farnese Gardens, Harry felt more than ever that
he should be studying some definite subject or language, doing
something more than merely swimming through this ocean of superb
sights. William urged him to consider some months in Germany,
concentrating on German as he and Sarg Perry had done two years
before, but at this Harry rebelled, holding out on the grounds that
"there were things more important" for him to do: "Here I am,"
he wrote Willy, "twenty-six with such a waste of lost time behind
me and such an accumulated ignorance of so many of the elements
and rudiments of my own tongue, literature piling up in my track,
and with the practical needs of my 'calling' facing me in the immediate future—with these things pressing on me to such a degree
that to branch off into the awful chaos of that portentous tongue
seems simply like an increase of cares and responsibility without an
increase in means. If I were to go to England a short time hence
and remain there until I go home (I am talking all the while on the
basis of my return a year hence, when I shall have been absent about
twenty months), I shall simply be getting in a different way a mass
of impressions which, if I had hitherto been well and able to develop
myself more freely and vigorously, I should probably have got from
study, or at least from more liberal habits of reading. For mere
pleasure alone, I can think of none greater than to spend a summer
wandering through England with a certain freedom. It may be that
the great impression England has left on my mind is owing in measure to its being the first European country I saw, and saw first after
that long monotonous period of home life; and that after Italy it
will seem comparatively pale and colorless. But with all abate-
ments I am sure it will yield me great delights and rich instructions.
The principal drawback I see to going there—to going anywhere
in fact—is the possible—not to say probable dearth of society. I
feel as if 'society' were not destined to play a very large part in lift-
ing me fairly onto my legs. It is an agent I have never fairly tried,
but I have great hopes of it. The only trouble is to get hold of it.
If I were to settle here in Rome I should probably be able to see, as
much as I pleased, plenty of Americans. This one consideration

almost outweighs several weighty matters. On the Continent alone
is American society to be found; and the apparent inaccessibility of
the natives is so great that save this there is little other. I got a
strong feeling while in England of the degree to which, to a lonely
and ailing man, society must remain obstructed and closed, and to go
there and be left wholly to my own resources, though it might be very
pleasant for a couple of months, would be rather dreary for six.
To have any but really *good* society there, moreover, would be rather
more intolerable than to have none at all. If I go, I shall try to drum
up a few introductions. . . . I went to Story's studio with Mrs. Ward
and saw Story in person. He was very civil and his statues very
clever. I likewise received the card of George Ripley of the New
York *Tribune* and of course (feeling very grateful for his attention) immediately returned his visit. He was very kind and agreeable and asked lovingly about father." [28]

Almost forty years later, Henry James published in 1903, *William
Wetmore Story and His Friends,* a two-volume biography of the
expatriated American sculptor who lived so many years in Rome.
To his father, Harry wrote fully of his responses to St. Peter's, the
Vatican, and other great monuments, which the elder James had
never seen and concerning which he replied: " . . . It was very good
to get your first impressions of Rome, and I can sympathize with you
very fully. I feel that I myself should be horribly affected there by
this historical picturesque. I should be extremely sensitive to its
objectivity, and would therefore all the more revolt from its sub-
jectivity, as hearing underneath it all the pent-up moaning and groan-
ing soul of the race, struggling to be free or to come to consciousness.
I am glad on the whole that my lot is cast in the land where life
doesn't wait on death, and where consequently no natural but only
an artificial picturesque is possible. The historical consciousness rules
to such a distorted excess in Europe that I have always been restless
there and ended by pining for the land of the future exclusively.
Condemned to *remain* there, I should stifle in a jiffy—especially on
Roman soil. . . . " [29]

To Harry, so different from his father, the historical consciousness
of Rome was not at all an artificial picturesqueness, but a magnificent

manifestation of the finest art and architecture produced by the
classical and Renaissance ages. Utterly free from the ardent religious
philosophy of the elder James, he heard no moanings or groanings
of a race held under the tradition and domination of the church.
To him the superb pageantry surpassed in beauty anything he had
ever witnessed, even the unforgettable baptism of Prince Napoleon
in Notre Dame. To William he wrote, at the end of his first day
in Rome: ". . . The effect is something indescribable. For the first
time I know what the picturesque is. In St. Peter's I stayed some
time. It's even beyond its reputation. It was filled with foreign
ecclesiastics—great armies encamped in prayer on the marble plains
of its pavements—an inexhaustible physiognomical study. To crown
my day, on my way home, I met his Holiness in person—driving in
prodigious purple state—sitting dim within the shadows of his coach
with two uplifted benedictory fingers—like some dusky Hindoo idol
in the depths of its shrine. Even if I should leave Rome tonight
I should feel that I have caught the keynote of its operation on the
scene. I have looked along the grassy vista of the Appian Way
and seen the topmost stone-work of the Coliseum sitting shrouded
in the light of heaven, like the edge of an Alpine chain. I've trod
the Forum and I scaled the Capitol. I've seen the Tiber hurrying
along, as swift and dirty as history! From the high tribune of the
great chapel of St. Peter's I have heard in the papal choir a strange
old man sing in a shrill unpleasant soprano. I've seen troops of
little tonsured neophytes clad in scarlet, marching and counter-
marching and ducking and flopping, like poor little raw recruits for
the heavenly hosts. In fine I've seen Rome, and I shall go to bed a
wiser man than I last rose—yesterday morning. . . . " [30] How much
wiser he was his father would have questioned, but how much richer
in impressions and responses there can be no doubt. He was, in
fact, more the passionate pilgrim in Italy than he was to be in
England in 1870, and never throughout his long years of expatriation in England was Italy to lose its charm for him.

By December 21, 1869, Rome had given way to Naples, with the
Isle of Capri in the distance and Pompeii, the Sorrento Drive, and
Vesuvius offering attractions which wove the Italian spell more

tightly around him. The fortnight he spent at the Hotel de Grand Bretagne brought Rome and Florence by retrospect into sharper focus, while the great semi-circle of the Bay of Naples swept out in a gesture of encircling arms in which Henry James felt he could clasp the whole magnificent vista. Moving reluctantly northward in late December, he stopped at Assisi, Perugia, and Genoa before going over for a brief visit at Avignon. By mid-January he was again in Geneva, reaching London early in February and arriving in Malvern in March, so exhausted that he remained for several weeks, satisfied with very restricted excursions about the Malvern Hills or over to Worcester.

That he returned to England as "a passionate pilgrim" so intoxicated and overwhelmed by England and the English people that he was from that very moment an Anglophile is far from the truth. Such a theory, precipitated by a popular but erroneous interpretation of the one story which resulted from James's English travels of 1869-1870, *A Passionate Pilgrim,* is clearly refuted by his letters written from London and Malvern at that time, as well as by the fact that in his fiction of 1870-1875, emanating from these fifteen months in Europe, six stories came out of the Italian and four from the French travels. To base an understanding of young Henry James's attitude toward England on the ravings of the character Searle, or even upon the narrator of *A Passionate Pilgrim,* without consideration of these other factors is indeed fallacious.[31] Even in his later years, as a celebrated figure in London or at his country house in Rye, Henry James suffered from no illusions about the strengths and weaknesses of the English character, for he was acutely sensitive to it from the beginning. In a letter to his brother William, written from Malvern on March 8, 1870, the day of Minny Temple's death, incidentally, though he did not receive word of it until more than two weeks later, he stated: "Never from a single Englishman of them all have I heard the first word of appreciation and enjoyment of the things here that I find delightful. To a certain extent this is natural: but not to the extent to which they carry it. As for the women, I give 'em up in advance. I am tired of their plainness and stiffness and tastelessness—their dowdy beads and their lindsey

woolsey trains. Nay, this is peevish and brutal. Personally (with all
their faults) they are well enough. I revolt from their dreary deathly
want of—what shall I call it?—Clover Hooper has it—intellectual
grace—Minny Temple has it—moral spontaneity. They live wholly
in the realm of the cut and dried. 'Have you ever been to Florence?'
'Oh yes.' 'Isn't it a most peculiarly interesting city?' 'Oh yes, I think
it's so very nice.' 'Have you read *Romola?*' 'Oh yes.' 'I suppose you admire it.' 'Oh yes, I think it so very clever.' The
English have such a mortal mistrust of anything like criticism or
'keen analysis' (which they seem to regard as a kind of maudlin
foreign flummery) that I rarely remember to have heard on English
lips any other intellectual verdict (no matter under what provocation)
than this broad synthesis—'so immensely clever.' What exasperates
you is not that they can't say more, but that they wouldn't if they
could. Ah, but they are a great people for all that. . . . " [32]

Ten days later, in a letter to his father, Harry described the utter
charm of a walk over to Worcester "through a region so thick-
grown with good old English 'effects'—with elm-scattered meadows
and sheep-cropped commons and the ivy-smothered dwellings of
small gentility, the high-gabled, heavy-timbered, broken-plastered
farmhouses, the stiles leading to delicious meadow footpaths and
lodge-gates leading to far-off manors—with all things suggestive of
the opening chapters of half-remembered novels, devoured in infancy—that I felt as if I were pressing all England to my soul. As I
neared the good old town I saw the great Cathedral tower, high and
square, rise far into the cloud-dappled blue. And as I came nearer
still I stopped on the bridge and viewed the great ecclesiastical pile
cast downward into the yellow Severn. And going further yet I
entered the town and lounged about the close and gazed my fill at
that most soul-sustaining sight—the waning afternoon, far aloft on
the broad perpendicular field of the Cathedral spire—tasted too, as
deeply, of the peculiar stillness and repose of the close—saw a ruddy
English lad come out and lock the door of the old foundation
school which marries its heavy gothic walls to the basement of the
church, and carry the vast big key into one of the still canonical
houses—and stood wondering as to the effect on a man's mind of

having in one's boyhood haunted the Cathedral shade as a King's scholar and yet kept ruddy with much cricket in misty meadows by the Severn. This is a sample of the meditations suggested in my daily walks. Envy me—if you can without hating! I wish I could describe them all—Colwell Green especially, where weather favouring, I expect to drag myself this afternoon—where each square yard of ground lies verdantly brimming with the deepest British picturesque, and half begging, half deprecating a sketch. . . . " [33]

His unrestricted admiration of "the English country, English houses, English colleges, English inns, and English ghosts," in the intense glow of his first adult discoveries of England is indeed understandable, but it was balanced, and substantially so, by the strong reservations he made on the English character. On the one hand his aesthetic sensitivities, highly conditioned for the beauties he found there, freed his pen for a refreshingly spontaneous pouring out of his delighted senses; on the other, his increasing acuteness in evaluating people, the Americans set off against the English, and they in turn contrasted with the French and Italians, laid the foundations for the structure of his international theme.

In 1855, upon arriving from Geneva as a twelve-year-old boy, Harry had been profoundly moved by the charms of Thackeray's London, in the mellowed rooms of the old Gloucester Coffee-House, for example, on Berkeley Street and Piccadilly; even more so was he delighted by the old Adelphi Hotel (Radley's, it was then called) at Liverpool in 1869, upon arriving from New York. The places, yes, but not the people, he succumbed to completely. His father's dislike of certain aspects of the English, flaring out in full force, for example at Newport in 1861, on the occasion of his Fourth of July oration, had been a topic of frequent discussion at the family dinner table. Henry knew too the opinions of Irving and Emerson, Hawthorne and Holmes, all of whom had treated the Englishman in broad and unprejudiced terms. James Russell Lowell, in The Atlantic Monthly for July, 1869, had published his famous essay, On a Certain Condescension in Foreigners, which struck out boldly against the prevalent English concept of Americans as wholly given over to money-getting, as vulgarians without a culture and unable to develop one.³⁴ Of all this interplay of opinion young Henry James was quite aware, maintaining by it that sense of balance which made him seriously consider France, and not England, as his possible home of expatriation in 1875-1876.

As much as he sympathized with the English and European view of American vulgarity, he held a lasting respect for Americans as "a people of *character*," having "energy, capacity, and intellectual stuff in ample measure." In the sort of super-national point of view which he was forming in 1869-1870, he saw American morality and character balance off favorably against the false standards of Europeans, a point on which he was so misunderstood in *Daisy Miller,* and which in varying degrees is found in all his international fiction. Because Henry James could see something on both sides of this whole question on conflicting civilizations and cultures, because he wished more than anything to arrive at the truth about human nature, he was destined to be misunderstood on both sides of the Atlantic. The comparatively raw, unpolished, granite strength of America stood up admirably against decadent Europe with its complicated mores of folly, shallowness, and artificiality; yet, America's untutored, frontier crudeness was an offense to those sensitivities which found great pleasure in Europe's deep-rooted, tradition-laden crucible of culture and civilization. Between the two, young Henry James at the end of his youth in 1870 found himself caught; his position, however, was not strange, for his boyhood and youth had continually trained him to be the detached observer, the cosmopolitan in tastes and temperament.

Just how cosmopolitan he really was and to what degree his whole future would be determined by this inclination, he had not realized in the decade of the 'Sixties. The fifteen months in Europe, however, in sharp contrast to the previous years at home, stirred deeply the question of repatriation. That sense of Europe which since the return to Newport in 1860 had been dormant and inactive came so forcefully into play in 1869-1870 that he was faced with a whole new adjustment of values and of loyalties. Ten years later, after the final step of expatriation had been taken, he understood the fate which was to be his for the rest of his life. Furthermore, he saw the price he was to pay and the rewards that would be his.

In his essay, "Occasional Paris," he describes the position, the occupation, actually, for which all his boyhood and youth had prepared him: "It is hard to say exactly what is the profit of comparing one race to another, and weighing in opposed groups the manners and customs of neighbouring countries; but it is certain that as we move about the world we constantly indulge in this exercise. This is especially the case if we happen to be infected with the baleful spirit of the cosmopolite—that uncomfortable consequence of seeing many lands and feeling at home in none. To be a cosmopolite is not, I think, an ideal; the ideal should be to be a concentrated patriot. Being a cosmopolite is an accident, but one must make the best of it. If you have lived about, as the phrase is, you have lost that sense of the absoluteness and the sanctity of the habits of your fellow-patriots which once made you so happy in the midst of them. You have seen that there are a great many *patriae* in the world, and that each of these is filled with excellent people for whom the local idiosyncrasies are the only thing that is not rather barbarous. There comes a time when one set of customs, wherever it may be found, grows to seem to you about as provincial as another; and then I suppose it may be said of you that you have become a cosmopolite. You have formed the habit of comparing, of looking for points of difference and of resemblance, for present and absent advantages, for the virtues that go with certain defects, and the defects that go with certain virtues. . . . It is good to think well of mankind, and this, on the whole, a cosmopolite does. . . . The consequence of the cosmopolite spirit is to initiate you into the merits of all peoples; to convince you that national virtues are numerous, that they may be very different, and to make downright preferences really very hard. . . . Compare, then, I say, as often as the occasion presents itself. The result as regards any particular people, and as regards the human race at large, may be pronounced agreeable, and the process is both instructive and entertaining." [35]

On March 29, 1870 at Malvern, as he sat over his writing desk, pouring out to his mother, then to William, the shock and grief he suffered from the news of Minny Temple's death, young Henry James was not yet a true cosmopolite. The homesickness that had plagued him for a year came upon him now in great waves, and the physical exhaustion and discomfort which had threatened more than once to terminate his travels again turned him towards home. Minny's death brought to him an overwhelming swarm of recollections and associations that took him back to the very small boy in Albany and New York, to the son and brother in London, Paris, and Boulogne, to the youth in Newport and Cambridge. Hovering above it all was the vision of Europe—the peasant woman in a black bodice, a white blouse, a red petticoat, and sabots, bending over her work in the French countryside, and high above her the ruins of a castle—he would never forget that. Europe was still a vision in 1870. But so was America. There would be another try in America, another year in Europe, then a last vain effort at home and a futile attempt in Paris. There would be five, six, seven years of searching, of crossing and recrossing the Atlantic, of circling about and moving forward. The mere feeding on the picturesque, indulging in a vast sea of impressions, he was to learn, would never establish him as an artist. He must work, as hard as the peasant woman worked. He must dig deep into the very texture of the English nature, become as much as possible a part of the English spirit, send down strong roots into the foreign soil that would nurture and support his life and his work as his native soil had failed to do—and he must do it alone.

This was the end of youth; yet, as a man of seventy he could write: "We are never old, that is we never cease really to be young, for all *life* at the same time . . . youth is an army, the whole battalion of our faculties and our freshness, our passions and our illusions, on a considerably reluctant march into the enemy's country, the country of the general lost freshness: and I think it throws out at least as many stragglers behind as skirmishers ahead—stragglers who often catch up belatedly with the main body, and even in many cases never catch up at all." [36] Young Henry James had been a straggler; he was still a straggler in 1870, but he was a skirmisher too, and the years were to prove him the victor in the long battle which he fought alone on foreign soil.

NOTES

1. Henry James, *The Middle Years,* New York, Charles Scribner's Sons, 1917, 2.
2. *Ibid.,* 1.
3. Garth Wilkinson James and Robertson James were established by their father on a plantation in Florida after their service in the Civil War. By 1870 the project was given up under the pressure of overwhelming economic and financial troubles which proved insurmountable. So different from the two oldest sons, they chose to strike out for themselves far from the family hearth in Cambridge. They settled in Milwaukee after marrying substantial but undistinguished girls, and struggled for years with depressions, unemployment, and hard toil, in circumstances utterly unlike the happy affluence of their childhood and youth. Alice James, who suffered a nervous breakdown at Newport during the War years, became a semi-invalid for the rest of her life and by 1870 was spending much time in New York under medical care. William James, having been appointed an instructor at Harvard in 1869, lived on Quincy Street with his parents, as did Harry when he was not travelling in Europe.
4. MS. letter from Henry James, Jr., to Mrs. Henry James, Sr., March 29, 1870.
5. The few letters from Minny Temple to Henry James, found among the James Papers in Houghton Library at Harvard University, were published by the author in "Henry James and Minny Temple," *American Literature,* vol. 21, March, 1949, 35-48.
6. *Notes of a Son and Brother,* 457, 458.
7. *Ibid.,* 461, 462. Concerning the friendship between Henry James, Jr., and Oliver Wendell Holmes, Jr., see Mark DeWolfe Howe, "The Letters of Henry James to Mr. Justice Holmes," The *Yale Review,* Spring, 1949, 410-433.
8. MS. letter from Henry James, Jr., to Alice James, January 4, 1867, Houghton Library, Harvard University.
9. MS. letter from Mrs. Henry James, Sr., to Alice James, January, 1867, Houghton Library, Harvard University.
10. *Life in Letters,* I, 137.
11. Henry James, Sr., who had permitted his paternal enthusiasm to expand too generously over his son's work while talking to Mr. Fields in the office of The *Atlantic,* wrote a charming note of apology to the kindly editor: "My dear Fields, I had no sooner left your sanctum yesterday than I was afflicted to remember how I profaned

it by my unmeasured talk about poor H——. Please forget it entirely.
I don't know how it is with better men, but the parental sentiment is
so fiendish a thing with me, that if anyone attempt to slay my
young, especially in a clandestine way, or out of a pious regard (*e.g.*)
to the welfare of the souls comprehended in the doctrine of The
Atlantic Monthly, I can't help devoting him bag and baggage with
all my vows to the infernal gods. I am not aware of my animus until
I catch, as yesterday, a courteous ear; then the unlovely fire flames
forth at such a rate as to leave me no doubt or reflection when it
was originally lighted. Please pray for your sinful and suffering but
cordial friend, H. J." MS. letter from Henry James, Sr., to James
T. Fields, May 2, 1868, Houghton Library, Harvard University. The
"poor H——" referred to was in all probability Thomas Wentworth
Higginson (1823-1911) who was then in Cambridge, devoting himself to writing, teaching, and social reform. He had made very unfavorable comments upon Harry's stories, mentioned by Minny
Temple to Harry in her letter of June 3, 1869.

12. Concerning evidences of George Sand's influence, one critic states:
"This country setting (of *Gabrielle*) and all its attributes, however,
were influenced by, and possibly directly borrowed from, George Sand
—from her novels of country life and the passion which may develop there between young girls of noble birth and poor young men.
The situation, with the omission of minor complicating elements, is
the situation found in *Valentine*—one girl, two lovers, and the parents
who wish to dominate. Gabrielle has the independence of spirit, the
intensity of passion of a George Sand heroine, and she is portrayed
in the same gentle, understanding way, though some of the minor
characters, notably the baron and the baroness, are, because of the
slight irony with which James handles them, more nearly related to
the characters of Balzac's novels. The tale has the open air spirit of
George Sand's novels; it is not a story of the city or the drawing
room; it is a story of the out of doors. The passion which develops
there is of the same strong, imperative kind as the passion treated by
George Sand. And James employed the method of the French writer
in treating it; he did not analyze it himself but allowed his characters to do it for him, in long, thoughtful yet emotional conversations
as lovers are wont to ponder, so that character is revealed and artistry
is not sacrificed to analysis but gained by this new way of treating it.
Many of the minor details and incidents employed in the development
—the contrast of Gabrielle with her friend Marie de Chalais, the
incident of the dying peasant and Gabrielle consoling the family,
the long walks in the country, the way in which the danger of
death may make the full force of one's love for the first time apparent—all these have frequent counterparts in the novels of the
French writer. They are the trademarks of her style. Thus the story
is not exactly Henry James's. It is more George Sand's." Cornelia
Pulsifer Kelley, *op. cit.,* 90.

13. During June, July, and August of 1869, as the story was appearing
in The *Atlantic,* Howells wrote very encouraging reports of its
public reception: "I'll enclose some scraps of print, by which you'll
see that *Gabrielle de Bergerac* is thought well of by those whose
good opinion ought not to be of any consequence, but is. It really
promises to make a greater impression than anything else you've
done in The *Atlantic.* . . . I'm not sure that the August *Atlantic* will
reach you, and so I shall tear out the installment of *Gabrielle* and
Jubilee Days (by Howells) and send them in this letter. Your story
is universally praised, and is accounted the best thing you've done.
There seems at last to be a general waking-up to your merits; but
when you've fame as great as Hawthorne's, you won't forget who
was the first, warmest, and truest of your admirers, will you?" *Life
in Letters,* I, 141, 144.

14. *Notes to a Son and Brother,* 468-470. Mary Temple's relation to
the Emmet family came through her father, Colonel Robert Emmet
Temple. Another connection was established when her oldest sister,
Katherine, married Richard Stockton Emmet of Pelham, New York,
the first of whose six children, William Temple Emmet, was born at
Pelham, July 28, 1869, during Minny's visit there. Minny's younger
sister, Ellen, married Christopher Temple Emmet, M. D., on September 15, 1869, so that Minny's summer with her sisters was
domestically a very exciting one. The intermarrying of the James,
Emmet, and Temple families thus brought about the vast cousinage
of which Henry James wrote so affectionately.

15. *The Middle Years,* 5, 6. This autobiographical fragment of one-
hundred and nineteen pages was never completed or revised by James.
In contrast with the published and unpublished letters which Henry
James wrote to his family from England in 1869-1870, the tone of
The Middle Years is more highly colored by his long English residence of later years than are either of the two previous autobiog-
raphies, *A Small Boy and Others* and *Notes of a Son and Brother.*
It is, therefore, more desirable to call upon the available sources
that were contemporary with these years of his first adult trip to
Europe for a correct understanding of his actual thoughts and feelings.

16. MS. letter from Henry James, Jr., to Mrs. Henry James, Sr., March
2, 1869, Houghton Library, Harvard University.

17. MS. letter from Henry James, Jr., to William James, March 19, 1869,
Houghton Library, Harvard University.

18. Malvern, or Great Malvern, was then a celebrated health resort and inland watering-place in Worcestershire, near the Severn, on the
slopes of the Malvern Hills. About eight miles from Worcester, it
was comprised of the villages of Malvern Link, Malvern Wells, and
Little Malvern. The climate and mineral springs had made the resort
one of the most popular in England, and the charm of the area
was enhanced by an eleventh-century Benedictine priory that was re-

stored as a parish church. The hills, ranging along the borders of Worcestershire and Herefordshire, extended for nine or ten miles, with abrupt heights, such as Worcestershire Beacon, on which highest point was an ancient British fortress.

19. MS. letter from Henry James, Jr., to William James, April 8, 1869, Houghton Library, Harvard University. In this same letter he expresses deep appreciation to his father for enabling him to take this extensive trip abroad: "I wrote only a week ago today to father but I nevertheless find it necessary to my comfort to write again. . . . I haven't yet attempted to answer his three notes 'in kind.' I don't know that I can, better than by telling him that I haven't had a moment of self-satisfaction and enjoyment here (and I have had many), but I have immediately thought of him as being the real author of my pleasure—having placed it in my power to be here at all, and having taught me all my life to think and feel properly, so that my thoughts and feelings are possibly not idle. . . . "

20. MS. letter from Henry James, Jr., to William James, April 26, 1869, Houghton Library, Harvard University.

21. Henry James, Sr., wrote an appreciative note to James Russell Lowell for the latter's favorable notice of the story: "My dear Mr. Lowell, I hoped to be able to see you yesterday at the Club, and to tell you how much my paternal pride has been gratified by your 'munificent' notice of Harry's literary exploits, as he himself characterizes it. Nothing in fact could have been more grateful to me than that generous tribute from a veteran of your tried renown to this youthful aspirant in the field of letters, and I thank you with all my heart. I rejoice in it especially that the poor lad, whose literary aims, it seems to me, are anything but frivolous, will himself feel your charming appreciation of him to be the very blessing he could most vocet. I have never had any pretense to any literary repute myself, nor felt how good it is *laudari laudato viro*: but I think I can understand the satisfaction this good boy must feel in having his merits passed upon by so exquisite a master as yourself. Believe me ever affectionately and gratefully yours, Henry James." MS. letter from Henry James, Sr., to James Russell Lowell, June 27, 1869, Houghton Library, Harvard University.

22. *Letters of Henry James,* I, 22, 23. In this same letter he added: "I *have* seem some nice Americans and I still love my country."

23. Henry James, "Preface," *The Reverberator,* London, Macmillan and Co., 1922, xx.

24. MS. letter from Henry James, Jr., to Mrs. Henry James, Sr., March 29, 1870. In this same letter he wrote: "I have had a long walk this afternoon and feel already strangely familiar with the idea of Minny's death. But I can't help wishing that I had been in closer relation with her during her last hours—and find a sweet comfort at all events in thinking of that never-to-be-answered letter

I wrote to her from Florence. If ever my good genius prompted me, it was then."

25. MS. letter from William James to Henry James, Jr., December 5, 1869, Houghton Library, Harvard University. Upon learning of Minny Temple's death, William James wrote in his diary: "By that big part of me that's in the tomb with you, may I realize and believe in the immediacy of death! May I feel that every torment suffered here passes and is as a breath of wind,—every pleasure too. Acts and examples stay. Time is long. One human life is an instant. Is our patience so short-winded, our curiosity so dead or our grit so loose, that that one instant snatched out of the endless age should not be cheerfully sat out. Minny, your death makes me feel the nothingness of all our egotistic fury. The inevitable release is sure; wherefore take our turn kindly whatever it contain. Ascend to some sort of partnership with fate, and since tragedy is at the heart of us, go to meet it, work it in to our ends, instead of dodging it all our days, and being run down by it at last. *Use* your death (or your life, it's all one meaning), *tut twam asi* ('Thou art that')."

26. MS. letter from Mary Temple to Henry James, Jr., November 7, 1869. Houghton Library, Harvard University.

27. From Promfret, late in July, 1869, Mrs. James wrote him: ". . . If you were only here for an hour, and we could talk over this subject of expense, I could, I know, exorcise all these demons of anxiety and conscientiousness that possess you, and leave you free as air to enjoy to the full all that surrounds you, and drink in health of body and of mind in following out your own safe and innocent attractions. Just here we desire, dear Harry, to have you, only exacting from you the promise that you will henceforth throw away prudence and think only of your own comfort and pleasure, for our sake as much as your own. I am sure you may confide in your prudent old mother to take care of that side of the question. You must have got my letter suggesting your going to Italy for the winter *very* soon after writing your last; so you see we are quite of one mind. Italy will be just the place for you; and so do not, I pray you, cramp yourself in any way to hinder your fullest enjoyment of it. You dear, reasonable, over-conscientious soul! Take the fullest liberty and enjoyment your tastes and inclinations crave, and we will promise heartily to foot the bill." MS. letter from Mrs. Henry James, Sr., to Henry James, Jr., July 24, 1869, Houghton Library, Harvard University.

28. MS. letter from Henry James, Jr., to William James, November 30, 1869, Houghton Library, Harvard University. William Wetmore Story (1819-1895) had gone to Rome to become a sculptor in 1847 and resided there much of his remaining life. Such works as *Cleopatra* and *Medea,* the former described at length in Hawthorne's *Marble Faun,* are representative of his choice of subjects, his style being strongly influenced by the sentimental neo-classicism then

prevalent. George Ripley (1802-1880) was an intimate friend of Henry James, Sr., and a prominent transcendentalist, having helped to found The *Dial* and to organize Brook Farm. He was strong in his support of *The Harbinger,* for which the elder James had written extensively, and was the book reviewer for The New York *Tribune,* in which the Jameses had a financial interest. In 1866 and in 1869-1870, he made trips to Europe where he became acquainted with many of the authors and philosophers whose views he had long championed in his writing.

29. MS. letter from Henry James, Sr., to Henry James, Jr., December 26, 1869, Houghton Library, Harvard University.

30. *The Letters of Henry James,* I, 25.

31. In *The Pilgrimage of Henry James,* Van Wyck Brooks, in 1925, inaugurated this theory of Henry James's almost religious passion for England as a young man, establishing the thesis upon the character Searle as spokesman for the author of *A Passionate Pilgrim.* Rebecca West, Ford Madox Hueffer, and others followed this interpretation, apparently without access to or consideration of extensive family letters and papers containing much evidence to the contrary. Cornelia Pulsifer Kelley in 1930, in *The Early Development of Henry James,* by understanding the narrator of the story as the channel of James's ideas on England contributed a substantial note of reëvaluation in the whole scholarly dispute. Recent scholarship tends to set aside Brooks's theory, taking a more balanced point of view.

32. *Letters of Henry James,* I, 26, 27.

33. *Ibid.,* I, 28, 29.

34. Concerning these issues Lowell wrote: "This (that Americans are vulgar) was one of those horribly vague accusations, the victim of which has no defence. An umbrella is of no avail against a Scotch mist. It envelopes you, it penetrates at every pore, it wets you through without seeming to wet you at all. Vulgarity is an eighth deadly sin, added to the list in these latter days, and worse than all the others put together, since it perils your salvation in *this* world,—far the more important of the two in the minds of most men. . . . 'How am I vulgar?' asks the culprit, shudderingly. 'Because thou are not like unto Us,' answers Lucifer, Son of the Morning, and there is no more to be said. The god of this world may be a fallen angel, but he has us *there!* We were as clean,—so far as my observation goes, I think we are cleaner, morally and physically, than the English, and therefore, of course, than everybody else. But we did not pronounce the diphthong *ou* as they did, and we said *eether* and not *eyther,* following therein the fashion of our ancestors, who unhappily could bring over no English better than Shakespeare's; and we did not stammer as they had learned to do from the courtiers, who in this way flattered the Hanoverian king, a foreigner among the people he had come to reign over." "On a Certain Condescension

in Foreigners," *My Study Window*, Boston, Houghton Mifflin Co., 1871, 23. In the same essay Lowell suggests the Englishman's growing awareness that America gave promise of becoming a great nation: "Till after the Civil War it never seemed to enter the head of any foreigner, especially any Englishman, that an American had what could be called a country, except as a place to eat, sleep, and trade in. Then it seemed to strike them suddenly. 'By Jove, you know, fellahs don't fight like that for a shop-till!' No, I rather think not. To Americans America is something more than a promise and an expectation. It has a past and a tradition of its own. . . . " *Ibid.*, 75, 76.

35. Henry James, *Portraits of Places,* ed. George Alvin Finch, New York, Lear Publishers, Inc., 1948, 114. (First published in 1883.)
36. *The Middle Years,* 1, 2.

Bibliography

The Collection of James Papers in the Houghton Library of Harvard University contains scores of manuscript letters, written to and from members of the James family, many of which have not been published. Upon this wealth of material the author has drawn extensively, using numerous letters in the text of this book, previously not available in printed form, or published only in part. He is grateful for the privilege of using these James Papers.

* * * *

Anonymous, "Newport, Historical and Social," *Harper's New Monthly Magazine,* vol. IX (August 1854), pp. 289-317.

Alcott, Bronson, *The Journals of Bronson Alcott,* ed. Odell Shepard, Boston, Little, Brown and Company, 1938.

Barrett, Laurence, "Young Henry James, Critic," *American Literature,* vol. XX, (January 1949), pp. 385-400.

Baudelaire, Charles, *Eugene Delacroix, His Life and His Work,* (Translated by Joseph M. Berstein), New York, Lear Publishers, 1947.

Beach, Joseph Warren, *The Method of Henry James,* New Haven, Yale University Press, 1918.

Blackmur, Robert P., "Henry James," *Literary History of the United States,* vol. II, New York, The Macmillan Company, 1948.

Bowen, Catherine Drinker, *Yankee from Olympus,* Boston, Little, Brown and Company, 1944.

Bradford, Gamaliel, *American Portraits,* Boston, Houghton Mifflin Company, 1922.

——————, *The Journal of Gamaliel Bradford,* ed. Van Wyck Brooks, Boston, Houghton Mifflin Company, 1933.

Brooks, Van Wyck, *The Pilgrimage of Henry James,* New York, E. P. Dutton and Company, 1925.

Brown, Henry Collins, *Old New York,* New York, Privately Printed, 1913.

Brown, T. Allston, *History of the American Stage,* New York, Dick and Fitzgerald, 1870.

——————, *A History of the New York Stage from the First Performance in 1732 to 1901,* 3 Vols., New York, Dodd, Mead and Company, 1903.

Charging Ledgers, New York Society Library, vols. 1839-1841, 1846-1847, 1849-1850, 1851-1854.

Clayton, Ellen Creathorne, *Queens of Song (Being Memoirs of Some of the Celebrated French Vocalists),* New York, Harper and Brothers, 1865.

Coad, Oral Sumner and Edwin Mims, Jr., *The American Stage* (The Pageant of America), New Haven, Yale University Press, 1929.

Cortissoz, Royal, *John La Farge, A Memoir and a Study,* Boston, Houghton Mifflin Company, 1911.

Cunningham, George H., *London,* New York, E. P. Dutton and Company, 1927.

Dewey, David Rich, *Financial History of the United States,* New York, Longmans, Green and Company, 1931.

Edel, Leon, ed. *The Complete Plays of Henry James,* New York, J. B. Lippincott, 1949.

——————, *Henry James, The Untried Years,* New York, J. B. Lippincott, 1953.

Edgar, Pelham, *Henry James, Man and Author,* New York, Houghton Mifflin Company, 1927.

Elliott, Maud Howe, *This Was My Newport,* Cambridge, The Mythology Company, 1944.

Emerson, Edward Waldo, *The Early Days of the Saturday Club, 1855-70,* Boston, Houghton Mifflin Company, 1918.

Fields, James T., *Yesterday with Authors,* Boston, Houghton Mifflin Company, 1900.

Fleury, Comte, *Memoirs of the Empress Eugénie,* New York, Appleton and Company, 1920.

Francis' Picture of New York and Strangers Guide, New York, C. S. Francis and Company, 1851.

Godkin, Edwin, *Life and Letters of Edwin Lawrence Godkin,* 2 vols. ed. Rollo Odgen, New York, The Macmillan Company, 1907.

Granger, Ernest, *Les Merveilles de La France, Le Pays, Les Monuments, Les Habitants,* Paris, Hachette, n.d.

Grattan, C. Hartley, *The Three Jameses, A Family of Minds (Henry James, Sr., William James, Henry James),* New York, Longmans, Green and Company, 1932.

Harlow, Virginia, *Thomas Sergeant Perry,* Durham, N. C., Duke University Press, 1950.

Hastings, Katherine, *William James (1771-1832) of Albany,* Reprinted from *New York Genealogical and Biographical Record,* vol. LV, 1924.

Haswell, Charles H., *Reminiscences of an Octogenarian,* New York, Harper Brothers, 1896.

Häusermann, H. W., *The Genevese Background,* London, Routledge & Kegan Paul Ltd., 1952.

Hawthorne, Julian, *The Memoirs of Julian Hawthorne,* ed. Edith Garrigues Hawthorne, New York, The Macmillan Company, 1938.

Hayward, Arthur L., *The Days of Dickens,* London, George Routledge and Sons Ltd., n. d.

Helps, Arthur, *The Correspondence of Sir Arthur Helps,* ed. E. A. Helps, London, John Lane, 1917.

Hornblow, Arthur, *A History of the Theatre in America,* vol. II, Philadelphia, J. B. Lippincott, 1919.

Howe, Julia Ward, *Reminiscences, 1819-1899,* Boston, Houghton Mifflin Company, 1899.

Howe, Mark A. DeWolfe, *Barrett Wendell and His Letters,* Boston, The Atlantic Monthly Press, 1924.

————, "The Letters of Henry James to Mr. Justice Holmes," *The Yale Review,* Spring 1949, pp. 410-433.

————, *Memories of a Hostess,* Boston, The Atlantic Monthly Press, 1922.

Howells, William Dean, "Henry James, Jr.," *Century* Magazine, 3 n. s., vol. 25 (November 1882), pp. 25-29.

————, *Life in Letters of William Dean Howells,* 2 vols., ed. Mildred Howells, Garden City, New York, Doubleday, Doran, 1928.

Hutton, Laurence, *Plays and Players,* New York, Hurd and Houghton, 1875.

Index of Conveyances Recorded in the Office of Register of the City and County of New York (Grantors), New York, McSpedon and Baker, 1857.

Index to Personal Names in the Historical Portions of the Manual of the Corporation of the City of New York (As issued by David T. Valentine, Clerk of the Common Council for the Successive Years, 1841-42 to 1866), compiled by Louis Dow Scisco, Washington, D. C. Presented to the New York Genealogical and Biographical Society, 1948.

Ireland, Joseph N., *Records of the New York Stage from 1750-1860,* 2 vols., New York, T. H. Morrell, 1867.

James, *Alice James, Her Brothers, Her Journal,* ed. Anna Robeson Burr, New York, Dodd, Mead and Company, 1934.

James, Henry, *The American Scene,* New York, Harper and Brothers, 1907.

—————, *The Art of the Novel,* ed. Richard P. Blackmur, New York, Charles Scribner's Sons, 1934.

—————, "A Day of Days," The *Galaxy,* June, 1866.

—————, "DeGrey: A Romance," The *Atlantic Monthly,* July 1868.

—————, "Gabrielle de Bergerac," The *Atlantic Monthly,* July-September, 1869.

—————, "A Landscape Painter," The *Atlantic Monthly,* February, 1866.

—————, *The Letters of Henry James,* 2 vols., ed. Percy Lubbock, New York, Charles Scribner's Sons, 1920.

—————, "A Light Man," The *Galaxy,* July, 1869.

—————, Manuscript Letters in "Miscellaneous Papers," *James Papers,* New York City Public Library, New York City, New York.

—————, Manuscript Letters to William Conant Church, *James Papers,* New York City Public Library, New York City, New York.

—————, *The Middle Years,* New York, Charles Scribner's Sons, 1917.

—————, "A Most Extraordinary Case," The *Atlantic Monthly,* April, 1868.

—————, "My Friend Bingham," The *Atlantic Monthly,* March, 1867.

—————, *The Notebooks of Henry James,* ed. F. O. Matthiessen and Kenneth B. Murdock, New York, Oxford University Press, 1947.

—————, *Notes of a Son and Brother,* New York, Charles Scribner's Sons, 1914.

—————, "Osborne's Revenge," The *Galaxy,* July, 1868.

—————, *Partial Portraits,* New York, The Macmillan Company, 1888.

—————, "A Passionate Pilgrim," The *Atlantic Monthly,* March-April, 1871.

—————, "Poor Richard," The *Atlantic Monthly,* June-August, 1867.

—————, *Portraits of Places,* ed. George Alvin Finch, New York, Lear Publishers, Inc., 1948.

—————, "A Problem," The *Galaxy,* June, 1868.

—————, *The Reverberator,* London, Macmillan and Company, 1922.

—————, "The Romance of Certain Old Clothes," The *Atlantic Monthly,* February, 1868.

—————, *A Small Boy and Others,* New York, Charles Scribner's Sons, 1913.

—————, "The Story of a Masterpiece," The *Galaxy,* January-February, 1868.

—————, "The Story of a Year," The *Atlantic Monthly,* March, 1865.

—————, "Travelling Companions," The *Atlantic Monthly,* November-December, 1870.

—————, *The Wings of the Dove,* 2 vols., New York, Charles Scribner's Sons, 1909.

——————, "Within the Rim," *Fortnightly Review*, vol. 108 (July-December, 1917), pp. 161-171.

James, Henry, Sr., *The Church of Christ Not an Ecclesiasticism*, London, W. White, 1865.

——————, *The Literary Remains of Henry James*, ed. William James, his son, Boston, James R. Osgood, 1885.

——————, Manuscript letters in the "Bryant-Godwin Papers," *James Papers*, New York City Public Library, New York City, New York.

——————, *The Nature of Evil* (Considered in a letter to the Rev. Edward Beecher), New York, D. Appleton and Company, 1915.

——————, *Society the Redeemed Form of Man*, Boston, Houghton, Osgood and Company, 1879.

James, William, *The Letters of William James*, 2 vols. ed. by his son Henry James, New York, The Atlantic Monthly Press, 1920.

Jenkins, Stephens, *The Greatest Street in the World, Broadway*, New York, G. P. Putnam's Sons, 1911.

Johnson, Charles, *English Painting from the Seventeenth Century to the Present Day*, London, G. Bell and Sons, Ltd., 1934.

Jubilee Volume, Published by the Scotch Presbyterian Church, New York, Thomas Nelson and Sons, 1906.

Kelley, Cornelia Pulsifer, *The Early Development of Henry James*, Urbana, Illinois, University of Illinois Press, 1930.

Le Clair, Robert C., "Henry James and Minny Temple," *American Literature*, vol. 21, March 1949, pp. 35-48.

——————, *Three American Travellers in England: James Russell Lowell, Henry Adams, Henry James*, Philadelphia, Privately Printed, 1945.

Leonard, John William, *History of the City of New York, 1609-1909*, New York, The Journal of Commerce and Commercial Bulletin, 1910.

Life in America (A special Loan Exhibition of Paintings Held During the Period of the New York World's Fair, April 24 to October 29, 1939), New York, The Metropolitan Museum of Art, 1939.

Lowell, James Russell, *My Study Window*, Boston, Houghton Mifflin Company, 1871.

Lyall, Sir Alfred, *The Rise and Expansion of the British Domain in India*, London, John Murray, 1920.

Mackaye, Percy M., *Epoch, the Life of Steele Mackaye*, 2 vols., New York, Boni and Liveright, 1927.

Mather, Frank Jewett, Jr., *Modern Painting*, New York, Henry Holt and Company, 1927.

Matthews, Brander, *French Dramatists of the 19th Century*, New York, Charles Scribner's Sons, 1905.

Matthiessen, F. O., *The James Family,* New York, Alfred A. Knopf, 1947.

Maurice, Arthur Bartlett, *The Paris of the Novelists,* New York, Doubleday, Page and Company, 1919.

Morse, John T., Jr., *Thomas Sergeant Perry,* Boston, Houghton Mifflin Company, 1929.

Munsell, Joel, *The Annals of Albany,* vol. 9, Albany, New York, Munsell and Rowland, 1858.

————, *Collections on the History of Albany,* vol. I, Albany, New York, J. Munsell, 1865-1871.

Murray, John, *A Handbook for Visitors in Paris,* London, John Murray, 1864.

New York *Daily-Tribune,* September 3, 1855, September 8, 1855, January 16, 1856.

Nicoll, Allardyce, *A History of the Late Nineteenth Century Drama,* 2 vols., Cambridge, At the University Press, 1946.

Norton, Charles Eliot, *Letters of Charles Eliot Norton,* 2 vols., ed. Sara Norton and M. A. DeWolfe Howe, Boston, Houghton Mifflin Company, 1913.

Nowell-Smith, Simon, *The Legend of the Master,* New York, Charles Scribner's Sons, 1948.

Orr, A. (Mrs. Sutherland), "Mr. Henry James, Sr.," The *Athenaeum* (London), July 24, 1880, pp. 113-115.

Pattee, Fred Lewis, *The Development of the American Short Story,* New York, Harper Brothers, 1923.

Pelliana, *Pell of Pelham* (*1635-1919*), New York, Privately Printed, 1934.

Perry, Bliss, ed., *The Heart of Emerson's Essays,* Boston, Houghton Mifflin Company, 1933.

————, *The Heart of Emerson's Journals,* Boston, Houghton Mifflin Company, 1926.

————, *Life and Letters of Henry Lee Higginson,* Boston, the Atlantic Monthly Press, 1921.

Perry, Ralph Barton, "The Common Enemy: Early Letters of Oliver Wendell Holmes, Jr. and William James," The *Atlantic Monthly,* vol. 156 (September, 1935), pp. 293-303.

————, *The Thought and Character of William James,* 2 vols., Boston, Little, Brown and Company, 1935.

Phelps' New York City Guide, New York, T. C. Fanning, 1852.

Phillips, Le Roy, *A Bibliography of the Writings of Henry James,* New York, Coward, McCann, 1930.

Preble, George Henry, Rear Admiral, U. S. N., *A Chronological History of the Origin and Development of Steam Navigation,* Philadelphia, Hamersly and Company, 1883.

Quinn, Arthur Hobson, *A History of the American Drama from the Beginning to the Civil War,* New York, Harper and Brothers, 1923.

——————, *A History of the American Drama from the Civil War to the Present Day,* New York, Harper and Brothers, 1927.

——————, *American Fiction, An Historical and Critical Survey,* New York, D. Appleton-Century Company, 1936.

Roberts, Morris, *Henry James's Criticism,* Cambridge, Harvard University Press, 1929.

Rhode Island, Federal Writers Project, (American Guide Series), Boston, Houghton Mifflin Company, 1937.

Rourke, Constance, *Trumpets of Jubilee,* New York, Harcourt, Brace and Company, 1927.

Saint-Gaudens, Homer, *The American Artist and His Times,* New York, Dodd, Mead and Company, 1941.

Shannon, Martha A. S., *Boston Days of William Morris Hunt,* Boston, Marshall Jones Company, 1923.

Smith, Eugene W., *Trans-Atlantic Passenger Ships Past and Present,* Boston, George H. Dean Company, 1947.

Smith, S. C. Kaines, *An Outline of Modern Painting in Europe and America,* New York, William Morrow and Company, 1931.

Spender, Stephen, *The Destructive Element,* London, Jonathan Cape, 1935.

Thackeray, William Makepeace, *The Newcomes,* 2 vols., London, Bradbury and Evans, 1855.

Van Dyke, John C., *History of Painting,* New York, Longmans, Green and Company, 1901.

Walsh, Rev. William, *Hugh Walsh's Family,* Newburgh, New York, Newburgh Journal Print, 1903.

Ware, Ralph Hartman, *American Adaptation of French Plays on the New York and Philadelphia Stages from 1834 to the Civil War,* Philadelphia, Privately Printed, 1930.

Warren, Austin, *The Elder James,* New York, The Macmillan Company, 1934.

Watson, Ernest Bradlee, *Sheridan to Robertson,* Cambridge, Harvard University Press, 1926.

West, Rebecca, *Henry James,* London, Nisbet and Company, Ltd., 1916.

Wharton, Edith, *A Backward Glance,* New York, D. Appleton-Century Company, 1934.

Williams, W., *New York City Guide,* New York, D. Appleton and
    Company, 1851.

Wilson, James Grant, *The Memorial History of the City of New York,*
    vols. III, IV, New York, New York History Company, 1893.

Young, Frederic Harold, *The Philosophy of Henry James, Sr.,* New
    York, Bookman Associates, 1951.

Index